ESOTERIC PSYCHOLOGY

VOLUME ONE

BOOKS BY ALICE A. BAILEY

Initiation, Human and Solar
Letters on Occult Meditation
The Consciousness of the Atom
A Treatise on Cosmic Fire
The Light of the Soul
The Soul and its Mechanism
From Intellect to Intuition
A Treatise on White Magic
From Bethlehem to Calvary
Discipleship in the New Age–Vol. I
Discipleship in the New Age–Vol. II
Problems of Humanity
The Reappearance of the Christ
The Destiny of the Nations
Glamour: A World Problem
Telepathy and the Etheric Vehicle
The Unfinished Autobiography
Education in the New Age
The Externalisation of the Hierarchy

A Treatise on the Seven Rays:

Vol. I–Esoteric Psychology
Vol. II–Esoteric Psychology
Vol. III–Esoteric Astrology
Vol. IV–Esoteric Healing
Vol. V–The Rays and the Initiations
The Labours of Hercules
The Master Index

ESOTERIC PSYCHOLOGY

VOLUME I

A TREATISE ON THE SEVEN RAYS

by

ALICE A. BAILEY

LUCIS PUBLISHING COMPANIES

COPYRIGHT © 1964 BY LUCIS TRUST

First Printed Edition, 1936

Revised Edition 1964

Nineteentth Printing, 2024

ISBN No. 978-085330-118-9
0-85330-118-2
Library of Congress Catalog Card Number: 53-19914

All rights reserved. Permissions to be sought from the Publisher.

The non-profit Lucis Publishing Companies are owned by the Lucis Trust. As the original publishers of all books of esoteric philosophy by Alice A. Bailey, the Companies are dedicated to ensuring the ongoing availability, authenticity, and production quality of these books. No royalties are paid and new publications are financed by the Tibetan Book Fund which has been established by Lucis Trust for the perpetuation of the teachings of the Tibetan and Alice A. Bailey.

Esoteric Psychology Vol I is also available in
eBook, Audiobook and Clothbound editions.

This book has been translated into Danish, Dutch, French, German, Greek, Italian, Portuguese, Russian, Spanish and Swedish. Translation into other languages is proceeding.

LUCIS PUBLISHING COMPANY
866 United Nations Plaza, Suite 482, New York, N.Y. 10017

LUCIS PRESS LIMITED
Suite 54, 3 Whitehall Court, London SW1A 2EF

www.lucistrust.org
PRINTED IN THE UNITED KINGDOM

DEDICATED TO

D.M.M.M.　　　M.K.A.P.　　　E.A.S.L.

EXTRACT FROM A STATEMENT BY THE TIBETAN

Published August 1934

Suffice it to say, that I am a Tibetan disciple of a certain degree, and this tells you but little, for all are disciples from the humblest aspirant up to, and beyond, the Christ Himself. I live in a physical body like other men, on the borders of Tibet, and at times (from the exoteric standpoint) preside over a large group of Tibetan lamas, when my other duties permit. It is this fact that has caused it to be reported that I am an abbot of this particular lamasery. Those associated with me in the work of the Hierarchy (and all true disciples are associated in this work) know me by still another name and office. A.A.B. knows who I am and recognises me by two of my names.

I am a brother of yours, who has travelled a little longer upon the Path than has the average student, and has therefore incurred greater responsibilities. I am one who has wrestled and fought his way into a greater measure of light than has the aspirant who will read this article, and I must therefore act as a transmitter of the light, no matter what the cost. I am not an old man, as age counts among the teachers, yet I am not young or inexperienced. My work is to teach and spread the knowledge of the Ageless Wisdom wherever I can find a response, and I have been doing this for many years. I seek also to help the Master M. and the Master K.H. whenever opportunity offers, for I have been long connected with Them and with Their work. In all the above, I have told you much; yet at the same time I have told you nothing which would lead you to offer me that blind obedience and the foolish devotion which the emotional aspirant offers to the

Guru and Master whom he is as yet unable to contact. Nor will he make that desired contact until he has transmuted emotional devotion into unselfish service to humanity,—not to the Master.

The books that I have written are sent out with no claim for their acceptance. They may, or may not, be correct, true and useful. It is for you to ascertain their truth by right practice and by the exercise of the intuition. Neither I nor A.A.B. is the least interested in having them acclaimed as inspired writings, or in having anyone speak of them (with bated breath) as being the work of one of the Masters. If they present truth in such a way that it follows sequentially upon that already offered in the world teachings, if the information given raises the aspiration and the will-to-serve from the plane of the emotions to that of the mind (the plane whereon the Masters *can* be found) then they will have served their purpose. If the teaching conveyed calls forth a response from the illumined mind of the worker in the world, and brings a flashing forth of his intuition, then let that teaching be accepted. But not otherwise. If the statements meet with eventual corroboration, or are deemed true under the test of the Law of Correspondences, then that is well and good. But should this not be so, let not the student accept what is said.

THE TIBETAN.

THE GREAT INVOCATION

From the point of Light within the Mind of God
    Let light stream forth into the minds of men.
    Let Light descend on Earth.

From the point of Love within the Heart of God
    Let love stream forth into the hearts of men.
    May Christ return to Earth.

From the centre where the Will of God is known
    Let purpose guide the little wills of men—
    The purpose which the Masters know and serve.

From the centre which we call the race of men
    Let the Plan of Love and Light work out.
    And may it seal the door where evil dwells.

Let Light and Love and Power restore the Plan on Earth.

"The above Invocation or Prayer does not belong to any person or group but to all Humanity. The beauty and the strength of this Invocation lies in its simplicity, and in its expression of certain central truths which all men, innately and normally, accept—the truth of the existence of a basic Intelligence to Whom we vaguely give the name of God; the truth that behind all outer seeming, the motivating power of the universe is Love; the truth that a great Individuality came to earth, called by Christians, the Christ, and embodied that love so that we could understand; the truth that both love and intelligence are effects of what is called the Will of God; and finally the self-evident truth that only through *humanity* itself can the Divine Plan work out."

ALICE A. BAILEY

A TREATISE ON THE SEVEN RAYS

Volume	I.	Esoteric Psychology
Volume	II.	Esoteric Psychology
Volume	III.	Esoteric Astrology
Volume	IV.	Esoteric Healing
Volume	V.	The Rays and the Initiations

SYNOPSIS OF
A TREATISE ON THE SEVEN RAYS

VOLUME I

SECTION ONE
I. Introductory Remarks
II. Certain Questions and Answers
III. Ten Basic Propositions

SECTION TWO
I. The Seven Creative Builders—the Seven Rays
II. The Rays and the Kingdoms in Nature
III. The Rays and Man
Some Tabulations on the Rays

VOLUME II
I. The Egoic Ray
II. The Ray of the Personality
III. Humanity Today

VOLUME III
I. The Zodiac and the Rays
II. The Nature of Esoteric Astrology
III. The Science of Triangles
IV. The Sacred and Non-Sacred Planets
V. The Three Major Constellations
VI. The Three Crosses
II. The Rays, Constellations and Planets

VOLUME IV
I. The Basic Causes of Disease
II. The Basic Requirements for Healing
III. The Fundamental Laws of Healing

VOLUME V
I. Stanzas for Disciples
II. The Fourteen Rules for Disciples and Initiates
III. The Rays and the Initiations

TABLE OF CONTENTS

Foreword xvii

SECTION ONE

I. *Introductory Remarks:*
   1. The Three Objectives in studying the Rays: 3
      a. Light is thrown on history 3
      b The nature of man is clarified 4
      c. The new psychology is formulated 8

   2. A definition of the words:
     Life-Quality-Appearance 14

   3. The Seven Rays enumerated 22

   4. The Function of Christianity 28

II. *Certain Questions and their Answers:*
   1. What is the Soul and its Nature? 36
      a. It is the Son of Father-Sprit and Mother-Matter 36
      b It is the Principle of Intelligence 38
      c. It is Light and Energy 41
      d. It is the Principle of Sentiency 53

   2. What are the Origin, Goal, Purpose and Plan of the Soul? 59
      a. The Three Rays of Aspect 62
      b. The Four Rays of Attribute 70

   3. Can the Fact of the Soul be proved? 89

   4. Of What Value is it to study the Rays? 109

Table of Contents

    5. What is the meaning of:
       a. Sentiency — 130
       b. Consciousness or Awareness — 131
       c. Energy of Light — 132

III. *Ten Basic Propositions:*
    1. There is one Life — 141
    2. There are Seven Rays — 141
    3. Life-Quality-Appearance constitute Existence — 141
    4. The seven Rays are the seven Creative Forces — 141
    5. The seven Rays manifest through the seven Planets — 142
    6. Every Human Being is on one of the Rays — 142
    7. There is one Monad, seven Rays and myriads of Forms — 142
    8. The Laws of Evolution embody the Life Purpose of the seven Rays — 142
    9. Man develops through Self-expression and Self-Realisation — 142
   10. Individualisation leads eventually to Initiation — 143

SECTION TWO

I. *The Seven Creative Builders, the Seven Rays:*
    1. The Rays and Life-Quality-Appearance — 157
    2. The Present Ray Plan and the Workers:
       The Origin of the Plan and its immediate Application — 170
    3. Three Major Propositions — 191
       a. Every Ray Life is an expression of a Solar Life — 191
       b. Every Ray Life is the recipient and Custodian of energies — 191
       c. The Quality of a Ray Life determines its phenomenal Appearance — 191
    4. Quality in the World of Appearances — 193
    5. An Analysis of the Rays and their Expression — 200

II. *The Rays and the Kingdoms in Nature:*
Introductory Remarks — 215

Table of Contents

1. The Mineral Kingdom:	223
2. The Vegetable Kingdom:	223
a. Life, Radiance and Magnetism	235
b. The Five Secrets of the Kingdoms in Nature	238
c. The Planets and the Kingdoms in Nature	245
3. The Animal Kingdom:	251
a. Human Relations to Animals	254
b. Individualisation	258
c. The Five Points of Contact	262
d. Cyclic Manifestation	265
e. The Problem of Sex	268

III. *The Rays and Man:*

Introductory Remarks	311
1. The Ray of the Solar System	334
2. The Planetary Ray—Earth	335
3. The Ray of the Fourth Kingdom	342
4. The Racial Rays	348
5. The Rays in Cyclic Manifestation:	357
a. The outgoing sixth Ray	358
b. The incoming seventh Ray	363
c. The functioning Ray Laws	375
6. The Nations and the Rays	381
a. The major Nations and their Rays	381
b. The Jewish Problem	393
7. The Ray of the Ego	401
Some Tabulations on the Rays	411
Index	433

"Matter is the Vehicle for the manifestation of Soul on this plane of existence, and Soul is the Vehicle on a higher plane for the manifestation of Spirit, and these three are a Trinity synthesized by Life, which pervades them all."

The Secret Doctrine 1st Ed. p.17

THREE SOULS, ONE MAN

Three souls which make up one soul: first, to wit,
A soul of each and all the bodily parts,
Seated therein, which works, and is what Does,
And has the use of earth, and ends the man
Downward: but, tending upward for advice,
Grows into, and again is grown into
By the next soul, which, seated in the brain,
Useth the first with its collected use,
And feeleth, thinketh, willeth,– is what Knows:
Which, duly tending upward in its turn,
Grows into, and again is grown into
By the last soul, that uses both the first,
Subsisting whether they assist or no,
And, constituting man's self, is what Is –
And leans upon the former, makes it play,
As that played off the first: and, tending up,
Holds, is upheld by, God, and ends the man
Upward in that dread point of intercourse,
Nor needs a place, for it returns to Him.
What Does, what Knows, what Is; three souls, one man.

From "Death in the Desert"
by Robert Browning.

Foreword

THE question arises, each time a book is written which is to be read by earnest aspirants: What line of instruction will carry forward their training with the most speed?—for speed is an essential factor, if the present day unfoldment is to be rightly utilised and the stress and strain in the world relieved. The teaching to be given must likewise increase their mental competency, and lead to that stabilisation of the emotional body which will most rapidly set them free for service. It must be remembered that constant study (of papers), and the apprehension by the ear and eye of statements anent the Ageless Wisdom, serve only to increase responsibility, or produce brain fatigue and staleness, with subsequent revolt from instruction. Only that which is brought into use in the life is of practical value and retains its livingness. Sincerity is the first thing for which those of us who teach inevitably look.

Let me remind those I reach through these books that the main result I look for is one of *group* co-operation and understanding, and not that of individual benefit. By studying and reading with care, a group interplay is set up, the group becomes more closely integrated, the units in it more closely linked together and as a group more closely blended in the unfolding Plan of the great Ones. We are building and planning for the future and for humanity, and not for the personal unfoldment of any particular aspirant. The individual growth is of no tremendous significance. The formation and development of a band of pledged aspirants, trained to work together and to respond in unison to a teaching, is of real moment to those of us who are responsible for the training and for the preparation of the group of world disciples who will function with freedom and power in a later cycle. You see a tiny portion of the Plan. We see the Plan as it unfolds for a series of lives ahead, and we are today seeking those who can be taught to work in group formation and who can constitute one of the active units in the vast happenings that lie ahead, connected with that two-thirds of humanity who will stand upon the Path at the close of the age, and with that one-third who will be held over for later unfoldment. We are training men and women everywhere so that they can be sensitive to the Plan, sensitive to their group vibration, and thus able to co-operate intelligently with the unfolding purpose. It is a mistake to think that the Plan is to train aspirants to be sensitive to the vibration of a Master or to the Hierarchy. That is but incidental and of minor importance.

It is for the purpose of training aspirants so that group awareness may be developed that these books have been written. Recognise clearly that you *personally* do not count, but that the *group* most surely does. Teaching is not given only in order to train you or to provide you with opportunity. All life is opportunity, and individual reaction to opportunity is one of the factors which indicate soul growth. For this, the training school of the world itself suffices.

There should be in all impartation of truth no imposition of authority. Aspirants must be left free to avail themselves of the teaching or not, and spiritual work must go forward because of the free choice and self-initiated effort of the individual student.

In the books already published three basic lines of teaching can be traced:

First, a relatively new technique has been given as to the control of the body.

Second, teaching has been given anent the formation of the New Group of World Servers.

Third, the general lines of the magical work of creation have received attention.

The first line of teaching concerns the individual and his development; the second indicates the nature and ideals of the group into which he may find his way if he profits by the teaching and learns control; the third, could you but realise it, details in some measure the methods and modes of work during the coming new age.

Ponder upon these three main approaches to truth, and think upon them with clarity of thought. Mental appreciation of their significance will produce understanding and will likewise increase the group apprehension of the teaching which I have sought to impart. Any student who thinks clearly and applies the teaching to his daily life is contributing most valuably to the group awareness.

Oft an aspirant says to himself: "Of what real use am I? How can I, in my small sphere, be of service to the world?" Let me reply to these questions by pointing out that by thinking this book into the minds of the public, by expressing before your fellow men the teaching it imparts, and by a life lived in conformity with its teaching, your service is very real.

This will necessarily involve a pledging of the entire personality to the helping of humanity, and the promise to the Higher Self that endeavour will be made to lose sight of self in service—a service to be rendered in the place and under the circumstances which a man's destiny and duty have imposed upon him. I mean a renewal of the effort to bring about the purification of all the bodies so that the entire lower man may be a pure channel and instrument through which spiritual force may flow unimpeded. I mean the attaining of an attitude wherein the aspirant desires nothing for the separated self, and in which he regards all that he has as something which he can lay upon the altar of sacrifice for the aiding of his brethren. Could all who read this book see the results of such a united effort, there would emerge a group activity, intelligently undertaken, which would achieve great things. So many people run hither and thither after this individual or that, or this piece of work or that, and, working with lack of intelligent co-ordination, achieve nothing and no group results. But united group effort would eventuate in an inspired reorganisation of the entire world, and the elimination of hindrances; there would be the making of real sacrifices and the giving up of personal wishes and desires in order that group purposes may be served.

Above all, there must be the elimination of fear. With this I have dealt at length in *A Treatise on White Magic*, and have given likewise certain rules and formulas for its control. How many who have read the teaching profited by the information imparted? Will you not, with determination and because the world cries out for help, cast away fear and go forward with joy and courage into the future?

There has been, behind all the books which I have written, a definite purpose and a planned sequence of teaching. It may be of interest to you if I trace them for you:

The first book issued was *Initiation, Human and Solar*. This book was intended for the average aspirant, to lead him on from where he was to a vision of an organised band of teachers who were seeking to aid humanity (and incidentally himself), and to give some idea of their technique of work and modes of procedure.

Letters on Occult Meditation indicated how these teachers could be reached and the discipline of life that the treading of the Path involved. These two are especially for aspirants.

A Treatise on Cosmic Fire is in an entirely different category. In the last analysis, it is for the guidance of the initiates of the world, and will lift the aspirant's eyes away from himself and his own growth to a vaster conception and a universal ideal. The mark of the initiate is his lack of interest in himself, in his own unfoldment and his own personal fate, and all aspirants who become accepted disciples have to master the technique of disinterestedness. Their eyes have also to be lifted away from the group of workers and from the hierarchy which they constitute and to be fixed on wider horizons and vaster realms of activity. The great creative Plan, its laws and technique of unfoldment, and the work of the Builders of the Universe was dealt with; emerging out of the mass of imparted facts, and underlying all the teaching, was the idea of a great Life with its own psychology and ideas. It was an attempt to give a synthetic picture of the unfolding Mind of God as It works out Its plans through the lesser Sons of Mind. In symbolism and archaic phrases it veiled the truths and principles which lie at the root of the creative process, and in its entirety is beyond the grasp of the advanced student. At the same time, it is a most valuable compendium of information, and will serve to convey truth and to develop the intuition.

The last book, *A Treatise on White Magic*, is a parallel volume to *A Treatise on Cosmic Fire*. Just as the first dealt with the psychology of Deity, the work of the Macrocosm, and the laws whereby the Solar Logos works, so this book constitutes a treatise on the psychology of the Son of God and the work of the Microcosm. It intimately concerns His place in the larger whole and is of practical application to daily life in that whole.

I have also aided A.A.B. in getting out a translation of the *Yoga Sutras of Patanjali*, which is a bridging book, intended to show the aspirant the rules whereby the light within him may be developed and the power of the intuition be brought to bear on all problems and on the phenomena of life itself.

This book was given the name *The Light of the Soul.*

Here I am fulfilling my intention to write a book on the subject of the *Seven Rays*. This topic has always been of real interest for students, but about these rays little is known. We know, from *The Secret Doctrine*, that they are the building Forces and the sum total of all that is in the manifested universe, but their effect in the human kingdom, and their essential quality and nature, remain as yet a mystery. It will be necessary for me to avoid the cosmic note, if I may so call it, for I seek to make the information of practical value to the student and to the intelligent reader. I shall therefore approach the subject entirely from the standpoint of the human family and deal with the subject in terms of psychological values, laying the foundation for that new psychology which is much needed, and so dealing primarily with the human equation. What I have to say will be a commentary upon an expansion of the words found in the proem of *The Secret Doctrine*, 1st Ed. p.17 that "All Souls are one with the Universal Over-soul."

We shall, from the outset, accept the fact of the soul. We shall not consider the arguments for or against the hypothesis of there being a soul—universal, cosmic, and divine, or individual and human. For our purposes of discussion, the soul exists, and its intrinsic reality is assumed, as a basic and proven principle. Those who do not admit this assumption can, however, study the book from the angle of a temporarily accepted hypothesis, and thus seek to gather those analogies and indications which may substantiate the point of view. To the aspirant, and to those who are seeking to demonstrate the existence of the soul because they believe in its existence, this expression of its laws and tradition, its nature, origin and potentialities will become a gradually deepening and experienced phenomenon.

What I indicate and the suggestions I may make, will, I forecast, be demonstrated, in the scientific sense, during the coming Aquarian Age. Science will then have penetrated a little further into the field of intangible yet real phenomena; it will have discovered (mayhap it has already made this discovery) that the dense and concrete do not exist; it will know that there is but one substance, present in nature in varying degrees of density and of vibratory activity, and that this substance is impelled by urgent purpose and expressive of divine intent.

We shall seek to avoid as far as possible those loose generalities which are so distressing to the academic and critical mind, and in which the mystic finds such relief and joy. I will however ask those who study this treatise to reserve their opinion and come to no crystallised judgment until the entire proposition has been presented to them, and its outlines have been clearly sensed and its detail somewhat elaborated.

It will be necessary for us to introduce the subject on a wide basis and to link the individual with the general, and this may (at the first) seem too vast a theme, too speculative a presentation and too misty and vague an outline. But this situation cannot be avoided, for the argument—as must be the case in all truly occult work—must be considered from the universal to the particular, from the cosmic to the individual. Men are, as yet, too interested in the particular and the individual to find it easy to apply the same interest to the greater Whole in which they "live and move and have their being," nor do they at this time (as a general rule) possess that inner mechanism of thought and that intuitive perception of truth which will enable them easily to grasp the significance of that which underlies the symbolism of words, or to see clearly the subjective outline under the objective form. But the effort to understand carries its own reward, and the attempt to grasp and comprehend the Soul—cosmic, universal, planetary and individual—leads inevitably to an unfoldment of the mental apparatus (with a subsequent development of the, as yet, quiescent brain cells) which must eventually produce a co-ordination of the thinking faculty, and resultant illumination.

The nature of our septenary universe must be considered, and the relation of the threefold human being to the divine Trinity must be noted. A general idea of the entire symbolic picture is of value. Each student, as he takes up the study of the rays, must steadily bear in mind that he himself—as a human unit—finds his place on one or other of these rays. The problem thus produced is a very real one. The physical body may be responsive to one type of ray force, whilst the personality as a whole may vibrate in unison with another. The ego or soul may find itself upon still a third type of ray, thus responding to another type of ray energy. The question of the monadic ray brings in still another factor in many cases, but this can only be implied and not really elucidated. As I have oft told you, it is only the initiate of the third initiation who can come in touch with his monadic ray, or his highest life aspect, and the humble aspirant cannot as yet ascertain whether he is a monad of Power, of Love or of Intelligent Activity.

In concluding, I ask for your sincere cooperation in the work which we are undertaking. It may be of more general and public value than any other of my writings. I shall seek to make this treatise upon the soul relatively brief. I shall seek to express these abstract truths in such a way that the general public, with its profound interest in the soul, may be intrigued and won to a deeper consideration of what is as yet a veiled surmise. The Aquarian Age will see the fact of the soul demonstrated. This is an attempt, carried forward in the difficulties of a transition period which lacks even the needed terminology, to aid that demonstration.

Let me also add that your attitude to the imparted instruction should be that of the student who is seeking truth that can be verified and information that can be applied to the daily life and tested in the crucible of life experience. If, for instance, there are indeed seven rays, embodying seven types of divine energy, then a man should be able to recognise these types and energies in the particular field of phenomena in which he plays his little part. If the truth given is veiled in symbolism and offered as an hypothesis, it should at the same time be unveiled sufficiently so as to be recognisable, and should have in it sufficient intelligent appeal to warrant its investigation. The words "All souls are one with the Uniersal Over-soul" may and do, I believe, embody a basic and essential piece of information, but unless there is evidence in the world that there is appearing a living relation between all sentient beings, then the statement is meaningless. But the fact is that universal sentiency and a general awareness are recognised everywhere as existing and as developing. The world is full of *knowledge,* which is in the last analysis sentient response to conditions which exist, by minds which are developing but are not fully developed. It is becoming gradually apparent that under diversity lies a basic unity, and that our awareness is right and true and correct in so far as we can identify ourselves with this unity.

In closing, may I beg all of you to go forward. Let nothing in the past—physical inertia, mental depression, lack of emotional control—keep you from taking fresh hold and with joy and interest making that needed progress which will fit you for more active and useful service. That none of you may be hindered by the past or by the present, but may live as Onlookers, is the prayer, constant and believing, of your teacher.

THE TIBETAN.

Section One

I. *Introductory Remarks*:

1. The three Objectives in studying the Rays.
2. Definition of the words: Life-Quality-Appearance.
3. The Seven Rays enumerated.
4. The Function of Christianity.

CHAPTER I

Introductory Remarks

---

1. *The Three Objectives in Studying the Rays*

THE study of the rays, and a true and deep comprehension of the inner significance of the teaching, will do for us three things:

A. It will throw much light upon the times and cycles in the unfolding panorama of history. In the last analysis, history is an account of the growth and development of man from the stage of the cave man, with his consciousness centred in his animal life, up to the present time wherein the human consciousness is steadily becoming more inclusive and mental, and so on and up to the stage of a perfected son of God. It is an account of the apprehension, by man, of the creative ideas which have moulded the race and are establishing its destiny. It gives us a dramatic picture of the progress of those souls who are carried in or out of manifestation by the appearance or disappearance of a ray. We shall find, as we study, that words will greatly handicap our expression of the realities involved, and we must endeavour to penetrate beneath the surface meaning to the esoteric structure of truth. These rays are in constant movement and circulation, and demonstrate an activity which is progressive and cyclic and evidences increasing momentum. They are dominant at one time and quiescent at another, and according to the particular ray which is making its presence felt at any particular time, so will be the quality of the civilisation, the type of forms which will make their appearance in the kingdoms of nature, and the consequent stage of awareness (the state of consciousness) of the human beings who are carried into form life in that particular era. These embodied lives (again in all four kingdoms) will be responsive to the peculiar vibration, quality, colouring and nature of the ray in question. The ray in manifestation will affect potently the three bodies which constitute the personality of man, and the influence of the ray will produce changes in the mind content and the emotional nature of the man and determine the calibre of the physical body.

I am aware, therefore, that in giving out this relatively new teaching upon the rays I may, in my endeavour to shed fresh light, temporarily increase the complexity of the subject. But as experiment is made, as people are studied in the laboratories of the psychologists and the psychoanalysts in connection with their ray indications, and as the newer sciences come into wise use and their proper sphere, we shall gain much and the teaching will find corroboration. We shall see emerging a new approach to the ancient truths, and a new mode of investigating humanity. In the meantime let us concentrate upon the clear enunciation of the truth anent the rays, and seek to tabulate, outline and indicate their nature, purpose and effects.

The seven rays, being cyclic in appearance, have continuously passed in and out of manifestation and have thus left their mark down the ages upon mankind, and therefore hold the clue to any true historical survey. Such a survey still remains to be made.

B. A second result of the study of the rays will be to clarify our knowledge as to the nature of man. Modern psychology, experimental and academic, has done much to gather information as to how a man functions, what is the nature of his reactions, the calibre of his thought apparatus and the quality of his physical mechanism, the mode of his thinking and the sum total of complexes, psychoses, neuroses, instincts, intuitions and intellectual fixations which he undoubtedly is. Medical psychology has also given us much, and we have learnt that the human being is entirely conditioned by his instrument of expression and can express no more than his nervous system, brain and glands permit. We find, however, that some of the theories, even the best proven, break down, given varying conditions. The field covered by psychology today is so vast, its schools so many and varied, and its terminology so cumbersome, that I can make no attempt to deal with it here.

The indebtedness of the world to the trained psychologists cannot be estimated, but unless there is a key idea interjected into the whole field of thought, it will fall of its own weight, and produce (as it is already producing) problems, complexes and diseases of the mind which are direct results of its own methods. The knowledge we now have of how men work on the physical plane as integrated personalities, and of how they can be expected to work, given certain conditions, is broad and sound, and the wideness of its grasp can be somewhat gauged if we compare what we know today with what was known a hundred and fifty years ago. But it has been largely based upon a study of the abnormal, and upon the form aspect (this latter being the true scientific method), and is therefore limited and circumscribed when it is put to the test in the last analysis and in the light of the undoubtedly existent supernormal. What I seek to do, and the contribution I seek to make to the subject, have to do with the emphasis we shall lay upon the nature of the integrating principle found within all coherent forms and on that which can (for lack of a better word) be called the soul or self. This principle, which informs the body nature and expresses its reactions through the emotional and mental states, is of course recognised by many schools of psychology, but remains nevertheless an unknown and undefinable quantity. They find it impossible to discover its origin; they know not what it is, whether or not it is an informing entity, detached and separate from the body nature; they question whether it is an integrated energetic sum total brought into existence through the fusion of the body cells, and therefore, through the process of evolution, constituting a thinking, feeling entity; or whether it is no more than the aggregated life and consciousness of the cells themselves.

The above is a generalisation which will serve our purpose and will cover the general proposition. It will appear, as we study, that the energies which inform the personalities and which constitute the nature of the human being fall naturally into three groups:

1. Those energies which we call "the spirits in men." You note here the utter superficiality of that phrase. It is meaningless and misleading. Spirit is *One*, but within that essential unity the "points of fire" or "the divine sparks" can be seen and noted. These unities, within the unity, are coloured by and react qualitatively to, three types of energy, for it is scientifically true, and a spiritual fact in nature, that God is the Three in One and the One in Three. The spirit of man came into incarnation along a line of force emanation from one or other of these three streams, which form one stream, emanating from the Most High.

2. These streams of energy differentiate into a major three,

yet remain one stream. This is an occult fact worthy of the deepest meditation. In their turn they differentiate into seven streams which "carry into the light," as it is called, the seven types of souls. It is with these seven that we shall deal.

3. The energies into which the three distribute themselves, thus becoming seven, in their turn produce the forty-nine types of force which express themselves through all the forms in the three worlds and the four kingdoms in nature. You have therefore:

   a. Three monadic groups of energies. The essential Unity expresses, through these three, the qualities of Will, Love and Intelligence.
   b. Seven groups of energies which are the medium through which the three major groups express the divine qualities.
   c. Forty-nine groups of forces to which all forms respond and which constitute the body of expression for the seven, who in their turn are reflections of the three divine qualities.

In some mysterious ways, therefore, the differentiations which manifest in nature are found in the realm of quality and not in the realm of reality.

It is with the seven groups of souls (or soul energies) that we shall deal, and with the threefold forms in the fourth kingdom of nature which they create, and through which they have to express the quality of their ray group and the energy of that one of the three essential groups to which their soul ray is related. We shall therefore, if possible, endeavour to add to modern psychology and enrich its content with that esoteric psychology which deals with the soul or self, the ensouling entity within the form.

C. The third effect of the study of these rays should be twofold. Not only shall we understand somewhat the inner side of history, not only shall we gain an idea of the divine qualities emerging from the three aspects and determining the forms of expression on the physical plane, but we shall have a practical method of analysis whereby we can arrive at a right understanding of ourselves as ensouling entities, and at a wiser comprehension of our fellowmen. When, through our study, we ascertain for instance that the tendency of our soul ray is that of will or power, but that the ray governing the personality is that of devotion, we can more truly gauge our opportunity, our capacities and our limitations; we can more justly determine our vocation and service, our assets and our debits, our true value and strength. When we can add to that knowledge an analysis which enables us to realise that the physical body is reacting pre-eminently to the soul ray, whilst the emotional body is under the influence of the personality ray which is historically in manifestation at the time, we are then in a position to gauge our particular problem with judgment. We can then deal more intelligently with ourselves, with our children and with our friends and associates. We shall find ourselves able to cooperate more wisely with the Plan as it is seeking expression at any particular time.

It is a platitude to say that the true meaning of "psychology" is the "word of the soul." It is the sound, producing an effect in matter, which a particular ray may make. This is in some ways a difficult way of expressing it, but if it is realised that each of the seven rays emits its own sound, and in so doing sets in motion those forces which must work in unison with it, the entire question of man's free will, of his eternal destiny and of his power to be self-assertive comes up for solution. These questions we shall seek to answer as

Introductory Remarks

we proceed.

Some of the points which I may seek to make clear will not be capable of substantiation and cannot be proved by you. These it would be wise to accept as working hypotheses, in order to understand that whereof I seek to speak. Some of the points I may make you may find yourself capable of checking up in your own life experience, and they will call forth from you a recognition coming from your concrete mind; or they may produce in you a reaction of the intensest conviction, emanating from your intuitively aware Self. In any case, read slowly; apply the laws of analogy and of correspondence; study yourself and your brethren; seek to link what I say to any knowledge you may possess of the modern theories, and remember that the more truly you live as a soul the more surely you will comprehend that which may be imparted.

As you study you must not forget the basic concept that in all occult work one is occupied with energy—energy units, energy embodied in forms, energy streams in flow; and that these energies are made potent and embody our purpose through the use of thought; they follow along the well-defined thought currents of the group.

It must be remembered, however, that it is in this region of thought that the cleavage comes between black and white magic. It is in the use of thought power that the two aspects of magic can be seen functioning, and therefore it is true that there is no black magic, per se, until one reaches the realm of mind. No one can be a black magician until the will and the thought work in unison, until mind control and the creative work of the focussed mind can be seen. It has oft been said the black magician is rare, indeed, and that is verily true, because the creative thinker, with power to use the sustained will, is also rare.

Let me illustrate. There is need for clear thinking on these matters, for as we study the psychology of the microcosm and arrive at an understanding of his ray impulses and energies we shall need to see clearly the way we go so that we shall tread the path of selflessness, leading to group awareness, and not the path of individualism, leading eventually and inevitably (as the mind aspect becomes organised) to the left hand path of black magic.

Those strong souls who consciously and knowingly enter into the realms of spiritual force and take thence that which they need and that which they choose, must work with intelligence, so that there may be a subsequent wise distribution of force within a chosen area. Those who know themselves to be in the rank and file of aspirants, but who possess the persistence which will drive them forward to the goal, need to remember that theirs is the responsibility of adding their quota to the sum total, and that this is done every time they think of the group, correspond with a fellow aspirant or meditate.

Extend the idea, then, from the student in a group to the group itself, regarding it as a group unit within a larger group. You have there a perfect analogy to the way the Great Ones work at this time. Regard, therefore, all your work as group work, causing effects which are inevitable and contributing to the potency of the group thought form.

The second thing upon which I seek to touch concerns the testing going on inevitably among the aspirants and disciples at this time. This is not so much a testing of their place upon the Path, as of their power to live in the world as citizens of another kingdom, and as the custodians of that which the world as a rule does not recognise. In so far as that testing is applied, and in so far as it can be gauged, I seek to point out that the testing is not applied, as some think, because of their affiliation with any group or because of their one-pointed determination to tread the Path. It is applied because the aspirants' own souls so ordained it, prior to incarnation, and it was the will of their souls that a certain measure of growth, hitherto unknown, should be attained, a certain degree of detachment from form should be achieved, and a certain preparation should be undergone which would lead to a liberation from the form life. The idea that a renewed effort towards the goal of spiritual light is the cause of trouble or precipitates disaster is not a statement of fact. The extent of the discipline to be undergone by a disciple is settled and known by his soul before he even takes a body; it is determined by law.

It is this problem of energy units and their mutual interplay which underlies the entire subject of the rays which we shall seek to investigate. Every group in the world is a nucleus for the focussing and interplay of the seven types of force, just as every human being is also a meeting place for the seven types of energy,—two in the ascendant and five less potent. Every group can consequently be a creative centre and produce that which is an expression of the controlling energies and of the directed thought of the thinkers in the group. From the standpoint of Those Who see and guide, therefore, every group is constructing something that is relatively tangible and governed by certain building laws. The great work of the Builders proceeds steadily. Often that which is built is inchoate, futile and without form or purpose, and of no use to either gods or men. But the race as a whole is now coming into an era wherein the mind is becoming a potent factor; many are learning to hold the mind steady in the light, and consequently are receptive to ideas hitherto unrecognised. If a group of minds can be so drawn together and fused into an adequate synthesis, and if they (in their individual and daily meditation) keep focussed or oriented towards that which can be apprehended, great concepts can be grasped and great ideas intuited. Men can train themselves—as a group—to think these intuited ideas of the true and the beautiful and of the Plan into manifested existence, and thus a creation of beauty, embodying a divine principle, can be built. Ponder on this, seek to fit yourselves for the registering of these ideas, and train yourselves to formulate them into thoughts and to transmit them so that others can apprehend them also. This is the nature of the real work to be done by the new groups, and students today who can grasp this idea have the opportunity to do some of this pioneering work.

Always the individual of advancement and of poise has been able to do this intuiting, and to concretise the idea. Groups of students meditating synchronously should now attempt to do the same. The effort to synchronise effort does not relate so much to the time element as to unity of intent and of purpose.

There is to be found today in the realm of the intuition much of wonder; this can be contacted. It is now the privilege of the race to contact that "raincloud of knowable things" to which the ancient seer Patanjali refers in his fourth book; the race, through its many aspirants, can today precipitate this "raincloud" so that the brains of men everywhere can register the contact. Hitherto this has been the privilege of the illumined and rare seer. In this way the New Age will be ushered in and the new knowledge will enter into the minds of humanity.

This can be practically demonstrated if those who are interested in this *Treatise on the Seven Rays* can attune themselves to think clearly, and with a poised and illumined mind seek to understand what is relatively a new aspect of truth.

In undertaking to reveal something anent the nature of the seven rays, I feel it necessary to remind all of you who take up this study that any speculation as to the emanating source of the rays must remain profitless until there is developed within each student that apparatus of response and that sensitive mechanism which will enable him to register a wider

Introductory Remarks 13

field of contacts than is at present possible. Many are as yet in the initial stage of registering an awareness of a field of expression which they know exists—the field of soul awareness—but which is not yet for them their normal field of expression. Many know a great deal about it, theoretically, but the practical effects of applied knowledge are not yet theirs. Many are conscious of consciousness, and are aware of the kingdom of the soul and of an occasional reaction to impression from that kingdom, but they are not yet consciousness itself, nor so identified with the soul that consciousness of all else drops away. To achieve that is their aim and objective.

Let me also remind you that the career of the Monad (an aspect of energy found on one or other of the three major rays) can be roughly divided into three parts, leading to a fourth:

1. A lower realisation of a unity which is the unity of the form nature. In this unity, the soul is so closely identified with the matter aspect that it sees no distinction, but *is* the form, and knows not itself as soul. This often reaches its height in some life of full personality expression, wherein the soul is completely centred in personality reactions; the lower life is so strong and vital that a powerful and material expression eventuates.
2. A subsequent and painful differentiation of the consciousness into a realised duality. In this condition, the man is distinctly aware of what is termed his essential duality; he knows he is spirit-matter, is form-life, and is the soul in manifestation. During this stage, which covers many lives and carries the man along the path of probation and discipleship as far as the third initiation, the centre of gravity (if I may so express it) shifts steadily out of the form side and centres itself more and more in that

of the soul. There is a growing consciousness that there is a Reality which embraces, and at the same time extinguishes, duality.

Remember that the entire story of evolution is the story of consciousness, and of a growing expansion of the "becoming-aware" principle, so that from the microscopic interest of the self-conscious man—for we shall retain the parable within the confines of the fourth kingdom in nature—we have a slowly developing inclusiveness which finally leads him into the consciousness of the cosmic Christ.

3. The higher realisation of unity follows upon this sense of duality, and in this final stage the sense of being soul and body is lost. The consciousness identifies itself with the indwelling Life of the planet and of the solar system. When this happens, there is the registering of a state of being which lies beyond word, mind and form expression of any kind.

The great Jewish seer sought to convey these three stages in the words, *I Am—That—I Am*. He thus expressed them tritely and succinctly and adequately, had we but the development to know it. The third (however understood) defies expression, and hints at a fourth type of realisation which is that of Deity itself, about which it profits us not to speculate.

2. *Life-Quality-Appearance*

In our study of the rays it must therefore be remembered that we are dealing with life-expression, through the medium of matter-form. The highest unity will be cognised only when this dual relation is perfected. The theory of the One Life may be held, but I deal not basically with theory but with that which may be known, provided there is growth and intelligent application of truth. I deal with possibility and with that which is capable of achievement. Many these days like to talk and think in terms of that One Life, but it remains but speech and thought, whilst the true awareness of that essential Unity remains a dream and an imagining. Whenever this reality is put into words duality is emphasised and the spiritual controversy (using the word in its basic meaning and not in its ordinary warlike connotation) is enhanced. Take for example the words: "I believe in the One Life" or "To me, there is but one Reality," and note how they are in their phraseology an expression of duality. Life cannot be expressed in words nor can its realised perfection. The process of "becoming," which leads to "being," is a cosmic event, involving all forms, and no son of God lies separated from that mutable process as yet. As long as he is in form he cannot know what Life is, though, when he has attained certain steps and can function on the higher planes of the system in full awareness, he can begin to glimpse that awful Reality. Certain great initiates, down the ages, have fulfilled their function of revealers, and have held before the eyes of the pioneering disciples of life the ideal of Oneness and of Unity. It has nevertheless been a matter of shifting the focus of attention progressively out of one form into another, and thus, from a higher standpoint getting a fresh glimpse of a possible truth. Each age (and the present is no exception) has believed its grasp of Reality and its sensitivity to the inner Beauty to be greater and nearer the True than was ever previously possible. The highest realisation of what is termed the One Life is the awareness (of the initiate of high degree) of the embodied Logos, of Deity, and his identification with the consciousness of that stupendous Creator Who is seeking expression through the medium of the solar system. No initiate on the planet can identify himself with the consciousness of that Identified Being (in the esoteric sense of the term) Who, speaking in the *Bhagavad Gita*, says: "Having pervaded the entire universe with a fragment of Myself, I remain."

These thoughts I commend to your consideration and to your careful pondering, begging you to see to it that there is a steady expansion of your sense of awareness and a growing capacity to make understanding contacts with that emerging Truth, Reality and Beauty which the universe declares. Guard yourself at the same time from mystical rhapsodies anent the One Life, which are apt to be no more than the negation of all mental apprehension and a luxuriating in the sensuous perception of a highly developed and high grade emotional nature.

All our considerations therefore in this *Treatise on the Seven Rays* will necessarily be held within the realm of thought which involves awareness of duality. I shall employ the language of duality, and this I shall do, not because I seek to emphasize it to the neglect of unity (for this unity is to me somewhat of a reality and I glimpse more than a possibility), but because all aspirants and disciples and all initiates up to the third initiation—as I earlier said—are swinging as a pendulum between the pairs of opposites, spirit and matter. I speak not here of the pairs of opposites of the astral or emotional plane, which are illusory reflections of the true pairs of opposites, but of the basic duality of manifestation. I seek to deal with that material which is of practical value and which can be grasped by the illumined intelligence of the average man. It is necessary for all students who seek illumination and a right apprehension of truth to drop the emphasis so often laid upon certain aspects and presentations of truth being *spiritual* and others being *mental*. It is in the realm of so-called mind that the great principle of separateness is found. It is also in the realm of mind that the great at-one-ment is made. The words of the initiate Paul have here a fitting place, wherein he says: "Let this mind be in you which was also in Christ," and adds in another place that Christ had made "in himself, of twain, one new man". It is through the mind that theory is formulated, truth distinguished and Deity apprehended. When we are more advanced upon the Path, we shall see naught but spirit everywhere, and the aphorism, enunciated by that great disciple, H.P.Blavtsky, that "matter is spirit on the lowest point of its cyclic activity." and "Spirit is matter *on the seventh plane*," *The Secret Doctrine* 1st Ed. p.693 & p.633 or the highest, will be a realised fact in our consciousness. It is as yet but an intellectual phrase which means little except the enunciation of a truth, incapable of proof. Everything is an expression of a spiritual consciousness, which spiritualises by its inherent life all matter-forms. A grub or worm working out its little life in a mass of decaying substance is as much a spiritual manifestation as an initiate working out his destiny in a mass of rapidly changing human forms. It is all manifested Deity; it is all divine expression and all a form of sensitive awareness and of response to environment, and therefore a form of conscious expression.

The seven rays are the first differentiation of the divine triplicity of Spirit-Consciousness-Form, and they provide the entire field of expression for the manifested Deity. We are told in the scriptures of the world that the interplay, or the relation between, Father—Spirit and Mother—Matter produces eventually a third, which is the Son, or the consciousness aspect. That Son, the product of the two, is esoterically defined as "the One Who was third but is the second." The reason for this wording is that there first existed the two divine aspects, Spirit-Matter, or matter impregnated with life, and it was only when these two realised their mutual unity (note the necessary ambiguity of that phrase) that the Son emerged. The esotericist, however, regards Spirit-Matter as the first unity, and the Son therefore is the second factor. This Son, Who is divine Life incarnate in matter, and consequently the producer of the diversity and immensity of forms, is the embodiment of divine quality. We might therefore utilise—for the sake of clarity—the terms Life-Quality-Appearance as interchangeable with the more usual trinity of Spirit-Soul-Body, or Life-Consciousness-Form.

I shall utilise the word *Life* when referring to Spirit, to energy, to the Father, to the first aspect of Divinity, and to that essential dynamic electric Fire which produces all that is, and is the sustaining, originating Cause and Source of all manifestation.

I shall use the word *Appearance* to express that which we call matter, or form, or objective expression; it is that illusory tangible outer appearance which is animated by life. This is the third aspect, the Mother, overshadowed and fertilised by the Holy Ghost, or Life, united with intelligent substance. This is fire by friction—a friction brought about by life and matter and their interplay, and producing change and constant mutation.

I shall use the word *Quality* as expressive of the second aspect, the Son of God, the cosmic Christ incarnate in form—a form brought into being by the relation of spirit and matter. This interplay produces that psychological Entity which we call the Christ. This cosmic Christ demonstrated to us His perfection, as far as the human family is concerned, through the medium of the historical Christ. This psychological Entity can bring into functioning activity a quality within all human forms which esoterically can "obliterate the forms" and so engross the attention as to be regarded eventually as the main factor and as constituting all that is. This truth as to life and quality and form is made most clearly apparent to us in the story of the Christ of Galilee. He was constantly reminding the people that He was not what He appeared to be, neither was He the Father in Heaven, and He is ever referred to by those who know and love Him in terms of quality. He demonstrated to us the quality of the love of God, and in Himself He embodied not only that which He had evolved of the seven ray qualities, but also—as do few of the sons of God—a basic principle of the ray of the Solar Logos Himself, the quality of Love. This we shall study more closely when we take up the consideration of the second Ray of Love-Wisdom.

The seven rays are therefore embodiments of seven types of force which demonstrate to us the seven qualities of Deity. These seven qualities have consequently a sevenfold effect upon the matter and forms to be found in all parts of the universe, and have also a sevenfold interrelation between themselves.

Life-quality-appearance are brought together into a synthesis in the manifested universe and in man incarnate, and the result of this synthesis is sevenfold, producing seven types of qualified forms which emerge on all planes and in all kingdoms. It must be remembered that all the planes which we, from our little point of view, regard as formless are not really so. Our seven planes are but the seven subplanes of the cosmic physical plane. We shall not deal with the planes, except in their relation to man's unfoldment, nor shall we deal with the macrocosm, or with the developing life of the Cosmic Christ. We shall confine our attention entirely to man and to his psychological reactions to the qualified forms in three directions: to those in the subhuman kingdoms in nature, to those with whom he associates in the human family and to the guiding Hierarchy and the world of souls. The seven ray types must be dealt with entirely from the human angle, for this treatise is intended to give the new psychological approach to man through an understanding of the energies, seven in number, with their forty-nine differentiations, which animate him and make him what he is. Later, as we take up each ray type, we shall subject man to a close analysis and study his reactions in these three directions.

These seven rays are the seven streams of force issuing from a central energy after (in point of time) that vortex of energy had been set up. Spirit and matter became mutually interactive and the form or appearance of the solar system began its process of becoming,—a process leading to an eventual *being*. This idea is ancient and true. We find reference to the seven aeons and the seven emanations and to the life and nature of the seven "Spirits which are before the Throne of God" in the writings of Plato and of all initiates who laid down in ancient times the basic propositions which have guided the human mentality down the ages. These great Lives, functioning within the boundaries of the solar system, gathered to Themselves that substance which They required for manifestation and built it into those forms and appearances through which They could best express Their innate qualities. Within the radius of Their influence, They gathered all that now appears. This aggregated, qualified material constitutes Their body of manifestation, just as the solar system is the body of manifestation of the Trinity of aspects.

This idea can best be apprehended if one remembers that every human being is, in his turn, an aggregate of atoms and cells built into form and having scattered throughout that form organs and centres of differentiated life which function in rhythm and relation, but which have varying influences and differing purposes. These aggregated and animated forms present an appearance of an entity or central life which is characterised by its own quality, and which functions according to the point in evolution, thus making an impress by its radiation and life upon every atom and cell and organism within the radius of immediate influence and also upon every other human being contacted. Man is a psychic entity, a Life Who, through radiatory influence, has built a form, coloured it with His own psychic quality and thus presented an appearance to the environing world which will persist for as long a time as He lives in form.

This statement covers also the life story and the qualified appearance of any one of the seven rays. God, Ray, Life, and Man are all psychological entities and builders of forms. Therefore a great psychological life is appearing through the medium of a solar system. Seven psychological lives, qualified by seven types of force, are appearing through the medium of the seven planets. Each planetary life repeats the same technique of manifestation—life-quality-appearance—and in its second aspect of quality demonstrates as a psychological entity. Every human being is a miniature replica of the entire plan. He is also spirit-soul-body, life-quality-appearance. He colours his appearance with his quality and animates it with his life. Because all appearances are expressions of quality and the lesser is included in the greater, every form in nature and every human being is found upon one or other of the seven qualifying rays and his appearance in a phenomenal form is coloured by the quality of his basic ray. It is qualified predominantly by the ray of the particular life upon whose emanation he issued forth, but it will include also in a secondary measure the six other ray types.

Let us therefore posit—as a symbolical analogy—the fact of a Central Life (extraneous and outside our solar system yet within it during the process of manifestation) Which decides within Itself to take a material form and to incarnate. A vortex of force is set up as a preliminary step and we then have God immanent and God transcendent at the same time. This vortex, as a result of this initial activity, demonstrates through the medium of what we call substance or (to use a technical term of modern science, which is the best we can do at this time) through the ether of space. The consequence of this active interplay of life and substance is that a basic unity is constituted. Father and mother are at-one. This unity is characterised by quality. Through this triplicity of life-quality-form, the central Life evokes and manifests consciousness, or awareness of response to all that is eventuating, but in a degree which it is impossible for us to cognise, limited as we are by our present relatively undeveloped point in evolution.

Students of this treatise must bear in mind, from the very start of their studies, the necessity for familiarising themselves with these four conditioning factors—life-quality-appearance—and their result or synthesis which we call *Consciousness*.

Always, therefore, we predicate that which stands outside of the appearance and which is conscious of that appearance. This involves awareness of its material development and consequent adequacy of expression, and also awareness of its psychic unfoldment. No study of the rays is possible apart from this fourfold recognition. Our grasp of the subject will be much facilitated if we train ourselves to regard ourselves as an accurate (though as yet undeveloped) expression and reflection of this initial creative quaternary. We are lives, making an appearance, expressing quality and slowly becoming aware of the process and the objective, as our consciousness becomes more like that of Divinity Itself.

3. *The Seven Rays Enumerated*

As part of the initial Plan, the one Life sought expansion, and the seven aeons or emanations came forth from the central vortex and actively repeated the earlier process in all its details. They too came into manifestation and in the work of

Introductory Remarks

expressing active life, qualified by love and limited by an outward phenomenal appearance, they swept into a secondary activity and became the seven Builders, the seven Sources of life and the seven Rishis of all the ancient scriptures. They are the original psychic Entities, imbued with the capacity to express love (which involves the concept of duality, for the loving and the loved, the desiring and the desired, must here be posited) and to emerge from subjective being into objective becoming. We call these seven by various names, as follows:

1. *The Lord of Power or Will.* This Life wills to love, and uses power as an expression of divine beneficence. For His body of manifestation He uses that planet for which the sun is regarded as the esoteric substitute.
2. *The Lord of Love-Wisdom*, Who is the embodiment of pure love, is regarded by esotericists as being as close to the heart of the Solar Logos as was the beloved disciple close to the heart of the Christ of Galilee. This Life instils into all forms the quality of love, with its more material manifestation of desire, and is the attractive principle in nature and the custodian of the Law of Attraction, which is the life-demonstration of pure Being. This Lord of Love is the most potent of the seven rays, because He is on the same cosmic ray as the solar Deity. He expresses Himself primarily through the planet Jupiter, which is His body of manifestation.
3. *The Lord of Active Intelligence.* His work is more closely linked to matter and He works in cooperation with the Lord of the second ray. He is the motivating impulse in the initial work of creation. The planet Saturn is His body of expression within the solar system, and through the medium of matter (which beneficently obstructs and

hinders) He provides humanity with a vast field of experiment and experience.

I should like to point out here that when I speak in terms of personality and perforce employ the personal pronoun, I must not be accused of personalising these great forces. I speak in terms of entity, of pure Being, and not in terms of human personality. But the handicap of language persists; and in teaching those who think in terms of the lower concrete mind, and whose intuition is dormant or only manifesting in flashes, I am compelled to speak in parables and use the language of word symbols. Let me point out also that all statements which I may make are in relation to our particular planet and couched in terms that can be understood by the humanity which our planet has produced. The work, as I outline it, constitutes only a fraction of the work undertaken by these Beings; They each have Their own purpose and radius of influence, and as our Earth is not one of the seven sacred planets (nor the body of manifestation of one of the basic seven rays), They have purposes and activities in which our Earth plays only a minor part.

4. *The Lord of Harmony, Beauty and Art.* The main function of this Being is the creation of Beauty (as an expression of truth) through the free interplay of life and form, basing the design of beauty upon the initial plan as it exists in the mind of the solar Logos. The body of manifestation of this life is not revealed, but the activity emanating from it produces that combination of sounds, colours and word music that expresses—through the form of the ideal—that which is the originating idea. This fourth Lord of creative expression will resume activity upon the Earth about six hundred years hence, though already the first faint impress of His influence is

being felt and the next century will see a re-awakening of creative art in all its branches.
5. *The Lord of Concrete Knowledge and Science.* This is a Great Life in close touch with the mind of the creative Deity, just as the Lord of the second ray is in close touch with the heart of that same Deity. His influence is great at this time, though not as potent as it will be later. Science is a psychological unfoldment in man due to this ray influence, and is only entering into its real work. His influence is waxing in power, just as the influence of the sixth Lord is waning.
6. *The Lord of Devotion and Idealism.* This solar Deity is a peculiar and characteristic expression of the quality of the solar Logos. Forget not that in the great scheme of the universal universe (not just our universe) our solar Logos is as differentiated and distinctive in quality as are any of the sons of men. This ray force, with the second ray, is a true and vital expression of the divine nature. A militant focussing upon the ideal, a one-pointed devotion to the intent of the life urge, and a divine sincerity are the qualities of this Lord, and set their impress upon all that is found within His body of manifestation. Advanced esotericists debate as to whether Mars is, or is not, the planet through which He manifests. You must remember that only a few of the planets are the bodies of expression of the Lords of the rays. There are ten "planets of expression" (to use the term employed by the ancient Rishis), and only seven ray Lives are regarded as the Builders of the system. The great mystery, which is finally revealed in the higher initiations, is the relation of a ray to a planet. Therefore seek not full information at this time. The influence of this sixth Lord is now passing out.

7. *The Lord of Ceremonial Order or Magic* is now coming into power and is slowly but surely making His pressure felt. His influence is most potent upon the physical plane, for there is a close numerical interrelation between (for instance) the Lord of the seventh ray and the seventh plane, the physical, just as the seventh root race will see complete conformity to and a perfect expression of law and order. This ray of order and its incoming is partially responsible for the present tendency in world affairs toward governmental dictatorship and the imposed control of a central governing body.

It may be of value here if I give you the following statement as to the activity, or non-activity, of the rays, begging you to bear in mind that this statement refers only to our Earth and its evolutions:

Ray One ...... Not in manifestation.
*Ray Two ...... In manifestation since 1575 A.D.
*Ray Three ..... In manifestation since 1425 A.D.
Ray Four ..... To come slowly into manifestation after 2025 A.D.
*Ray Five ...... In manifestation since 1775 A.D.
Ray Six........ Passing rapidly out of manifestation. It began to pass out in 1625 A.D.
*Ray Seven ..... In manifestation since 1675 A.D.

These are of course all lesser cycles within the influence of the sign Pisces. You will see that four rays are in manifestation at this time,—the second, third, fifth, and seventh.

The question arises here: How does it happen that we find people in incarnation on all the rays at practically the same time? The reason is that, as you can easily see, the fourth is beginning to approach and the sixth is passing out, which puts six of the rays in the position of having their egos in manifestation. There are however very few of the fourth ray egos on the Earth at this time, and a very large number of sixth ray egos, for it will be about two hundred years before all the sixth ray egos pass out of incarnation. As to the first ray egos, there are no pure first ray types on the planet. All so-called first ray egos are on the first subray of the second ray, which is in incarnation. A pure first ray ego in incarnation at this time would be a disaster. There is not sufficient intelligence and love in the world to balance the dynamic will of an ego on the ray of the destroyer.

Just as the human family has a relation to the planetary Logos of our Earth which is best expressed by stating that it constitutes His heart and brain, so does the sum total of analogous evolutions within the entire solar system constitute the heart and brain of the solar Logos. Intelligent activity and love are the outstanding characteristics of a developed son of God, whilst their lower reflections—sex and desire—are the characteristics of the average man and the undeveloped sons of God.

These seven living qualified emanations from the central vortex of force are composed of untold myriads of energy units which are inherently and innately aspects of life, endowed with quality and capable of appearance. Below the human, the combination of these three produces conscious response to the environment, regarding the environment as composed of the sum total of all lives, qualities and appearances,—the synthesis of the seven rays or emanations of the Deity. They produce in the human kingdom a self-conscious awareness, and in the superhuman world a synthetic inclusiveness. All human monads, carried into manifestation by the will and desire of some ray Lord, are part of His body of manifestation. Potentially they express His quality and appear phenomenally according to the point in evolutionary expression which has been reached. "As He is, so are we in this world," but only as yet potentially,—the goal of evolution being to make the potential into the real, and the latent into the expressed. The work of the esotericist is just this very thing: to bring out of latency, the hidden quality.

4. *The Function of Christianity*

I have now laid down the basic premise that all that is known to us is a manifesting divine Entity, expressing Itself through three aspects which (for the purposes of this treatise and because they are more in line with the terminology of emerging modern thought) I choose to call Life-Quality-Appearance. These are but other names for the Trinity of all the great religions, and are synonymous with the Christian phrase, Father, Son and Holy Ghost (those old anthropomorphic terms!); with Spirit, Soul and Body, the current phraseology; and with the Life, Consciousness and Form of the Indian philosophy.

May I interpolate here the comment that modern thinkers would do well to bear in mind that the importance of Christianity lies in the realisation that it is a bridging religion. This is symbolised for us by the fact that the Master of all the Masters took incarnation in Palestine, that slice of land which is midway between Asia and Europe, and which partakes of the character of both. Christianity is the religion of the transitional period which links the era of self-conscious existence with that of a group-conscious world. It is extant in the age which will see that type of thought prevailing which (when rightly applied) will serve as the connecting link between the worlds of concrete and of abstract mind. The *Old Commentary* puts it thus:

> "When the hour arrives wherein the light of the soul reveals the antahkarana (the bridge between the personality consciousness and the soul consciousness, A.A.B.) then shall men

be known by their knowledge, be coloured by the despair of desire unappeased, be divided into those who recognise their dharma (meet all implied obligations and duties) and those who only see the working out of karma, and from the very nature of their need find light and peace at last."

Christianity is primarily a religion of cleavage, demonstrating to man his duality and so laying the foundation for future unity. This is a most needed stage and has served humanity well; the purpose and intent of Christianity has been definite and high, and it has done its divine work. Today it is in the process of being superseded, but by what new formulation of truth is not yet revealed. The light is slowly pouring into man's life, and in this lighted radiance he will formulate the new religion and arrive at a fresh enunciation of ancient truth. Through the lens of the illumined mind, he will shortly see aspects of divinity hitherto unknown. Has it ever dawned on you that there may be qualities and characteristics of the divine nature, latent as yet within the form, that have hitherto remained totally unknown and not even dimly sensed, and which, as yet, are literally unprecedented and for which we have neither words nor other adequate medium of expression? So it is. Just as the phrase "group-consciousness" would carry, for early primitive man, no significance whatsoever, and would have been only a meaningless string of alphabetical forms, so (lingering just below the surface of our manifested world) lie divine qualities and a purpose which is as far removed from the consciousness of our present humanity as the idea of collective awareness was from the consciousness of prehistoric humanity. Take courage from this thought. The past guarantees the infinite expansion of the future.

II. *Certain Questions and their Answers.*

1. What is the soul and its nature?
2. What is the origin, goal, purpose and plan of the soul?
3. Can the fact of the soul be proved?
4. Of what value is it to study the rays?
5. What is the meaning of: Sentiency; Consciousness or Awareness; Energy or Light?

CHAPTER II

Certain Questions and Their Answers

I INDICATED that in this treatise we would give our main attention to the central one of the three aspects, and would concentrate upon *quality*. What do I mean by this? I mean that we shall occupy ourselves with that which is emerging through the medium of form, with that which veils or hides itself behind the appearance, which is expressive of life or spirit, and which is produced through the interplay of life with matter. This, when posited of man, the reflection of divinity, and when applied to the subject of his quality, involves three recognitions:

1. That a human being is, as earlier said, an embodied Life, expressing quality and registering that quality in consciousness or as sensitive response to the interplay going forward, during the evolutionary process, between spirit and matter.
2. That man, being a synthesis (and the only complete synthesis, except the Macrocosmic Deity), registers a self-recognition which is potent enough today to enable him to differentiate reactions to. . . .
   a. The triplicity (as the *Bhagavad Gita* calls it) of the Knower, the field of knowledge, and knowledge.
   b. A growing realisation that the field of knowledge is but an appearance or an illusion, that knowledge itself can be a hindrance unless transmuted into wisdom.

c. An evolutionary growth in responsiveness to one or other of these three, and which indicates a developing sensitivity.

   This is leading to a growth of interest in the Knower and to a belief that this Knower is the Soul, one with Deity, illimitable and eternal and—in time and space—the determining factor in human existence.

3. That the endless diversity of forms hides a subjective synthesis. Man can therefore eventually see, expressing itself through all forms in all kingdoms, a universal *septenate*, and when this happens, he is then entering into the world of subjective unity, and can proceed on his way consciously towards the One. He cannot as yet enter into the consciousness of that basic essential Unity, but he can enter into that of his own ray-life, of the emanating source of his own temporarily specialised life.

This triplicity of ideas requires careful study. It might be expressed thus:

```
     o  . . . . . . . . . .  The One Life. Unity.
   o o o  . . . . . . . . .  The Major three Rays ⎫
 o o o o  . . . . . . . . .  The Minor four Rays  ⎬ Making seven
                                                  ⎭
     o  . . . . . . . . . .  The Unity of Appearance
```

With the one Life we shall not concern ourselves. We accept it as a basic truth and we realise that we are on our way back from the unity of form-identified existence, through the varying unfoldments of a conscious response to divine interplay and activity, to a final identification with the one Life. Form awareness has to give place to the qualified radiation of the self-conscious spiritual identity which is that of a son of God, appearing through form. This will be finally superseded by two phases of expression wherein there is:

1. A sense of divine synthesis, of which our bodily "well-

being" is the lowest form of material, yet symbolic, reflection. It is a sense of coordinated blissful satisfaction, based on realised Being.

2. A withdrawal from even this life-awareness to a phase still more intensive and detached, which involves an awareness of the life of God Itself, free from form, but still, in a mysterious sense, aware of quality.

In the language of mysticism it might be expressed this way:

"I take a body. That body is alive. I know its life. I therefore know my mother.

"I use a body. That body is not me. I serve the group and in this serving live within the body, detached, a son of God. I know my Self.

"I infuse a body. I am its life and in that life shall I see life. That life is known as love. I am the love of God. I know the Father, and know His life is love.

"I am the body and its loving life. I am the Self, whose quality is love. I am the life of God Himself. The Mother-Father-Son am I.

"Behind these three there stands the unknown God. That God am I."

Let us be perfectly clear even at the expense of reiteration. In this treatise, though we may touch upon form and consider its nature, we shall lay emphasis upon self-consciousness as it expresses itself as responsiveness, as awareness of a peculiar kind which we call the "quality of consciousness," or its inherent characteristic. We have always the subsidiary triplicities, which are only adjectival terms employed to express the quality of the appearing life.

Form . . . . Mutability, conscious response to radiation.
                         Matter.
Self-Consciousness . . Responsiveness. Awareness of identity.
                         Soul.
Life . . . . Immutability. Emanation. Cause. Source.
                         Spirit.

The synthesis of all these in manifestation we call God, the Isolated, the All-pervading, the Detached and the Withdrawn.

The above abstract truths are difficult of apprehension, but need here to be expressed, so that our platform is understood and we are not open to the criticism that we neglect reality and regard diversity as the only truth.

We shall now answer five questions that I have formulated and answered for the reader.

Question 1. What is the soul? Can we define it? What is its nature?

Here I shall give but four definitions which will serve as a basis for all that follows.

A. The soul can be spoken of as the Son of the Father and of the Mother (Spirit-Matter) and is therefore the embodied life of God, coming into incarnation in order to reveal the quality of the nature of God, which is essential love. This life, taking form, nurtures the quality of love within all forms, and ultimately reveals the purpose of all creation. This is the simplest definition for average humanity, being couched in the language of mysticism, thus linking the truth as found in all religions. It is necessarily inadequate, for it fails to emphasize the truth that what can be posited of man can also be posited of the cosmic reality, and that just as a human appearance on Earth veils both the quality and purpose (in varying degree), so does that synthesis of all forms or appearances, within that unity which we call a solar system, veil the quality and purpose of Deity. It is only when man is no longer deluded by appearance and has freed himself from the veil of illusion that he arrives at a knowledge of the quality of God's consciousness and at the purpose which it is revealing. This he does in a triple way:

a. He discovers his own soul, the product of the union of

his Father in heaven with the Mother or the material nature. This last is the personality. He then, having discovered the personality, discovers the quality of his own soul life, and the purpose for which he has "appeared."

b. He finds that this quality expresses itself through seven aspects or basic differentiations, and that this septenate of qualities colours, esoterically, all forms in all kingdoms in nature, thus constituting the totality of the revelations of the divine purpose. This, he finds, is essentially a septenary aggregation of energies, each energy producing differing effects and appearances. This discovery he makes by finding that his own soul is tinctured by one of the seven ray qualities, that he is identified with his ray purpose—whatever it may be—and is expressing a particular type of divine energy.

c. From this point he proceeds to a recognition of the entire septenate, and upon the Path of Initiation he gains a glimpse of a Unity, hitherto unrealised, nor even sensed.

Thus from a consciousness of himself, man arrives at an awareness of the interrelation between the seven basic energies or rays; and from that he proceeds to a realisation of the triple deity, until at the final initiation (the fifth) he finds himself consciously at-one with the unified divine intent lying behind all appearances and all qualities. It might be added that initiations, higher than the fifth, reveal a purpose wider and deeper than that which is working out within our solar system. The purpose of our manifested Logos is but a part of a greater intent. It might also be noted that in the fourth kingdom of nature, on the path of evolution and of probation, a man arrives at a knowledge of his individual soul, and glimpses the quality and purpose of that soul. On the path of discipleship and of initiation, he glimpses the quality and purpose of his planetary Life, and discovers himself as a part of a ray Life, Which is appearing through the form of a planet and is embodying an aspect of the divine purpose and energy. After the third initiation he glimpses the quality and purpose of the solar system; he sees his ray life and energy as a part of a greater whole. These are but modes of expressing the emerging quality and the hidden purpose of the graded Lives which inform all appearances and colour them with quality.

B. The soul can be regarded as the principle of intelligence—an intelligence whose characteristics are mind and mental awareness, which in turn demonstrate as the power to analyse, to discriminate, to separate, and to distinguish, to choose or to reject, with all the implications conveyed in these terms. As long as a man is identified with the appearance, these aspects of the mental principle produce in him the "great heresy of separateness." It is the appearance of the form nature that glamours him and completely deludes him. He regards himself as the form, and then proceeds from a realisation of himself as the material form, and as identified with the outer appearance, to a realisation of himself as an insatiable desire. He then becomes identified with his desire body, with his appetites, good and bad, and considers himself as one with his moods, his feelings, his longings, whether they ray out in the direction of the material world or inward toward the world of thought or the kingdom of the soul. He is torn by a sense of duality. Later, he becomes identified with still another of the appearances,—with the mind body or nature. Thoughts become to him so tangible that he is swayed, turned and influenced by them; and to the world of material appearances, and to the world of the great Illusion is added the world of thought forms. He is then subjected to a triple illusion, and he, the conscious life behind the illusion, begins to unify the forms into one coordinated whole, in order the better to control them.

Thus the *Personality* of the soul makes its appearance. He stands then on the verge of the probationary path. He enters the world of quality and of value, and begins to discover the nature of the soul and to shift the emphasis from the appearance to the quality of the Life which has produced it. This identification of the quality with the appearance grows steadily upon the path until the fusion of quality and appearance, of energy and that which it energises, is so perfect that appearance no longer veils the reality, and the soul is now the dominant factor; consciousness is now identified with itself (or with its ray) and not with its phenomenal appearance. Later, the soul itself is superseded by the Monad, and that Monad becomes, in verity, embodied purpose.

The process can be expressed by a very simple symbology, as follows:—o.o.o. or o.o...o or o...o.o., thus portraying the separateness of the three aspects. The union, then, of the aspects of appearance—quality—purpose or life, results in an abstraction from the appearance, and therefore the end of phenomenal existence. Ponder on the simple arrangement of these signs, for they portray your life and progress:

Unevolved man. . .o o o. appearance, quality, life.
Disciple. . . . . .o o..o. appearance—quality. . . . . .life.
Initiate. . . . . .o..o o. appearance. . . . . . quality—life.

Finally. . . . . (o o) within the circle of infinity.

This is true of the human being, of the Christ in incarnation; it is equally true of the cosmic Christ, of God incarnate in the solar system. In the system a similar fusion and blending is going on, and the separated aspects are entering into an evolutionary relationship, resulting in an eventual synthesis of appearance and quality, and then of quality and purpose. It might be noted here that the Hierarchy as a whole is distinguished by the sign o..oo; the New Group of World

Servers by the sign oo..o; and the unevolved masses by o o o. Forget not, that in all three groups, as in nature, there are the intermediate stages composed of those who are on their way to a transitional accomplishment.

The work before all students of this *Treatise on the Seven Rays* is the fusion of quality and appearance, and therefore they need to study the nature of that quality in order to produce a true appearance. In the ancient rules given to mystics in Atlantean times we find these words:

> "Let the disciple know the nature of his Lord of Love. Seven the aspects of the love of God; seven the colours of that manifesting One; sevenfold the work; seven the energies and sevenfold the Path back to the centre of peace. Let the disciple live in love, and love in life."

In those olden days no thought of *purpose* entered into the minds of men, for the race was not mental nor was it intended so to be. The emphasis was laid upon the *quality* of the appearance in all preparation for initiation, and the highest initiate of that time endeavoured to express only the quality of God's love. The Plan was the great mystery. The Christ, cosmic and individual, was sensed and known, but *purpose* was as yet veiled and unrevealed. The "noble eightfold path" was *not* known, and only seven steps into the Temple were seen. With the coming in of the Aryan race, the purpose and the plan began to be revealed. Only when the appearance is beginning to be dominated by quality, and consciousness is expressing itself in directed awareness through the form, is the purpose dimly sensed.

I seek in various ways to convey through the symbol of words the significance of the soul. The soul is therefore the son of God, the product of the marriage of spirit and matter. The soul is an expression of the mind of God, for mind and intellect are terms expressing the cosmic principle of intelligent love,—a love which produces an appearance through the nature of mind and thus is the builder of the separate forms or appearances. The soul also, through the quality of love, produces the fusion of appearance and of quality, of awareness and of form.

C. The soul is (and here words limit and distort) a unit of light, coloured by a particular ray vibration; it is a vibrating centre of energy found within the appearance or form of its entire ray life. It is one of seven groups of millions of lives which in their totality constitute the One Life. From its very nature, the soul is conscious or aware in three directions. It is God-conscious; it is group-conscious; it is self-conscious. This self-conscious aspect is brought to fruition in the phenomenal appearance of a human being; the group-conscious aspect retains the human state of consciousness, but adds to it awareness of its ray life, progressively unfolded; its awareness then is the awareness of love, of quality, of spirit in its relationships; it is God-conscious only potentially, and in that unfoldment lies, for the soul, its own growth upward and outward after its self-conscious aspect is perfected and its group-awareness is recognised. The soul therefore has the following points, or appearances:

    o. . . .Consciousness of God, of solar system. Unity.

The Soul ooo. . . .o. Consciousness of the ray, of one of the seven, of divine quality. Group Consciousness.

Aspirant o. . . .Self consciousness, awareness of appearance. Diversity of form life.

Aspirants who are studying and training themselves to live the life of service might be regarded as having reached the point where the line is to be found. To visualise this correctly the sign should be regarded as in rapid revolution, thus producing a turning wheel, which is the wheel of life.

Let me again repeat:

1. The soul is the son of God, the product of the union of spirit and matter.
2. The soul is an embodiment of conscious mind, the expression, if one might so phrase it, of divine intelligent awareness.
3. The soul is a unit of energy, vibrating in unison with one of the seven ray Lives, and coloured by a particular ray light.

The personality of the soul is intended to be an embodiment of love, applied with intelligence and producing those "attractive" forms which will serve to express that loving intelligence. The soul in its turn is intended to be the embodiment of divine purpose or will, intelligently applied in the great creative work, which is produced through the power of creative love.

Each son of God can say: I am born of the love of the Father for the Mother, of the desire of life for form. I express, therefore, the love and the magnetic attractiveness of the God nature, and the responsiveness of the form nature, and am consciousness itself, aware of Deity or Life.

Each intelligent point of life can say: I am the product of intelligent will, working through intelligent activity and producing a world of created forms which embody or veil the loving purpose of Deity.

Each vibrating unit of energy can say: I am part of a divine whole, which in its septenary nature expresses the love and life of the One Reality, coloured by one of the seven qualities of the love of Deity and responsive to the other qualities.

For our purposes in this treatise, we must grasp the fact

that the world of appearances is energised by and vibrating to the world of qualities or values, which world, in its turn, is energised by or vibrating to the world of purpose or of will. Therefore, as is stated in *The Secret Doctrine* and in *A Treatise on Cosmic Fire*, the electric fire of will, and the solar fire of love, in cooperation with fire by friction, produce the world of created and creative forms. These proceed under the law of attractive magnetic love towards the evolutionary accomplishment of a purpose at present inscrutable. This purpose remains unknown only on account of the limitations of the "appearance" which is not yet responsive to the quality. When the illusory appearance and the veiled quality of the life are known and comprehended the underlying purpose will emerge with clarity. Indications of this can be dimly sensed and the attribute of this growing awareness can be noted in the tendency of modern thought to speak of patterns and of plans, of blue prints and synthetic formulations of ideas, and in the tracing of historical developments—national, racial, human and psychological. As we read, ponder and study, the dim outlines of the Plan appear, but until the consciousness has transcended all human limitations and has included the subhuman, as well as the superhuman, within its range of contacts, the true Plan cannot be rightly grasped. The will, lying behind the purpose, cannot be understood until the consciousness has transcended even that of the superhuman man, and has become one with the divine.

Will or the energy of life are synonymous terms and are an abstraction, existing apart from all form expression. The will-to-be emerges from outside the solar system altogether. It is the all-pervading energy of God which informs with a fraction of itself the solar system, and yet remains outside. Plan and purpose concern the emanating energies of that central Life and involve duality,—will or the life urge plus attractive magnetic love which, in its turn, is the response of the vibrating universal substance to the impact of the energy of will. This initial activity precedes the creative process of form building; and the play of the divine will on the ocean of space, matter, or etheric substance produced the first differentiation into the major rays, and their mutual interplay produced the minor four rays. Thus the seven emanations, the seven potencies and the seven rays came into manifestation. They are the seven breaths of the one Life, the seven basic energies; they streamed forth from the centre formed by the impact of the will of God on divine substance, and divided into seven streams of force. The radius of the influence of these seven streams determined the extent or scope of activity of a solar system and "outlined" the limits of the form of the incarnated cosmic Christ. Each of these seven streams or emanations of energy was coloured by a divine quality, an aspect of love, and all of them were needed for the ultimate perfecting of the latent and unrevealed purpose.

The will of Deity coloured the stream of energy units which we call by the name of the Ray of Will or Power, the first ray, and the impact of that stream on the matter of space insured that the hidden purpose of Deity would inevitably and eventually be revealed. It is a ray of such dynamic intensity that we call it the ray of the Destroyer. It is not as yet functioning actively. It will come into full play only when the time comes for the purpose to be safely revealed. Its units of energy in manifestation in the human kingdom are very few. As I earlier said, there is not a true first ray type in incarnation as yet. Its main potency is to be found in the mineral kingdom, and the key to the mystery of the first ray is to be found in radium.

In the vegetable kingdom the second ray is peculiarly active, producing among other things the magnetic attractiveness of flowers. The mystery of the second ray is found to be hidden in the significance of the perfume of flowers. Perfume and radium are related, being emanatory expressions of ray effects upon differing groupings of material substance. The third ray is, in its turn, peculiarly related to the animal kingdom, producing the tendency to intelligent activity which we note in the higher domestic animals. The correspondence to radioactivity and to emanatory perfumes which we found in the mineral and vegetable kingdoms, we here call devotion, the characteristic of the attractive interplay between the domestic animals and man. Devotees of personalities might more rapidly transmute that devotion into its higher correspondence—love of principles—if they realised that they were only displaying an animal emanation.

The desire of the Deity expresses itself through the second Ray of Love-Wisdom. Desire is a word which has been prostituted to cover the tendency of humanity to crave material things or those pleasures which bring satisfaction to the sensuous nature. It is applied to those conditions which will satisfy the personality, but in the last analysis, desire is essentially love. This desire expresses itself by attractiveness, by its capacity to draw to itself and into the radius of its influence that which is loved. It is the bond of coherence, and is that principle of magnetic cohesion which lies behind all creative work and which produces the emergence into the light of manifestation of those forms or appearances through which it is possible to satisfy desire. This second ray is pre-eminently the ray of applied consciousness, and works through the creation and development of those forms which are found throughout the universe. They are essentially mechanisms for the development of responsiveness or awareness; they are sensitive machines, responsive to an enveloping environment. This is true of all forms, from that of a crystal to that of a solar system. They have been created in the great process of satisfying desire and of providing the media of contact which will guarantee a progressive satisfaction. In the human family, the effect of this dual interplay of Life (desiring satisfaction) and of form (providing the field of experience) is a consciousness which is striving towards a love of the formless instead of desire for form, and the wise adaptation of all experience to the process of transmuting desire into love. Hence this ray is, par excellence, the dual ray of the solar Logos Himself, and hence colours all manifested forms, directing all consciousness in all forms in all kingdoms of nature, and in all fields of development; it carries the life through the range of forms in that basic search or urge for the attainment of bliss through the satisfaction of desire. This urge and the interaction of the pairs of opposites produced the varying types of conscious reaction to experience which, in their main stages, we call consciousness, animal consciousness, and allied differentiating phrases.

This second ray is the ray of Deity Itself, and is coloured by distinctive aspects of desire or love. They produce the totality of the manifested appearances, animated by the Life Which determines the quality. The Father, Spirit or Life, wills to seek the satisfaction of desire. The Mother or matter meets the desire and is attracted also by the Father. Their mutual response initiates the creative work, and the Son is born, inheriting from the Father the urge to desire or love, and from the Mother the tendency actively to create forms. Thus, in the language of symbolism, have the form worlds come into being, and through the evolutionary work the process is going forward of satisfying the desire of spirit. Thus in the two major rays of Will and Love we have the two main characteristics of the divine nature, which lie latent behind all the myriad of forms. The aeons will see these two energies steadily dominating all appearance and driving the created world on to a full display of the divine nature. This is true of gods and men.

But in the same way in which the Father contributes to the Son the divine qualities of will and love, so the Mother contributes much also, and the initial duality is increased and the qualities are enhanced by the addition of a quality inherent in matter itself,—the quality or Ray of Intelligent Activity. This is the third of the divine attributes and completes, if I may so express it, the equipment of the appearing forms, and predisposes all creation to an intelligent appreciation of the true goal of desire and to an intelligent use of the technique of form building in order to reveal divine purpose. The Knower (man) is the custodian of that wisdom which will enable him to further the divine plan and bring the will of God to fruition. The field of knowledge is so constituted that it vibrates with intelligent response to the slowly emerging will. Knowledge itself is that which knows its own ends and works towards those ends through the process of experiment, expectation, experience, examination and exaltation which produces a final exit. Words such as these are synthetic symbols, conveying a cosmic story in terms of constructive brevity.

Thus the three rays of Will, Love and Intelligence produce appearance, donate quality and, through the life principle which is the underlying aspect of unity, ensure continuity of growth until such time as the will of God has evidenced itself as power, has attracted to itself the desired, has with wisdom utilised the experience of a gradually growing satisfaction, and has intelligently applied the gain of experience to the production of forms more sensitive, more beautiful and more fully expressive of the quality of the life.

Each of these rays is dual in time and space, though only the second ray is dual when they are regarded from the standpoint of the final abstraction. In their temporary duality can be seen, for each of them, the interplay which we call cause and effect.

Ray I .... Will, dynamically applied, emerges in manifestation as power.
Ray II ... Love, magnetically functioning, produces wisdom.
Ray III .. Intelligence, potentially found in substance, causes activity.

The result of the interplay of these three major rays can be seen in the activity of the four minor rays. *The Secret Doctrine* speaks of the Lords of Knowledge and of Love, and also of the Lords of Ceaseless Devotion. We might, in order more clearly to understand the mystical significance of these names, point out that the dynamic persistent will of the Logos expresses itself through the Lords of Ceaseless Devotion. Here devotion is not the quality to which I referred earlier in this treatise, but is the persistent directed one-pointed will of God, embodied in a Life which is that of the Lord of the first ray. The Lords of Love and of Knowledge are the two great Lives Who embody or ensoul the Love-Wisdom and the creative Intelligence aspects of the two major rays. These three are the sum total of all forms or appearances, the givers of all qualities, and the emerging Life aspect behind the tangible manifestations. They correspond, in the human family, to the three aspects of Personality, Soul and Monad. The Monad is dynamic will or purpose, but remains unrevealed until after the third initiation. The Monad is Life, the sustaining force, a Lord of persevering and ceaseless devotion to the pursuit of a seen and determined objective. The soul is a Lord of love and wisdom, whilst the personality is a Lord of knowledge and of intelligent activity. This use of terms involves the realisation of an achieved goal. It is not true of the present stage as regards expression, for this is the intermediate stage. None are as yet working with full intelligent activity, though some day each will do so. None are as yet manifesting Lords of love, but they sense the ideal and are striving towards its expression. None are as yet Lords of ceaseless will and none realise as yet the plan of the monad nor the true goal towards which all are striving. Some day all will. But potentially every human unit is all these three, and some day the appearances which were called personalities, that mask or veil reality, will fully reveal the qualities of Deity. When that time comes, the purpose for which all creation waits will burst upon the awakened vision, and we shall know the true meaning of bliss, and why the morning stars sang together. Joy is the strong basic note of our particular solar system.

One of the foundational septenate of rays embodies in itself the principle of harmony, and this fourth Ray of Harmony gives to all forms that which produces beauty and works towards the harmonising of all effects emanating from the world of causes, which is the world of the three major rays. The ray of beauty, of art and harmony is the producer of the quality of *organisation through form*. It is in the last analysis the ray of mathematical exactitude and is not the ray of the artist, as so many seem to think. The artist is found on all rays, just as is the engineer or the physician, the homemaker or the musician. I want to make this clear, for there is much misunderstanding on this matter.

Each of the great rays has a form of teaching truth to humanity which is its unique contribution, and in this way develops man by a system or technique which is qualified by the ray quality and is therefore specific and unique. Let me point out to you the modes of this group teaching:

Ray I . . .	Higher Expression:	The science of statesmanship, of government.
	Lower Expression:	Modern diplomacy and politics.
Ray II. . .	Higher Expression:	The process of initiation as taught by the hierarchy of adepts.
	Lower Expression:	Religion.
Ray III . .	Higher Expression:	Means of communication or interaction. The radio, telephone, telegraph and the power to travel.
	Lower Expression:	The use and spread of money and gold.
Ray IV . .	Higher Expression:	The Masonic work, based on the formation of the hierarchy, and related to the second ray.
	Lower Expression:	Architectural construction. Modern city planning.
Ray V . . .	Higher Expression:	The science of the soul. Esoteric psychology.
	Lower Expression:	Modern educational systems and mental science.
Ray VI . .	Higher Expression:	Christianity and diversified religions. (Notice here relation to Ray II.)
	Lower Expression:	Churches and organised religions.
Ray VII .	Higher Expression:	All forms of white magic.
	Lower Expression:	Spiritualism of "phenomena."

The fourth ray is essentially the refiner, the producer of perfection within the form, and the prime manipulator of the energies of God in such a way that the Temple of the Lord is indeed known in its true nature as that which "houses" the Light. Thus the Shekinah will shine forth within the secret place of the Temple in its full glory. Such is the work of the seven Builders. This ray is expressive primarily on the first the formless planes, counting from below upwards, and its true purpose cannot emerge until the soul is awakened and consciousness is adequately recording the known. The planes or manifested spheres of expression are influenced in manifestation in a numerical order:

Ray I . . . . . . Will or Power . . . . Plane of divinity.
Ray II . . . . . Love-Wisdom . . . . Plane of the monad.
Ray III. . . . . Active Intelligence . . . . . . Plane of spirit, atma.
Ray IV. . . . . Harmony . . . . Plane of the intuition.
Ray V . . . . . Concrete Knowledge . . . . Mental Plane.
Ray VI. . . . . Devotion, Idealism . . . . . . Astral Plane.
Ray VII . . . . Ceremonial Order . . . . Physical Plane.

The fifth ray therefore works actively on the plane of the greatest moment to humanity, being, for man, the plane of the soul, and of the higher and the lower mind. It embodies the principle of knowledge, and because of its activity and its close relation to the third Ray of Active Intelligence might be regarded as a ray having a most vital relation to man at this time in particular. It is the ray which—when active, as it was in Lemurian times,—produces individualisation, which is literally the shifting of the evolving life of God into a new sphere of awareness. This particular transference into higher forms of awareness tends, at the beginning, to separativeness.

The fifth ray has produced what we call science. In science we find a condition which is rare in the extreme. Science is separative in its approach to the differing aspects of the divine manifestation which we call the world of natural phenomena, but it is non-separative in actuality, for there is little warring between the sciences and little competition between scientists. In this the workers in the scientific field differ profoundly from those of the religious. The reason for this is to be found in the fact that the true scientist, being a coordinated personality and working therefore on mental levels, works very close to the soul. The developed personality produces the clear distinctions of the dominant lower mind, but (if one may use such a symbolic way of expression) the close proximity of the soul negates a separative attitude. The religious man is pre-eminently astral or emotional and works in a more separative manner, particularly in this Piscean age which is passing away. When I say the religious man I refer to the mystic and to the man who *senses* the beatific vision. I refer not to disciples nor to those who are called initiates, for they add to the mystical vision a trained mental apprehension.

The sixth Ray of Devotion embodies the principle of recognition. By this I mean the capacity to see the ideal reality lying behind the form; this implies a one-pointed application of desire and of intelligence in order to produce an expression of that sensed idea. It is responsible for much of the formulation of the ideas which have led man on, and for much of the emphasis on the appearance which has veiled and hidden those ideals. It is on this ray primarily—as it cycles in and out of manifestation—that the work of distinguishing between appearance and quality is carried forward, and this work has its field of activity upon the astral plane. The complexity of this subject and the acuteness of the feeling evolved become therefore apparent.

The seventh Ray of Ceremonial Order or Magic embodies a curious quality which is the outstanding characteristic of the particular Life which ensouls this ray. It is the quality or principle which is the coordinating factor unifying the inner quality and the outer tangible form or appearance. This work goes on primarily on etheric levels and involves physical energy. This is the true magical work. I should like to point out that when the fourth ray and the seventh ray come into incarnation together, we shall have a most peculiar period of revelation and of light-bringing. It is said of this time that then "the temple of the Lord will take on an added glory and the Builders will rejoice together." This will be the high moment of the Masonic work, spiritually understood. The Lost Word will then be recovered and uttered for all to hear, and the Master will arise and walk among His builders in the full light of the glory which shines from the east.

The spiritualising of forms might be regarded as the main work of the seventh ray, and it is this principle of fusion, of coordination and of blending which is active on etheric levels every time a soul comes into incarnation and a child is born on earth.

D. The soul is the principle of sentiency, underlying all outer manifestation, pervading all forms, and constituting the consciousness of God Himself. When the soul, immersed in substance, is simply sentiency, it produces through its evolutionary interplay an addition, and we find emerging quality and capacity to react to vibration and to environment. This is the soul as it expresses itself in all the subhuman kingdoms in nature.

When the soul, an expression of sentiency and quality, adds to these the capacity of detached self-awareness, there appears that self-identified entity which we call a human being.

When the soul adds to sentiency, quality and self-awareness, the consciousness of the group, then we have identification with a ray-group, and there appears the disciple, the initiate and the master.

When the soul adds to sentiency, quality, self-awareness and group consciousness, a consciousness of divine synthetic purpose (called by us the Plan), then we have that state of being and knowledge which is distinctive of all upon the Path of Initiation, and includes those graded Lives, from the more advanced disciple up to the planetary Logos Himself.

But forget not that when we make these distinctions it is nevertheless one Soul that is functioning, acting through vehicles of varying capacities, of differentiated refinements and of greater and lesser limitations, in just the same sense as a man is one identity, working sometimes through a physical body and sometimes through a feeling body or a mental body, and sometimes knowing himself to be the Self—a rare and unusual occurrence for the majority.

Every form in manifestation does two things:

1. Appropriates, or is pervaded by, as much of the world soul as its capacity will permit. The atom of substance, the molecule or the cell all have soul, but not in the same degree as has an animal; and an animal has soul, but not in the same degree as has a Master, and so on up or down the scale.
2. Through the interaction between the indwelling soul and the form, two things occur:
   a. Sentiency and quality are expressed according to the type of body and its point of evolution.
   b. The pervading soul drives the body nature into activity, and forces it forward along the path of development, and thus provides for the soul a field of experience and for the body the opportunity to react to the higher soul impulse. Thus the field of expression is benefited, and the soul masters the technique of contact which is its objective in any particular form.

The soul therefore, viewed from one angle, is an aspect of the body, for there is a soul in every atom comprising all bodies in all kingdoms in nature. The subtle coherent soul which is the result of the bringing together of spirit and matter exists as an entity apart from the body nature, and constitutes (when separated from the body) the etheric body, the double, as it is sometimes called, or the counterpart of the physical body. This is the sum total of the soul of the atoms constituting the physical body. It is the true form; it is the principle of coherence in every form.

The soul, in relation to the human being, is the mind principle in two capacities, or the mind expressing itself in two ways. These two ways are registered and become part of the organised equipment of the human body when it is adequately refined and sufficiently developed:

1. The lower concrete mind, the mental body, the "chitta" or mind stuff.
2. The higher spiritual or abstract mind.

These two aspects of the soul, its two basic qualities, bring into being the human kingdom and enable man to contact both the lower kingdoms in nature and the higher spiritual realities. The first, the quality of mind in its lower manifestation, is owned potentially by every atom in every form in every kingdom in nature. It is a part of the body nature, inherent and potential, and is the basis of brotherhood, of absolute unity, of universal synthesis and divine coherence in manifestation. The other, the higher aspect, is the principle of self-awareness, and when combined with the lower aspect produces the self-consciousness of the human being. When the lower aspect has informed and pervaded the forms in the subhuman kingdoms, and when it has worked upon those forms and their latent sentiency so as to produce adequate refinement and sentiency, the vibration becomes so potent that the higher is attracted and there is a fusion or at-one-ing. This is like a higher recapitulation of the initial union of spirit and matter which brought the world into being. A human soul is thus brought into existence and begins its long career. It is now a differentiated entity.

"Soul" also is a word used to express the sum total of the psychic nature—the vital body, the emotional nature and the mind stuff. But it is also more than that, once the human stage is reached. It constitutes the spiritual entity, a conscious psychical being, a son of God, possessing life, quality and appearance—a unique manifestation in time and space of the three expressions of the soul as we have just outlined them.

1. The soul of all the atoms, composing the tangible appearance.
2. The personal soul or the subtle coherent sum total which we call the Personality, composed of the subtle bodies, etheric or vital, astral or emotional, and the lower mental apparatus. These three vehicles humanity shares with the animal kingdom as regards its possession of vitality, sentiency, and potential mind; with the vegetable kingdom as regards vitality and sentiency; and with the mineral kingdom as regards vitality and potential sentiency.
3. The soul is also the spiritual being, or the union of life and quality. When there is the union of the three souls, so called, we have a human being.

Thus in man you have the blending or fusion of life, quality and appearance, or spirit, soul and body, through the medium of a tangible form.

In the process of differentiation these various aspects have attracted attention, and the underlying synthesis has been overlooked or disregarded. Yet all forms are differentiations of the soul, but that soul is one Soul, when viewed and considered spiritually. When studied from the form side, naught but differentiation and separation can be seen. When studied from the consciousness or sentiency aspect, unity emerges. When the human stage is reached and self-awareness is blended with the sentiency of forms and with the tiny consciousness of the atom, some idea of a possible subjective unity begins dimly to dawn on the thinker's mind. When the stage of discipleship is reached, a man begins to see himself as a sentient part of a sentient whole, and slowly reacts to the purpose and intent of that whole. He grasps that purpose little by little as he swings consciously into the rhythm of the sum total of which he is a part. When more advanced stages and more rarefied and refined forms are possible, the part is lost in the whole; the rhythm of the whole subjects the individual to a uniform participation in the synthetic purpose, but the realisation of individual self-awareness persists and enriches the individual contribution, which is now intelligently and willingly offered, so that the form not only constitutes an aspect of the sum total (which has always and inevitably been the case, even when unrealised), but the conscious thinking entity knows the *fact* of the unity of consciousness and of the synthesis of life. Thus we have three things to bear in mind as we read and study:

1. The synthesis of life . . . . spirit.
2. The unity of consciousness . . . . soul.
3. The integration of forms . . . . body.

These three always have been at-one, but the human consciousness has not known it. It is the realisation of these three factors and their integration into the technique of living which is, for man, the objective of his entire evolutionary experience.

Let us, talking necessarily in symbols, consider the universal Soul, or the consciousness of the Logos Who brought our universe into being. Let us regard the Deity as pervading the form of His solar system with life, and as being conscious of His work, of His project and His goal. This solar system is an appearance, but God remains transcendent. Within all forms God is immanent, yet persists aloof and withdrawn. Just as a thinking, intelligent human being functions through his body but dwells primarily in his mental consciousness or in his emotional processes, so God dwells withdrawn in His mind nature; the world that He has created and pervaded with His life, goes forward towards the goal for which He has created it. Within, however, the radius of His appearing form, greater activities are going forward; varying states of consciousness and stages of awareness are to be seen; developing degrees of sentiency emerge, and even in the symbolism of the human form we have such differing states of sentiency as are registered by the hair, by the internal organisms in the body, by the nervous system, by the brain, and by the entity we call the self (who registers emotion and thought). In the same way does the Deity, within the solar system, express as wide a divergence of consciousness.

There is a body consciousness; there is a sensory apparatus, registering reaction to the environment; there is a consciousness of moods, of quality, of mental reactions to a world of ideas; there is a higher consciousness of plan and of purpose; there is a consciousness of life.

It is interesting to note in connection with the Deity that this sensory response to environment provides the entire basis for astrology and for the effect of the constellations upon the solar system and the interplanetary forces.

We might sum it all up in relation to man as follows:

Man's form nature reacts in its consciousness to the form nature of Deity. The outer garment of the soul (physical, vital and psychic) is part of the outer garment of God.

Man's self-conscious soul is en rapport with the soul of all things. It is an integral part of the universal Soul, and because of this can become aware of the conscious purpose of Deity; can intelligently cooperate with the will of God, and thus work with the plan of Evolution.

Man's spirit is one with the life of God and is within him, deep-seated in his soul, as his soul is seated within the body.

This spirit will in some distant time put him en rapport with that aspect of God which is transcendent, and thus each son of God will eventually find his way to that centre—withdrawn and abstracted—where God dwells beyond the confines of the solar system.

These are words which are formulated in an endeavour to convey an idea of order, of plan, of universal synthesis, of the integration and incorporation of the fragment in the whole, and of the part with the all.

Let us endeavour now to answer the second question, remembering as we proceed, that it is not possible for us to do more than enter symbolically into the practical purposes of Deity. As I write for simple aspirants, I cannot convey the truth until such time as their rapport with their own souls is complete, or more complete than is now the case. The effort, however, to grasp that which cannot be expressed in words produces a downpouring of the abstract mind or of the intuition, and this, in its turn, stimulates and develops the brain cells and produces a steady stabilisation of the power to stand in "spiritual being"; then it becomes possible to grasp the inexpressible and to live by its power.

Question 2. What are the origin, goal, purpose and plan of the soul?

The seven rays are the sum total of the divine Consciousness, of the universal Mind; They might be regarded as seven intelligent Entities through Whom the plan is working out. They embody divine purpose, express the qualities required for the materialising of that purpose, and They create the forms and are the forms through which the divine idea can be carried forward to completion. Symbolically, They may be regarded as constituting the brain of the divine Heavenly Man. They correspond to the ventricles of the brain, to the seven centres within the brain, to the seven centres of force, and to the seven major glands which determine the quality of the physical body. They are the conscious executors of divine purpose; They are the seven Breaths, animating all forms which have been created by Them to carry out the plan.

It may perhaps be easier to understand the relation of the seven rays to Deity if we remember that man himself (being made in the image of God) is a seven-fold being, capable of seven states of consciousness, expressive of the seven principles or basic qualities which enable him to be aware of the seven planes upon which he is, consciously or unconsciously, functioning. He is a septenate at all times, but his objective is to be consciously aware of all the states of being, to express consciously all the qualities, and to function freely on all the planes.

The seven ray Beings, unlike man, are fully conscious and entirely aware of the purpose and the Plan. They are "ever in deep meditation," and have reached the point where, through Their advanced stage of development, They are "impelled toward fulfillment." They are fully self-conscious and group-conscious; They are the sum total of the universal mind; They are "awake and active." Their goal and Their purpose is such that it is idle for us to speculate about it, for the highest point of achievement for man is the lowest point for Them. These seven Rays, Breaths and Heavenly Men have the task of wrestling with matter in order to subjugate it to divine purpose, and the goal—as far as one can sense it—is to subject the material forms to the play of the life aspect, thus producing those qualities which will carry the will of God to completion. They are therefore the sum total of all the souls within the solar system, and Their activity produces all forms; according to the *nature* of the form so will be the grade of consciousness. Through the seven rays, the life or spirit aspect flows, cycling through every kingdom in nature and producing thus all states of consciousness in all fields of awareness.

For the purpose of this treatise students will have to accept the hypothesis that every human being is swept into manifestation on the impulse of some ray, and is coloured by that particular ray quality, which determines the form aspect, indicates the way he should go, and enables him (by the time the third initiation is reached) to have sensed and then to have cooperated with his ray purpose. After the third initiation he begins to sense the synthetic purpose towards which all the seven rays are working; but as this treatise is written for aspirants and disciples, and not for initiates of the third degree, it is needless to speculate upon this ultimate destiny.

The human soul is a synthesis of material energy, qualified by intelligent consciousness, plus the spiritual energy which is, in its turn, qualified by one of the seven ray types.

Thus the human being emerges, a son of God incarnate in form, with one hand (as the *Old Commentary* says) holding firmly to the rock of matter and with the other hand plunged into a sea of love. An ancient scripture puts it thus:

"When the right hand of the man of matter grasps the flower of life and plucks it for himself, the left hand remains in emptiness.

"When the right hand of the man of matter grasps the golden lotus of the soul, the left descends seeking the flower of life, though he seeks it not for selfish ends.

"When the right hand holds the golden lotus firm and the left hand grasps the flower of life, man finds himself to be the seven-leaved plant which flowers on earth and flowers before the Throne of God."

The purpose of Deity, as it is known to the Creator, is totally unknown to all save the higher initiates. But the purpose of each ray Life may be sensed and defined, subject of course to the limitations of the human mind and to the inadequacy of words. The planned activity of every ray qualifies every form found within its body of manifestation.

We come now to a technical statement which must be accepted for the sake of argument, being incapable of proof.

All the Lords of the rays create a body of expression, and thus the seven planets have come into being. These are their major expressions.

>   The Sun (Veiling Vulcan)
>   Jupiter
>   Saturn
>   Mercury
>   Venus
>   Mars
>   The Moon

The energies of these seven Lives however are not confined to their planetary expressions, but sweep around the confines of the solar system just as the life impulses of a human being—his vital forces, his desire impulses, and his mental energies—sweep throughout his body, bringing the various organs into activity and enabling him to carry out his intent, to live his life, and to fulfill the objective for which he created his body of manifestation.

Each of the seven kingdoms in nature reacts to the energy of some particular ray Life. Each of the seven planes similarly reacts; each septenate in nature vibrates to one or another of the initial septenates, for the seven rays establish that process which assigns the limits of influence of all forms. They are that which determines all things, and when I use these words I indicate the necessity of Law. Law is the will of the seven Deities, making its impression upon substance in order to produce a specific intent through the method of the evolutionary process.

A. The Three Rays of Aspect.

We shall now express the ray purpose in the form of an ancient teaching preserved on leaves that are so old that the writing is slowly fading. I now translate it into modern language though much is lost thereby.

THE FIRST PURPOSE OF DEITY

Ray I. Will or Power.

Behind the central sacred sun, hidden within its rays, a form is found. Within that form there glows a point of power which vibrates not as yet but shines as light electric.

Fierce are its rays. It burns all forms, yet touches not the life of God incarnate.

From the One who is the seven goes forth a word. That word reverberates along the line of fiery essence, and when it sounds within the circle of the human lives it takes the form of affirmation, an uttered fiat or word of power. Thus there is impressed upon the living mold the thought of . . . . . . (the hidden, inexpressible ray name.)

Let dynamic power, electric light, reveal the past, destroy the form that is, and open up the golden door. This door reveals the way which leads towards the centre where dwells the one whose name cannot be heard within the confines of our solar sphere.

His robe of blue veils his eternal purpose, but in the rising and the setting sun his orb of red is seen.

His word is power. His light, electric. The lightning is his symbol. His will is hidden in the counsel of his thought. Nought is revealed.

His power is felt. The sons of men, reacting to his power, send to the utmost bounds of light a question:

Why this blind power? Why death? Why this decay of forms? Why the negation of the power to hold? Why death, Oh Mighty Son of God?

Faintly the answer comes: I hold the keys of life and death. I bind and loose again. I, the Destroyer, am.

This ray Lord is not yet in full expression, except as He causes destruction and brings cycles to an end. The Monads of power are much fewer in number than any others. Egos upon the power ray are relatively not so few. They are characterised by a dynamic will, and their power within the human family works out as the force of destruction, but in the last analysis it is a destruction that will produce liberation. We shall see as we continue to study first ray egos and personalities that death and destruction are always to be found in their work, and hence the apparent cruelty and impersonality of their reactions. Form does not count with first ray types; their energy produces death to form, but ushers in great periods of cyclic pralaya; the first ray is the controller of the death drama in all kingdoms—a destruction of forms which brings about release of power and permits "entrance into Light through the gateway of Death." The intent of the Lord of the first ray is to stand behind His six Brothers, and when They have achieved Their purpose, to shatter the forms which They have built. This He does by passing His power through Their bodies, and Their united effort leads to abstraction and a return to the centre whence the initial impulse came. The first ray purpose therefore is to produce death, and some idea of that purpose may be gleaned if we study some of the names by which the ray Lord is called:

> The Lord of Death
> The Opener of the Door
> The Liberator from Form
> The Great Abstractor
> The Fiery Element, producing shattering
> The Crystallizer of the Form
> The Power that touches and withdraws
> The Lord of the Burning Ground
> The Will that breaks into the Garden
> The Ravisher of Souls
> The Finger of God
> The Breath that blasts
> The Lightning which annihilates
> The Most High

The qualities and characteristics of this Lord Who brings release may be gathered from the following six aphorisms which, an ancient legend says, His six Brothers gave to Him, as They begged Him to hold His hand till They had had time to work out Their purposes:

1. Kill out desire when desire has fulfilled its work. Thou art the one who indicates fulfillment.
   Quality . . . . . . clear vision.
2. Seek out the gentle way, Oh Lord of Power. Wait for thy brother on the path of Love. He builds the forms that can withstand thy power.
   Quality . . . . . . dynamic power.
3. Withhold thy hand until the time has come. Then give the gift of death, Oh Opener of the Door.
   Quality . . . . . . sense of time.
4. Stand not alone, but with the many join thyself. Thou art the One, the Isolated. Come forth unto thine own.
   Quality . . . . . . solitariness.
5. Lead thine own forth but learn to know thine own. Hate not attachment but see its plan and purpose.
   Quality . . . . . . detachment.
6. Through thee the life pulsates, the rhythm is imposed. The life is all. Love life in all its forms.
   Quality . . . . . . singleness of purpose.

The six qualities enumerated above express the force of this ray as it makes its presence felt in the fourth kingdom in nature. The effects in other kingdoms differ, but we shall confine our attention to the standpoint of humanity. The purpose of the first ray, and its main work, is to produce cessation and the death of all forms in all kingdoms in nature and on all planes. The energy of this ray Lord brings about the death of an ant or of a solar system, of an organisation, a religion, or a government, of a race type or of a planet. His will or purpose works out through the law of periodicity.

THE SECOND PURPOSE OF DEITY

Ray II. Love-Wisdom

The Word is issuing from the heart of God, emerging from a central point of love. That Word is love itself. Divine desire colours all that life of love. Within the human hierarchy, the affirmation gathers power and sound.

The Word in the beginning was. The Word hath dwelt and dwells with God. In Him was light. In Him was life. Within His light we walk.

His symbol is the thunder, the Word that cycles down the ages.

Some of the names of this ray Lord which convey his purpose are as follows:

> The Displayer of Glory
> The Lord of Eternal Love
> The Cosmic Magnet
> The Giver of Wisdom
> The Radiance in the Form
> The Master Builder
> The Conferrer of Names
> The Great Geometrician
> The One Who hides the Life
> The Cosmic Mystery
> The Light Bringer
> The Son of God Incarnate
> The Cosmic Christ

The legend tells us that the six Brothers summarise His qualities in the following aphorisms:

1. Send forth the Word and speak the radiant love of God. Make all men hear.
    Quality . . . . . . love divine.
2. Let the glory of the Lord shine forth. Let there be radiant light as well as radiant love.
    Quality . . . . . . radiance.
3. Draw to thyself the object of thy search. Pull forth into the light of day from out the night of time the one thou lovest.
    Quality . . . . . . attraction.
4. When light and love are shewn forth then let the power within produce the perfect flower. Let the word that heals the form go forth. That secret word that then must be revealed.
    Quality . . . . . . the power to save.
5. Salvation, light, and love, with the magnetic power of God, produce the word of wisdom. Send forth that word, and lead the sons of men from off the path of knowledge on to the path of understanding.
    Quality . . . . . . wisdom.

6. Within the radius of the love of God, within the circle of the solar system, all forms, all souls, all lives revolve. Let each son of God enter into this wisdom. Reveal to each the oneness of the many lives.

    Quality . . . . . .expansion or inclusiveness.

The third ray, which is one that has a very long cycle, having been in manifestation since A.D. 1425, has a direct effect upon the fifth root race, the Aryan, and has connected with it a set of curious phrases which express its purpose.

THE THIRD PURPOSE OF DEITY

Ray III. Active Intelligence or Adaptability

    Let the Warden of the South continue with the building. Let him apply the force which will produce the shining living stone that fits into the temple's plan with right exactitude. Let him prepare the corner stone and wisely place it in the north, under the eye of God Himself, and subject to the balance of the triangle.

    Let the Researcher of the past uncover the thought of God, hidden deep within the mind of the Kumaras of Love, and thus let him lead the Agnishvattas, waiting within the place of darkness, into the place of light.

    Let the Keeper of the sparks breathe with the breath divine upon the points of fire, and let him kindle to a blaze that which is hidden, that which is not seen, and so illumine all the spheres whereon God works.

I would call attention to the fact that all I can do here is to put into words certain ancient symbols, and so emphasize the process (adopted by the early initiate-teachers) of enunciating a word or sound, which produces a symbolic form, which in its turn, is capable of translation into words. These must in their turn be comprehended intuitively and adapted to individual need, and thus be assimilated into the life practice. Otherwise these ancient and interesting ideas, these interpretative names, and these aphorisms, conveying the "power of qualities", are worse than useless and serve but to increase responsibility. The capacity to see objective significances and then apply them to life is an expression of the true esoteric sense. If one studies these tabulations and phrases with care, they will be found to convey indication as to one's individual ray, life tendencies and purpose; if the appeal the various statements make anent a particular ray evoke an intuitive understanding on the part of the student, so that he recognises himself, his ray energy and aspects of his latent and deeply desired spiritual nature, then these communications I am making here as to Purpose, Name and Quality will be profitable and useful.

Some of the names of the Lord of the third ray indicate His use of force and His real nature. They are as follows:

>The Keeper of the Records.
>The Lord of Memory
>The Unifier of the lower Four
>The Interpreter of That Which is seen
>The Lord of Balance
>The Divine Separator
>The Discriminating Essential Life
>The One Who produces Alliance
>The Three-sided Triangle
>The Illuminator of the Lotus
>The Builder of the Foundation
>The Forerunner of the Light
>The One Who veils and yet reveals
>The Dispenser of Time
>The Lord of Space
>The Universal Mind
>The Threefold Wick
>The Great Architect of the Universe

and many others terms which indicate relation to light, to time, to space, to the manifested Logos, to matter and to the "power which evokes the form."

If all these names are studied in connection with modern developments or modern culture and science, it will become apparent how potent and influential in our day and time is this particular ray Life, and how His energies (having produced the tangible objective worlds) are turned to the manifestation of our modern civilisation, with its material emphasis, its search as to the nature of time and space, and that mental unfoldment which it is the glory and the destiny of our particular race to demonstrate.

The qualities which characterise this ray Lord might be enumerated in the following phrases. We must bear in mind that the seventh or synthetic characteristic of each of the rays is denoted by the ray name and is not specifically stated in the other six qualities. His six Brothers, Sons of the one Father, chanted these injunctions to Him on the day of His renewed activity (on what we call the day of creation):

1. Produce the dual form and veil the life. Let form appear, and prove itself divine. All is of God.
    Quality . . . . . .the power to manifest.
2. Conform the shell to that which dwells within. Let the world egg appear. Let ages pass, then let the soul appear. Let life emerge within a destined time.
    Quality . . . . . .the power to evolve.
3. Let mind control. Let the clear shining of the sun of life reveal the mind of God, and set the shining one upon his way. Then lead him to the central point where all is lost within the light supernal.
    Quality . . . . . .mental illumination.
4. God and His form are one. Reveal this fact, Oh sovereign Lord of form. God and His form are one. Negate the dual concept. Lend colour to the form. The life is one; the harmony complete. Prove thus the two are one.
    Quality . . . . . .the power to produce synthesis on the physical plane.
5. Produce the garment of the Lord; set forth the robe of many colours. Then separate that robe from That Which hides behind its many folds. Take off the veiling sheaths. Let God be seen. Take Christ from off the cross.
    Quality . . . . . .scientific investigation.
6. Let the two paths converge. Balance the pairs of opposites

and let the path appear between the two. God and the Path and man are one.

Quality . . . . . . balance.

Thus the three major rays sum up in themselves the process of creation, of energising, through the urge of the divine will; and the work of the four minor rays (as they are called, though with no idea of there being lesser or greater) is to elaborate or differentiate the qualities of the life, and so produce the infinite multiplicity of forms which will enable the life to assume its many points of focus and express—through the process of evolutionary manifestation—its diverse characteristics.

B. *The Four Rays of Attribute.*

THE FOURTH PURPOSE OF DEITY

Ray IV. Harmony, Beauty, Art

Colour, and yet no colour now is seen. Sound and the soundless One meet in an infinite point of peace. Time and the timeless One negate the thoughts of men. But time is not.

Form is there found, and yet the psychic sense reveals that which the form is powerless to hide,—the inner synthesis, the all-embracing prism, that point of unity which—when it is duly reached—reveals a further point where all the three are one, and not the two alone.

Form and its soul are merged. The inner vision watches o'er the fusion, knows the divine relation and sees the two as one. But from that point of high attainment, a higher vision blazes forth before the opened inner eye. The three are one, and not alone the two. Pass on, O pilgrim on the Way.

In reading these words, the student must bear in mind that the antechamber has been left behind and man stands (when he has allowed the fourth ray to do its work and can therefore function on the fourth or buddhic plane) within the temple of the Lord. He has found a measure of light, but in that light he now sees light, and visions a greater revelation and brilliance. This now becomes the object of his search.

He has mastered the uses of duality and has learnt to at-one soul and body into one instrument for spirit. Now he passes on his way to achieve the greater synthesis.

The Lord of the fourth ray has many names which warrant careful study and much consideration. In less than a hundred years this Lord of harmonising power will have more influence and will offset some of the Saturn disruption of the first decanate of Aquarius. In the meantime a study of His names will produce a simplification of His efforts and build up a body of constructive thought which will facilitate His work when He is again in active manifestation. He is always, however, more or less in power where the human family is concerned, for there is a numerical alliance between the fourth ray, the fourth Creative Hierarchy, or the human monads, and the fourth kingdom in nature. His power is always consequently active.

> The Perceiver on the Way
> The Link between the Three and Three
> The Divine Intermediary
> The Hand of God
> The Hidden One
> The Seed, that is the Flower
> The Mountain whereon Form dies
> The Light within the Light
> The Corrector of the Form
> The One Who marks the parting of the Way
> The Master
> The Dweller in the Holy Place
> The Lower than the Three, the Highest of the Four
> The Trumpet of the Lord.

The aphorisms connected with this fourth ray are not easy of comprehension. They require an exercise of the intuition and are conveyed by six short and excessively brief commands uttered, curiously enough, late in the creative period and at the time when the fourth Creative Hierarchy came into incarnation:

> 1. Speak low the Word. Speak low.
>
>   Quality . . . . . .power to penetrate the depths of matter.
> 2. Champion desire. Give what is needed to the seeker.
>
>   Quality . . . . . .the dual aspects of desire.
> 3. Lower the thread. Unfold the Way. Link man with God. Arise.
>
>   Quality . . . . . .power to reveal the path.
> 4. All flowers are thine. Settle the roots in mud, the flowers in sun. Prove mud and sun, and roots and flowers are one.
>
>   Quality . . . . . .power to express divinity. Growth.
> 5. Roll and return, and roll again. Cycle around the circle of the Heavens. Prove all is one.
>
>   Quality . . . . . .the harmony of the spheres.
> 6. Colour the sound. Sound forth the colour. Produce the notes and see them pass into the shades, which in their turn produce the sounds. Thus all are seen as one.
>
>   Quality . . . . . .the synthesis of true beauty.

This instruction on the rays is of deeper significance than can as yet be comprehended. Careful systematic study and a sane refraining from the forming of rapid deductions will be the wisest way in which to approach its consideration. It is not possible for me to deal with the definite human psychological applications at this early stage. I am occupied with stating a general outline, with the impartation of ideas, with the grounding of a few basic concepts in the consciousness of the reader, and with an attempt to clothe this most abstruse and difficult subject in such a form that some new rhythm of thought may be set in motion, and some new realisations be grasped and held. These concern at present a prototypal cosmic process, and will lead eventually to an understanding of the part an individual may play in a stupendous cosmic whole. We begin with the universal and end with the particular, which is ever the truly occult method.

However, all that I am positing about a ray Life may be equally well posited anent a human life, but it should be borne in mind that the pure ray type does not as yet exist, for there is not to be found that perfect form, mechanism or expression of the ray quality, nor that absolutely purified appearance in the human family, except in such rare cases as the Buddha, or Christ, and (in another field of expression) an Alexander or Julius Caesar. Leonardo da Vinci was an analogous expression. The rays concern energy and consciousness, and determine expression, but where the matter utilised and the vehicle informed is as yet imperfectly evolved, there is then limitation and the "tuning out" automatically of much of the energy. The effect of ray force, working through imperfect forms, must be distorted and curtailed and misapplied. Let me illustrate. I have said that first ray energy works out as the destruction of forms; it must be remembered that a pure destroyer is utterly unknown, and mercifully for the race this is so. It is a beneficent condition that as yet a first ray ego is so handicapped and limited by the form nature and the quality of that form nature that it is unable to make adequate or intelligent use of its destructive force. First ray personalities are oft destructive, as well you know, but the energy generated is insufficient to work much harm. Again, pure love is incapable of expression today, its flow being impeded by the form nature. A consideration of these two cases will help the reader to appreciate the situation. But the time is near at hand wherein there will be a fuller expression of ray purpose, type or quality, and therefore a truer appearance.

This is owing to the imminent appearance, or manifestation, of certain great Lives Who will embody the energy of rays two, three, five and seven. They will thus constitute focal points for the inflow of these four types of divine energy and, this will produce a tremendous stimulation of their corresponding and responding units of life. These four Beings, Who will appear as human beings in the field of the modern world, may be looked for before the end of this century and Their united effort will inaugurate definitely the New Age, and usher in the period which will go down in history as the time of glory for the fifth root race. Each of these four Masters, for that They will be, is also subjectively the focal point for a triple inflow of energy from the centre in the Body of God which is symbolically spoken of as "the heart of the Sun." For each ray is in its turn a triple manifesting entity as is the solar Deity Himself. Love will be Their outstanding characteristic, and through that attractive magnetic force the new forms will come into being which will permit of purer ray types, and thus of more truly expressive appearances. A great deal of the destructive energy extant in the world today is due to the presence on the astral plane of a first ray disciple of the planetary Logos. His work it is to clear the way for the manifestation of these other four major Disciples, Who are primarily Builders; They will enter on Their work when the task of the wreckers of form has been accomplished.

I should like here to give a suggestion, for it is necessary that some of the methods of the Hierarchy should begin to be understood. The work of what in the West is called "the Christ Principle" is to build the forms for the expression of quality and life. That is the characteristic work of the second aspect of divinity. The work of the Antichrist is to destroy forms, and this is essentially the work of the first expression of divinity. But the work of the destroyer is *not* the work of black magic, and when ignorant humanity regards Antichrist as working on the black side, their error is great. His work is as beneficent as that of the building aspect, and it is but man's hatred of the death of forms which makes him regard the work of the destroyer as "black," as being against the divine will, and as subversive of the divine programme. The work of the representatives of that mysterious power which we call cosmic evil, and their responding representatives, is indeed worthy of the word "black"; but it is not applicable to the work of Antichrist. It might be added that the work of the black forces wells up from below, whilst the work of the destroyers is impelled from above. The symbols of these two ways are the sword and the cross.

After these preliminary remarks, which are intended to indicate the magnitude of the subject, we shall now proceed to an analysis of the three rays which still remain to be considered.

THE FIFTH PURPOSE OF DEITY

Ray V. Concrete Knowledge or Science
   The thunders crash around the mountain top; dark clouds conceal the form. The mists, arising from the watery sphere, serve to distort the wondrous . . . . . . found within the secret place. The form is there. Its note is sounding forth.
   A beam of light illuminates the form; the hidden now appears. Knowledge of God and how He veils Himself finds consummation in the thoughts of man. The energies and forces receive their secret names, reveal their inner purpose, and all is seen as rhythm, a returning on itself. The great scroll can now be read. God's purpose and His plans are fixed, and man can read the form.
   The plan takes form. The plan is form. Its purpose is the revelation of the mind of God. The past reveals the form, but the present indicates the flowing in of energy.
   That which is on its way comes as a cloud which veils the sun. But hid behind this cloud of immanence is love, and on the earth is love and in the heaven is love, and this,—the love which maketh all things new—must stand revealed. This is the purpose back of all the acts of this great Lord of Knowledge.

Before enumerating the names of this great Life, I should

like to point out that the fifth ray is one of unique and peculiar potency in relation to the human kingdom. The reason is that the fifth plane of mind is the sphere of His major activity and it is on this plane that we find the triple aspects of mind:

1. Abstract or higher mind, the embodiment of a higher triad.
2. The concrete or lower mind, the highest aspect of the lower self.
3. The ego or solar Angel, the pure Son of Mind, Who expresses intelligence, both abstractly and concretely, and is the point of unification.

This Life has also much power today in connection with the fifth root-race and with the transference of the consciousness of humanity into the fifth or spiritual kingdom. Students would learn much if they contrasted the building power of the higher mind with the destroying power of the lower. Just as the personality has no other function in the divine plan than to be a channel for, and the medium of expression of, the soul, so the lower mind is intended to be the channel for the pure inflow of higher mind energy.

This fifth ray is a Being of the intensest spiritual light and in His manifestation on this fifth plane, which is peculiarly His, He symbolises the three aspects in a way achieved by no other ray. Through His quality of higher mind, this ray is a pure channel for the divine will. Through the septenary grouping of the solar lives on the mental levels whereon they appear, He brought into functioning activity seven corresponding reflections of the seven centres of Deity, as far as our planet is concerned, a thing which none of His six brother rays have done. This statement means little to you, but the tremendous sacrifice and effort thus involved are paralleled only by the life of the Buddha, and this is one of the reasons why, in this fifth race, love and mind must eventually and mutually reveal each other.

Some of the names given to the Lord of this ray are as follows:

> The Revealer of Truth
> The great Connector
> The Divine Intermediary
> The Crystallizer of Forms
> The Three-fold Thinker
> The Cloud upon the Mountain-top
> The Precipitator of the Cross
> The Dividing Sword
> The Winnower of the Chaff
> The Fifth great Judge
> The Rose of God
> The Heavenly One
> The Door into the Mind of God
> The Initiating Energy
> The Ruler of the Third Heaven
> The Guardian of the Door
> The Dispenser of Knowledge
> The Angel with the Flaming Sword
> The Keeper of the Secret
> The Beloved of the Logos
> The Brother from Sirius
> The Master of the Hierophants

This fifth ray has so many names, owing to His close connection with man (since man was originally created), that it has not been easy to choose those which are of the most use in enabling the student to form an idea of the fifth ray characteristics and mission; but the study of the six aphorisms, and the qualities which they indicate, will show how potent and important is this ray Lord. These six aphorisms were chanted by His six Brothers at that momentous crisis wherein the human family came into existence and the solar Angels sacrificed themselves. Esoterically speaking, they "went down into hell, and found their place in prison." On that day souls were born. A new kingdom of expression came into being, and the three highest planes and the three lower were brought into a scintillating interchange.

> 1. God and His Angels now arise and see. Let the mountain-tops emerge from out the dense wet mist. Let the sun touch their summits and let them stand in light. Shine forth.
>
>   Quality . . . . . .emergence into form and out of form.
>
> 2. God and His Angels now arise and hear. Let a deep murmur rise and let the cry of seeking man enter into their ears. Let man listen. Let man call. Speak loud.
>
>   Quality . . . . . .power to make the Voice of the Silence heard.
>
> 3. God and His Angels now arise and touch. Bring forth the rod of power. Extend it outward toward the sons of men; touch them with fire, then bring them near. Bring forth.
>
>   Quality . . . . . .initiating activity.
>
> 4. God and His Angels now arise and taste. Let all experience come. Let all the ways appear. Discern and choose; dissect and analyse. All ways are one.
>
>   Quality . . . . . .revelation of the way.
>
> 5. God and His Angels now arise and sense the odor rising from the burning-ground of man. Let the fire do its work. Draw man within the furnace and let him drop within the rose-red centre the nature that retards. Let the fire burn.
>
>   Quality . . . . . .purification with fire.
>
> 6. God and His Angels now arise and fuse the many in the One. Let the blending work proceed. Let that which causes all to be produce the cause of their cessation. Let one temple now emerge. Produce the crowning glory. So let it be.
>
>   Quality . . . . . . the manifestation of the great white light. (The Shekinah. A.A.B.)

There is much of practical usefulness to the reader in a study of these qualities. When he believes himself to be upon a particular ray, they will indicate to him some of the characteristics for which he may look, and perhaps demonstrate to him what he has to do, what he has to express, and what he has to overcome. These qualities should be studied from two angles: their divine aspect and their reverse aspect or the form side. This ray, for instance, is shown to be the revealer of the way, and it should be remembered therefore that this fifth ray reveals the way down into death or into incarnation (which is the death-like prison of the soul), or it reveals the way up and out of darkness into the pure light of God's day. I mention this as I am exceedingly anxious that all who read this treatise should make application of this teaching to their daily lives. I am not interested in imparting weird or unusual items of information anent these matters for the delectation of an unhealthy mental appetite. The stocking of the memory with occult detail which serves no useful purpose only strains the brain cells and feeds the pride.

THE SIXTH PURPOSE OF DEITY

Ray VI. Devotion or Idealism

This ray which is just going out of manifestation, is of vital interest to us, for it has set its mark upon our western civilisation in a more definite way than any of the others. It is for us the most familiar and the best known of the rays. The mantram which defines its purpose is unlike the others and might be expressed somewhat as follows:

> The Crusade is on. The warriors march upon their way. They crush and kill all that impedes their way, and aught that rises on their onward path is trampled under foot. March towards the light.
>
> The work goes forward. The workers veil their eyes from pity as from fear. The work is all that counts. The form must disappear so that the loving spirit may enter into rest. Naught must arrest the progress of the workers with the plan. They enter upon the work assigned with paean and with song.
>
> The cross is reared on high; the form is laid thereon, and on

that cross must render up its life. Each builds a cross which forms the cross. They mount upon the cross.

Through war, through work, through pain and toil, the purpose is achieved. Thus saith the symbol.

It will be noted how this purpose, when applied by man to himself, works his release. When applied by man to man, it has produced the corrupt and awful story of man's cruelty to man. In the above mantram you will find the clue to the sixth ray purpose as it appears in the human kingdom, and a close expansive study (note that paradoxical phrase) of the underlying ideas will reveal a little of the larger purpose. The soul is and should be pitiless to its form and its problem. The soul can, however, comprehend the need for pain and difficulty in the world, for he can extend a knowledge of his own technique with himself to the technique of God with His world; but he does nothing knowingly that could possibly increase the world's pain or sorrow.

Some of the names for this beneficent yet somewhat violently energised Lord of a ray are as follows:

> The Negator of Desire
> The One Who sees the Right
> The Visioner of Reality
> The Divine Robber
> The Devotee of Life
> The Hater of Forms
> The Warrior on the March
> The Sword Bearer of the Logos
> The Upholder of the Truth
> The Crucifier and the Crucified
> The Breaker of Stones
> The Imperishable Flaming One
> The One Whom Naught can turn
> The Implacable Ruler
> The General on the Perfect Way
> The One Who leads the Twelve

Curiously enough, this sixth ray Lord has always been a

loved enigma to His six Brethren. This comes out in the questions which They addressed to Him on one occasion when They met "under the eye of the Lord" to interchange Their plans for united, divine, harmonious action. They asked these questions in a spirit of heavenly joy and love, but with the intent to throw some light upon the somewhat obscure quality of Their loved Brother.

1. Why is desire red? Why red as blood? Tell us, Oh Son of God, why thy way is red with blood?
    Quality . . . . . .power to kill out desire.
2. Why do you turn your back upon the sphere of earth? Is it too small, too poor? Why kick it as a ball upon a playing field?
    Quality . . . . . .spurning that which is not desired.
3. Why set the cross from earth to heaven? But earth can be a heaven. Why mount the cross and die?
    Quality . . . . . .self-immolation.
4. Why battle thus with all that is around? Seek you not peace? Why stand between the forces of the night and day? Why thus unmoved and calm, untired and unafraid?
    Quality . . . . . .endurance and fearlessness.
5. See you not God in all, the life in all, and love in all? Why separate yourself and leave behind the loved and the well-known?
    Quality . . . . . .power to detach oneself.
6. Can you arrest the waters of the sixth great sphere? Can you stem the flood? Can you recover both the raven and the dove? Can you, the Fish, swim free?
    Quality . . . . . .overcoming the waters of the emotional nature.

This out-going ray of devotion to the ideal, and the incoming ray of magical order or organisation are largely responsible for the type of man's consciousness today. Man is essentially devoted (to the point of fanaticism) to whatever may be the goal of his life's attention. This goal may be to achieve discipleship, or to raise a family, or to get money, or to achieve popularity, or any other objective to which he consecrates his time and energy; but whatever it may be, to it he devotes all that he is or has. Man also is essentially and inherently a producer of law and order, though this quality is only just beginning to make its presence felt. This is because mankind is, at last, becoming mentally centred, and hence we have in the world at this time the many and varied attempts to straighten out affairs along business, national, economic, social and other lines, to produce some system and order, and to bring about the re-arranging of all energies with the objective (unrealised consciously as yet) of inaugurating the New Age. Owing, however, to defective mental control and to an almost universal ignorance as to the laws of thought, and in addition, to a profound lack of knowledge as to man's own nature, man works blindly. The ideals sensed are not correctly interpreted by the mind nor applied in such a way that they are of general and appropriate application. Hence the confusion and the chaotic experimentation going on, and hence also the imposition of personal authority to enforce an individual's idea of the ideal.

The need today is for sound teaching as to the laws of thought, and the rules which govern the building of those thought-forms which must embody the ideas sent forth from the universal divine Mind. Men must begin on the subjective planes of life to work out the needed order. When this is realised, we shall have every important group of men engaged in world affairs, or in the work of government in all its branches, aided on the mental plane by trained thinkers, so that there may be right application and correct adjustment to the Plan. This time is as yet far away, and hence the distortions and misrepresentations on earth of the Plan as it exists in heaven, to use the Christian phraseology.

It was the realisation of the present world need for illumined thinkers and subjective workers which prompted Those Who guide so to direct the incoming spiritual energies that the formation of the esoteric groups everywhere came about; it led also to the publication of the mass of mystical and Oriental literature on meditation and allied topics which has flooded the world today. Hence also the effort that I, a worker on the inner side of life, am making to teach the newer psychology in this treatise, and so show to man what is his equipment and how well suited he is to the work for which he has been created, and which he has as yet failed to comprehend. The force and the effect of the seventh ray influence will, however, reveal to him the magical work, and the next twenty five hundred years will bring about so much change and make possible the working of so many so-called "miracles" that even the outer appearance of the world will be profoundly altered; the vegetation and the animal life will be modified and developed, and much that is latent in the forms of both kingdoms will be brought into expression through the freer flow and the more intelligent manipulation of the energies which create and constitute all forms. The world has been changed beyond belief during the past five hundred years, and during the next two hundred years the changes will be still more rapid and deep-seated, for the growth of the intellectual powers of man is gathering momentum, and Man, the Creator, is coming into possession of His powers.

THE SEVENTH PURPOSE OF DEITY

Ray VII. Ceremonial Order or Magic

"Let the Temple of the Lord be built", the seventh great Angel cried. Then to their places in the north, the south, the west and east, seven great sons of God moved with measured pace and took their seats. The work of building thus began.

The doors were closed. The light shone dim. The temple walls could not be seen. The seven were silent and their forms were veiled. The time had not arrived for the breaking forth of light. The Word could not be uttered. Only between the seven Forms the work went on. A silent call went forth from each to each. Yet still the temple door stayed shut.

As time went on, the sounds of life were heard. The door was opened, and the door was shut. Each time it opened, the power within the temple grew; each time the light waxed stronger, for one by one the sons of men entered the temple, passed from north to south, from west to east and in the centre of the heart found light, found understanding and the power to work. They entered through the door; they passed before the Seven; they raised the temple's veil and entered into life.

The temple grew in beauty. Its lines, its walls, its decorations, and its height and depth and breadth slowly emerged and entered into light.

Out from the east, the Word went forth: Open the door to all the sons of men who come from all the darkened valleys of the land and seek the temple of the Lord. Give them the light. Unveil the inner shrine, and through the work of all the craftsmen of the Lord extend the temple's walls and thus irradiate the world. Sound forth the Word creative and raise the dead to life.

Thus shall the temple of the light be carried from heaven to earth. Thus shall its walls be reared upon the great plains of the world of men. Thus shall the light reveal and nurture all the dreams of men.

Then shall the Master in the east awaken those who are asleep. Then shall the warden in the west test and try all the true seekers after light. Then shall the warden in the south instruct and aid the blind. Then shall the gate into the north remain wide open, for there the unseen Master stands with welcoming hand and understanding heart, to lead the pilgrims to the east where the true light shines forth.

"Why this opening of the temple?" demand the greater Seven. Because the work is ready; the craftsmen are prepared. God has created in the light. His sons can now create. What can else be done?"

"Naught!" came the answer from the greater Seven. "Let the work proceed. Let the sons of God create."

These words will be noted by many as of deep significance and as indicating a wide intention (during the coming cycle) to open the door wide into the temple of the hidden mystery to man. One by one we shall undergo the esoteric and spiritual counterpart of the psychological factor which is called "a mental test." That test will demonstrate a man's usefulness in mental work and power, it will show his capacity to build thought-forms and to vitalise them. This I dealt with in *A Treatise on White Magic*, and the relation of that treatise to the magical work of the seventh ray and its cycle of activity will become increasingly apparent. *A Treatise on White Magic* is an attempt to lay down the rules for training and for work which will make it possible for the candidate to the mysteries to enter the temple and to take his place as a creative worker and thus aid in the magical work of the Lord of the Temple.

The names whereby this ray Lord is known are many, and their meaning is of prime significance today. The work of the future can be seen from a study of these names.

> The Unveiled Magician
> The Worker in the Magical Art
> The Creator of the Form
> The Bestower of Light from the Second Lord
> The Manipulator of the Wand
> The Watcher in the East
> The Custodian of the Seventh Plan
> The Invoker of Wrath
> The Keeper of the Magical Word
> The Temple Guardian
> The Representative of God
> The One Who lifts to Life
> The Lord of Death
> The One Who feeds the Sacred Fire
> The Whirling Sphere
> The Sword of the Initiator
> The Divine Alchemical Worker
> The Builder of the Square
> The Orienting Force

The Fiery Unifier
The Key to the Mystery
The Expression of the Will
The Revealer of Beauty

This ray Lord has a peculiar power on earth and on the physical plane of divine manifestation. His usefulness to His six Brothers is therefore apparent. He makes Their work appear. He is the most active of all the rays in this world period, and is never out of manifestation for more than fifteen hundred years. It is almost as if He whirled in and out of active work under a very rapid cycle, and His closest relation, symbolically, is to His Brethren of the second and fifth rays *in this world period.*

He builds (using second ray cooperation) through the power of thought (thus cooperating with the Lord of the fifth ray and on the physical plane, which is His own essential and peculiar sphere). In another world period His relation with the other ray Lords may undergo change, but at this time His work will be more easily understood when He is recognised as aiding the building Lord of the second ray and utilising the energies of the Lord of concrete thought.

The aphorisms embodying His qualities run as follows, and were esoterically whispered into His ears when He "left the most high place and descended into the seventh sphere to carry out the work assigned."

1. Take thy tools with thee, brother of the building light. Carve deep. Construct and shape the living stone.
    Quality . . . . . .power to create.
2. Choose well thy workers. Love them all. Pick six to do thy will. Remain the seventh in the east. Yet call the world to enter into that which thou shalt build. Blend all together in the will of God.
    Quality . . . . . .power to cooperate.
3. Sit in the centre and the east as well. Move not from there.

Send out thy force to do thy will and gather back thy forces. Use well the power of thought. Sit still.

    Quality . . . . . .power to think.

4. See all parts enter into the purpose. Build towards beauty, brother Lord. Make all colours bright and clear. See to the inner glory. Build the shrine well. Use care.

    Quality . . . . . .revelation of the beauty of God.

5. Watch well thy thought. Enter at will into the mind of God. Pluck thence the power, the plan, the part to play. Reveal the mind of God.

    Quality . . . . . .mental power.

6. Stay in the east. The five have given thee a friendly Word. I, the sixth, tell thee to use it on the dead. Revive the dead. Build forms anew. Guard well that Word. Make all men seek it for themselves.

    Quality . . . . . .power to vivify.

Thus we have studied a little the work of the seven rays. The teaching has had to be conveyed symbolically and its understanding necessitates an awakened esoteric sense; to comprehend it all is not as yet possible.

The Chohans of the sixth initiation have the guidance of those units of consciousness in whom their particular ray vibration and colour predominate. The vast importance of this fact is often overlooked, even when theoretically acknowledged by aspirants to initiation. Hence the importance of determining the ray of the ego and of the Monad,—something of vital moment after the third initiation. A majority and a minority always exist in every department of life. So it is in the work of the Logos, for at the end of the greater cycle (manvantara) the majority will find their way to the synthetic love ray; a small minority will find their way to the power ray. This minority are destined for an important function. They will constitute the nucleus which (in the next solar system) will constitute the majority, finding their synthesis on ray one. This is a great mystery and not easily understood.

Some hint towards its solution will be found hidden in the real meaning of the words "exoteric" and "esoteric."

The fact should be remembered that only five rays dominate at any one time. All manifest, but only five dominate. A distinction should be made between the rays dominating in a solar system and those dominating in a scheme, or a chain. To this reference has been made in *A Treatise on Cosmic Fire*. Three rays out of the seven synthesise. One ray out of the three will synthesise at the culmination. For the first solar system the third ray was the synthetic ray, but for this solar system the second ray is the synthetic ray, and for the next solar system the first ray will perform a similar function.

Two rays are largely the goal of human endeavour, the first ray and the second ray. One ray is the goal of the deva or angel evolution, the third ray. All these three rays contact the two poles, and the attainment of the goal at the end of the cycle marks the achievement of the solar Logos. This again is hidden in mystery. The seventh ray and the first ray are very closely allied, with the third ray linking them, so that we have the relation expressed thus,— 1. 3. 7. There is a close association also between rays 2. 4. 6., with the fifth ray in a peculiar position, as a central point of attainment, the home of the ego or soul, the embodied plane of mind, the point of consummation for the personality, and the reflection in the three worlds of the threefold monad.

Ray I . . . . Will, demonstrating as power in the unfolding of the Plan of the Logos.

Ray III . . . Adaptability of activity with intelligence. This ray was the dominant one in the past solar system; it is the foundation or basis of this system, and is controlled by the Mahachohan.

Ray VII . . Ceremonial ritual or organisation. This is the reflection on the physical plane of the two above, and is likewise connected with the Mahachohan. It controls the elemental forces and the involutionary process and the form side of the three kingdoms in nature. It holds hid the secret of physical colour and sound. It is the law.

These three rays together embrace and embody all. They are Power, Activity and the Law in manifestation.

Ray II . . . .Love and Wisdom, the synthetic ray which is the goal for this system, holding all in close harmony and relation.

Ray IV . . . The expression of Harmony, beauty, music and unity.

Ray VI . . . The ray of Devotion to the ardour of aspiration, and of the sacrifice of the personal self for the good of all, with the object in view of harmony and beauty, impelled thereto by love.

These two groups of rays might be related to each other as follows:

Rays 1. 3. 7   are the great rays connected with the form, with the evolutionary process, with the intelligent functioning of the system, and with the laws controlling the life in all forms in all the kingdoms in nature.

Rays 2. 4. 6   are the rays connected with the inner life, expanding through those forms,—the rays of motive, aspiration and sacrifice. Rays pre-eminently of quality.

Rays 1. 3. 7   deal with things concrete and with the functioning of matter and form from the lowest plane to the highest.

Rays 2. 4. 6   deal with things abstract, with spiritual expression through the medium of form.

Ray 5 . . . . . . forms the connecting link of the intelligence.

Our third question comes up now for consideration and is as follows:

Question 3. Can the fact of the Soul be proved?

The soul has been satisfactorily disproved from the standpoint of academic science. For ages the search has gone on, with the objective of the search—scientifically speaking—being laid on the demonstration of the location of the soul in the human body. That has been the emphasis and the important factor to the scientific mind, which is so different to that of its more mystically inclined brother.

All research, especially that carried on lately in connection with the modern materialistic schools and with the fuller understanding of the mechanism of the human body, has tended to prove that the soul is a superstition, a defense mechanism, and that conscious thought with all the higher manifestations of the human mind (and hence also the lower expressions of personality, selfhood and conscious integration) can well be provided for and accounted for by man's present equipment of brain, nervous system and the endocrine system. All these in their turn are understood to be the result of a long evolutionary and selective process. The wonder of the machine itself is divine in its completion and in its scope. From a primeval germ, developing under the pressure of nature's laws, and of environing conditions plus a consistent adaptation to requirements and a most careful selection, man has developed; he now possesses a mechanism which is responsive to the natural world, to sensation and to thought. That which is called the soul is regarded frequently as the result of this selective process and as constituting the sum total of the responsive and discriminating powers of the cells and organs of the body, plus the life principle. All, we are told, is inherent in the parental germ, and the conditions of the environment, added to heredity and education, are sufficient to account for the phenomena of the human consciousness. Man is a machine, a part of a still greater machine which we call nature, and both man and nature are run on immutable laws. There is no free will except within certain clearly defined limits, which are defined by equipment and by circumstance.

Certain Questions

There can be no immortality, for when the machine breaks down and disintegrates there is nothing left but the dissociated cells and atoms of which it was originally composed. When the principle of coherence or of integration ceases to function, that which it produced—the coherent functioning body—likewise ceases to function. Consciousness and choice, awareness and affection, thought and temperament, life and love, character and capacities—all disappear, and there is nothing left but the atoms of which the body had been composed. These in their turn are dissipated and disappear, and all has finally been reabsorbed into the general reservoir of forces and atoms.

Of the countless millions of human beings who have lived and loved, suffered and rejoiced upon our planet, what is left today to guarantee to us their existence in the past, not to speak of their continuing existence in the present? A few bones, a few buildings, and, later, traces of their historical influence; later still, we note what they have left behind of beauty in the field of literature, of architecture, of painting, and in those forms in which they have embodied their thought and aspiration, their visions and their ideals. On the planet today we find a humanity at all stages of development, with mechanisms of varying kinds, adequate and inadequate. We find all of them, without exception, breaking down under test and limited by disease, or hiding the seeds of disease; the perfect equipment is totally unknown, and every man harbors the germs of trouble. No man possesses a perfect mechanism, but owns one that must inevitably break down at some point that is conditioned by an under-developed or over-developed glandular system, that hides at some point inherited disease and racial weaknesses, and that fails somewhere, in some portion of the mechanism, to meet the needs (physical, emotional, and mental) of the day and hour. Of what does this speak? Of the sum total of the united cell life; of the environing group in which a particular form finds itself; of the life, impersonal and abstract in nature, which pervades it; of a vague group spirit that is expressing itself through the fourth kingdom in nature; of a temporary and impermanent self; or of an immortal entity who is the dweller in the body?

Such are some of the questions which arise today; and in the last analysis, belief in the soul can be posited as being largely a matter of temperament, of the wish and desire of the ages wherein man struggled and suffered and relieved the strain of living by constructing a body of thought around a happy immortal being, who was to be free, eventually and finally, from all the difficulties of physical existence. The soul can be regarded as a beautiful vision or as an hallucination, for all that tends to prove its existence is the testimony of the many mystics down the ages to a contact and an experience which can be accounted for in terms of dream life, of brain lesions or of escape reactions, but which rests on no sure foundation. So say the materialists and the upholders of proven scientific facts. Belief, verbal testimony, hope, curious and inexplicable psychic happenings, the mass of untrained opinion and the findings of visionary people (who were probably psychopathic cases) are not enough to prove the fact of the soul. They prove only man's power to imagine, to build images and pictures, and to lose himself and his dreadful present in a dream world of a possible and ardently desired future in which frustration will end, in which full expression will be achieved, and in which each man will enter into an impossible heritage which he has himself constructed out of the unrealised hopes and dim unuttered longings of his deeply hidden thought life. Belief in God and Heaven and in an immortal future have grown out of the ancient awe and ignorant terror of infant humanity. They saw in all the phenomena of nature (incomprehensible and terrifying) the activity of a gigantic man, built on lines which were the projection of their own consciousness, and who could be propitiated or angered by the behaviour of a human being. The result of a man's effect upon this deity provided man's destiny, which was either good or bad according to the reactions of this God to his deeds. Thus we have the origin of the heaven or hell complexes of the present religious faiths. From this grew, automatically, the idea of a persistent entity called the soul, which could enjoy heaven or suffer hell at the will of God and as the result of actions done whilst in the human form. As the forms of man grew in sensitivity; as they became more and more refined under the influence of the law of selection and of adaptation; as the group life grew closer and the group integration was improved; as the heritage of history, of tradition and of the arts grew richer and made its impress, so that ideas of God grew, and likewise ideas of the soul and of the world, man's concepts of reality grew richer and deeper, so that today we are faced with the problem of a thought inheritance which testifies to a world of concepts, ideas and intuitions which deal with the immaterial and the intangible, and which testify to an age-long belief in a soul and its immortality for which there is no true justification. At the same time we have demonstrated to us by science that all we can really know with certainty is the tangible world of phenomena, with its forms, its mechanisms, its test tubes and its laboratories, and the bodies of men "fearfully and wonderfully made," diverse and different. These in some mysterious way produce thoughts and dreams and imaginings, and which, in their turn, find expression in the formulated schemes of the past, the present and the future, or in the fields of literature, art and of science itself, or in the simple everyday life of the ordinary human being who lives and loves and works and plays and bears children and eats food and earns money and sleeps.

And then what? Does man disappear into nothingness, or does, somewhere, a part of him (hitherto unseen) live on? Does this aspect survive for a time and then in its turn disappear, or is there an immortal principle, a subtle intangible entity which has an existence either in the body or out of the body, and which is the undying immutable Being, belief in Whom has sustained countless millions down the ages? Is the soul a fiction of the imagination and has science satisfactorily disproved its existence? Is consciousness a function of the brain and of the allied nervous system, or shall we accept the idea of a conscious dweller in the form? Does our power to become aware of and to react to our surroundings find its source in the body-nature, or is there an entity who beholds and takes action? Is this entity different to and separable from the body, or is it the result of the body type and life, and so either persists after the body disappears, or disappears with it and is lost? Is there nothing but matter or energies in constant movement which produce the appearances of men who react in their turn and express the energy that is pouring through them blindly and unconsciously, having no individual existence? Or are all these theories partially true, and shall we really comprehend the nature and being of man only in the synthesis of all of them and in the acceptance of the general premises? Is it not possible that the mechanically minded and scientific investigators are right in their conclusion anent the mechanism and the form nature, and that the spiritually minded thinkers who posit an immortal entity are also right? As yet perhaps something is lacking which would bridge the gap between the two positions. Is it possible that we may discover a something which will link the intangible world of true being with the tangible world (so-called) of form life?

When humanity is assured of divinity and of immortality, and has entered into a state of knowledge as to the nature of the soul and of the kingdom in which that soul functions, its attitude to daily life and to current affairs will undergo such a transformation that we shall verily and indeed see the emergence of a new heaven and a new earth. Once the central entity within each human form is recognised and known for what it essentially is, and once its divine persistence is established, then we shall necessarily see the beginning of the reign of divine law on earth—a law imposed without friction and without rebellion. This beneficent reaction will come about because the thinkers of the race will be blended together in a general soul awareness, and a consequent group consciousness will permit them to see the purpose underlying the working of the law.

Let us put this a little more simply. We are told in the New Testament that we must endeavour to let the mind which was in Christ also be manifest in us. We are working towards the perfecting of the rule of Christ on earth; we are aiming at the development of the Christ consciousness and at the bringing in of the rule or law of Christ, which is Love. This will come to fruition in the Aquarian Age, and we shall see brotherhood established on earth. The rule of Christ is the dominance of the basic spiritual laws. The mind of Christ is a phrase conveying the concept of the rule of divine intelligent love, which stimulates the rule of the soul within all forms, and brings in the reign of the Spirit. It is not easy to express the nature of the revelation which is on the way. It involves the recognition by men everywhere that the "mind-stuff," as the Hindus call it, to which their own minds are related and of which their mental bodies are an integral part, is also part of the mind of Christ, the cosmic Christ, of Whom the historical Christ is—upon our planet—the ordained representative. When men, through meditation and group service, have developed an awareness of their own controlled and illumined minds, they will find themselves initiated into a consciousness of true being and into a state of knowledge which will prove to them the fact of the soul, beyond all doubt or questioning.

The Mystery of the Ages is on the verge of revelation, and through the revelation of the soul that mystery which it veils will stand revealed. The scriptures of the world, we know, have ever prophesied that at the end of the age we shall see the revelation of that which is secret, and the emergence into the light of day of that which has hitherto been concealed and veiled. This, our present cycle, is the end of the age, and the next two hundred years will see the abolition of death, as we now understand that great transition, and the establishing of the fact of the soul's existence. The soul will be known as an entity, as the motivating impulse and the spiritual centre back of all manifested forms. The next few decades will see certain great beliefs substantiated. The work of Christ, and His main mission two thousand years ago, was to demonstrate the divine possibilities and powers latent in every human being. The proclamation which He made to the effect that we were all sons of God and own one universal Father will, in the future, no longer be regarded as a beautiful, mystical and symbolic statement, but will be regarded as a scientific pronouncement. Our universal brotherhood and our essential immortality will be demonstrated and realised to be facts in nature. He came, He said, not to bring peace but a sword, and esoterically, He has been the "Cosmic Divider." Why? Because, in establishing unity, He also makes a distinction between body and soul. Body and soul are, however, only two parts of one whole, and this must not be forgotten. In establishing the fact of the soul and its expression, the body, the totality emerges in completeness.

How will this revelation come? We enter here into the realm of foretelling and of prevision to which many have an objection on the ground that the thing of the moment is that which aids the soul's spiritual living; they feel that the holding out of promises of future help and revelation, and the encouragement in the aspirant of a happy speculation and an idle expectancy carry the seeds of danger, of static inertia, and of idle imaginings. But "where there is no vision, the people perish," and so much has happened during the last two hundred years, and so much has already been revealed, that we are provided with a firm basis for all our forward looking. Had the unfoldments of the nineteenth and twentieth centuries, in the departments of science and psychology alone, been forecast to the thinkers of the world in the sixteenth century, how strange and impossible it would all have seemed to them! Stranger than anything I might here prophecy to you, for we have already seen so much occur, and the testimony to the world of true being is accumulating so fast, that we can no longer stand amazed at any occurrence.

The fact of the soul will be brought to the racial recognition in many ways, and the revelation will come along so many lines that all types of minds will be satisfied. I shall indicate only a few.

The psychics of the world are increasing greatly in number, and the growing sensitivity of the race to impression is a cause of rejoicing and of danger. All over the world aspirants are registering contacts hitherto unknown, are seeing a phenomenal world usually hidden to them, and are generally becoming aware of an expansion of consciousness. They are registering a world of phenomena—often astral, sometimes mental, and occasionally egoic—which does initiate them into a new dimension of consciousness and into a different state of being. This expansion of consciousness serves both to encourage them in their endeavour and to complicate the way of the aspirant. This growing sensitivity is universal;

hence the rapid growth of spiritualism and of the psychic sciences, and hence also the increase among men of nervous tension, of neurotic conditions, and of the greatly increased problems of the psychiatrist; hence also the spread of new nervous and mental diseases. This sensitivity is the response of the mechanism of man to the approaching developments, and the race as a whole is being brought into a condition wherein it will be ready to "see and hear" that which has been up to the present unrevealed.

The growth of the colour sense and the capacity to respond musically to quarter tones and subtle nuances indicate a thinning of the veil which separates the world of external and tangible phenomena from that of subjective being and of more subtle matter. The growth also of etheric vision and the largely increased numbers of clairvoyant and clairaudient people are steadily revealing the existence of the astral plane and the etheric counterpart of the physical world. More and more people are becoming aware of this subjective realm; they see people walking around who are either the so-called "dead," or who in sleep have dropped the physical sheath. They become aware of colours and distinctive hues and streams of organised light which are not of this physical world; they hear sounds and voices which emanate from those who are not using the physical vocal apparatus, and from forms of existence which are not corporeal.

The first step towards substantiating the fact of the soul is to establish the fact of survival, though this may not necessarily prove the fact of immortality. It can nevertheless be regarded as a step in the right direction. That something survives the process of death, and that something persists after the disintegration of the physical body, is steadily being proved. If that is not so, then we are the victims of a collective hallucination, and the brains and minds of thousands of

Certain Questions

people are untrue and deceiving, are diseased and distorted. Such a gigantic collective insanity is more difficult to credit than the alternative of an expanded consciousness. This development along psychic lines does not prove the fact of the soul, however; it only serves to break down the materialistic position.

It is among the thinkers of the race that the first assured recognition of the soul will come, and this event will be the result of the study and analysis, by the psychologists of the world, of the nature of genius and the significance of creative work.

Some men and women in the world tower above their fellow men, and produce that which is superlative in its own field; their work has in it the element of divinity and of immortality. The work of creative artists, the intuitive perception of great scientific investigators, the inspired imagination of the poets of the world and the vision of the illumined idealists, have all to be accounted for and explained, for the laws under which such men and women work have yet to be discovered. The close study, by the psychologist, of the abnormal and the subnormal, of warped and distorted minds and of defective equipments, has been over-emphasized, and due attention has not been given to the divinely abnormal, and to those types of consciousness which transcend the ordinary human state of intelligent awareness. These latter super-normal states find expression through the medium of the great artists, musicians, dramatists, writers, and the many other types of creative workers who have been the glory of the human kingdom down the ages, and who will flame forth during the coming century with greater glory still.

When the hypothesis of the soul is accepted, when the nature of the spiritual energy which flows through the soul is admitted, and when the mechanism of the force centres is studied, we shall make rapid progress towards knowledge. When, through meditation, experiment is made to produce creatively some of the beauty contacted, some of the ideas revealed and some of the patterns seen, we shall learn to cultivate genius and understand how to train people to work creatively. Then much will be discovered about the centres in man where the divine principle has its dwelling, and from which the Christ within can work. The study of the superconscious must be undertaken, and not simply the study of the self-conscious or of the sub-conscious. Through this study, carried forward with an open mind, modern psychology will eventually arrive at a recognition of the soul.

The range of investigation is so wide that I can only indicate some of the possible fields of research:

1. The investigation of the nature of genius, and its definite and specialised cultivation.

2. Training in creative work and a study of the difference between this kind of training and training for vocational work. Creative work proves the fact of the soul; vocational training demonstrates the type of the personality.

3. Scientific investigation of the powers in man, with particular attention to telepathy. It will be found that telepathic work is from mind to mind, or from soul to mind, and does not necessarily imply brain to brain communication and contact. This is one of the most promising fields of investigation, though it still presents much difficulty. The fact of the existence of the soul will not be proved through the medium of telepathy until after the year 1945. By that time an event will have happened in the world and a particular new teaching will have been given which will put the entire subject of telepathic phenomena in a new light.

4. The scientific training of clairvoyants and the intelligent development of clairvoyant powers by the intelligentsia

of the world leaves as yet much to be desired, but it will come as the result of mind control and illumination. Men will learn to subject the mechanism of the body to a downflow of spiritual energy and stimulation, and thus will bring the powers of the psychic nature into activity, and the old method of sitting for development in order to awaken the centres will be seen as dangerous and unnecessary.

In the field of modern psychology we can look for a gradual recognition of the fact of the self. The problem of the psychologists is to comprehend the relationship or the identity of that self with the soul.

It is, however, from the field of science that the greatest help will come. The fact of the soul will eventually be proved through the study of light and of radiation and through a coming evolution in particles of light. Through this imminent development we shall find ourselves seeing more and penetrating deeper into that which we see today. One of the recognised facts in the realm of natural science has been the cyclic change in the fauna and flora of our planet. Animals, plentiful and familiar many thousands of years ago, are now extinct, and by means of their bones we endeavour to reconstruct their forms. Flowers and trees that once covered the surface of our planet have now entirely disappeared and only their fossilized remains are left to indicate to us a vegetation vastly different to that which we now enjoy. Man himself has changed so much that we find it difficult to recognise *homo sapiens* in the early primitive races of the far distant past. This mutability and obliteration of earlier types is due to a major factor among many. The quality of the light which promotes and nurtures growth, vitality and fertility in the kingdoms of nature has changed several times during the ages, and as it has changed it has produced corresponding mutations in the phenomenal world. From the standpoint of the esotericist, all forms of life on our planet are affected by three types of light substance, and at the present time a fourth type is gradually making its presence felt. These types of light are:

1. The light of the sun.
2. The light in the planet itself—not the reflected light of the sun but its own inherent radiance.
3. A light seeping in (if I may use such a phrase) from the astral plane, a steady and gradual penetration of the "astral light" and its fusion with the other two types of radiance.
4. A light which is beginning to merge itself with the other three types and which comes from that state of matter which we call the mental plane—a light in its turn reflected from the realm of the soul.

An intensification of the light is going on all the time, and this increase in intensity began on the earth at about the time when man discovered the uses of electricity, which discovery was a direct result of this intensification. The electrification of the planet through the wide-spread use of electricity is one of the things which is inaugurating the new age, and which will aid in bringing about the revelation of the presence of the soul. Before long this intensification will become so great that it will materially assist in the rending of the veil which separates the astral plane from the physical plane; the dividing etheric web will shortly be dissipated, and this will permit a more rapid inflow of the third aspect of light. The light from the astral plane (a starry radiance) and the light of the planet itself will be more closely blended, and the result upon humanity and upon the three other kingdoms in nature cannot be over-emphasized. It will, for one thing, profoundly affect the human eye and make the present sporadic etheric vision a universal asset. It will bring within the radius of our range of contact the

Certain Questions

infra-red and ultra-violet gamut of colours, and we shall see what at present is hidden. All this will tend to destroy the platform upon which the materialists stand, and to pave the way, first, for the admission of the soul as a sound hypothesis, and secondly, for the demonstration of its existence. We only need more light, in the esoteric sense, in order to see the soul, and that light will shortly be available and we shall understand the meaning of the words, "And in Thy light shall we see light."

This intensification of the light will continue until A.D. 2025, when there will come a cycle of relative stability and of steady shining without much augmentation. In the second decanate of Aquarius these three aspects will again be augmented by increased light from the fourth aspect, that is the light from the soul realm, reaching us via the universal "chitta" or mind stuff. This will flood the world. By that time, however, the soul will be recognised as a fact, and as a consequence of this recognition our entire civilisation will have changed so radically that we cannot today even guess at the form it will take. The next ten years will see a greatly increased merging of the first three forms of light, and those of you who are awake to these issues and happenings will find it interesting to note what is going on. The consensus of opinion in the religious and spiritualistic fields and in the field of biblical prophecy, and likewise a study of the symbolism of the Pyramid, lead students to believe that the immediate future will see some great event and some unforeseen spiritual happening. This should be duly anticipated, and careful preparation should be made for it. I refer not to any coming of any individual. I refer to a natural process with far-reaching effects.

There are certain other fields of activity which will all do their part in demonstrating the fact of the soul.

There is an aspect of human consciousness which has for

long baffled the materialistic psychologist, and this is the curious power of prevision, the ability to foresee and foretell with accuracy events coming in the immediate future, or distant happenings. There are warnings given by some inner monitor which have again and again saved man from death and disaster; there are the appearances, to their friends and relatives, of men or women who have just died, before any word of their death has been received. This is not in the field of telepathic knowledge of the death, but involves the appearance of the person. There is the power to participate in events in distant places and to recover the recollection of what transpired with accuracy as to place, personnel and detail. These powers and many similar previsions and recognitions have long bewildered investigators and must find correct explanation. In their wise investigation, in the accumulation of responsible evidence, and in the later substantiation of the prevision, it will begin to be seen that some factor exists in man which is not bound by space-time limitations, but which transcends the normal human consciousness. The present attempted investigation and explanations are inadequate and do not account satisfactorily for all the facts. When, however, they are approached from the standpoint of the soul, with its faculty of omniscience and its freedom from categories of past, present and future (for they are lost in the consciousness of the Eternal Now), we shall begin to understand the process a little more clearly. When the true Dweller in the body is recognised and the laws of prevision are discovered, and when the power to foresee is generally prevalent, then we shall begin to find ample proof of the existence of the soul. It will be impossible to account for the ordinary phenomena then current without admitting its existence.

Along these various lines proof of the soul will accumulate. In the massing of testimony and of evidence a fruitful field of activity lies. In the training of the higher types of men in the use of the soul force and soul powers, and in the trained control of the mechanism, that evidence so produced will be seen to be of so high an order and will be so scientifically presented that it will be regarded as of as much importance and as justifiable as any views presented by our leading scientists in their various fields of research today. The study of the soul will before long be as legitimate and respectable an investigation as any scientific problem, such as research into the nature of the atom. The investigation of the soul and its governing laws will, before long, engross the attention of our finest minds. The newer psychology will eventually succeed in proving the fact of its existence, and the paralleling intuitive and instinctive response of mankind to soul nurture, emanating from the invisible side of life, will steadily and successfully prove the existence of a spiritual entity in man,—an entity all-wise, immortal, divine and creative.

But the process would be slow were it not for the work now being done by a group of disciples and initiates working in collaboration with the Master P——, Who has His headquarters in America and Who, with His disciples, is doing much to stimulate the various psychological schools in the world today. It is needless for students to endeavour to ascertain His identity. He works through movements and schools of thought, and does no work with private individuals. He works practically entirely on the mental plane, with the power of thought, and is quite unknown and unrecognised, except by His fellow workers in the various countries in the world, and by the disciples on His ray, the fourth ray. Much that is opening in the world of psychology today is due to the work He does in stimulating the minds of the leaders of movements. He works with them on the mental plane, but does not contact them as physical plane individuals.

The urgency of the time is great, and the Masters are exceedingly active and profoundly concerned at this time with the work of salvaging the world. They have not the time for personal work, except with Their own groups of accepted chelas, all of whom are active in the world work, or they would not be in the Masters' group. Also They may work intermittently with small groups of probationers to whom They offer opportunity and give an occasional hint. Each of Them has a few, a very few, probationers in training, to take the place of chelas who pass on to initiation, but beyond these two groups, during this century, They do no personal work, leaving the many aspirants to the care of lesser initiates and chelas. Even Their work and Their personal chelas at this time are much restricted, and word has been sent out to the working disciples in the world to stand on their own feet, to use their own judgment and not handicap the Masters at this time of intense strain and danger by attracting Their attention needlessly. The world issues today are of such importance, and the opportunity before humanity is so great, and the Masters are so entirely occupied with world affairs and with the dominant and prominent figures in high places in the nations, that the instruction of unimportant people in the various little occult groups and societies is temporarily suspended. The time is relatively so short in which to accomplish and carry out certain aspects of the Plan as entrusted to the Great Ones, that all true chelas are going about their work and endeavouring to solve their own problems without having to call on the Master's help, thus leaving Him free for more important work. The closer a disciple is to a Master, the more deeply he realises this fact, and the more he endeavours to fulfill his duty, learn his lessons, serve humanity, and lift some of the load of work off the shoulders of the Master.

The world today is full of disciples of varying degree,

and each of them is, in his place, able to guide and help some aspirants. The world is full of teaching and of books able to inspire and help all true seekers after spiritual knowledge. The last fifty years have seen much teaching given out and much esoteric training given to the world and available now to all who earnestly seek it. Aspirants have much to work upon and much theory to render into practice, and this leaves the Masters free for more important work.

One of the interesting things that is happening, and one of the factors which will serve eventually in the work of demonstrating the fact of the soul, is the mass of communications, inspired writings, and telepathic dictations which is flooding the world today. As you know, the spiritualistic movement is producing a vast amount of this inspired or pseudo-inspired literature, some of it of the very highest order and unquestionably the work of highly evolved disciples, and some of it most mediocre in quality. The various theosophical societies have been the recipients of similar communications, and they are found in every occult group. True communications are frequently of deep spiritual value, and contain much teaching and help for the aspirant. Students of the times would do well to remember that it is the teaching that is of moment, not the supposed source; by their intrinsic value alone these writings and communications must be judged. These communications emanate in the majority of instances from the soul plane, and the recipient or the communicator (the intermediary or scribe) is either inspired by his own soul or has tapped the thought level and knowledge of the ray group to which his soul belongs. He tunes in on a reservoir of thought, and his mind and brain translate these thoughts into words and phrases.

In a lesser number of cases, the man who is receiving a dictation or writing is in telepathic rapport with some more advanced disciple than himself, and his mind is being impressed by some chela in his group. This chela, who is closer to the Master than he is, passes on to him some of the knowledge that he has absorbed through being able to live within the Master's aura. But the Master is not concerned in the process; it lies between the chela and the aspirant. In these cases the receiver of the communication is often misled, and thinks that the Master Himself is dictating to him, whereas in reality he has—through a more advanced chela than himself—tuned in on the Master's thought atmosphere.

None of the Masters of the sixth initiation (such as the Masters M. and K. H.) are at this time working through dictation with Their disciples. They are too much engrossed with world problems, and with the work of watching over the destinies of the prominent world figures in the various nations, to have any opportunity to dictate teaching to any particular disciple in some small field of activity and upon subjects of which sufficient is already known to enable the disciple to go ahead alone and unaided. Two of the Masters are working telepathically and through dictation with several accepted disciples, and Their effort is to inspire these disciples, who are active in world work, to greater usefulness in the Plan. They are working in this way in order to impress a few of the prominent thinkers in the field of science and of social welfare with the needed knowledge which will enable them to make the right moves in the emergence of the race into greater freedom. But I know of no others, in this particular generation, who are so doing, for They have delegated much of this work to Their initiates and disciples. The bulk of the communicators today (working through aspirants on the physical plane) are active working chelas of accepted degree who (living as they do in the thought aura of the Master and His group) are steadily endeavouring to reach all kinds of people, all over the world, in all groups. Hence the increasing flood of communications, of inspired writings, and of personal messages and teaching.

When you add to the above the equally large flood of communications which emanate from the transmitters' own souls and from the realm of the subconscious, you have accounted for the mass of the material going out now. In all this there is need for deep thankfulness at the growing responsiveness and sensitivity of man.

That the first reaction and effect of such an outpouring of communications is oft an increase of spiritual pride and ambition, and that the stepping down of the teaching from the mind to the brain and from the brain into words and sentences often fails in adequacy is sadly true, and that there is frequently misapprehension as to the emanating source of the instructions is also true, for the lack of humility in man and the lack of a true sense of proportion are great. But out of this inflow from the subjective side of life are coming new knowledge, increased devotion to the Plan, and those indications which will eventually bring us assurance. Men will know, and know soon, that the soul is not an imaginary fiction, that it is not just a symbolic way of expressing a deep-seated hope, and is not man's method of building a defense mechanism; nor is it an illusory way of escape from a distressing present. They will know that the soul is a Being, a Being that is responsible for all that appears upon the phenomenal plane.

We have two more questions to consider now, and they are as follows:

Question 4. Of what value is it to know about the seven rays?

Question 5. What is the significance of the outstanding soul qualities such as sentiency, consciousness, awareness, and light?

Question four is of importance on account of its vital practicality. In the last analysis, definition conveys mental satisfaction but is no criterion as to applied knowledge.

Above everything else, it is necessary that the aspirant be practical. The days of a mystical and dreamy consciousness are rapidly passing away, and as man, through understanding of psychology, comes to a more accurate knowledge of himself he will begin to act with precision and with intelligence; he will know with exactitude the way that he should go, and will comprehend the forces in his own nature which will lead to specific action when brought into touch with the forces of his environment. Aspirants should endeavour to make practical application of the imparted truths, and so minimise their responsibility. Where there is acquired knowledge and when no use is made of it there exists a condition of danger and subsequent penalty.

Much has been given in previous books which awaits your adaptation and useful service. Much will be given in the present volume, but students need to remember that they themselves evoke and call forth the teaching they receive. The position between me and those who are reading is not that of a teacher imposing a system of knowledge upon a group of waiting pupils. The group is simply the channel through which a particular aspect of the Ageless Wisdom can reach a waiting world. I do not regard you as a body of good men and women, who, because of your point in evolution, are deemed worthy to receive something esoteric and unusual, and hence withheld from the rest of the race. I regard you as sincerely interested in the spiritual life, as concerned with the endeavour to be intelligent, and as willing (more or less) to try to live as souls, and to use as much of the imparted teaching as can be understood. What use students make of it is entirely their own affair. But the value of any group of aspirants and disciples consists in this: They can—if they so choose and if their united aspiration is strong enough—draw forth the teaching, and so form a centre through which that teaching may go forth and begin its work of moulding human thought, of throwing light upon the problems of psychology, and of so expanding the point of truth (anent the seven rays, an ancient septenate, but little comprehended) that a new realisation may be evolved and a new science of psychology may be launched upon its career.

You ask, therefore: What must we as a group do that we may be of service, and so constitute a good channel for the helping of humanity?

First of all, you must see to it that your attitude towards all teaching is that of willing service, with no thought of self. The growth in spiritual realisation and the lifting of humanity is that which is of moment, and not your own personal growth or development, nor your own satisfaction at receiving special and new information. You *will* grow, and your soul will take increasing hold upon its instrument, when your mind and effort are turned towards group service, and when your tongue is rendered harmless, through the inflow of Love.

Secondly, let not your mind be occupied with idle speculations as to the identity of the teacher. What matters it who he is? Can you prove his identity in one way or another? And of what value is it to accept the statements of any fellow student who may claim to be informed on the matter, be he who he may? You cannot prove him right or wrong, and therefore it remains a waste of time which could well be given to more fruitful service, to closer study of the life-essentials, and to meditation.

What is taught should matter. The aspects of truth which I present to your consideration should count; the measure of help which I can give and the spiritual and mental stimulation which I may impart are of moment to you. The training of the intuition to recognise spiritual truth should be the subject of your effort. The sole authority is the teaching, and not the teacher; upon the rock of authority many schools have foundered. There is but one authority—each man's own immortal soul, and that is the only authority which should be recognised.

Learn to grasp the teaching correctly, and see it for what it is. Some of it is written for a distant time, and the true significance of this *Treatise on the Seven Rays* will begin to emerge as part of the general knowledge of humanity only towards the close of this century, unless the imminent outpouring evokes greater change than is now deemed possible by the watching Hierarchy. Some of the teaching is of immediate usefulness to all of you. Some of it will throw light upon the problems of modern psychology, and link the many aspects of the science of the soul. Disciples grow these days by finding out the reservoir of their soul's nourishment; they will discover that the source of their strength is to be found in group teaching and in group endeavour. We are training men to live as souls and not as children to be nursed and cared for in a protected nursery run by rules and orders. As souls, men derive their life from the ocean of the universal, and not from the tiny well of the particular. Carrying their little pitchers, they find their way to that ocean, and for themselves they draw into that receptacle that which they need. In the light of your own intuition and illumined mind (developed and brought to usefulness through meditation) take that aspect of the teaching which suits and aids you, and interpret it in the light of your own need and growth.

The days of *personality* contact, of *personality* attention and of personal messages are over, and have been over for quite a while, save in the vale of illusion, on the astral plane. This is a hard message, but no true disciple will misunderstand. From the depths of his own experience and struggle he knows it to be so. It is the group of Masters, the Hierarchy as a whole, that is of moment and its interaction with humanity; it is the Masters' group of disciples that counts, and its relation to probationary disciples on the physical plane, who are seen by the group as existing in group formation all over the world, no matter where its units may be; it is the body of teaching that can be made available, and its effect upon the collective mind of the thinkers of the race, that is of vital importance; it is the interplay between the subjective group of world workers and—on the outer plane of objectivity—the lovers of humanity which seems to us, the teachers, to be of supreme importance. The satisfying of individual aspiration, the meeting of the desire of the probationers and the feeding of spiritual ambition appeal to us not at all. The times are too serious, and the crisis too acute.

It is of course a fact that there are today groups of aspirants receiving definite instruction, and disciples being subjected to definite training. But it must be remembered (in spite of all statements by the devotees of the world to the contrary) that no training is given in these cases as to the handling of the details of the personality life; the specific problems of health, finance and family concerns are not dealt with nor considered; nor is comfort given or time taken to reassure or satisfy the unstable personality. Training aspirants as to the technique of spiritual growth *is* undertaken; correction of the hidden factors producing emotional conditions may be suggested; meditations may be arranged in order to bring about certain results; and instruction in the laws governing soul union may be offered; but no personality work is attempted. Disciples handle their own personalities. In the pressure of world work, the Masters are finding Themselves with less and less time to give even to Their disciples. How then do those who are not in the ranks of accepted disciples expect the Master to have the time to deal with their little affairs?

In the future, however, groups will be formed increasingly, which will function on a new basis, and some of these new "group organisms" are forming in the world at this time. They are still in the nature of an experiment and may prove premature or undesirable. The teaching given in these new groups, the suggestions made, the experiments in training to be attempted, and the technique imparted will not be given personally and privately to an individual group member, but all of it is open and can be read, known and considered by every other member in the group. These groups are as yet necessarily few, and very small in number. They are in the nature of an attempt to see if it will be possible eventually to externalise the groups gathered around a Master on the inner planes. These groups of accepted disciples on the inner side are sensitive organisms, and each member of these circles gathered around a Master is aware of that which concerns his fellow disciples' spiritual unfoldment, within the radius of the circle in which he finds himself. These small outer attempts at a tentative duplication are in an embryonic condition as yet. It is a test and a trial effort, and may fail. The members of these tiny outer groups (whose membership and grouping are known only to those who form part of them) have to be willing to be instructed and developed as group units, with the other members of their group aware of their failures or successes. They have also to preserve complete silence as to the existence of the group, and a breaking of this silence warrants their elimination from the group. The personnel of these groups is forgotten in the life of the group entity as a whole. The members are trained in the group, and the group is trained as a whole, with no emphasis upon the individual but only on the group interplay and interaction, its integration and growth.

Only those factors in the life of the individual are noted and handled which would hinder the growth of the group life and expression. It is the group note, the group colour, and the group development which count with the training staff of workers, and the individual is never considered as an individual, but only in his relation to the group. What he is told to do, and the discipline applied, is all based on the desire to preserve the group balance, and not on any *personal* interest in the individual. In this experiment a man is tried out to see his fitness. He will be tested early in his career as a group unit. If he passes the test and makes the grade, the group is enriched and grows thereby. If he fails, he drops out and others take his place until such time as the group unit is attuned and completed, and those who are sincere and true, impersonal and mentally poised, self-forgetful and loving, are found to work together in harmony. Thus they can, as a group entity, form a focal point for the transmission of spiritual force to a needy and waiting world.

But it is important to remember that the attitude of the training initiate or teacher is one of complete detachment and impersonality; he is aware of the soul light and condition, and of the mental state, but he does not turn his attention to the handling of the affairs of the aspirant on the physical plane, nor to the training of his emotional nature and his astral development. Aspirants learn to be master and adept by handling their own physical plane affairs and their astral idiosyncrasies. This they must do in the light and strength of their own souls. We who teach would break a law and hinder their development if we attempted to enforce conditions which come not naturally. We should also overstimulate their lower natures. When will aspirants learn that the teachers and senior disciples in charge of them work only on mental levels and with the soul? When will they grasp the fact that until a man has contacted his own soul, and has learned to function as a controlled mind as well, there is little we can do for him? Again I say, we are not interested in personalities and their small affairs. We have neither the time nor the inclination to interfere with the way and method of a man's daily life. Why should we, when enough has been printed and taught to occupy the attention of the aspiring man for many a day? When a man is beginning to live as a soul, and when his consciousness has shifted away from the world of illusion, then he can be useful. The first lesson he has to learn is a sense of values in time and space, and to know that we work with souls and do not nurse the personality.

Seems this too hard a saying to you? If it is indeed so to you, it means that you are as yet somewhat self-centred and in love with your own individual soul, having not yet duly contacted it, and having but perhaps sensed its vibration and no more. You have not yet that true picture of the world's need which will release you from your own ambition and set you free to work as we (on the subjective side) work, with no thought of self or of spiritual happiness, and with no desire for any self-appointed task; with no longing for glittering promises of future success, and with no demanding ache for the tender touch and contact with those greater in consciousness than ourselves. If this lies still beyond your realisation, recognise the fact, and understand that there is no blame attached. It only indicates to you the ground whereon you stand, and that the illusion of the astral plane still holds you in its thrall and still leads you to place personality reactions before group realisation. As long as you walk on that plane and function on that level of consciousness, it is not possible to draw you consciously into the Masters' groups on mental levels. You are still too destructive and personal; you would be apt to hurt the group and cause trouble; you would see things (through the group stimulation) with a clarity for which you are not yet ready, and would be shattered thereby. You have need to learn the lessons of accepting guidance from your own soul, and of learning to work with harmony and impersonality on the physical plane with the group or groups to which your destiny impels you. When you have learnt the lesson of self-forgetfulness, when you seek nothing for the separated self, when you stand firmly on your own feet and look for aid within yourself, and when the trend of your life is towards cooperation, then you may pass from the stage of Observer to that of Communicator. This will happen because you can be trusted to communicate only that which is impersonal and truly constructive, and which will not feed the emotional nature and satisfy the desire-self.

An interesting point might here be noted and a question answered. In *A Treatise on White Magic* I referred to the two groups of Observers and Communicators (the third group lies outside our present discussion), and the question was asked: Who trains these Observers and Communicators? I should like to make it clear that the observers train themselves or—more accurately—the soul of each trains the personality in true observation. In the case of the communicators, they are slowly and gradually trained by senior disciples, working from the subjective side of life. This training is never organised and arranged for on the physical plane, nor are any disciples—working on the physical plane—engaged in training groups of communicators to be employed later by the Hierarchy. In this matter (as in all else in the spiritual life) the disciple first trains himself to be responsive to his own soul, and then trains himself to be responsive to the inner group of workers, who later, as a result of his self-initiated effort, teach him to be a communicator, an intermediary. The hallmark of such communicators is mental clarity, true impersonality, spiritual tolerance, and a frugality in the use of words, when embodying concepts. It should be remembered that in the wealth of psychic writings pouring into the world today, the work of the true communicators will concern itself with the Plan and not with personalities; with principles and not with individual purposes; and that all such communicators will be mental types, channels for the love of God, and group conscious. There will be nothing in their work to produce separativeness, and nothing to feed the fires of controversy, antagonism or partisanship. Much of value may come along other lines than through this group of communicators, and you may look for an increased flood of inspirational writings of a high order, and for an outpouring of wisdom from the world of souls through the hundreds who are in touch with their own souls; there will also be much emanating from the highest level of the astral plane, of a high order along devotional lines, but none of this will be the work of the band of communicators now in process of forming. Only a handful are doing this work as yet, and the true influx of communicators will not start for another fifteen years.

To return to our two questions, and particularly to the one concerning the value of studying the rays. I have felt the need to write on this matter for the following reasons:

1. Modern psychology is in a cul-de-sac. The many psychologies have made their contribution to the whole subject, and all of them have value, for all have embodied an aspect of truth. Through them we have arrived at an amazing knowledge of man, of his instincts and animal mechanisms, of his reactions to his environment and of his sensitive apparatus; we have learnt much about the sub-conscious, through which ancient racial sins and knowledges, suppressed complexes and latent desires, as well as highly organised psychic reactions,

well up into the conscious mind so disastrously. We know much anent the man as a whole functioning unity, and of the interactions existing between the nervous system, the glandular system, the muscles, and their expression, in forms of quality, character, personality, and the environment. We have learnt much, therefore, about that composite being called Man, and man, as a psychic entity, is an established fact in nature, as is man, the animal. But man, the soul, remains still a speculation, a hope, a belief. The fact of the soul is not yet substantiated; and in helping the truth into the light I seek to bring the subject of the seven rays to the notice of the thinkers of modern times, so that the light of this esoteric knowledge may be thrown upon the science of psychology. Thus may the work of revelation be aided.

2. If there is one thing that has emerged into the minds of investigators, as they have studied man, it is the fact that he is essentially dual. Psychology has shown that in the consciousness of every human being is a sense of duality, that man is in some mysterious sense two beings, and that it is the warfare between these two which has led to all the neuroses and complexes which tax the ingenuity of trained psychologists to solve. The initiate Paul referred to this when he spoke of the eternal warfare going on between the carnal mind and the heavenly nature, and all aspirants who are occupied with an intelligent struggle towards liberation bear witness to the same. Paul points out that victory is won through Christ, and I give a clue to the importance of this study of the rays when I state that, esoterically, these seven rays are the sevenfold expressions of the Cosmic Christ, the second Person of the Trinity. Bewildered men and women go in their thousands to the clinics of the psychologists, carrying with them the burden of their dual natures; and psychologists in their thousands recognise this

duality and seek to unify the dissociated aspects. When the true nature of the seven rays is grasped, and when their effect on humanity in expressing the seven types of men is also understood, we shall then approach the subject of man's duality with greater intelligence. We shall comprehend better the nature of the forces which constitute one or another of these dualities. This is the true esoteric science. The science of the seven qualities or rays, and their effect upon the myriad forms which they mould and energise, is the coming new approach to the correct method of training and developing the human family. Modern exoteric science knows much about the outer form, or matter aspect, and its electrical nature. Esoteric science knows much about the nature of the subjective energies and the qualities which colour and condition the form. When these two knowledges are brought intelligently together, we shall evolve a truer and more accurate psychology and a new science of human culture. Then the work of unifying man—man, the psychic entity, and man, the conditioning soul—will go rapidly forward.

3. A knowledge of the rays and their tendencies and energies will bring much illumination to the workers in the field of the various sciences. All the sciences find themselves on some one or other of the rays, and a science is literally the light thrown by a ray into a particular field of divine manifestation. The four kingdoms in nature are embodiments of four great Lives Who are found, each on one of the four minor rays. The Being Who is the life of the fourth or human kingdom in nature (regarding that kingdom as a distinct organism, just as man's body nature or personality is a distinct organism, separable from him as a soul) is on the fifth ray. The Being Who ensouls similarly the third kingdom, the animal kingdom, vibrates to the sixth ray. The Being Who is the expression and

active force of the entire vegetable kingdom is to be found upon the fourth ray. Therefore we have:

Humanity. . . 4th Kingdom . . .5th Ray . . . . Concrete Knowledge.
Animal . . . . 3rd Kingdom . . .6th Ray . . . . Devotion upwards or forwards.
Vegetable. . .2nd Kingdom . . 4th Ray . . . . Harmony and Beauty,
Mineral . . . . 1st Kingdom . . .7th Ray . . . . Organisation and Ritual.

These statements mean little to you at present, but we shall elaborate them later, when we come to the consideration of these rays in greater detail. I am but giving a general impression at this time. It is apparent nevertheless that when the nature of the energy permeating and animating any particular kingdom in nature is recognised and accepted (even if hypothetically) by the scientists, much light will be thrown upon the outer form qualified by a particular force and life.

There is, for instance, a definite reason why the bulk of the wild flowers and garden flowers in the occident, and also those found during the autumn season, are at this time found in tones of yellow and orange; and the mental calibre of the later sub-races of the Aryan race, as well as its general tone throughout the Aryan age, is also related to the same reason. The influence of the fourth Ray of Harmony and Beauty, and the developing power of the fifth Ray of Knowledge (synonymous to the merging of the intuition and the intellect in highly evolved man) have a definite effect upon the vegetable kingdom and upon the human aura. Yellow-orange shines forth in both. I mention this as an illustration of an externalisation of ray force, and as an indication of the value of the esoteric science when applied to the exoteric.

The blue ray of devotion passes now into the violet of what we term the ceremonial ray. What do these words mean? Simply that the great Musician of the universe is moving the keys, is sounding another note and thus bringing in another turn of the wheel, and swinging into the arc of manifestation the ray of violet, the great note G. These rays bring with them—in every kingdom in nature—all that is attuned to them: Human beings, devas of order high or low, elementals of a desirable or undesirable nature, flowers, fruits, and vegetable life of a certain kind, and animals and forms of varying species. It is the passing out of a ray that signals the ultimate extinction of some particular form, some type of animal life, and leads to some vegetable aspect coming to an end. Hence the confusion among the scientists at this time. The process of coming in is slow, as is all work in nature, and as is the process of passing out. Simultaneously with the cyclic birth and emergence of a new ray is the slow return to its source of the prevailing ray, present at the advent of the new.

At this time the sixth ray is passing out and is taking with it all those forms whose keynote is blue—those people, for instance, who with devotion (misplaced or not) followed some particular object, person or idea. With it passes, therefore, those whom we term fanatics, those who with one-pointed zeal work towards some sensed objective. Many of the flowers in which you now rejoice are passing out, the bluebell, the hyacinth and the olive for example; the sapphire will become scarce and the turquoise will lose its hue. Flowers of violet colour, of lavender and of purple will come into favour. Behind all this lies a purpose profound.

The physical plane, in its densest aspect, holds little of mystery for man today; he has knowledge on these matters. But the rarer levels of the physical plane lie hid and are, for man, his next field of discovery. The ceremonial ray brings with it the means whereby that knowledge may be acquired and revealed to all, and thus not be the sole property of the wise and of the occultists. The three higher etheric levels, with their denizens, are waiting to become the property of all, and with their inhabitants comes the next approximation.

It is possible at this time to foretell certain events which will come to pass during the next one hundred years.

First, in about ten years time the first ether, with all that is composed of that matter, will be recognised scientific fact, and the scientists who work intuitionally will come to recognise the devas of that plane. People coming into incarnation on this seventh ray will have the eyes that see, and the purple devas and the lesser devas of the etheric body will be visioned by them.

Secondly, when He Whom both angels and men await, will approach near unto this physical plane, He will bring with Him not only some of the Great Ones and the Masters, but some of the Devas who stand to the deva evolution as the Masters to the human. Forget not that the human evolution is but one of many, and that this is a period of crisis among the devas likewise. The call has gone forth for them to approach humanity, and with their heightened vibration and superior knowledge unite their forces with those of humanity, for the progression of the two evolutions. They have much to impart anent colour and sound, and their effect upon the etheric bodies of men and animals. When that which they have to give is apprehended by the race, physical ills will be nullified and attention will be centred upon the infirmities of the astral or emotional body.

These violet devas of the four ethers form, as you may imagine, four great groups with seven subsidiary divisions. These four groups work with the four types of men now in incarnation, for it is a statement of fact that at no time in this round are more than four types of men in incarnation at any one time. Four rays dominate at any given period, with one in excess of the other three. I mean by this, that only four rays are in physical incarnation; for on the plane of the soul all seven types are of course found. This idea is brought out in the four castes in India, and you will find that these four are found universally. The four groups of devas are a band of servers to the Lord, and their special work is to contact men and to give them definite and experimental teaching.

They will instruct in the effect of colour in the healing of disease, especially the effect of the violet light in the lessening of human ills and in the cure of those physical plane sicknesses which have their origin in the etheric body or double.

They will teach men to see etherically, by heightening human vibration by action of their own.

They will demonstrate to the materialistic thinkers of the world the fact that the superconscious states exist—not the superhuman only—and will also make clear the hitherto unrecognised fact that other beings, besides the human, have their habitat on earth.

They will also teach the sounding of the tones that correspond to the gradations of violet, and through that sounding enable man to utilise the ethers, as he now utilises physical plane matter for his various needs.

They will enable human beings so to control the ethers that weight will be for them transmuted, and motion will be intensified, becoming more rapid, more gliding, noiseless, and therefore less tiring. In the human control of the etheric levels lie the lessening of fatigue, rapidity of transit, and the ability to transcend time. Until this prophecy is a fact in consciousness, its meaning is obscure.

They will also teach men how rightly to nourish the body and to draw from the surrounding ethers the requisite food. Man will in the future concentrate more on the sound condition of the etheric body, and the functioning of the dense physical body will become practically automatic.

They will enable human beings, as a race, and not as individuals, to expand their consciousness so that it will embrace the superphysical. Forget not the important fact that in the accomplishment of this the *web* that divides the physical plane from the astral plane will be discovered by the scientists, and its purpose will eventually be acknowledged. With that discovery will come the power to penetrate the web, and so link up consciously with the astral body. Another material unification will have been accomplished.

Then what else will occur, and what will be the method of approach to these devas?

More and more, during the next fifteen years, will men receive definite teaching, often subconsciously, from devas to whom they are linked. This will be done telepathically at first. Doctors today get much information from certain devas. There are two great devas belonging to the green group on mental levels who assist in this work, and some physicians get much knowledge subjectively from a violet deva working on the atomic subplane of the physical plane, aided by a deva of the causal level who works with, or through, their egos. As men learn to sense and recognise these devas, more and more teaching will be given. They teach in three ways:

a. By means of intuitional telepathy.
b. Through demonstration of colour, proving the accomplishment of certain things in this way.
c. By definite musical sounds, which will cause vibrations in the ethers, which in their turn will produce forms.

The ether will eventually appear to the enhanced vision of humanity to have more substance than it now has, and as etheric vision increases, the ethers will be recognised as being strictly physical plane matter. Therefore when in sickness men shall call a deva, when that deva can destroy diseased tissue by sounding a note that will result in the elimination of the corrupt tissue, when by the presence caused by the vibration new tissue is visibly built in, then the presence of these devas will be generally acknowledged and their power will be utilised.

By what means will their presence be realised and their powers employed?

First of all, by a definite development of the human eye, which will then see that which is now unseen. It will be a change within the eye, and not a form of clairvoyance.

Next, by a steady experimentation with invocations, and through their use the method of calling the devas will be discovered. This development must be approached with caution, for to the unprotected it leads to disaster. Hence the necessity to inculcate pure living, the learning of protective invocations and formulas, and the power of the church and of Masonry to protect. Forget not that evil entities exist on other planes than the physical, that they can respond to analogous vibrations, and that the invocations that call a deva may, if sounded inaccurately, call a being that will work havoc. In ritual lies protection. Hence the emphasis laid upon church forms and on the Masonic rituals,—an emphasis which will increase and not grow less as the years slip by. The force of invocations will be known later.

Every individual vibrates to some particular measure. Those who know and who work clairvoyantly and clairaudiently find that all matter sounds, all matter pulsates, and all matter has its own colour. Each human being can therefore be made to give forth some specific sound; in making that sound he flashes into colour, and the combination of the two is indicative of some measure which is peculiarly his own.

Every unit of the human race is on some one of the seven

rays; therefore some one colour predominates, and some one tone sounds forth; infinite are the gradations and many the shades of colour and tone. Each ray has its subsidiary rays which it dominates, acting as the synthetic ray. These seven rays are linked with the colours of the spectrum. There are the rays of red, blue, yellow, orange, green and violet. There is the ray that synthesises them all, that of indigo. There are the three major rays—red, blue and yellow—and the four subsidiary colours which, in the evolving Monad, find their correspondence in the spiritual Triad and the lower quaternary. The Logos of our system is concentrating on the love or blue aspect. This—as the synthesis—manifests as indigo. This matter of the rays and their colours is confusing to the neophyte. I can but indicate some thoughts, and in the accumulation of suggestion light may eventually come. The clue lies in similarity of colour, which entails a resemblance in note and rhythm. When, therefore, a man is on the red and yellow rays, with red as his primary ray, and meets another human being who is on the blue and yellow rays, with a secondary resemblance to the yellow, there may be recognition. But when a man on the yellow and blue rays, with yellow as his primary colour, meets a brother on the yellow and red rays, the recognition is immediate and mutual, for the primary colour is the same. When this fundamental cause of association or dissociation is better understood, the secondary colours will be made to act as the meeting ground, to the mutual benefit of the parties concerned.

Of the colours, red, blue and yellow are primary and irreducible. They are the colours of the major rays.

        a. Will or Power . . . . Red
        b. Love-Wisdom . . . . Blue
        c. Active Intelligence . . . . Yellow

We have then the subsidiary rays:

    d. Orange.
    e. Green.
    f. Violet.

and the synthesising ray, Indigo.

4. It is of course to the human interest that a study of the rays makes its main appeal. It is this study that will vivify and awaken psychologists to the true understanding of man. Every human being finds himself upon one of the seven rays. His personality is found, in every life, upon one of them, in varying rotation, according to the ray of the ego or soul. After the third initiation he locates his soul (if one may use such an inappropriate word) on one of the three major rays, though until that time it may be found in one of the seven ray groups. From that exalted attitude he strives towards the essential unity of the Monad. The fact of there being seven ray types carries great implications, and the intricacy of the subject is baffling to the neophyte.

A ray confers, through its energy, peculiar physical conditions, and determines the quality of the astral-emotional nature; it colours the mind body; it controls the distribution of energy, for the rays are of differing rates of vibration, and govern a particular centre in the body (differing with each ray) through which that distribution is made. Each ray works through one centre primarily and through the remaining six, in a specific order. The ray predisposes a man to certain strengths and weaknesses, and constitutes his principle of limitation, as well as endowing him with capacity. It governs the method of his relations to other human types and is responsible for his reactions in form to other forms. It gives him his colouring and quality, his general tone on the three planes of the personality, and it moulds his physical appearance. Certain attitudes of mind are easy for one ray type and difficult for another, and hence the changing personality shifts from ray to ray, from life to life, until all the qualities are developed and expressed. Certain souls, by their ray destiny, are found in certain fields of activity, and a particular field of endeavour remains relatively the same for many life expressions. A governor or statesman has learnt facility in his craft through much experience in that field. A world Teacher has been teaching for age-long cycles. A world Saviour has been, for many lives, at the task of salvaging. When a man is two-thirds of the way along the evolutionary path his soul ray type begins to dominate the personality ray type and will therefore govern the trend of his expression on earth, not in the spiritual sense (so-called) but in the sense of pre-disposing the personality towards certain activities.

A knowledge therefore of the rays and their qualities and activities is, from the standpoint of psychology, of profound importance, and hence this treatise.

5. Groups of people, organisations, nations and groups of nations are all the result of ray activity and magnetism. Hence an understanding of the forces which stream forth from the divine creative centre, and which we call the rays, is of value in understanding the quality, nature, and destiny of vast human masses. The seven planets are governed by one or other of the rays. Countries (viewed independently of their nationals) are likewise the result of ray activity, and thus the importance of the subject cannot be overestimated.

Question 5. What is the meaning of the following words: Sentiency; Consciousness or Awareness; The Energy of Light?

We shall now consider our last question, and I shall indicate to you, in general terms,—necessarily limited by the inadequacy of language,—the significance of the outstanding soul qualities:

a. Sentiency, or sensitive response to contact, and by that means the subsequent growth in knowledge.
b. Consciousness, awareness of environment, and the development of instruments whereby consciousness may be increasingly developed.
c. Light, or radiation, the effect of the interplay between the life and the environment.

The first point that I seek to make is a difficult one to grasp for those beneath the rank of initiate or accepted disciple of the higher stages. The soul is that factor in matter (or rather that which emerges out of the contact between spirit and matter) which produces sentient response and what we call consciousness in its varying forms; it is also that latent or subjective essential quality which makes itself felt as light or luminous radiation. It is the "self-shining from within" which is characteristic of all forms. Matter, per se, and in its undifferentiated state, prior to being swept into activity through the creative process, is *not* possessed of soul, and does not therefore possess the qualities of response and of radiation. Only when,—in the creative and evolutionary process,—these two are brought into conjunction and fusion does the soul appear and give to these two aspects of divinity the opportunity to manifest as a trinity and the chance to demonstrate sentient activity and magnetic radiatory light. As all that we shall posit in this treatise is to be approached from the angle of human evolution, it might be stated that only when the soul aspect is dominant is the response apparatus (the form nature of man) fulfilling its complete destiny, and only then does true magnetic radiation and the pure shining forth of light become possible. Symbolically, in the early stages of human evolution, man is, from the angle of consciousness, relatively unresponsive and unconscious, as is matter in its early stages in the formative process. The achievement of full awareness is of course the goal of the evolutionary process. Again symbolically speaking, the unevolved man emits or manifests no light. The light in the head is invisible, though the clairvoyant investigators would see the dim glow of the light within the elements which constitute the body, and the light hidden in the atoms which constitute the form nature.

As evolution proceeds, these dim points of "dark light" intensify their glow; the light within the head flickers at intervals during the life of the average man, and becomes a shining light as he enters upon the path of discipleship. When he becomes an initiate, the light of the atoms is so bright, and the light in the head so intense (with a paralleling stimulation of the centres of force in the body), that the light body appears. Eventually this body of light becomes externalised and of greater prominence than the dense tangible physical body. This is the body of light in which the true son of God consciously dwells. After the third initiation, the dual light becomes accentuated and takes on a still greater brilliancy through the blending with it of the energy of spirit. This is not really the admission or the re-combining of a third light, but the fanning of the light of matter and the light of the soul into a greater glory through the *Breath* of the spirit. Something anent this light has been earlier indicated in *A Treatise on Cosmic Fire*. Study it and seek to understand the significance of this process. In the understanding of these aspects of light comes a truer perspective as to the nature of the fires in the human expression of divinity.

It must never be forgotten that the soul of all things, the *anima mundi*, as it expresses itself through all the four kingdoms in nature, is that which gives to our planet its light in the heavens. The planetary light is the sum total of the light, dim and uncertain, to be found in all atoms of radiatory and vibratory matter or substance, which compose all forms in all kingdoms. Added to this, there is, within the planet and also within each kingdom in nature, the correspondence to the etheric body with its centres of radiant energy, found underlying or "substanding" the outer physical form. Man's etheric body is a corporate part of the planetary etheric body, and constitutes its most refined and most highly developed aspect. As the aeons pass away there is a growing intensity of light radiating forth from our planet. This does not necessarily mean that a dweller on Neptune would see our planet glowing with an increasingly brighter light, though this does happen in a few cases in the universe. But it means that, from the standpoint of a clairvoyant vision, the etheric planetary body will grow in vivid radiation and glory as that radiation expresses more and more the true light of the soul.

The soul is light *essentially*, both *literally* from the vibratory angle, and *philosophically* from the angle of constituting the true medium of knowledge. The soul is light *symbolically*, for it is like the rays of the sun, which pour out into the darkness; the soul, through the medium of the brain, causes revelation. It throws its light into the brain, and thus the way of the human being becomes increasingly illumined. The brain is like the eye of the soul, looking out into the physical world; in the same sense the soul is the eye of the Monad, and in a curious and occult sense, the fourth kingdom in nature constitutes on our planet the eye of the planetary Deity. The brain is responsive to the seven senses:

1. Hearing
2. Touch
3. Sight
4. Taste
5. Smell
6. The mind, the common-sense
7. The intuition or the synthetic sense.

Through these seven senses contact with the world of matter and of spirit becomes possible. The seven senses are, in a peculiar way, the physical plane correspondences of the seven rays, and are closely related to and governed by them all. The following tabulation will be found suggestive. That is all that it is intended to be:

1. Hearing . . . . . 7th Ray . . Magic . . . . The Word of Power.
2. Touch . . . . . . 1st Ray . . Destroyer . . . . . The Finger of God.
3. Sight . . . . 3rd Ray . . Vision . . . . The Eye of God.
4. Taste . . . . 6th Ray . . Idealism . . . . . . The Desire of Nations.
5. Smell . . . . . . 4th Ray . . Art . . . . The Beauty of Revelation.
6. The Intellect . 5th Ray . . Mind . . . . The Knowledge of God.
7. The Intuition . 2nd Ray . . Love-Wisdom . Understanding of God.

Through the Words of Power the worlds came into ordered being, and the Lord of the Ray of Ceremonial Magic brings about the organisation of the divine organism.

Through the application of the Finger of God in its directing and forceful work, we have the cyclic destruction of forms, so that the manifestation of Deity may grow in power and beauty. Thus the Lord of Power or Will performs the task of destruction, thereby bringing beauty into being and the revelation of God's will and His beneficent purpose.

By means of the Eye of God light shines forth upon the way of the sun, the path of the planets, and the path of man. The Lord of Adaptability and the Intellect brings into expression and into objectivity the intelligent working out of the divine idea and Plan.

When the "Desire of all nations" shall come, and the Cosmic Christ shall stand revealed, all men and all creatures shall occultly "taste" or share in that great happening, and the Lord of the Ray of Devotion and Idealism shall see the consummation of His work and be "satisfied."

Also the Lord of the fourth Ray of Harmony, Beauty and Art will add His share to the great creative work, and it will be found that, in the elusive following to its source of that mysterious revelation which we call beauty, there will be expressed that subtle quality of which "smell," in the animal sense, is the symbol. The great search and the esoteric "following of the scent" will come to an end. This fourth ray is pre-eminently the way of the seeker, the searcher and the sensitive reflector of beauty. The Jewish nation has a close relation to this fourth ray and to the fourth root race, and hence their eminence at this time in the world of art, and hence the magnitude of their endless symbolic wandering and searching.

When the Knowledge of God shall shine forth universally (and this is not the knowledge of, or awareness of a great Being but the expression through human instrumentality of the divine omniscience), then will the Lord of Concrete Science, Who is the embodiment of the fifth principle of mind, see His work brought to a conclusion. He stimulates the sense of awareness in humanity and nurtures the consciousness aspect in the subhuman kingdoms, producing the response, therefore, of matter to spirit, and bringing about the interpretation of that to which there has been a sentient rapport.

The intuition is literally the synthetic and immediate grasp of the truth, as it essentially exists, and the Lord of the second ray will bring to a conclusion the entire evolutionary process through the development in humanity of that perfect insight which will make every human being a complete and intelligent cooperator with the Plan.

Certain Questions

A close study of these ray forces in relation to the creative work and the furthering of the Plan (in so far as we can, at this time, grasp it) will reveal how closely the entire building-wrecking-rebuilding process is tied up with the question of the three qualities of the soul, sentiency, consciousness and awareness, and will demonstrate how the problem of light, with which I have just been dealing, has a definite relation to our ability to interpret and comprehend these three qualities.

Consciousness, in the esoteric teaching, concerns the response of the form aspect in the three subhuman kingdoms:

1. To the world of living, vibratory and magnetic forms, in which each form is immersed. Every form, through its radiation, affects every other form, and according to the quality of the form and according to its evolutionary status, so will be its response to its environment.
2. To the subjective world of forces which we call the etheric world. All forms in all four kingdoms thus respond in some degree and manner.
3. To the world of quality, or of desire intent. All forms in all kingdoms respond, en masse, to the urge or the desire aspect of divinity which lies at the root of the entire evolutionary process. This is recognised as an incentive and is more or less self-directed in the human family; it is blindly followed by the forms in the other kingdoms, who respond according to the nature of their response mechanisms to these varying urges.

When we deal with the inflow of mental energy and with the forces emanating from the fifth plane of mind (higher mind, lower mind and the egoic intelligent entity) we enter more entirely into the domain of human evolution itself, and the vague word "consciousness" could well be superseded by the word "awareness." In varying degree man is aware, but only man is aware that he is aware. His response apparatus responds to, and is influenced by, all the contacts to which the subhuman forms respond, but he is also aware of himself, and his response mechanism is capable of reacting, not only to external stimuli but to contacts emanating from within himself, from the Self so called, and also from the worlds of introspection and of mystical vision which seem sealed to all subhuman forms of life.

In the larger picture, with which we are not to occupy ourselves in this treatise, the planet constitutes the response apparatus of a superhuman Life, and that Life responds consciously to impacts emanating from the solar system as a whole, and from certain constellations (embodied Lives) with which our solar system is linked. Similarly the solar Logos functions through the medium of that gigantic response apparatus which is bounded by the ring-pass-not of a solar system. Each form, from that of the tiniest atom to that of a vast constellation, is an embodiment of a life, which expresses itself as consciousness, awareness, and responsive sentiency through the medium of some type of response mechanism. Thus we have the establishing of a universe of lives, interacting and interrelated, all of them conscious, some of them self-conscious, and others group-conscious, but all grounded in the universal mind, all possessing souls, and all presenting aspects of the divine Life.

Life, quality, appearance remain thus the primal triplicity. Appearance is objective, and forms have been studied scientifically, analysed and classified, for ages. Now we are introverting and introspecting, and have the commencement of a cycle wherein the world of quality and of meaning will be subjected to a similar investigation and classification. This will result in the giving of new values to life, to an enriching of our understanding, and will produce, as a result, the growth and substitution of the intuition for the intellect.

May I urge upon all to live more continuously in the world of meaning and less in the world of appearances? It is a truer world and less full of illusion. When the understanding is developed, when men have learnt to see below the surface and have cultivated true vision, then we shall have the steady emergence of the quality of the soul in all forms and the relative subsiding into the background of the power of the form nature. It is this world of meaning which it is the privilege of humanity to reveal, and all true esoteric students should be pioneers in this field.

III. *Ten Basic Propositions.*

1. There is one Life
2. There are seven Rays.
3. Life-Quality-Appearance constitute Existence.
4. The seven Rays are the seven creative Forces.
5. The Rays manifest through the seven Planets.
6. Every Human Being is on one of the Rays.
7. There are one Monad, seven Rays and myriads of Forms.
8. The Laws of Evolution embody the Life Purpose of the seven Rays.
9. Man develops through Self-expression and Self-realisation.
10. Individualisation leads eventually to Initiation.

CHAPTER III

Ten Basic Propositions

IN CONCLUDING this section of our treatise, and before starting on our real study of the rays, I seek to formulate for you the fundamental propositions upon which all this teaching is founded. They are for me, a humble worker in the Hierarchy, as they are for the Great White Lodge as a whole, a statement of fact and of truth. For students and seekers they must be accepted as an hypothesis:

One: There is one Life, which expresses Itself primarily through seven basic qualities or aspects, and secondarily through the myriad diversity of forms.

Two: These seven radiant qualities are the seven Rays, the seven Lives, who give Their life to the forms, and give the form world its meaning, its laws, and its urge to evolution.

Three: Life, quality and appearance, or spirit, soul and body constitute all that exists. They are existence itself, with its capacity for growth, for activity, for manifestation of beauty, and for full conformity to the Plan. This Plan is rooted in the consciousness of the seven ray Lives.

Four: These seven Lives, Whose nature is consciousness and Whose expression is sentiency and specific quality, produce cyclically the manifested world; They work together in the closest union and harmony, and cooperate intelligently with the Plan of which They are the custodians. They are the seven Builders, Who produce the radiant temple of the Lord, under the guidance of the Mind of the Great Architect of the Universe.

Five: Each ray Life is predominantly expressing Itself through one of the seven sacred planets, but the life of all the seven flows through every planet, including the Earth, and thus qualifies every form. On each planet is a small replica of the general scheme, and every planet conforms to the intent and purpose of the whole.

Six: Humanity, with which this treatise deals, is an expression of the life of God, and every human being has come forth along one line or other of the seven ray forces. The nature of his soul is qualified or determined by the ray Life which breathed him forth, and his form nature is coloured by the ray Life which—in its cyclic appearance on the physical plane at any particular time—sets the quality of the race life and of the forms in the kingdoms of nature. The soul nature or quality remains the same throughout a world period; its form life and nature change from life to life, according to its cyclic need and the environing group condition. This latter is determined by the ray or rays in incarnation at the time.

Seven: The Monad is the Life, lived in unison with the seven ray Lives. One Monad, seven rays and myriads of forms,—this is the structure behind the manifested worlds.

Eight: The Laws which govern the emergence of the quality or soul, through the medium of forms, are simply the mental purpose and life direction of the ray Lords, Whose purpose is immutable, Whose vision is perfect, and Whose justice is supreme.

Nine: The mode or method of development for humanity is self-expression and self-realisation. When this process is consummated the self expressed is the One Self or the ray Life, and the realisation achieved is the revelation of God as the quality of the manifested world and as the Life behind appearance and quality. The seven ray Lives, or the seven soul types, are seen as the expression of one Life, and diversity is lost in the vision of the One and in identification with the One.

Ten: The method employed to bring about this realisation is experience, beginning with individualisation and ending with initiation, thus producing the perfect blending and expression of life-quality-appearance.

This is a brief statement of the Plan. Of this the Hierarchy of Masters in Its seven divisions (the correspondences of the seven rays) is the custodian, and with Them lies the responsibility in any century of carrying out the next stage of that Plan.

Section Two

I. *The Seven Creative Builders, the Seven Rays.*

1. The Rays and Life-Quality-Appearance.
2. The Present Ray Plan and the Workers.
3. Three Major Propositions.
4. Quality in the World of Appearances.
5. An Analysis of the Rays and their Expression.

CHAPTER I

The Seven Creative Builders, the Seven Rays

WE HAVE now completed our first section, and have therefore laid the groundwork for our future studies. First, I seek to give a brief exegesis of the basic theory of *The Secret Doctrine*, called the hylozoistic theory. This posits a living substance, composed of a multiplicity of sentient lives which are continuously swept into expression by the "breath of the divine Life." This theory recognises no so-called inorganic matter anywhere in the universe, and emphasizes the fact that all forms are built up of infinitesimal lives, which in their totality—great or small—constitute a Life, and that these composite lives, in their turn, are a corporate part of a still greater Life. Thus eventually we have that great scale of lives, manifesting in greater expression and reaching all the way from the tiny life called the atom (with which science deals) up to that vast atomic life which we call a solar system.

This is a briefly and inadequately expressed definition of the doctrine of hylozoism, and is an attempt to interpret and find a meaning in the manifested phenomenal world, with its three main characteristics of life-quality-appearance. Forget not to find the meaning behind all forms and life experiences, and thereby learn to enter into that world of subjective forces which is the true world wherein all occultists work.

Let us take these three words and seek to understand their significance in relation to the rays.

As to the significance of the word "life" our task is well-nigh insuperable, for no human being has, or can have, any comprehension of the nature of life until he has attained the third initiation. I repeat this with emphasis, and in order to impress upon you the futility of idle speculation upon this subject. Disciples who have undergone the third initiation and have climbed the mount of Transfiguration can—from that high point—glimpse the radiance of the subjective centre of energy (the central spiritual sun of *The Secret Doctrine*) and so gain a flash of realisation as to the meaning of the word "life." But they cannot, and they dare not, pass on the knowledge gained. Their efforts to convey such information would be futile, and language itself would be inadequate to the task. Life is not what anyone has hitherto surmised. Energy (in contradistinction to force, and using the word to express the emanating centre which differentiates into forces) is not what idle speculation has portrayed it to be. Life is the synthesis of all activity—an activity which is a blend of many energies, for life is the sum total of the energies of the seven solar systems, of which our solar system is but one. These, in their totality, are the expression of the activity of that Being Who is designated in our hierarchical archives as the "One About Whom Naught May Be Said." This seven-fold cosmic energy, the fused and blended energies of seven solar systems, including ours, sweeps automatically through each of the seven, carrying the qualities of

1. Impulse towards activity.
2. Active impulse towards organisation.
3. Active organised impulse towards a definite purpose.

I have worded these impulses as above in order to show the emergent tendency through their mutual interplay. This triple energetic impulse, borne on the impetus of the seven

The Creative Builders

great breaths or rays, started the world process of Becoming, and manifested as the urge towards evolution,—towards an evolution which is active, organised, and which works undeviatingly and unerringly towards a specific goal. This goal is known in its fullest measure only to that incomprehensible Existence Who works through seven solar systems (in their turn the expression of seven great Lives) just as our solar Deity works through the seven planetary Logoi. All this has been hinted at and outlined in *A Treatise on Cosmic Fire*, and I do not propose enlarging upon it here. I would point out, however, because it has a definite bearing on the evolution of quality in the human family, that the seven creative Builders or planetary Logoi of our solar system are embodiments of the will, energy, and magnetic force which streams through Them from the seven solar systems into Their various spheres of activity. Thus, through Their united activity, the organised solar system is produced, whose energies are in constant circulation and whose emerging qualities are balanced and demonstrated throughout the entire system. All parts of the solar system are interdependent; all the forces and energies are in constant flux and mutation; all of them sweep in great pulsations, and through a form of rhythmic breathing, around the entire solar atom; so that the qualities of every solar life, pouring through the seven ray forms, permeate every form within the solar ring-pass-not, and thus link every form with every other form. Note therefore the fact that each of the seven rays or creative Builders embodies the energy, will, love and purpose of the Lord of the solar system, as that Lord in His turn embodies an aspect of the energy, will, love and purpose of the "One About Whom Naught May Be Said." Therefore the first proposition to be grasped by the student of the rays is as follows:

I. *Every ray Life is an expression of a solar Life, and every planet is consequently . . .*
   1. Linked with every other planetary life in the solar system.
   2. Animated by energy emanating from one or other of the seven solar systems.
   3. Actuated by a triple stream of life forces coming from:
       a. Solar systems outside our own.
       b. Our own solar system.
       c. Its own planetary Being.

It is impossible for the average thinker to grasp the significance of this statement, but he can understand somewhat the statement that every planet is a focal point through which forces and energies circulate and flow ceaselessly, and that these energies emanate from the outer cosmos or universe itself, from the solar system of which his own planet is a part, and of which our sun is the centre, and from that Being Who constitutes our own particular planetary Lord or Life.

I should like at this point to make clear the distinction between a constellation and a solar system, according to the esoteric teaching, even though the modern scientist may not agree.

A *solar system* consists of a sun as the central focal point, with its series of attendant planets, which are held in magnetic rapport in their orbits around that sun.

A *constellation* consists of two or more solar systems or series of suns with their attendant planets. These systems are held together as a coherent whole by the powerful interrelation of the suns, whose magnetic rapport is so balanced that occultly "they tread the Path together within the radius of each other's power;" they preserve their relative distances, and vitalise their planets, but at the same time they preserve an equality of balance and of influence. In a few rare cases this balance is disturbed, and there is a waxing or a waning of influence and of magnetic power.

This condition is governed by a cosmic law of rhythm so obscure as to be incomprehensible at this time.

An illustration of this waxing and waning of influence and of radiance (synonymous terms in occultism) on a large scale can be seen today in the constellation Gemini, wherein one of the twins is increasing in brilliance and power, and the other is decreasing. But this is a somewhat unique example, esoterically.

The relation of the constellations to the solar system, which is the basis of astrological research, will be considered later. I seek to point out here only the dual fact that the seven rays are themselves

1. Expressions of energies emanating from the seven solar systems, which are, in their turn, animated by the Life of the "One About Whom Naught May Be Said."
2. Influenced by, and therefore under the astrological control of, the twelve constellations whose energies are contacted by our solar system during the course of the journey of our sun through the greater Zodiac, during the vast period of approximately 25,000 years, and in a lesser degree during the course of the twelve months of the year, wherein the lesser path of the Zodiac is trodden.

The complexity of the subject is very great, and only the broad general outline of the system, and the basic principles governing the law of evolution, can be dimly sensed and grasped. The sweep of the subject is so vast that the concrete mind and the rationalising nature lose themselves in the realised complexities and problems. But the illumined intuition, with its power to synthesise (which is the emerging characteristic of the disciples and initiates under training), can and does lead them into a measured sequence of expansions of consciousness which eventually land them at last on the summit of the Mount of Transfiguration. From that eminence the disciple can gain the vision which will enable him to see the whole scheme in a moment of time, and to share with Arjuna the experience of the *Gita* wherein he "saw all forms gathered together in the body of that God of Gods." He can then descend from that mountain with his personality transfigured and radiant. Why? Because he now knows that spirit is a fact and the basis of immortality; he knows, past all controversy, that there is a Plan, and that the love of God is the basic law of all manifestation and the origin of all evolutionary momentum; and he can rest back upon the knowledge that the fact of spirit, the immediacy of love and the synthetic scope of the Plan provide a foundation upon which he can place his feet, take his stand with assurance, and then go forward in certain confidence of an assured goal.

Our second statement of fact is therefore:

II. *Each one of the rays is the recipient and custodian of energies coming from*
   1. The seven solar systems.
   2. The twelve constellations.

   Each ray passes these energies through its body of manifestation (a planet), and thereby imparts them to the planetary form, and to all forms upon and within it. These differentiated forms are therefore animated by energy coming from the cosmic Life, from the solar Deity, and from the planetary Life, and are consequently coloured by qualities from the seven solar systems and the twelve constellations. This blend of energies, working on substance, produces the forms, and each subjective form, in its turn, produces the outer appearance.

It is not possible for us to study these forces and qualities in detail, especially in connection with an individual human being, for the scale is so minute, relatively, and the detail to be considered is so intricate. But the nature of the qualities and energies can be somewhat grasped as we study the seven ray Lives with their seven psychological types, and the twelve creative Hierarchies, as outlined for us in *The Secret Doctrine*. The 7+12=19, and if you add to these 19 expressions of the Life the 3 major aspects of Deity, which we call the life of God the Father, the love of God the Son, and the active intelligence of God the Holy Ghost, you arrive at the mystic number 22 which is called (in esotericism) the number of the adept. This simply means that the adept is one who comprehends the nature of the 19 forces as they express themselves through the medium of the triple divine manifestation, as it in its turn relates itself to human consciousness. It does *not* mean that the adept has mastered and can wield these 19 types of energy. They are consciously wielded only by the three synthetic Builders or Creators, Who are:

1. The Life which expresses Itself through seven solar systems.
   The One About Whom Naught May Be Said.
2. The Life which expresses Itself through seven planets.
   The Solar Deity . . . . . . God.
3. The Life which expresses Itself through seven planetary centres, or continents.
   The Planetary Logos . . . . . . The Ancient of Days.

What the adept has done has been to bring his seven centres of force, located in the etheric body, into a responsive condition to the higher *spiritual* forces; as he progresses he will find that he will gradually and sequentially become equally responsive to the above three types of *synthetic* force.

On the path of discipleship, and until the third initiation, he learns to respond to the energy and to the spiritual purpose of the Life of his own planet. At the first and second initiations, and until the third initiation, he has been led on and initiated by the influence of the Christ, and under His direction he has submitted to two expansions of consciousness and has prepared himself for a third. When ready for this, he comes under the initiatory power of the planetary Logos; and through the mediating activity of that great Being the initiate becomes actively aware of energy emanating from the solar Deity. He is therefore learning to respond to the second type of synthetic force.

After he has taken the highest initiation possible on this planet, he is, for the first time, responsive to energy emanating from the outer cosmic *Centre*. This last stage of expansion is rare indeed, and only one hundred and eleven human beings, during our planetary history, have passed on to this state of awareness.

Of what use is this information to you or to any student? Practically none, beyond indicating the vastness of the Plan and the amazing scope of the human consciousness. What that contact with the highest type of synthetic force may mean, I cannot tell you. The planetary Logoi themselves walk in the light of that sublime Consciousness, and towards that privilege the Christ Himself, and His great Brother, the Buddha, with the three Buddhas of Activity, are at this time aspiring. More than that I know not, nor may I further enlarge upon the matter. But the wonder and the immensity of the drama unfolding in the universe is a proof of its reality, and the grasp of man, small though it may appear to be, is a guarantee of his divinity. Stage by stage we slowly make our approach to the goal of conscious and intelligent awareness. Step by step we are mastering matter and making more adequate the mechanism of awareness and of contact. Little by little we (and by that I mean the human family, as a whole) are approaching the "place of recognition," and are preparing to climb the mountain of vision. If aspirants but realised the wonders of that revelation, and if they grasped the magnificence of the reward given to their efforts, we would have less failure, more courage, a greater and steadier achievement, and consequently a more rapidly illumined world.

The scope of that imparted vision warrants careful study, and the proffering of the divine ambition to the soul for recognition. It is not the multitude of words read which is of moment, but the accuracy of the recording by the brain and the adaptation of the teaching to the individual need. The vision cannot be appropriated. It is ever on ahead, but if the entire life is given to vision, and if the serving of one's fellow man is overlooked, the vision profits not. I have sought to convey the magnitude of the Plan and the steps upon the evolutionary stairway which lie ahead of every aspirant and of every member of the hierarchy.

1. *The Rays and Life-Quality-Appearance*

WE COME at this time to consideration of the rays, which brings us immediately into the realm of psychology and of the various psychological influences. As we deal with the second of the ray manifestations, with the *Quality* aspect, we are dealing with those pre-determining factors which produce the myriad differentiations in the phenomenal world. The quality, the colouring, or the type nature of living energy (which is our inadequate definition of the word "life") settles or determines the aspect assumed and the characteristics expressed by all the forms in the four kingdoms of nature; the individual form emanations are settled thereby, and under the modifying influence of the contact of the living quality with the substance affected and with the kingdom which is the focus of attention, there is consequently produced the characteristic appearance, the specialised activity and the intrinsic emanation of any form in any kingdom. In my earlier books, I divided the rays into two groups:

Group I . . . Rays of Aspect, the three major rays.
Group II . . Rays of Attribute, the four minor rays.

The three great rays, which constitute the sum total of the divine manifestation, are aspect rays, and this for two reasons:

First, they are, in their totality, the manifested Deity, the *Word* in incarnation. They are the expression of the creative purpose, and the synthesis of life, quality and appearance.

Secondly, they are active in every form in every kingdom, and they determine the broad general characteristics which govern the energy, the quality and the kingdom in question; through them the differentiated forms come into being, the specialised lives express themselves, and the diversity of divine agents fulfill their destiny in the plane of existence allocated to them.

Along these three streams of qualified life-force the creative agencies of God make their presence powerfully felt, and through their activity every form is imbued with that inner evolutionary attribute which must eventually sweep it into line with divine purpose, inevitably produce that type of consciousness which will enable the phenomenal unit to react to its surroundings and thus fulfill its destiny as a corporate part of the whole. Thus intrinsic quality and specific type radiation become possible. The interplay of these three rays determines the outer phenomenal appearance, attracts the unity of life into one or other of the kingdoms in nature, and into one or other of the myriad divisions within that kingdom; the selective and discriminating process is repeated until we have the many ramifications within the four kingdoms, the divisions, groups within a division, families and branches. Thus the creative process, in its wondrous beauty, sequence and unfoldment, stands

The Creative Builders

forth to our awakening consciousness, and we are left awestruck and bewildered at the creative facility of the Great Architect of the Universe.

Looking at all this beauty from a symbolic angle, and thereby simplifying the concept (which is ever the work of the worker in symbols), we might say that Ray I embodies the dynamic idea of God, and thus the Most High starts the work of creation.

Ray II is occupied with the first formulations of the plan upon which the form must be constructed and the idea materialised, and (through the agencies of this great second emanation) the blue prints come into being with their mathematical accuracy, their structural unity and their geometrical perfection. The Grand Geometrician comes thus to the forefront and makes the work of the Builders possible. Upon figure and form, number and sequences will the Temple be built, and so embrace and express the glory of the Lord. The second ray is the ray of the Master Builder.

Ray III constitutes the aggregate of the active building forces, and the Great Architect, with His Builders, organises the material, starts the work of construction, and eventually (as the evolutionary cycle proceeds upon its way) materialises the idea and purpose of God the Father, under the guidance of God the Son. Yet these three are as much a unity as is a human being who conceives an idea, uses his mind and brain to bring his idea into manifestation, and employs his hands and all his natural forces to perfect his concept. The division of aspects and forces is unreal, except for the purpose of intelligent understanding.

The readers of this treatise who really want to profit by this teaching must train themselves ever to think in terms of the whole. The arbitrary tabulations, the divisions into triplicities and septenates, and the diversified enumeration of forces which are seen as emanating from the seven constellations, the ten planets, and the twelve mansions of the zodiac, are but intended to give the student an idea of a world of energies in which he has to play his part. From the standpoint of esoteric psychology, it should be noted that all the schools of psychology go astray in their handling of the human unit, for just this reason; they do not judge a man as a synthetic whole, and—owing to the lack of knowledge, and to the failure, as yet, of the intuitive faculty—the average psychologist seldom enters into the realms of true quality and of the life aspect; the man under investigation is considered more or less objectively, and the true sources of the phenomenal nature are seldom touched. The determining aspects of the personality ray which produce the sum total of the physical, emotional and mental qualities is in process of tabulation and research and much has been done of a valuable nature. A man's physical reactions, his emotional habits, and his mental processes—normal and abnormal—are far better understood than they were twenty-five years ago. Nevertheless, until there is a more adequate knowledge of ray qualities, and until a man's soul ray is determined and the effect of that ray upon the personality ray is charted and known, the true nature of his temperament and the real subjective cause of his varied reactions, his complexes and inhibitions will remain a problem most difficult to handle. When, for instance, psychologists realise that it is the play of soul quality and energy which determines whether a man in any particular life will function as an introvert or an extrovert, then they will work to produce that balancing of the ray forces which will make the man able to express himself in such a way that the path to the outer world is left open, and that to the inner world is also cleared of obstacles.

What is the real nature of a true mystic or introvert? He

The Creative Builders

is one whose soul force, ray or quality is too strong for the personality to handle. The man then finds that the path to the inner worlds of desire-emotion, of mind and of spiritual vision are, for him, the line of least resistance, and the physical plane integration and expression suffer as a consequence. The "pull" of the soul offsets the outer "pull," and the man becomes a visionary mystic. I refer not to the practical mystic who is on the way to becoming a white occultist. The reverse condition can also be true, and then you have the pure extrovert. The personality ray focusses itself upon the physical plane, and the inner lure of the soul is temporarily offset, sometimes for several lives. Where this outer condition and "pull" is over-strong, and when all the personality ray qualities are focussed to a point, you will have either a display of exhibitionism, as it is called, or a constructive high grade personality, expressing genius and the creative possibilities of a coordinated physical, emotional and mental expression. The manifestation of this coordination will be outward into the world of doing, and not inward into the world of being or of the soul. Both these conditions indicate the "genius towards perfection"; where the equipment is mediocre, you have a thwarted or frustrated complex and a strong sense of inferiority which may diverge towards an abnormal exhibitionism. Where the equipment is fine and trained, you will have a brilliant worker in the varying fields of human endeavour. When, as is occasionally the case, you have added to the above a tendency to introvert, with the consequences of soul knowledge and of intuitional development, you then have a leader of men, a teacher from the gods, and a spiritual power. Hence the value to psychologists in these modern days (temporarily at least) if they will interest themselves in the hypotheses of the school of esoteric psychology. They may gain thereby, and in any case they lose nothing.

The four rays of attribute, which find their synthesis in the third ray of aspect, produce the varying qualities in greater detail than do the three rays of aspect. It might generally be stated, as we endeavour to clarify our problem, that the three rays of aspect find their main expression in relation to mankind through the medium of the three periodical vehicles:

Ray I . . Power . . . . Life . . . . Ideas . . The Monad
Ray II . Love-Wisdom . . . . Consciousness. . Ideals . The Soul
Ray III Active Intelligence . Appearance . . . . Idols . . Personality

They find their secondary expression in the three bodies which form the personality of man:

Ray I . . . . Power . . . . . . Ideas . . . Mental body . . . Purpose. Life.
Ray II . . . Love . . . . Ideals . . Astral body . . . Quality.
Ray III . . Intelligence . . Idols . . . Physical Body . Form.

The rays of attribute, though expressing themselves equally on all the planes and through the periodical vehicles and the three aspects of the personality, find their main expression through one or other of the four kingdoms in nature:

Ray IV . . Harmony, Conflict . . . . 4th kingdom . . . Human.
                                                                   The Balance.
Ray V . . . Concrete Knowledge . . 3rd kingdom . . .Animal.
Ray VI . . Devotion . . . . 2nd kingdom . . Vegetable.
Ray VII . Ceremonial Ritual . . . . 1st kingdom . . .Mineral.

These are their main fields of influence in the three worlds, and upon this we shall later enlarge.

In relation to mankind, these four rays of attribute find a wide expression in connection with the four aspects of the personality, or with the quaternary. The relationship is as follows:

Ray IV . . . . . Harmony through Conflict . . the Physical body.
Ray V . . . . . Concrete Knowledge . . . . the Etheric body.
Ray VI . . . . . Devotion . . . . the Astral body.
Ray VII . . . . Organisation . . . . the Mental body.

But again remember that the interrelation and interplay is synthetic on all planes, on the formless levels and also on the planes of form, and in this connection, with all states of consciousness and throughout the created universe.

THE SEVEN RAYS

We are told that seven great rays exist in the cosmos. In our solar system only one of these seven great rays is in operation. The seven sub-divisions constitute the "seven rays" which, wielded by our solar Logos, form the basis of endless variations in His system of worlds. These seven rays may be described as the seven channels through which all being in His solar system flows, the seven predominant characteristics or modifications of life, for it is not to humanity only that these rays apply, but to the seven kingdoms as well. In fact there is nothing in the whole solar system, at whatever stage of evolution it may stand, which does not belong and has not always belonged to one or other of the seven rays.

The following table may explain the various characteristics of the seven rays:

No.	Characteristics.	Methods of development.	Planet.	Colour. (according to Besant.)
I	Will or Power	Raja Yoga	Uranus	Flame. representing Sun.
II	Wisdom. Balance. Intuition.	Raja Yoga	Mercury	Yellow. Rose.
III	Higher Mind	Exactitude in thought. Higher Mathematics. Philosophy.	Venus	Indigo. Blue. Bronze.

IV. Conflict	Intensity of struggle	Saturn	Green.
Birth of Horus	Hatha Yoga, the most dangerous method of psychic growth.		
V..Lower Mind	Exactitude in action	The Moon	Violet
	Practical Science.		
VI. Devotion	Bhakti Yoga	Mars	Rose. Blue.
	Necessity for an object.		
VII.Ceremonial Order	Ceremonial observances	Jupiter	Bright. Clear. Blue.
	Control over forces of nature.		

It will be clear that each of the kingdoms—elemental, mineral, vegetable, and animal as well as the human—is divided into seven primary types or rays, and as individualisation (i.e. the transition from the animal to the human kingdom) can take place at present only through association with man, it follows that there must stand at the head of the animal kingdom, on each ray, some species of animal susceptible to human influence through which such individualisation can take place. The elephant is said to stand at the head of the second ray type of animal, while the cat and dog occupy a similar position on the fourth and sixth rays respectively. We have had no information as to the others, with this exception, that the animals of the first ray are no longer in existence on earth.

Besides regarding the rays as the channels through which all being flows, we must recognise them as influences operating on the world in turn. Each ray has its period of greatest

The Creative Builders

influence to which all are subject to a considerable extent, not merely those belonging by nature to that particular ray, but those on all the other rays as well. The long period of influence of each is divided into seven stages, each of which is qualified by the influence of the greater ray period, being intensified when its own sub-ray period is reached (i.e. the sixth ray influence is greatest during the period of the sixth sub-ray). We must carefully note that the term "sub-ray" is used merely for convenience to designate the shorter period of influence, not as indicating any difference in the nature of the ray.

We are told that the dominant ray at the present time, though passing out, is the sixth, the Ray of Devotion, and that this ray was already in operation before the dawn of Christianity; also that the seventh sub-ray became the modifying influence about seventy-five years ago (1860), and of course will continue as such. The first outcome of this seventh subray influence was the Ecumenical Council at Rome (1870), with its declaration of Papal Infallibility. The Tractarian Movement in England started at the same time, whilst the progress of the seventh sub-ray influence, still going on, is marked by the steady increase of ritualism and sacerdotalism in the various churches, and even in the church of Rome there has been a distinct tightening of priestly authority in all matters of dogma and practice. So much for its influence on religious thought; its other aspects will be considered later.

We have also been told that the religious revival under Wesley and Whitfield in England was under the sixth sub-ray, and I think we are justified in drawing the inference that the rise of Molinos and the Quietists in Spain and Central Europe, and of St. Martin and his band of spiritual philosophers in France and elsewhere, may have also marked the progress of the same period, during which the Ray of Devotion was accentuated by its own sixth sub-ray.

With these few isolated facts before us we may perhaps conclude that the time during which each sub-ray exerts its modifying influence is between one hundred and fifty and two hundred years.

We do not know how often (perhaps seven times?) the sub-rays are repeated successively within the cycle of the great ray. It must manifestly be more than once, seeing that the great sixth ray was operating before the rise of Christianity. It is also apparent that Buddhism cannot have been, as was at one time thought, the last outcome of the great second ray period, for the interval between the rise of Buddhism and that of Christianity was only five hundred years. It seems probable that Buddhism arose under the influence of the second sub-ray of the great sixth ray period. In attempting to trace back the influence which was the last outcome of the sub-rays, 5.4.3.2. and 1, it has been suggested that this period of the Alchemists and Rosicrucians may have been dominated by the fifth sub-ray; the epoch of the Flagellants and other fanatical enthusiasts who practised self-torture and mutilation was influenced by the fourth sub-ray; and the time when astrology was widely practised as representing the third sub-ray; while the earlier epoch of the Gnostics may have been the outcome of the second sub-ray. But these are only conjectures, and while the last named is possible, there can be no such correspondence of time in the previous cases, as the Alchemists, Flagellants, and Astrologers were all more or less contemporary during the Middle Ages.

The rise of modern spiritualism is no doubt due to the seventh sub-ray influence, and it may also be a foreshadowing of the great seventh ray still to come. It is interesting to note that this movement was started by a secret society which has existed in the world since the last period of seventh ray dominance in Atlantean times.

Every great religion which arises is under the influence of one or other of the rays, but it does not necessarily follow that each successive ray should have a great far-reaching religion as its outcome. We have heard that Brahmanism is the last great religion which arose under first ray influence; we do not know what may have been the religion which was the outcome of the last second ray period; but the Chaldean, the Egyptian and the Zoroastrian religions may be taken as representing the third, the fourth, and the fifth rays respectively. Christianity and probably Buddhism were the result of sixth ray influence. Mohammedanism, which numbers so large a following, is also under sixth ray influence, but it is not a great root religion, being a hybrid offshoot of Christianity with the tinge of Judaism.

The rays are sometimes considered as divided into three classes; the first ray by itself, the second ray by itself, and the other five in a group. When regarded in this way, they are spoken of as the three rays, and typify the various Trinities. Another suggestive fragment of symbology describes the three rays as using respectively three kinds of fire to light the sacrifice of the altar,—the electric, the solar, and the artificial, or fire by friction.

Before proceeding to consider the virtues, the vices and the special human characteristics which differentiate the individual belonging to one ray from the individual on another ray, it will be well to refer to the origin of the two ray influences which constitute the dominant and the modifying factors in the character of every human being, as well as to the planetary influence, or the ray of the personality, which again modifies these two great influences during any given life.

We have seen that seven rays are seven differentiations of one great cosmic ray, effected within the very being of our solar Logos before He began His creation. Now we know that the divine spark, the divine centre of consciousness in each one of us, comes from the highest principle of our Logos; it has therefore within it the potentiality of all the rays, but from the time when our Logos formed within Himself the countless centres of divine consciousness, each one of these centres was coloured by the special attributes of one or other of the rays. Seeing that the moment each became limited (i.e. separated from the absolute consciousness of the Logos by even the finest veil of differentiation) it must necessarily belong to one or other of the rays, the very essence of our being, the central spark of the divine in each one of us, may thus be said to belong to one or other of the seven rays, and this may be spoken of as a man's primary ray.

It will be remembered that the first great outpouring from the Logos vivified universal substance and caused every atom of matter within the "ring-pass-not" of His system to vibrate in seven different measures of vibration. The second outpouring caused molecular combinations, thus forming the six subplanes below the atomic on each plane, and produced form. It was at the time of the second outpouring that each of the divine centres of consciousness put forth a thread of being into an atom of the highest sub-planes of the atmic, the buddhic, and the manasic planes,—atoms destined to be the nuclei of the future bodies, each on its respective plane, the three forming the upper triad so often referred to. Now every atom is under the influence of one or other of the rays, and the atmic, buddhic and manasic atoms referred to all belong to the same ray; but this is not necessarily the same ray as that to which the over-shadowing centre of consciousness belongs. In fact, in the majority of cases, the ray of the centre of consciousness and the ray of the triad are different; the one modifies the other, the former being the primary (called by Mrs. Besant the monadic ray), the other being the secondary or individual ray, since the manasic atom is the nucleus of the future causal body in which the individual passes from life to life. This body is of course gradually built up of particles of matter belonging to the same quality and type as its nucleus atom, and when it is so built through long ages of evolution, the over-shadowing divine centre of consciousness, which has through the ages also evolved individually, unites with it, and the immortal individual Ego starts on its upward climb through the human kingdom. This is the third outpouring for each soul. The influence of this secondary or individual ray constitutes the main factor in the earlier stages of evolution, i.e., in the elemental, mineral, vegetable and animal kingdoms; but of course the deepest rooted influence must be that which affects the divine centre of consciousness; therefore when the union above referred to takes place, and the entity has become the re-incarnating ego, the primary ray becomes and remains the dominant force.

But there is still another influence to be spoken of. This is the planetary ray under which each human being is born. It must of course be understood that the so-called influence of a planet is really the influence of the Hierarchy ruling over that planet. This personal ray is an important factor in the character of a man during the one lifetime of its operation. I say one lifetime, but it may of course be one or more, if the karmic conditions demand it, for the moment of birth for every individual is fixed in accordance with karmic necessities, and probably all of us—whatever our primary or individual rays—have passed lifetimes again and again under the personal influence of all the seven rays.

2. The Present Ray Plan and the Workers

THE work of the first and second rays is primarily instrumental in the work of materialising the Plan of God for our world and causing its manifestation. It would be of interest at this point to consider the Plan as it is at present working out, for the reason that these two types of ray force, that of power-will and that of love-wisdom, are predominantly operative at this time. All the workers along other lines of force—whether manifesting objectively or active subjectively—have temporarily subordinated their interests and to some degree cancelled their previous arrangements, in order to meet the need of the world. There is a Plan now coming into effect, and this has demanded the attention and called for the loyal cooperation of all departments of the world government. In all organised endeavour and in all wide schemes of construction and of work there must ever be the subordination of certain factors to other factors, and never more so than in the working out, at this time, of the Hierarchical Plan.

If the teachings in this treatise are to achieve the purpose for which they are intended, it is essential that scattered through the occult generalities and the universal concepts there should be those points of immediate and imperative interest which will make this treatise of practical usefulness and of living application.

In *A Treatise on White Magic* I outlined one of the first steps taken by the Hierarchy in the work of inaugurating the new Plan. This Plan was tentatively formulated in 1900, at one of the great quarterly meetings of the Hierarchy. In 1925, at the next great meeting for cooperation, the new Plan was discussed in greater detail, certain necessary changes (growing out of the results of the World War) were negotiated, and the members of that important Council determined two things:

First, that there should be a united effort by the collective members of the planetary Hierarchy, over a period of several years (that is until 1950), to bring about certain definite results, and that during that time the attention of the Great Ones should be turned towards a definite attempt to expand the consciousness of humanity and to institute a sort of forcing process, so that men's horizon of thought would be tremendously enlarged, and their faith, assurance and knowledge be equally increased and strengthened. It was decided that certain areas of doubt should be cleared up.

Secondly, it was determined to link more closely and subjectively the senior disciples, aspirants and workers in the world. To this end, all the Masters put Their personal groups of disciples in touch with each other, subjectively, intuitively, and sometimes telepathically. Thus the New Group of World Servers came into being.

Instead, therefore, of seven groups of workers in the world, all engrossed with activities along the seven major lines of force—their place in the scheme determined by their ray—the Masters, Their disciples and the probationers grouped themselves into three main divisions, so that the political, the religious, and the educational departments of human evolution might be adequately served.

At the same time They organised the intermediate group of World Servers, who could act as liaison officers, interpreters, and intermediaries between the inner active Hierarchy and the thinkers of the world, and also serve as agents in every country and in every group. Thus all groups which were animated by any desire to serve, and which were (in spite of errors in technique and method) of any usefulness in aiding their fellow men, were swept into a current of spiritual stimulation with the intent to increase their effectiveness. Groups that were crystallised and sectarian as a whole would fail to respond, but in all of them, even the most dead, there were found a few who were responsive to the new impulse.

The institution of this new Plan automatically brought about an augmented training of those men and women who showed signs of being responsive to subjective influences and to the intuition. It was found wise to bring about a forcing process, in order to make mankind more sensitive and to develop certain latent but hidden powers, and also to attempt to bring the more advanced types of men up to a standard of sensitivity and to a spiritual receptivity which had been hitherto the prerogative of the few mystics and intuitives. During the past few years this process has been going on, and the results have proved better than had been anticipated. The war, which devastated the world, cleared away much debris.

Roughly speaking, the Plan fell into three divisions in the minds of its organisers:

First, Political.

The objective of the work here planned was the development and the establishment of an international consciousness. This was an effort along the line of power or will, of government, or along the line of the first ray. Disciples and aspirants working in the field of organisation, and the mass of idealists, were organised in this work, and the seventh and sixth ray workers were brought into line. The groups therefore ranged themselves into one group in this endeavour. It was also determined to demonstrate the need for economic synthesis, as part of the work of relating the nations to each other, so that the spirit which is evidenced by such an organisation as the Red Cross, for instance, might also be evidenced internationally in the

The Creative Builders

interplay of the nations with each other. It is needless to point out that material stress and strain and the wrecking of old political parties and trade relations had to play their part. It was determined to demonstrate the necessity of establishing a spirit of international dependence and interrelation, so that the nations would be forced to realise politically that isolation, separativeness, and the cultivation of a national egoism must go, and that a national spirit coloured by a sense of superiority, by class hatreds and racial antagonisms, constitutes a barrier to the true development of humanity. The people must be taught that the longing to increase possessions is a deterrent to real expansion. Thus plans were laid whereby the Brotherhood of Nations, based on mutual need, mutual understanding, and mutual helpfulness, should gradually come into being.

It was the establishing of a state of mind which was the primary objective, and not the establishing of some impossible and mythical Utopia, or of those material conditions whereby one group is entirely subordinated by the will-to-power of another group which enforces a standardised and uniform condition through the use of power in some form or another. The work indicated, and therefore set before the New Group of World Servers, is to enunciate those principles of national relations which underlie a world state or federation, and their instructions were to get the ear of the leaders in various countries, and thus slowly and gradually awaken the masses (through them) to the true significance of that easily spoken, but little understood word, Brotherhood.

This work is perhaps one of the hardest of the tasks which the Society of Organised Minds has ever set itself. Racial hatreds and national aspirations are so strong, and the ignorance of the masses is so great, that all the resources of the workers along the line of government and power (the first ray) were necessary to make the needed impact upon the public consciousness. There has been, and there still is, much to destroy before the nations are reduced to the point where they will become sensitive to the new vision, and able to recognise their need of each other.

It has been interesting to note how the idea of the controlled and beneficently applied power of those who work with and through ideas has—during the past few years—materialised on the physical plane through the medium of the dictatorship of the proletariat, of the workers of a nation, as set up in Russia. This has been subversive of the rule and control of the aristocracy, of the bourgeoisie and of the intelligentsia; it has glorified work and the workers, and has driven out of the country (by death or exile) some of its best elements. Yet behind all the mistakes and cruelty, and behind the rank materialism, there lie great ideals,—the supply of the need of all, the beauty of mutual service, and the divinity of constructive work.

In Germany, you have the dictatorship of racial superiority, and the attempt to deify a race. Without humour and real understanding, one race is preparing to dictate terms to other races, by the weight of its thought and its achievements rather than by war. Yet the ideal of a superman is a true ideal, and it needs upholding before the world. Temporarily, it has been forgotten that the superman is the goal for all, and that Asiatics, Nordics, Jews, Gentiles, Americans, and Anglo-Saxons, the Africans and all other world races are children of the same Father, fed from the same source of Life, and saved by the same divine Christ principle. Therefore the superman has been and will be found emerging out of the ranks of every people, to find his way into the ranks of the Spiritual Hierarchy and the New Group of World Servers.

In America, you have the dictatorship of organised busi-

The Creative Builders 175

ness seeking to regulate and control every department of the economic life of the nation, and cutting deep down, through the trained minds in the government, to the very roots of the national existence. That certain types of mind may regard this as an infringement of the liberty of the subject is of small importance, relatively speaking, compared to the gradually emerging synthesis which aims subjectively to kill out greed and end the exploitation of the many by the few. In Great Britain, we find the dictatorship of empire (if such a paradoxical term may be employed), but it is an empire of the middle classes, controlling and balancing. In Italy, in Turkey and elsewhere other great experiments are going on.

The originators of these various national movements are often ignorant of the impulses which lie back of their work, and are frequently unable to explain the ideals toward which they are working, except in terms of human ambition and power. Nevertheless, unknown to themselves, they are really sensitive to the great ideas thrown into their minds by the Minds behind the scenes. They respond to the idea of general good, of human equality, of the superman, of universal trade requirements, and of the distribution of wealth, but—and here is the important point—because the inner synthesis of effort is not emphasised, because there is no general knowledge as to the source of the great concepts, and no understanding of the inner Brotherhood which is guiding humanity towards an outer Brotherhood, these great principles are being widely distorted, selfishly applied, and separately utilised. The fires of class hatreds, of racial antagonisms, and of national pride are burning intensely strong.

Such is the problem before the Great Ones at this time. What will They do to bring the nations, through the agency of the inner department of government and the political rule which we have been considering, to a realisation of their essential unity, and so further that "peace on earth, good will to men" of which we all dream.

Second, Religious.

The aim before this department is to establish a universal understanding of the nature of reality, and to foster the growth of the spiritual consciousness. Though in some ways religious differences are the hardest to bridge or heal, yet real progress has been made in this phase of the Hierarchical work. There is today in the world a very large number of those who fundamentally believe in the brotherhood of religions. Though the unintelligent masses everywhere have little or no idea of things spiritual, they can be more easily brought to believe in the one God and to the idea of a universal faith than to any other idea. Many thousands of them are frankly agnostic or believe in nothing, whilst many other thousands are restive under the control of theological authority. They have nevertheless within them that germ of the spirit of love which is normally inclusive and intuitive. Curiously enough, along this line the seething millions of the Orient present a more serious problem to the Great Ones than do the peoples of the Occident, for ignorance is deeply prevalent among the masses of Asia as to the trend of affairs in the world of religion, owing to the widespread illiteracy of the races, and their consequent easy exploitation and control by the religious demagogues, fervent prophets and reactionaries.

Disciples or workers on the second ray are now actively handling this problem. It is interesting to note that the reason for the success in breaking down old barriers and in bringing about a condition of spiritual readiness everywhere in the Occident, is largely due to the work of the Orientalist scholars in France, Germany and England. They have made the literature of the East available, in all its beauty, to the West,

The Creative Builders 177

and so have linked the spiritual truths of all ages with the truth of the Christian presentation, showing them all to be of equal progressive value. Now the masses in India, China, and northern Africa must be awakened to the inner significance of their own faiths, and to the part that Christianity plays in the same great religious programme. This is occupying the close attention of certain second ray teachers in India, Japan and Syria.

During the next ten years the work of the Fellowship of Religions (of which the outer organisations are an externalisation) will greatly increase. Soon we shall have the inner structure of a world-faith so clearly defined in the minds of many thousands that its outer structure will inevitably make its appearance before the end of the century.

The inner structure of the World Federation of Nations will eventually be equally well organised, with its outer form taking rapid shape by 2025. Do not infer from this that we shall have a perfected world religion and a complete community of nations. Not so rapidly does nature move; but the concept and the idea will be universally recognised, universally desired, and generally worked for, and when these conditions exist nothing can stop the appearance of the ultimate physical form for that cycle.

Third, Scientific.

The workers along this line have definitely set themselves the goal of expanding man's consciousness and so widening his horizon that a synthesis of the tangible and the intangible will take place. This will bring about the entrance of mankind into a new and subjective realm, and his apprehension of new states of awareness. These developments will be brought about by the workers in the fields of education, of science, and of psychology. Great things are on the way at this time, and the activities of workers on the third and fifth rays have never been so well directed nor so potent as today.

As I told you, and as I now repeat, the workers on all the rays are organised to take part in one supreme effort,—an effort towards which the entire Christian era has been tending and for which it has been a preparation. The seventh and sixth rays are occupied with the work of government and with the task of producing a new synthesis, and thus the force of all the workers along those lines is combining with the energy of the first ray. The energies of the aspirants and disciples on the third and fifth rays are turned to the work of expanding the human consciousness, of bringing to light the hidden wonders of the universe, and of hastening the unfoldment of the latent powers in mankind. These powers, when awakened, will be extensions of many of the present senses and will admit man into that world which lies behind the veil of ignorance and matter.

You will note that so strenuous is the work of breaking down national group isolation and separativeness that it takes the united energies of three groups of workers to bring about the desired results. The seven groups of workers are organised therefore as follows:

1. In the department of politics . . . . First, sixth and seventh rays.
2. In the department of religion . . . Second and fourth rays.
3. In the department of education . . Third and fifth rays.

Do not forget that, though the work is being carried forward in three fields of human thought and activity, the net result is one directed effort towards the production of synthesis and a great preparatory drive towards a revelation of such wonder that I cannot yet detail it. Recognition of its truth is dependent upon inner growth and illumination, and this growth is being speeded up, leading to an easier recognition of that which is on the way. Remember, revelation seldom comes along the expected lines. There will be a pouring in of light upon mankind which will alter his conditions of living, change his outlook upon world affairs, and inaugurate a new age which will be distinguished by an aptitude for group synthesis and cooperation, and by new mental powers, leading to a re-orientation of the mind so that it can function with equal facility in two directions. It will be able to turn outward into the world of manifested forms, and inward into the world of synthesis, of unity and of spirit. There will be a fresh attitude towards life which will evidence itself in a better sense of values, for life will have a meaning hitherto unknown, and we shall have an interpretation of that meaning which will enrich our daily experience. Towards this end all true workers are now bending every effort.

Earlier in this treatise I referred to the areas of doubt which now exist in man's mind, and I should like briefly to refer to the three major areas which—when cleared up—will facilitate the bringing in of the new age with its new civilisations, new sciences and new religion. There are three problems which the next few years will see well on the way towards an intelligent solution in the minds of the most conservative, but which will be regarded as definitely solved by the intuitive and illumined. These three problems might be regarded as constituting the three main objectives in the fields of science, of politics and of religion. With their solution will come the more rapid success of the world problems of government, of faith and of matter. Please note the distinction and significance of these last three words.

The Problem of Ideas

In the final analysis, the main problem of world government is the wise use of ideas. It is here that the power of speech makes itself felt, just as in the department of religion or of education the power of the written word, of the printed page, is felt. In the field of politics, the masses are swayed by their orators, and never more so than now through the use of the radio. Great ideas are dinned into the ear of the public without cessation—theories as to dictatorship, communism, nazism, fascism, marxism, nationalism, and democratic ideals. Methods of rule by this or that group of thinkers are presented to the public, leaving them no time for consideration, or for clear thinking. Racial antipathies are spread, and personal preferences and illusions find expression, bringing about the deception of the unthinking. The man who has a golden tongue, the man who has the gift of playing with words and can voice with emphasis people's grievances, the juggler in statistics, the fanatic with a certain and sure cure for social ills, and the man who loves to fan race hatreds, can ever get a following. Such men can with facility upset the balance of the community and lead a body of unthinking adherents to a transient success and power, or to obloquy and oblivion.

In the aggregate of this play with ideas, and in the constant impact upon the human consciousness of the great concepts which lie back of our evolutionary process, the race is developing the power to think, to choose, and to build a sure foundation. Through the evolutionary presentation of these ideas there is a steady march towards a liberty of thought (through the old method of experiment, of discard, and of renewed effort with ever newer concepts) which will enable mankind to build true to the great thought patterns which underlie the outer structure of our world. The attentive minds of the age are constantly being made sensitive to these patterns, so that the individual mind can recognise them and wrest them out of the darkness into the light of day. Thus

The Creative Builders

will the true patterns be made available, to play their part in leading the race towards its destiny, towards those deeper realisations which mould the racial types, and to that synthesis of understanding which will result in a realisation of Brotherhood. Thus thoughts play their part, and the problem of ideas will be increasingly understood, until the time may come when we shall have our trained intuitives and thinkers who will be able to work directly in the world of concepts and bring through (for the use of the race) the pattern ideas upon which to build. In saying this I realise that I may be accused of romancing and of communicating the impossible; but time will demonstrate the truth of that which I predict. The world structure emerges from and is built upon certain inner thought patterns, and it is these thought patterns which are producing the present flood of governmental experiments among all nations. But today there is no training given upon the process of contacting the world of patterns and upon the true interpretation of ideas, and hence the problems. Later, when the race sees its problem with clarity, it will act with wisdom and train with care its Observers and Communicators. These will be men and women in whom the intuition has awakened at the behest of an urgent intellect; they will be people whose minds are so subordinated to the group good, and so free from all sense of separativeness, that their minds present no impediment to the contact with the world of reality and of inner truth. They will not necessarily be people who could be termed "religious" in the ordinary sense of that word, but they will be men of good will, of high mental calibre, with minds well stocked and equipped; they will be free from personal ambition and selfishness, animated by love of humanity and by a desire to help the race. Such a man is a spiritual man.

The Problem of God

In the world of religion we shall see the solution of the second problem, and the ridding of the human consciousness of another area of doubt. The fact of God will be established and men's questioning in this respect will end. Such a God will not be a national or a racial God; not Christian, Hindu or Buddhist. Such a God will not be a figment of man's creative imagination or an extension of his own consciousness, but a Deity of essential life, who is the sum total of all energies; the energy of life itself, the energy of love, the energy of intelligence, of active experience, and that energy which produces the interplay between the seen and the unseen; a God most surely transcendent, but at the same time most assuredly immanent; a God of such immensity that the Heavens proclaim Him, and so intimate that the humblest child can recognise Him.

How can this be? you ask. I give a simple reply to your question, and yet one so scientific and so profound in meaning that only when it is realised to be a fact in a natural process will it be appreciated with accuracy. Out of the flesh God will be seen and known, yet with the eye of the inner vision can God be seen even when a man is occupying a body of flesh. Not with the physical eye can Deity be seen, though the hallmark of divinity is everywhere. There is an eye which can be developed and used, and which will enable its possessor to see God working on the inner side of Life, within Himself and within all forms, for "when thine eye is single, thy whole body is full of light." In that light shall we see light, and so see God. The three words: electricity, light and life, express divinity, and their synthesis is God. When we know the three as one in our own experience, then we know God. The lowest aspect we are now using, and of it we are

The Creative Builders

increasingly aware. The second aspect of light is on the point of revelation, through the right understanding of electrical phenomena. There lies the clue to the new age, the age of light, of illumination and of revelation. The esotericists of the world will understand a little of that to which I refer, and in their hands lies the training of humanity so that men may use that true vision and learn to utilise the "single eye." I would have you note, however, that the majority of true esotericists are found outside, and not within, the bulk of the schools which call themselves esoteric.

THE PROBLEM OF IMMORTALITY

The third area of doubt,—doubt as to the fact of immortality—will be solved before long in the realm of science, as the result of scientific investigation. Certain scientists will accept the hypothesis of immortality as a working basis upon which to base their search, and they will enter upon that search with a willingness to learn, a readiness to accept and a desire to formulate conclusions based upon reiterated evidence. These conclusions will, in their turn, form the basis for another hypothesis. Within the next few years the fact of persistence and of the eternity of existence will have advanced out of the realm of questioning into the realm of certainty. The problem will have shifted further back. There will be no question in anyone's mind that the discarding of the physical body will leave a man still a conscious living entity. He will be known to be perpetuating his existence in a realm lying behind the physical. He will be known to be still alive, awake and aware. This fact will be demonstrated in several ways. The development of a power within the physical eye of a human being (a power which has always been there, but which has been very little used) will reveal the etheric body, the "double," as it is sometimes called; and men will be seen occupying that body in some definite spatial area whilst their dead or disintegrating physical body has been left behind. Then again, the growth in the number of those people who have the power to use the "single eye," sometimes called the "reawakened third eye," will also add to the demonstration of the truth of immortality, for they will with facility see the man who has discarded his etheric body as well as his physical body. By the very weight of their numbers, and by the reputability of their position, they will carry their point. Through a discovery also in the field of photography, now being investigated, will the fact of survival be proven. Through the use of the radio by those who have passed over will communication be eventually set up, and reduced to a true science.

Nevertheless, certain imminent happenings will do more to annihilate the veil between the seen and the unseen than any other line of activity hitherto initiated. Of this I may not speak beyond telling you that an illumination will be set up and a radiance revealed which will result in a tremendous stimulation of mankind and bring about an awakening of a new order. Man will be keyed up to a perception and to a contact which will enable him to *see through*, which will reveal the nature of the fourth dimension, and will blend the subjective and the objective together into a new world. Death will lose its terrors, and that particular fear will come to an end.

Men are so occupied with their demand for light, so earnest in their cry for release from the present blindness, and so anxious for relief from the surrounding chaos, that they are apt to forget that from the inner side there is also a great effort and "push" to help, on the part of the Custodians of the Plan and Their assistants. This urge on Their part to help is more active than ever before, as human beings demand more

The Creative Builders 185

potently the privilege of light. A demand from the race, plus a response from the waiting Hierarchy, must inevitably produce potent results. The urge to know and the urge to teach are assuredly related and a part of the natural process of conscious development. The next few decades will mark a happening of such profound and widespread consequences that the present era in which we live will come to be looked upon as the dark ages. Science will penetrate deeper into the realm of the intangible, and work in mediums and with apparatus hitherto unknown. The release of the potencies in an atom will mark a revolutionary era, and science will have much to discard and much to give as it works with energies and forms of life hitherto unrecognised. The spiritualists will make a discovery whereby the means of contact with those who function out of the physical body will be greatly facilitated, and a group of mediums will begin to act as intermediaries for a number of scientists on the inner side of life and those who are still in physical bodies. Through the activity of the real esoteric schools, a technique of training will be instituted which will develop the new powers that will substantiate the old truth and turn men's beliefs into certainties. Through the stimulating and occultly scientific work of the department of religions, men will come to new knowledge and awareness, and will arrive at an uplift that will bring mankind to the Mount of Transfiguration. Through the work of the department of government, men will come to an understanding of those ideas which are needed to carry the nations the next step forward to mutual help.

I shall try to express the deepest objective of the Brotherhood, so that you can understand and cooperate. Humanity is intended to act as a power house through which certain types of divine energy can flow to the various forms of life found in the subhuman kingdoms. This flow of energy must be intelligently apprehended and intelligently directed, and thus will be brought to an end conditions of decay and of death now prevalent everywhere. Thus mankind can link the higher and the lower manifestations of Life, but this will be possible only when men themselves have (within themselves) linked their higher and their lower aspects. This is, and should be, one of the objectives of all esoteric training. Men are intended to acquire the facility to function freely in either direction, and so with ease contact the life of God as it flows through those forms we call superhuman, and those which are subhuman. Such is the emerging goal.

The next few years will mark an intensive effort on the part of the Hierarchy and on the part of the New Group of World Servers. There is a term set to their effort, and later this type of activity will end, and workers will enter into more extensive fields, if the work proves effective. Should the spiritually minded and intellectually constituted people of the race fail at this time to initiate the Plan, to wrest it out of the unseen and carry it into the realm of the seen, then we shall see a period of difficulty and of slower growth, but no entire collapse of the fabric of civilisation as the fear-mongers indicate. But we shall anticipate no such failure and no such setback to the carefully laid plans of the Watchers on the inner side. The word has gone out to rally all the disciples and aspirants of the world to an intensive work, and with that appeal from the Great Ones I seek to occupy myself. Everyone is needed and must go forward with hope and certainty. The Hierarchy is, with concentration, working and bending every effort to make the plan a success. The New Group of World Servers are being more closely integrated, and the work they are to do is being carefully planned. In London, in New York and in Geneva are three centres of their activity, and at Darjeeling and in Tokyo there is a mustering of forces.

The Creative Builders

I challenge the thinkers of the world to drop their sectarianism, their nationalism, and their partisanships, and in the spirit of brotherhood to work in their particular nation, regarding it as an integral part of a great federation of nations,—a federation that now exists on the inner side but waits for the activity of the world thinkers to bring it to materialisation on the outer side. I charge them to work in the cause of religion and in the field of that particular religion in which they, by an accident of birth or by choice, are interested, regarding each religion as part of the great world religion. They must look upon the activities of their group, society or organisation as demanding their help, just in so far, and only so far, as the principles upon which they are founded and the techniques which they employ serve the general good and develop the realisation of Brotherhood.

I ask you to drop your antagonisms and your antipathies, your hatreds and your racial differences, and attempt to think in terms of the one family, the one life, and the one humanity. I ask for no sentimental or devotional response to this challenge. I would remind you that hatred and separateness have brought humanity to the present sad condition. I would add to that reminder, however, the fact that there is in the world today a large enough number of liberated men to produce a change in the attitudes of mankind and in public opinion, if they measure up by an act of the will to what they know and believe.

I challenge you also to make sacrifices; to give yourself and your time and your money and your interest to carry these ideas to those around you in your own environment and to the group in which you find yourself, thus awakening your associates. I call you to a united effort to inculcate anew the ideas of brotherhood and of unity. I ask you to recognise your fellow workers in all the groups and to strengthen their hands. I ask you to seal your lips to words of hatred and of criticism, and to talk in terms of brotherhood and of group relationships. I beg of you to see to it that every day is for you a new day, in which you face new opportunity. Lose sight of your own affairs, your petty sorrows, worries and suspicions, in the urgency of the task to be done, and spread the cult of unity, of love and of harmlessness.

I ask you also to sever your connection with all groups which are seeking to destroy and to attack, no matter how sincere their motive. Range yourself on the side of the workers for constructive ends, who are fighting no other groups or organisations and who have eliminated the word "anti" out of their vocabulary. Stand on the side of those who are silently and steadily building for the new order—an order which is founded on love, which builds under the impulse of brotherhood, and which possesses a realisation of a brotherhood which is based on the knowledge that we are each and all, no matter what our race, the children of the One Father, and who have come to the realisation that the old ways of working must go and the newer methods must be given a chance.

If you cannot yourself teach or preach or write, give of your thought and of your money so that others can. Give of your hours and minutes of leisure so as to set others free to serve the Plan; give of your money so that the work of those associated with the New Group of World Servers may go forward with rapidity. Much time you waste on non-essentials. Many of you give little or nothing of time. The same is the case with money. Give as never before, and so make the physical aspects of the work possible. Some give of their very need, and the power they thereby release is great. Those on the inner side are grateful for the giving by those who can give only at great personal cost. Others give of what they can spare and only when it needs no sacrifice to give. Let that

The Creative Builders

condition also end, and give to the limit, with justice and understanding, so that the age of love and light may be more rapidly ushered in. I care not where or to whom you give, only that you give,—little if you have but little of time or money, much if you have much. Work and give, love and think, and aid those groups who are building and not destroying, loving and not attacking, lifting and not tearing down. Be not taken in by the specious argument that destruction is needed. It has been needed, no doubt; but the cycle of destruction is practically over, could you but realise it, and the builders must now get busy.

I challenge you above all to a deeper life, and I implore you for the sake of your fellow men to strengthen your contact with your own soul so that you will have done your share in making revelation possible; so that you will have served your part in bringing in the light, and will therefore be in a position to take advantage of that new light and new information, and so be better able to point the way and clear the path for the bewildered seeker at that time. Those who are not ready for the coming events will be blinded by the emerging light and bewildered by the revealing wonder; they will be swept by the living breath of God, and it is to you that we look to fit them for the event.

Before we proceed further I want to touch upon the apparent contradictions which occur (and which may continue to occur) in this treatise. Sometimes a ray will be spoken of as being in manifestation. At other times it may be referred to as being out of manifestation. We may speak about its influence upon a particular kingdom in nature, and then again still another ray may be regarded as of prime importance. These discrepancies are only apparent, and their cause lies hid in the right understanding of the Law of Cycles. Until this basic Law of Periodicity is comprehended (and this will not be possible until man has succeeded in developing fourth dimensional vision) it will not be easy to avoid what may look like contradictions. At one time a certain ray may be in incarnation and thus of paramount influence, and yet, at the same time, still another ray may govern the major cycle,—a cycle of which the ray under consideration may be only a temporary aspect. For instance, the seventh Ray of Ceremonial Organisation is now coming in, and the sixth Ray of Devotion is going out; yet this sixth ray is a major ray cycle and its influence will not entirely disappear for another 21,000 years. At the same time, this sixth ray might well be regarded as the sixth sub-ray of the fourth Ray of Harmony through Conflict, which has been in manifestation for several thousand years and will remain operative for another 40,000 years. Yet at the same time, this fourth ray *is* out of manifestation as regards its minor and cyclic influence.

I fully realise that this information is of a most confusing nature to the beginner in occultism, and only those students who conform to the requirement of grasping the general outline and the broad basic propositions will be able to gather out of these instructions the true, intended perspective. If the reader loses himself in the mass of possible analyses and intricacies of the imparted detail, he will not emerge into the realm of that clear vision which is intended. When he eliminates the detail and deals with the general conformation of the solar Plan, he will then be enabled to cooperate with the needed intelligence. Read therefore constructively and not critically, knowing that it is not easy to see the Plan as it exists in the minds of the Builders, Who work in the closest cooperation, conforming to the initial Plan, and yet carrying forward Their individual efforts with concentration and sustained enterprise.

3. *Three Major Propositions*

WE HAVE been studying the significance of the work of the seven creative Builders, as They express the life aspect and qualify the phenomenal appearance through which the One Life manifests. It is the quality in time and space that determines the phenomenal appearance, and this is the third major proposition of which the two previous are:

  a. Every ray Life is an expression of a solar Life, and every planet is therefore linked with every other planet, animated by energy from one or other of the seven solar systems, and actuated by a triple stream of force.
  b. Every one of the rays is the recipient and custodian of various energies, coming from varying sources.

To these two we add:

  c. It is the quality of a ray Life, in time and space, which determines the phenomenal appearance.

In these three propositions you have summed up the basic teaching of this Section. Here I can point out with success, I believe, the practical efficacy of a true understanding of these rather advanced occult teachings. If, for instance, you study the first proposition, you will note how a ray Life is an expression of a solar Life. Now take this broad idea and make it personally specific by referring the same proposition to an individual man, grasping the fact that every personality is intended to be an expression of a solar angel, and is consequently linked to every other solar angel in the kingdom of souls. Each is animated by the energies coming from all the seven groups of solar angels, and is likewise in touch with the life of the planet, of the solar system, and with extra-systemic force also. Is this not of vital, practical import? Does it not warrant close study and consideration of the attitude of the personality towards life, and of the measure of success of the solar angel at any given point in time and space (which is all that the personality is, in the last analysis) as it builds and qualifies its phenomenal appearance? Here we can see the scientific value of the study of ideals, of concentration upon the virtues and divine qualities, and upon an intellectual analysis of the divine attributes of any of the great sons of God.

Again, the second proposition states that the seven rays, being each the recipient and custodian of energies coming from the universe, bring in the basic concept of inter-relation, of inter-communication, of inter-dependence, of cooperative responsibility, and of *service*. These relationships, as we well know, underlie the principle of Brotherhood, which the race is just beginning to grasp and to discuss. Thus one of the major propositions which govern the building forces of the universe is of real practical application to the mental life and attitude of man today.

The first proposition relates to the ego, or solar angel, and its realisation.

The second proposition relates to the mental grasp of the "inspired" man—inspired from on high by his solar angel.

The third proposition, which states that quality determines the appearance, is intended to control or direct the feeling or desire life of the personality, for according to the quality of his desires will be the gradually emerging appearance.

Man is innately and truly divine, but the quality of the solar angel only makes its presence felt slowly and during the evolutionary cycle; it demonstrates only dimly as yet, and only emerges occasionally; though the sum total of characteristics in any one life is coloured by divine quality according to the egoic capacity to control or express, it is distorted by substance in the early stages almost past all recognition. These three propositions warrant careful thought and even meditation, for as they express the laws under which the seven creative Builders work, so do they express the laws under which the aspirant can now begin to work.

4. *Quality in the World of Appearances*

WE NOW take up the definition of the word "quality," which embodies the second ray aspect. This second aspect is the determining ray or the second manifesting aspect of divinity. It is the Christ or Vishnu aspect; it is the sentient consciousness aspect of deity in form. I stated also that we would consider its expression in the world of phenomena, meaning by this the world of external appearance and of tangible forms.

The quality that emerges through the process of manifesting, and under the impulse of the divine Life, is love, which functions through the medium of the Law of Attraction, with the aim of producing an ultimate synthesis in consciousness. Let us not forget that the objective of our present evolutionary process is the unfoldment of conscious awareness. The entire process is directed towards that consummation.

Quality, in the last analysis, is neither more nor less than the nature of that awareness, and the response in terms of quality to sentient contact. Through the gradually unfolding mechanism of contact (itself the result of active quality, determining the life of the unit cells which compose the form) the range of contacts extends indefinitely, and the response of the living entity to contact becomes more vital, more understanding in its capacity, and more synthetically comprehended. This response develops in two directions:

1. It leads to a comprehension of the response apparatus and to a wise use of the mechanism of contact.
2. It leads also to an understanding of the response of the individual consciousness to the consciousness contacted. This is brought about through the medium of the response mechanism. This other response apparatus may be either more developed or less developed than the one that does the contacting.

It is this interplay between the consciousnesses using the mechanisms that confers an understanding of quality. This interplay confers an understanding of the activity underlying the appearance, and motivating it. Exoteric science enables the activity aspect of the phenomenal forms to be apprehended and studied, and all the many manifestations of the many schools of human thought, which enlarge through their researches the range of human knowledge, have the same objective. At the same time, they increase our capacity to grasp the intense activity of every form in every kingdom in nature, and of every atom and cell within those forms. Science has led us on from pinnacle to pinnacle of achievement, till today we are lost in a world of energies. We have been taught to picture to ourselves a world of vibrating points of force which constitute in the aggregate all forms of life, and which present to our astonished and bewildered intellects a planetary life which is the sum total of all known forms. Each form is a universe in itself, and all forms are alive, vibrating with divine activity. We use the word "energy" to express this activity, and beyond that we are as yet unable to pass. Energy is life, and energy is also death. Activity is to be sensed and known in the organic and in the inorganic,—a vast series of atomic lives built up into structure after structure and found to be in ceaseless motion. A vast series of living structures, built up

The Creative Builders

into still greater and more inclusive forms, are all found, again, to be in equally ceaseless motion. These greater structures, in their turn, are found to be vibrant organisms, and so there unfolds before man's conscious vision nothing but life and activity, naught but motion and energy, and always a coherence, an ordered purpose, a growing synthesis, a Plan, and a *Will*. To this, science sets its seal, for scientific knowledge is the indication of man's response, through the collective response apparatus of humanity as a whole, to the mechanism of awareness of the great Life in which we live and move and have our being, the planetary Logos of our Earth.

The esoteric sciences carry us within the form or forms, and enable us to penetrate to the quality aspect. Students would do well to remember that occultism may be the study of forces, and that the occultist moves in the worlds of force, but these are also the worlds of quality and of those qualifying energies which are seeking to manifest through the world of appearances. As they achieve this, they will dominate the activity of the form units which constitute the phenomenal world. There are energies which lie behind the phenomena produced by the activity of the atomic structures; these are latent and unseen and often unfelt; they are subjective. The esoteric sciences have one purpose in view, and that is to produce the gradual emergence of these energies, so that the skilled occultist can eventually work in a dual yet unified world of force, and be the creative will which guides, blends and utilises the world of appearances and the realm of qualities. These two types of active creative energies must be controlled by the creating Will or Life aspect so that they function as one.

Therefore the aspirant is taught to turn within; to study motives; to acquaint himself with the qualities which are seeking expression in the outer world through the medium of his outer mechanism. As he learns to do this, the nature of that outer world of mechanisms alters, and he increasingly becomes aware of the qualities struggling for expression behind the outer forms. Thus the range of his conscious contacts extends, and he passes (through scientific research) from an exoteric understanding of the world of phenomenal appearances to an esoteric comprehension of the world of qualities. Never forget, therefore, that this dual apprehension must be emphasized, and that as a man learns to "know himself," he automatically learns to know the quality underlying all appearances. Look therefore for the quality everywhere. This is what we mean when we speak of seeing divinity on every hand, of recognising the note sounded by all beings, and of registering the hidden motif of all appearing. The unawakened man or woman sees the form, notes its forms of activity, and "judges by appearances." The awakening aspirant begins to sense some of the beauties that lie unrevealed behind all forms; the awakened disciple lays the focus of his attention upon the emerging world of qualities, and becomes steadily aware of colour, of new ranges of sound, of an inner evolving and newer response apparatus which is beginning to enable him to contact the unseen, the intangible, and the unrevealed. He becomes aware of those subjective impulses which condition the quality of the life, and which are slowly and gradually revealing themselves.

It is this unrevealed inner beauty which lies back of the emphasis laid by the churches upon the cultivation of the virtues, and by the occultists upon the use of a seed thought in meditation. These seed thoughts and virtues serve a valuable and constructive purpose. The Biblical truism that "as a man thinketh in his heart, so is he," is based on the same basic realisation, and the distinction between the spiritual man and the man of worldly and material purpose consists in the fact that one is attempting to work with the quality aspect of the life, and the other is focussing his attention upon the appearance aspect. He may and does employ certain qualities as he so works, but they are those qualities which have been developed during the evolutionary process of the divine Life as It has cycled through the subhuman and human kingdoms.

Each of the kingdoms in nature has developed, or is developing, one outstanding quality, with the other divine attributes as subsidiary.

The *mineral kingdom* has the quality of activity primarily emphasized, and its two extremes are the tamasic quality, or the static inert nature of the mineral world, and the quality of radio-activity, of radiation which is its beautiful and divinely perfected expression. The goal for all mineral atomic forms is this radio-active condition, the power to pass through all limiting and environing substances. This is initiation, or the entering into a state of liberation, for all mineral appearances, and the organising of all forms in this kingdom under the influence of the seventh ray.

The *vegetable kingdom* has the quality of attractiveness, expressed in colour, and its liberation, or its highest form of activity, is demonstrated by the perfume of its highest forms of life. This perfume is connected with its sex life, which has group purpose and which calls to its aid the initiating wind and the insect world. This is not just a pictorial way of portraying truth. The very nature of perfume, its purpose and intent, is to affect those agencies which will produce the spreading and the continuity of the life of the vegetable kingdom. The "aspirants" in the vegetable kingdom, and the most evolved of its forms, have beauty and perfume, and are susceptible to the hidden influences of Those to Whom is confided the initiating of the life-forms and their bringing to a desired perfection. Hence the influence of the sixth Ray of Devotion upon this kingdom, and the application of the Ray of Devotion which (symbolically expressed) "fixes the eye upon the sun; turns the life ever to the rays of warmth, and causes the blending of the colours and the glory of the perfumed radiance."

The *animal kingdom* has the quality of growing instinctual purpose which—in its highest form—works out as the domesticity of the more evolved animals, and their devotion to man. Behind the appearance of the animals is to be found a steady orientation towards understanding, and a consequent gravitation towards the forms of life which evidence that which they desire. Hence the influence of the fifth Ray of Concrete Knowledge, which pours through the human family upon the third kingdom in nature. Man is the initiating factor here, and to man is committed the task of leading the animal kingdom towards liberation—a liberation into the fourth kingdom, for that is the sphere of its next activity. The vegetable kingdom is liberated into another evolutionary process altogether, and its lives pass into the so-called deva, or angel, evolution. Hence the wind and the insect world are its agents, just as man and the agency of water are the initiators of the animal world. The secret of release for the animal nature is hidden in the "watery nature;" this is the blood aspect, and in the shedding of the blood, esoterically understood, lies the clue to the liberation of the animal kingdom. Hence certain initiatory processes are working out on a large scale in the shedding of blood through the slaughter of the animal form of the human being in the Great War, for instance. In the war the blood of thousands was poured out upon the soil, and from the standpoint of living purpose, certain esoteric results have been achieved. This fact is a difficult one for man to understand, for his awareness is as yet primarily that of the form and not of the quality of the life. It is difficult for men to comprehend the divine purpose working out behind the evils of animal slaughter and the shedding of blood down the ages, pre-human and human. But through the "pouring out of that water which is of the colour red" there is eventuating a liberation which will initiate the life of that kingdom into new states of consciousness and of awareness. The whole problem of slaughter, whether in the animal or the human kingdom, originated in events which occurred during the original "war in heaven," when Michael and his angels were cast down and our planetary system came into being. Until a man's consciousness is such that he can, through an inner mechanism as yet unevolved in the majority, respond to the planetary consciousness and "enter into the secrets of the Ancient of Days," the problem of pain, of bloodshed, of war and of suffering must remain an inscrutable mystery. It will be solved—and this is the keynote of most importance— only when man has himself changed the initiating process for the animals from that of bloodshed to that of domesticity and of mutual love. When the mentality of the race is more developed, then man can, by arbitration and the right use of speech, settle all differences, and thus change the mode of animal initiation, whether this refers to the animal kingdom or to his own animal body.

In the *fourth kingdom* the emerging quality is that aspect of synthetic love or understanding which is the intuition. This intuition is a quality of mental matter and of the "chitta" or mind stuff. Man is also intended to be radio-active; the incense or the perfume of his life must ascend, and thus attract the attention of the initiating factors which wait to lead him to liberation. These factors are the fire and the members of the fifth kingdom in nature. The growing purpose of his animal form must give place to the dynamic will of the spiritual entity, released from form limitations by the fire of life and of initiation. Thus he harmonises in himself all ways of approach and of release, and all achievements, and synthesises in his life the aspirations of the other three kingdoms.

Radio-activity, the perfume of the aspirant, the devotion to other human beings (the sublimation of domesticity), and the "shedding of blood" or the sacrifice of the life, the expression upon earth (the mineral kingdom) of the devotion and sex life of the vegetable kingdom, plus the sacrifice through blood of the animal kingdom, bring man to the portal of initiation. There the fire awaits him with its purifying uses, and thus earth, air, fire and water (the four elements) prepare him for the great liberation and for the release of that quality of synthetic apprehension of the underlying truth which we call the intuition. This is after all the response of the mechanism to the symbolic appeal of divine quality, expressed in the whole and seen as illumination. Thus the qualities emerge and appear in their full glory as man develops himself and unfolds within himself the needed apparatus of response, training himself to recognise the subjective realities or the divine qualities as they seek to manifest. The processes of manifestation produce results upon and in the gradually awakening consciousness of man.

5. *Analysis of the Rays and Their Expression, from an Earlier Manuscript.*

THERE is a vast fund of interesting knowledge as to the action and results of the ray activity in the lower kingdoms of nature, but on this point no details can be given; and

The Creative Builders

the following summary of what we have been told is necessarily imperfect and admits of endless amplification.

First Ray of Will or Power

Special Virtues:

Strength, courage, steadfastness, truthfulness arising from absolute fearlessness, power of ruling, capacity to grasp great questions in a large-minded way, and of handling men and measures.

Vices of Ray:

Pride, ambition, wilfulness, hardness, arrogance, desire to control others, obstinacy, anger.

Virtues to be acquired:

Tenderness, humility, sympathy, tolerance, patience.

This has been spoken of as the ray of power, and is correctly so called, but if it were power alone, without wisdom and love, a destructive and disintegrating force would result. When however the three characteristics are united, it becomes a creative and governing ray. Those on this ray have strong will power, for either good or evil, for the former when the will is directed by wisdom and made selfless by love. The first ray man will always "come to the front" in his own line. He may be the burglar or the judge who condemns him, but in either case he will be at the head of his profession. He is the born leader in any and every public career, one to trust and lean on, one to defend the weak and put down oppression, fearless of consequences and utterly indifferent to comment. On the other hand, an unmodified first ray can produce a man of unrelenting cruelty and hardness of nature.

The first ray man often has strong feeling and affection,

but he does not readily express it; he will love strong contrasts and masses of colour, but will rarely be an artist; he will delight in great orchestral effects and crashing choruses, and if modified by the fourth, sixth or seventh rays, may be a great composer, but not otherwise; and there is a type of this ray which is tone-deaf, and another which is colour-blind to the more delicate colours. Such a man will distinguish red and yellow, but will hopelessly confuse blue, green and violet.

The literary work of a first ray man will be strong and trenchant, but he will care little for style or finish in his writings. Perhaps examples of this type would be Luther, Carlyle, and Walt Whitman. It is said that in attempting the cure of disease the best method for the first ray man would be to draw health and strength from the great fount of universal life by his will power, and then pour it through the patient. This, of course, presupposes knowledge on his part of occult methods.

The characteristic method of approaching the great Quest on this ray would be by sheer force of will. Such a man would, as it were, take the kingdom of heaven "by violence." We have seen that the born leader belongs to this ray, wholly or in part. It makes the able commander-in-chief, such as Napoleon or Kitchener. Napoleon was first and fourth rays, and Kitchener was first and seventh, the seventh ray giving him his remarkable power of organisation.

The Second Ray of Love-Wisdom

Special Virtues:

Calm, strength, patience and endurance, love of truth, faithfulness, intuition, clear intelligence, and serene temper.

Vices of Ray:

Over-absorption in study, coldness, indifference to others, contempt of mental limitations in others.

Virtues to be acquired:

Love, compassion, unselfishness, energy.

This is called the ray of wisdom from its characteristic desire for pure knowledge and for absolute truth—cold and selfish, if without love, and inactive without power. When both power and love are present, then you have the ray of the Buddhas and of all great teachers of humanity,—those who, having attained wisdom for the sake of others, spend themselves in giving it forth. The student on this ray is ever unsatisfied with his highest attainments; no matter how great his knowledge, his mind is still fixed on the unknown, the beyond, and on the heights as yet unscaled.

The second ray man will have tact and foresight; he will make an excellent ambassador, and a first-rate teacher or head of a college; as a man of affairs, he will have clear intelligence and wisdom in dealing with matters which come before him, and he will have the capacity of impressing true views of things on others and of making them see things as he does. He will make a good business man, if modified by the fourth, fifth and seventh rays. The soldier on this ray would plan wisely and foresee possibilities; he would have an intuition as to the best course to pursue, and he would never lead his men into danger through rashness. He might be deficient in rapidity of action and energy. The artist on this ray would always seek to teach through his art, and his pictures would have a meaning. His literary work would always be instructive.

The method of healing, for the second ray man, would be to learn thoroughly the temperament of the patient as well as to be thoroughly conversant with the nature of the disease, so as to use his will power on the case to the best advantage.

The characteristic method of approaching the Path would be by close and earnest study of the teachings till they become so much a part of the man's consciousness as no longer to be merely intellectual knowledge, but a spiritual rule of living, thus bringing in intuition and true wisdom.

A bad type of the second ray would be bent on acquiring knowledge for himself alone, absolutely indifferent to the human needs of others. The foresight of such a man would degenerate into suspicion, his calmness into coldness and hardness of nature.

The Third Ray of Higher Mind

Special Virtues:

Wide views on all abstract questions, sincerity of purpose, clear intellect, capacity for concentration on philosophic studies, patience, caution, absence of the tendency to worry himself or others over trifles.

Vices of Ray:

Intellectual pride, coldness, isolation, inaccuracy in details, absent-mindedness, obstinacy, selfishness, overmuch criticism of others.

Virtues to be acquired:

Sympathy, tolerance, devotion, accuracy, energy and common-sense.

This is the ray of the abstract thinker, of the philosopher and the metaphysician, of the man who delights in the higher mathematics but who, unless modified by some practical ray, would hardly be troubled to keep his accounts accurately. His imaginative faculty will be highly developed, i.e., he can by the power of his imagination grasp the essence of a truth; his idealism will often be strong; he is a dreamer and a theorist, and from his wide views and great caution he sees every side

The Creative Builders

of a question equally clearly. This sometimes paralyses his action. He will make a good business man; as a soldier he will work out a problem in tactics at his desk, but is seldom great in the field. As an artist his technique is not fine, but his subjects will be full of thought and interest. He will love music, but unless influenced by the fourth ray he will not produce it. In all walks of life he is full of ideas, but is too impractical to carry them out.

One type of this ray is unconventional to a degree, slovenly, unpunctual and idle, and regardless of appearances. If influenced by the fifth ray as the secondary ray this character is, entirely changed. The third and the fifth rays make the perfectly balanced historian who grasps his subject in a large way and verifies every detail with patient accuracy. Again the third and the fifth rays together make the truly great mathematician who soars into heights of abstract thought and calculation, and who can also bring his results down to practical scientific use. The literary style of the third ray man is too often vague and involved, but if influenced by the first, fourth, fifth or seventh rays, this is changed, and under the fifth he will be a master of the pen.

The curing of disease by the third ray man would be by the use of drugs made of herbs or minerals belonging to the same ray as the patient whom he desires to relieve.

The method of approaching the great Quest, for this ray type, is by deep thinking on philosophic or metaphysical lines till he is led to the realisation of the great Beyond and of the paramount importance of treading the Path that leads thither.

THE FOURTH RAY OF HARMONY THROUGH CONFLICT

Special Virtues:

Strong affections, sympathy, physical courage, generosity, devotion, quickness of intellect and perception.

Vices of Ray:

Self-centredness, worrying, inaccuracy, lack of moral courage, strong passions, indolence, extravagance.

Virtues to be acquired:

Serenity, confidence, self-control, purity, unselfishness, accuracy, mental and moral balance.

This has been called the "ray of struggle" for on this ray the qualities of rajas (activity) and tamas (inertia) are so strangely equal in proportion that the nature of the fourth ray man is torn with their combat, and the outcome, when satisfactory, is spoken of as the "Birth of Horus," of the Christ, born from the throes of constant pain and suffering.

Tamas induces love of ease and pleasure, a hatred of causing pain amounting to moral cowardice, indolence, procrastination, a desire to let things be, to rest, and to take no thought of the morrow. Rajas is fiery, impatient, ever urging to action. These contrasting forces in the nature make life one perpetual warfare and unrest for the fourth ray man; the friction and the experience gained thereby may produce very rapid evolution, but the man may as easily become a ne'er-do-well as a hero.

It is the ray of the dashing cavalry leader, reckless of risks to himself or his followers. It is the ray of the man who will lead a forlorn hope, for in moments of excitement the fourth ray man is entirely dominated by rajas; of the wild speculator and gambler, full of enthusiasm and plans, easily overwhelmed by sorrow or failure, but as quickly recovering from all reverses and misfortunes.

It is pre-eminently the ray of colour, of the artist whose colour is always great, though his drawing will often be defective. (Watts was fourth and second rays.) The fourth ray man always loves colour, and can generally produce it. If untrained as an artist, a colour sense is sure to appear in other ways, in choice of dress or decorations.

In music, fourth ray compositions are always full of melody, and the fourth ray man loves a tune. As a writer or poet, his work will often be brilliant and full of picturesque word-painting, but inaccurate, full of exaggerations, and often pessimistic. He will generally talk well and have a sense of humour, but he varies between brilliant conversations and gloomy silences, according to his mood. He is a delightful and difficult person to live with.

In healing, the best fourth ray method is massage and magnetism, used with knowledge.

The method of approaching the Path will be by self-control, thus gaining equilibrium amongst the warring forces of the nature. The lower and extremely dangerous way is by Hatha Yoga.

THE FIFTH RAY OF LOWER MIND

Special Virtues:

Strictly accurate statements, justice (without mercy), perseverance, common-sense, uprightness, independence, keen intellect.

Vices of Ray:

Harsh criticism, narrowness, arrogance, unforgiving temper, lack of sympathy and reverence, prejudice.

Virtues to be acquired:

Reverence, devotion, sympathy, love, wide-mindedness.

This is the ray of science and of research. The man on this ray will possess keen intellect, great accuracy in detail, and will make unwearied efforts to trace the smallest fact to its source, and to verify every theory. He will generally be extremely truthful, full of lucid explanation of facts, though sometimes pedantic and wearisome from his insistence on trivial and unnecessary verbal minutiae. He will be orderly, punctual, business-like, disliking to receive favours or flattery.

It is the ray of the great chemist, the practical electrician, the first-rate engineer, the great operating surgeon. As a statesman, the fifth ray man would be narrow in his views, but he would be an excellent head of some special technical department, though a disagreeable person under whom to work. As a soldier, he would turn most readily to artillery and engineering. The artist on this ray is very rare, unless the fourth or seventh be the influencing secondary rays; even then, his colouring will be dull, his sculptures lifeless, and his music (if he composes) will be uninteresting, though technically correct in form. His style in writing or speaking will be clearness itself, but it will lack fire and point, and he will often be long-winded, from his desire to say all that can possibly be said on his subject.

In healing, he is the perfect surgeon, and his best cures will be through surgery and electricity.

For the fifth ray, the method of approaching the Path is by scientific research, pushed to ultimate conclusions, and by the acceptance of the inferences which follow these.

The Sixth Ray of Devotion

Special Virtues:

Devotion, single-mindedness, love, tenderness, intuition, loyalty, reverence.

Vices of Ray:

Selfish and jealous love, over-leaning on others, partiality, self-deception, sectarianism, superstition, prejudice, over-rapid conclusions, fiery anger.

Virtues to be acquired:

Strength, self-sacrifice, purity, truth, tolerance, serenity, balance and common sense.

This is called the ray of devotion. The man who is on this ray is full of religious instincts and impulses, and of intense personal feeling; nothing is taken equably. Everything, in his eyes, is either perfect or intolerable; his friends are angels, his enemies are very much the reverse; his view, in both cases, is formed not on the intrinsic merits of either class, but on the way the persons appeal to him, or on the sympathy or lack of sympathy which they shew to his favourite idols, whether these be concrete or abstract, for he is full of devotion, it may be to a person, or it may be to a cause.

He must always have a "personal God," an incarnation of Deity to adore. The best type of this ray makes the saint, the worst type, the bigot or fanatic, the typical martyr or the typical inquisitor. All religious wars or crusades have originated from sixth ray fanaticism. The man on this ray is often of gentle nature, but he can always flame into fury and fiery wrath. He will lay down his life for the objects of his devotion or reverence, but he will not lift a finger to help those outside of his immediate sympathies. As a soldier, he hates fighting but often when roused in battle fights like one possessed. He is never a great statesman nor a good business man, but he may be a great preacher or orator.

The sixth ray man will be the poet of the emotions (such as Tennyson) and the writer of religious books, either in poetry or prose. He is devoted to beauty and colour and all things lovely, but his productive skill is not great unless under the influence of one of the practically artistic rays, the fourth or seventh. His music will always be of a melodious order, and he will often be the composer of oratorios and of sacred music.

The method of healing for this ray would be by faith and prayer.

The way of approaching the Path would be by prayer and meditation, aiming at union with God.

THE SEVENTH RAY OF CEREMONIAL ORDER OR MAGIC

Special Virtues:

Strength, perseverance, courage, courtesy, extreme care in details, self-reliance.

Vices of Ray:

Formalism, bigotry, pride, narrowness, superficial judgments, self-opinion over-indulged.

Virtues to be acquired:

Realisation of unity, wide-mindedness, tolerance, humility, gentleness and love.

This is the ceremonial ray, the ray which makes a man delight in "all things done decently and in order," and according to rule and precedent. It is the ray of the high priest and the court chamberlain, of the soldier who is a born genius in organisation, of the ideal commissary general who will dress and feed the troops in the best possible way. It is the ray of the perfect nurse for the sick, careful in the smallest detail, though sometimes too much inclined to disregard the patients' idiosyncrasies and to try and grind them in the iron mill of routine.

It is the ray of form, of the perfect sculptor, who sees and produces ideal beauty, of the designer of beautiful forms and patterns of any sort; but such a man would not be successful as a painter unless his influencing ray were the fourth. The combination of four with seven would make the very highest type of artist, form and colour being both *in excelsis*. The literary work of the seventh ray man would be remarkable for its ultra-polished style, and such a writer would think far more of the manner than of the matter in his work, but would always be fluent both in writing and speech. The seventh ray man will often be sectarian. He will delight in fixed ceremonials and observances, in great processions and shows, in reviews of troops and warships, in genealogical trees, and in rules of precedence.

The bad type of seventh ray man is superstitious, and such a man will take deep interest in omens, in dreams, in all occult practices, and in spiritualistic phenomena. The good type of the ray is absolutely determined to do the right thing and say the right word at the right moment; hence great social success.

In healing, the seventh ray man would rely on extreme exactness in carrying out orthodox treatment of disease. On him the practices of yoga would have no physical bad results.

He will approach the Path through observance of rules of practice and of ritual, and can easily evoke and control the elemental forces.

From many of the above remarks it may have been inferred that the characteristics of any given ray find closer correspondence with one of the other rays than with the rest. This is a fact. The only one which stands alone and has no close relationship with any of the others is the fourth. This brings to mind the unique position which the number four occupies in the evolutionary process. We have the fourth root race, the fourth planetary chain, the fourth planet in the chain, the fourth planetary manvantara, etc.

Between the third and the fifth rays there is a close relationship. In the search after knowledge, for example, the most laborious and minute study of detail is the path that will be followed, whether in philosophy, the higher mathematics or in the pursuit of practical science.

The correspondence between the second and the sixth rays shews itself in the intuitive grasp of synthesised knowledge, and in the common bond of faithfulness and loyalty.

Masterfulness, steadfastness, and perseverance are the corresponding characteristics of the first and the seventh rays.

II. *The Rays and the Kingdoms in Nature.*

　　Introductory Remarks.
1. The Mineral Kingdom.
2. The Vegetable Kingdom.
3. The Animal Kingdom.

CHAPTER II

The Rays and the Kingdoms in Nature

Introductory Remarks

IN STARTING upon a consideration of the relation of the rays to the seven kingdoms I shall refer to the seven kingdoms on the upward or evolutionary arc, and not to the seven kingdoms as they can be enumerated on the involutionary or downward arc. This latter (according to the Theosophical literature) includes three kingdoms—nebulous, relatively formless, and unexpressed—and the four kingdoms as enumerated by modern science. With the involutionary arc we have nothing to do. The understanding of it is well nigh impossible to the finite mind of the average reader. Though these three involutionary kingdoms exist, and though the little known about them in the West has received written form, any real comprehension of the implied truths is entirely lacking. This is quite unavoidable. Their comprehension lies hid in the capacity to "recover" the past and to see that past as a whole.

The kingdoms which we shall consider in connection with the rays may be enumerated under the following terms:

1. The Mineral Kingdom	VII
2. The Vegetable Kingdom	VI
3. The Animal Kingdom	V
4. The Kingdom of Men	IV
5. The Kingdom of Souls	III
6. The Kingdom of Planetary Lives	II
7. The Kingdom of Solar Lives	I

These kingdoms might be regarded as differentiations of the One Life, from the angle of:

1. Phenomenal appearance, objective manifestation, or the externalisation of the solar Logos.
2. Consciousness or sensitivity to the expression of quality, through the medium of the phenomenal appearance.

Certain of the rays, as might be expected, are more responsible than certain others for the qualifying of any particular kingdom. Their effect is paramount in its determination. The effect of the other rays is subsidiary, but not absent. We must never forget that, in the close interrelation of forces in our solar system, no one of the seven possible forces is without effect. All of them function, qualify and motivate, but one or other will have a more vital effect than the rest. The following tabulation will give the major effect of the seven rays and the result of their influence upon the seven kingdoms with which we are concerned:

No.	Kingdom	Ray		Expression
1.	Mineral	VII.	Ceremonial Organisation	Radio-Activity.
		I	Will or Power	The basic Reservoir of Power.
2.	Vegetable	II.	Love-Wisdom	Magnetism.
		IV.	Beauty or Harmony	Uniformity of Colour.
		VI.	Idealistic Devotion	Upward Tendency.
3.	Animal	III.	Adaptability	Instinct.
		VI.	Devotion	Domesticity.
4.	Human	IV.	Harmony through Conflict	Experience. Growth.
		V.	Concrete Knowledge	Intellect.

5. Egoic or Souls	V.	Concrete Knowledge .. Personality.
	II.	Love-Wisdom .... Intuition.
6. Planetary Lives	VI.	Devotion to Ideas .... The Plan.
	III.	Active Intelligence ... Creative Work.
7. Solar Lives	I.	Will or Power .... Universal Mind.
	VII.	Ceremonial Magic .... Synthetic Ritual.

You will note one interesting difference in this tabulation, and that is the fact that the vegetable kingdom is the expression of three rays, whereas the others are expressions of two. Through these three the vegetable kingdom has been brought to its present condition of supreme beauty and its developed symbolism of colour. The vegetable kingdom is the outstanding contribution of our Earth to the general solar plan. Each of the planets contributes a unique and specialised quota to the sum total of evolutionary products, and the unique production of our particular planetary system is the vegetable kingdom. Other planets contribute forms and appearances which are their specific offering. It is needless for me to enumerate them here, for our language has no equivalent terms, and where there is no equivalent in language there is for mankind no equivalent in consciousness. The Earth, then, contributes the vegetable kingdom, and this is possible because it is the only kingdom in which three rays have finally succeeded in coalescing, in fusing and blending; they are also the three rays along a major line of forces, 2-4-6. When we come to a more detailed analysis of the rays and their effects on a kingdom in nature, we shall see why this has produced so unique a contribution. Its success is demonstrated in the uniformity of its production of green in the realm of colour, throughout the entire planet.

You will note also that the mineral kingdom and the

kingdom of solar lives (the first and seventh kingdoms) are the result of the activity of the first and the seventh rays. There is a close numerological interlocking here. These two kingdoms are respectively at the point of the greatest tenuity and the greatest density, and are produced by the will and the organising ability of the solar Deity. They embody the nebulous plan and the concretised plan. In the case of the seventh or highest kingdom (counting from below upwards) the Will aspect predominates and is the most powerful, whilst in the case of the mineral kingdom, the organisation aspect is of the most importance. This was to be anticipated, for the energy of Will is the first effect of the initiating divine activity, whilst the densest aspect of ceremonial organisation is the counterpart of the initial impulse, its concretisation, if I might so express it. The other kingdoms in nature, as can be seen in our tabulation, are not so related.

It will be of value if we now analyse our tabulation with a measure of care and get a little clearer grasp of the effect and influence of the seven rays.

As long as the true nature of the atom and its internal organisation remains a matter of investigation and of speculation and theory, the reader should regard what I here have to say in connection with this densest of all kingdoms as symbolically and pictorially true, but not to be taken literally. Just as the centre at the base of the spine is the last one to be aroused into full functioning activity, and is thus aroused only when the head centre is awakened and alive, so this lowest of all the kingdoms will be rightly understood only when all the seven kingdoms vibrate in unison. Until such time as this occurs, this kingdom and its life will remain an enigma, except to the initiate of high degree. All I can do is to make such suggestions as will arouse the abstract mind to activity and awaken interest to such a degree that the work of analysis and study will proceed. Conclusions cannot be reached, however, and this must be realised.

Two rays are of prime importance in the Life of God as It pours through this basic substance of our planet. In the work of the seventh ray, we have earthy substance, the solid material of our planetary life, organised into the varying mineral forms. These mineral forms, in their turn, hold latent those sustaining and vitalising elements from which other forms draw their sustenance. It must be remembered that each kingdom in nature is dependent upon and draws life from the kingdom which precedes it in the time sense, during the evolutionary cycle. Each Kingdom is a reservoir of power and of vitality to the next kingdom which emerges under the divine Plan.

The vegetable kingdom, for instance, draws its vital strength from three sources,—the sun, the water and the earth. In the building process it is the mineral content from the two latter sources that is of prime importance. The true structure of all forms is produced by the fabric of mineral products which is gradually built upon the etheric body, and which takes shape and form under a vital etheric urge, desire or impulse. It is the magnetic quality of the etheric body which attracts to itself the minerals needed for this skeleton form.

The animal kingdom, in turn, draws its sustenance primarily from the sun, the water and the vegetable kingdom. The mineral content required for the skeleton structure is therefore offered in a more advanced and sublimated form, being gathered out of the offering of the vegetable kingdom instead of out of that of the mineral kingdom. Each kingdom offers sacrifice to the next succeeding kingdom in the evolutionary sequence. The Law of Sacrifice determines the nature of each kingdom. Therefore each kingdom may be regarded as a laboratory wherein are prepared those forms of nutriment which are needed for the building of ever more refined structures. The human kingdom follows the same procedure, and draws its life (from the form angle) out of the animal kingdom as well as from the sun, water and the vegetable world. In the early stages of human unfoldment, animal food was, therefore, both karmically and in essence, the correct food for man; and for unevolved men, and from the standpoint of the animal form, such food is still right and proper. This brings up the whole question of vegetarianism, and I shall deal with it when we come to consider the fourth kingdom. The situation is not at all what is often thought, or as presented by the thinkers of today, and meat eating—at a certain stage of human unfoldment—incurs no evil doing.

Out of the great experimental school of human existence the kingdom of souls draws sustenance and vitality, and in the interlocking and interrelation of these four divine organisms does the world of form live and move and have its being. There are certain parallels in the human organism and certain correspondences which are of interest, and they may be presented in the following manner:

The human kingdom	Brain . . . . Vocal organs.	The two head centres.
The animal kingdom	Stomach . . . . . . Liver.	The solar plexus.
The vegetable kingdom . .	Heart . . . . Lungs	The heart centre. The throat centre.
The mineral kingdom	Generative . organs	The sacral centre. The base of spine.

The relation of the seven centres to the various kingdoms in nature can be here seen, and the symbolism of the human form can be noted. The seven kingdoms as a whole can also be seen as having the following relations:

1. Mineral kingdom . . . . base of spine . . . . Adrenals.
2. Vegetable kingdom . . . . . . heart centre . . . . Thymus.
3. Animal kingdom . . . . solar plexus . . . . Pancreas.
4. Human kingdom . . . . sacral centre . . . . Gonads.
5. Egoic kingdom . . . . throat centre . . . . Thyroid.
6. Planetary kingdom . . . . ajna centre . . . . Pituitary.
7. Solar kingdom . . . . head centre . . . . Pineal.

A study of these correspondences will be of value if the student will remember that these are the correspondences studied at the first initiation. They differ at the later expansions of consciousness.

The influence of the organising seventh ray is best seen in the amazing and geometrically perfect structure of the elements, as revealed by the microscope and by a study of the atom. As this treatise is intended for the reader who has no academic or scientific training, it will suffice to say that the mineral kingdom is a result of the "ritual of rhythm," as are all the basic forms upon which the myriad of structures in manifestation are constructed and founded. The system of numbers demonstrates in its fullest beauty in this kingdom, and there is no form and no numerological relation which cannot be discovered in minute form in this foundational kingdom, under the occult microscopic vision. Two factors determine the structures found in the mineral kingdom:

1. The seventh great impulse, or the will to organise.
2. The urge to create, or the initial rhythm which led the solar Logos to take form.

The work of the seventh Lord and of the first Lord is essentially the work of the architect and of the magician, and Their efforts are seen to perfection in the mineral world. This will not, however, be realised in full potency and magical revelation until the inner eye of true vision is developed and the forms underlying the creative work in the other kingdoms in nature are seen in their real values. The secrets of transmutation are the true secrets of this particular kingdom, and the two words expressing the process and the secret are condensation and transmutation. Each kingdom has its key words, which can be translated, though most inadequately, as follows:

Kingdom	Process	Secret	Objective
1. Mineral	Condensation	Transmutation	Radiation.
2. Vegetable	Conformation	Transformation	Magnetisation.
3. Animal	Concretisation	Transfusion	Experimentation.
4. Human	Adaptation	Translation	Transfiguration.
5. Egoic	Externalisation	Manifestation	Realisation.

A general picture of the creative intent emerges as one considers the significance of these words. The objectives and processes of the two highest kingdoms are too advanced for the average student to grasp, and constitute likewise two of the secrets of the higher initiation.

As this treatise is intended to be a practical attempt to elucidate the new psychology, and as its objective is to increase man's understanding of himself, it is not my intention to do more than convey a few ideas anent the rays and their relation to the three subhuman kingdoms in nature. In all esoteric writings it is necessary to show the synthesis and the continuity of the whole process of evolution, for only as man appreciates his position, midway between the higher three kingdoms and the lower three, will the true significance of the contribution of the fourth kingdom to the entire scheme of evolution appear. I have given several tabulations of correspondences and of the ray influences, and these warrant careful study. It is, for instance, apparent that if the seventh ray is now coming into power, and if its effect upon the lower kingdoms is beginning to be felt, then humanity must be prepared for such changes as are inevitable.

Left alone and unaided, man would eventually discover

for himself the designated events; but it would take much time and only in retrospect would the broad general outlines of the evolutionary process emerge from the mass of detail in which they are lost in the immediate present and foreground. By a willingness to study the truths that are sent out, from time to time, from the occult centres of the world, and through a readiness to act on suggested hypothesis will man increase his capacity to see life whole, and be able therefore to cooperate (with power and intelligence) in the working out of the Plan.

I dealt above with the Process, the Secret and the Purpose. For right understanding I shall now give you a synopsis of the information, concerning each kingdom, as it comes under consideration.

1. *The Mineral Kingdom*

Influence	The seventh ray of organisation and the first ray of power are the dominant factors.
Results	The evolutionary results are radiation and potency, a static potency, underlying the rest of the natural scheme.
Process	Condensation.
Secret	Transmutation. *A Treatise on Cosmic Fire* defines this as follows: "Transmutation is the passage from one state of being to another through the agency of fire."
Purpose	To demonstrate the radio-activity of life.
Divisions	Base metals, standard metals, precious stones.
Objective agency . . .	Fire. Fire is the initiating factor in this kingdom.
Subjective agency . .	Sound.
Quality	Extreme density. Inertia. Brilliance.

Students must remember that we are not dealing with the elements and atoms, as we study this kingdom. They are the substance out of which all the mineral forms are made. But we are dealing with the mineral forms as they manifest in the concrete world. We are considering the tangible and objective world. The internal constitution and geometrical formation of the minerals do not come under our subject matter. This is not a scientific treatise, as usually understood, but a study in quality and consciousness as they affect the form aspect. Much, if not nearly all that exoteric science has posited regarding the mineral kingdom can, for ordinary uses, be accepted as relative fact. But two points should be considered, and they are:

1. The consciousness aspect of the mineral world.
2. The transmutation of forms by fire in that kingdom, leading to an ultimate radiation.

The best known example of the effect of the initiation of the mineral by fire can be seen in the great transition and transformation, allotropically brought about, from the carbon stage to that of the perfect diamond. A further qualitative stage can be seen as the radiation or the throwing off of rays, as in radium.

That there are three stages in the evolutionary processes in the mineral kingdom must be borne in mind, and these (though apparently unrelated to each other from the angle of modern science) are nevertheless subjectively and essentially part of a tremendous inner process. These stages are the correspondences in the mineral kingdom to the stages of animal consciousness, of self-consciousness, and of the radiant group consciousness of the soul. There is a fourth stage of potency or of organised expressed power, but this lies ahead, and is the analogy in this kingdom to the life of the Monad, as expressed in the solar consciousness of the initiates of high degree.

The Kingdoms in Nature

Just as science has discovered the ninety-two elements so that the list of the possible elements is relatively complete, so eventually science will have arranged the progressive tables which will show the three stages of the life cycle of every mineral leading from the static mineral stage, such as carbon, through that of the crystal, semi-precious stone and precious stone to that of the radio-active substance. In the determining of this development it is impossible for man as yet to see the relations, for the cycles covered are so vast, the action of the fire in these tremendous periods so varying, and the recognition of the intermediate stages so difficult, that aught that I could say would but feed amusement and incredulity. But two basic premises can be laid down:

1. That the many mineral substances fall naturally into seven main groups, corresponding to the seven subdivisions of the influencing rays, those of organisation and power.

2. That only in those world cycles when the seventh ray is in manifestation, and therefore supremely powerful, do certain hidden changes take place in these seven groups. These are the correspondences, in the mineral evolution, to the seven initiations of man.

At these times there is an increased radiatory activity. This can be noted at this time in the discovery of radio-active substance, as the incoming ray increases its potency, decade by decade. A certain amount of radiation is basic and fundamental in any world cycle. But when the seventh ray comes in there is an intensification of that radiation, and new substances appear to come into new activity. This intensification leaves the entire mineral kingdom, as a whole, more radio-active than before, until this increased radiation becomes in its turn basic and fundamental. As the seventh ray passes cyclically out of manifestation a certain measure of inertia settles down on the kingdom, though that which is radiatory continues its activity. In this way the radiation of the mineral world steadily increases as the cycles come and go, and there is necessarily a paralleling effect upon the higher three kingdoms. People today have no idea what effect this radiation (due to the incoming ray) will have, not only upon the surrounding mineral world but on the vegetable kingdom (which has its roots in the mineral kingdom), and upon men and animals in lesser degree. The power of the incoming cosmic rays has called forth the more easily recognised radio-activity with which modern science is now concerned. It was three seventh ray disciples who "interpreted" these rays to man. I refer to the Curies and to Millikan. Being themselves on the seventh ray, they had the necessary psychic equipment and responsiveness to enable them intuitively to recognise their own ray vibration in the mineral kingdom.

The seventh ray is one of organised ritual, and in form building this quality is basic and necessary. The processes found in the mineral kingdom are profoundly geometrical. The first ray is that of dynamic will or power, and—speaking symbolically—when perfected forms and organised vehicles and dynamic power are related and unified, then we shall have a full expression, at the point of deepest and densest concretion, of the mind of God in form, with a radiation which will be dynamically effective.

Again speaking symbolically (and what else is possible when dealing with a mechanism as yet so inadequate as the mind and brain of the average aspirant?), the mineral kingdom marks the point of unique condensation. This is produced under the action of fire and by the pressure of the "divine idea". Esoterically speaking, we have, in the mineral world, the divine

Plan hidden in the geometry of a crystal, and God's radiant beauty stored in the colour of a precious stone. In miniature and at the lowest point of manifestation, we find the divine concepts working out. The goal of the universal concept is seen when the jewel rays forth its beauty, and when radium sends forth its rays, both destructive and constructive. If you could really understand the history of a crystal, you would enter into the glory of God. If you could enter into the attractive and the repulsive consciousness of a piece of iron or lead, you would see revealed the complete story of evolution. If you could study the hidden processes which go on under the influence of fire, you would enter into the secret of initiation. When the day comes when the history of the mineral kingdom can be grasped by the illumined seer, he will then see the long road that the diamond has travelled, and—by analogy—the long road that all sons of God traverse, governed by the same laws and unfolding the same consciousness.

The seventh ray, when manifesting on the seventh plane (as is now the case), is peculiarly potent, and its effect upon the mineral kingdom is consequently dynamically felt. If it is true that there is only one substance and one spirit, that "matter is spirit at the lowest point of its cyclic activity" and spirit is matter at its highest, then the ray of ceremonial order or ritual is but an expression of its polar opposite,—the first ray of will or power. It is the expression of the same potency under another aspect. This means therefore that:

1. The power or will of God expresses itself through the organised systematised processes of the seventh ray. The geometrical faculty of the Universal Mind finds its most material perfection on the physical or seventh plane, working through the seventh ray. So the mineral kingdom came into being as this major expression. It holds in solu-

tion all the forces and those chemicals and minerals which are needed by the forms in the other material kingdoms.
2. The mineral kingdom is therefore the most concrete expression of the dual unity of power and order. It constitutes the "foundation" of the ordered physical structure or the universe of our planet.
3. The rhythmic ritualistic adaptability of the seventh ray, plus the dynamic will of the power ray, are needed in conjunction for the full working out of the Plan, as it is found in the mind of God.

This is why, in this present period of transition, the Lord of the seventh ray is taking over the control of affairs and the ordered working out of the Plan, so as eventually to restore stability to the planet and give the incoming Aquarian influences a stable and extended field in which to work. This we shall later elaborate when we take up the study of the zodiacal signs and their relation to the rays.

We shall now touch upon the next two points,—condensation and its hidden secret, transmutation. From the standpoint of external matter, the mineral kingdom marks the densest expression of the life of God in substance, and its outstanding, though oft unrealised, characteristic is imprisoned or unexpressed power. Speaking in symbols, a volcano in eruption is a mild expression of this power. From the standpoint of esoteric substance, the four ethers are far more dense and "substantial". This modern science has also told us, positing the hypothetical ether. This fifth kingdom (counting occultly from the egoic kingdom downwards) is a reflection of these four ethers, and the point of their densest concretion. Just as they "substand" or form the basis of the manifested world, and are regarded as the "true form," so the mineral kingdom is the fundamental kingdom in the three worlds, under the Law of Correspondences. It is, in a most peculiar sense, "precipitated etheric substance", and is a condensation or externalisation of the etheric planes. This solidification or precipitation—resulting in the production of dense objective or solid matter—is the tangible result of the interplay of the energies and qualities of the first and seventh rays. Their united will and ordered rhythm have produced this Earth and the molten content of the planet, regarding the earth as the crust.

In the turning of the great wheel, cycle after cycle, these two rays come into functioning activity, and in between their objective cycles the other rays dominate and participate in the great work. The result of this interplay of psychic potencies will manifest in the eventual transmutation of the earth substance, and its resolution back again into that of which it is the objective condensation. Again language fails to find the needed terms. They are as yet non-existent. I mention this as an indication of the difficulty of our subject. Intangible etheric substance has been condensed into the dense tangible objective world. This—under the evolutionary plan—has to be again transmuted into its original condition, plus the gain of ordered rhythm and the tendencies and qualities wrought into the consciousness of its atoms and elements through the experience of externalisation. This resolution is noted by us as radiation and the radio-active substances. We are looking on at the transmutation process. The resolving agencies are fire, intense heat and pressure. These three agencies have already succeeded in bringing about the divisions of the mineral kingdom into three parts: the baser metals, as they are called, the standard metals (such as silver and gold and platinum), and the semi-precious stones and crystals. The precious jewels are a synthesis of all three,—one of the basic syntheses of evolution. In this connection, some correspondences between the mineral kingdom and the human evolutionary cycles might here be noted:

1. The base metals . . . . physical plane. Dense Consciousness.
   The first initiation.
2. The standard metals . . . . . . astral plane. Self-consciousness.
   The second initiation.
3. The semi-precious stones . . mental plane. Radiant consciousness.
   The third initiation.
4. The precious jewels . . . . egoic consciousness and achievement.
   The fourth initiation.

The correspondences of fire, heat and pressure in the evolution of the human being are self-evident, and their work can be seen paralleling that in the mineral kingdom.

The mineral kingdom is governed astrologically by Taurus, and there is a symbolic relation between the "eye" in the head of the Bull, the third eye, the light in the head, and the diamond. The consciousness of the Buddha has been called the "diamond-eye."

We have been technical, and much has been given which seems to have no bearing upon the psychological development of man. But to understand the rays and their bearing on life as a whole, it is necessary that man should grasp the fact that he is only a small fraction of that whole. Man has his roots in all the three kingdoms; all have contributed to his equipment; he is the macrocosm of the lower microcosm; he is the link which unites the three lower kingdoms to the three higher. Let it ever be borne in mind that the sign of man's spiritual unfoldment lies in his ability to include in his consciousness not only the so-called spiritual values and the power to react to soul contact, but also to include the material values, and to react divinely to the potencies which lie hid-

The Kingdoms in Nature 231

den from him in the custody of the other forms of divine life, found in the three sub-human kingdoms.

In the urgency of the present world situation, it might be well to ask: What need is there to study the rays and kingdoms of nature? Of what profit is it to speculate on matters of which it is as yet impossible for the average student to apprehend the truth? Such questions are intelligent and worth while and merit an intelligent reply. I shall make answer by asking another question: What indication has the would-be server that his mental equipment makes him of any use in this present world crisis?

One of the first things that any teacher of the race has to do is to increase the mental equipment of the would-be server. The work is oft times handicapped by the devoted offering of the emotional aspirant. The Plan is oft-times delayed in its fruition by the ill-timed and ill-judged efforts of the earnest follower of the Great Lord. Above all else the work is handicapped by the personality reactions of the leaders of the groups dedicated to esotericism. All personality reactions are, in the majority of cases, based upon emotion of some kind or another. Personal ambition, the desire (sometimes unrecognised) to be the supreme authority in a particular group, fear of interlopers and of terminologies (expressing identical truths), and jealousy of other leaders, plus a sincere though foggy and deluded interpretation of truth, are a great detriment to the cause of the Hierarchy. And everywhere these things are to be seen! The seat of all this trouble is to be found in the desire-feeling-emotional body, and in an undue attachment to externals and forms. These factors prevent that clear-seeing which leads to wise and co-operative action. If the mental equipment and the mental apprehension of truth can be increased, then it may be possible for real work to be done, and then the groups (that form the

One Group) can go forward into real usefulness. To this end it may be profitable to provide material whereby the mental bodies of the students can grow, and wherein they can find sustenance and the means to develop. Few people can evolve from within themselves the thoughts and the ideas which should lead them on in the realisation of truth; and those of us therefore who are responsible for the teaching of the race must perforce provide that which is required. Also, in so doing we work for the coming generation of enquirers, knowing full well that the advanced teaching of today, and the new ideas which influence the pioneers of humanity, become the inspiration of the thinking public in the succeeding generation, and the theology, in due time, of that which follows them. The beliefs and knowledges of the esotericists today (of the real spiritual esotericists, not of the so-called esoteric groups) are resolved into the formulas of faith of their successors, and become eventually identified with religious beliefs and organisations.

Mental comprehension of the ray teaching, and the study of the rays in relation to evolving nature, are of mental importance and of spiritual import, but of no practical value in the living of the daily life, except in so far as they serve to shift the polarisation of the aspirant off the emotional plane on to the mental, and thereby produce alignment and stabilisation.

We now come to a consideration of the rays and of the vegetable kingdom. It is difficult for us to grasp the significance of the consciousness and the activity of the mineral kingdom, for it is so far removed from our own. It is hard for us really to understand, with our seeing consciousness, the fact that, for instance, our nails and teeth and bony structure have a consciousness and an intelligent awareness that is the same in kind, though differing in degree, as that of the eye or of a sensory nerve. But so it is. As we approach the forms of life which approximate the living tissue of our animal bodies,

The Kingdoms in Nature

our appreciation of resemblance and of identical possibilities increases step by step. It is only by arguing from analogy that we grasp esoteric truth, and it might bring us some illumination if we realised that there are higher forms of life and consciousness in the cosmos who find it as difficult to throw their consciousness down into the animal forms of humanity as we would find it hard to project ourselves into the consciousness of an iron ploughshare. But again, so it is.

Let us now tabulate some of the available ideas and information.

2. *The Vegetable Kingdom*

Influences . . . . The second Ray of Love-wisdom, working out in a vastly increased sensibility.

The fourth Ray of Harmony and Beauty, working out in the general harmonization of this kingdom throughout the entire planet.

The sixth Ray of Devotion or (as it has been expressed symbolically in the ancient wisdom) the "urge to consecrate the life to the Sun, the giver of that life," or again, the "urge to turn the eye of the heart to the heart of the sun."

Results . . . . These work out in the second kingdom as magnetism, perfume, colour and growth towards the light. These words I commend to you for your earnest study, for it is in this kingdom that one first sees clearly the glory which lies ahead of humanity:

    a. Magnetic radiation. The blending of the mineral and vegetable goals.
    b. The perfume of perfection.
    c. The glory of the human aura. The radiant augoeides.
    d. Aspiration which leads to final inspiration.

Process . . . . Conformation, or the power to "conform" to the pattern set in the heavens, and to produce below that which is found above. This is done in this kingdom with greater pliability than in the mineral kingdom, where the process of condensation goes blindly forward.

Secret . . . . Transformation. Those hidden alchemical processes which enable the vegetable growths in this kingdom to draw their sustenance from the sun and. soil, and to "transform" it into form and colour

Purpose . . . . Magnetism. That inner source of beauty, loveliness and attractive power which lures to it the higher forms of life, leading the animal forms to consume it for food, and the thinking entities to draw from it inspiration, comfort and satisfaction of a mental kind.

Divisions . . . . Trees and shrubs.
The flowering plants.
The grasses and the lesser green things which do not come under the other two categories. A group of vegetable growths which are found under the general heading of sea growths.

Objective agency . . . Water.

Subjective agency . . . Touch.

Quality . . . . Rajas or activity.

It is not my intention to give in this treatise what the reader can discover in the academic textbooks of our colleges. It is not my work to parallel the information found in the exoteric teachings and theologies of our modern sciences. I seek to indicate the synthesis which underlies the whole, and to point out the continuity of consciousness which can be noted by the esotericist. In so doing the part is seen to be integrated in the sum total, in a manner different to that which can be seen when considering the form. It is the world of causes with which we are primarily concerned, and even when we consider and study that which we include under the heading of "results", it is as they demonstrate as initiated causes that we best arrive at their significance. It is as we grasp the radiatory potency of the mineral kingdom that we can begin to investigate the base of the evolutionary ladder and grasp the first steps taken by the life of God, through the medium of manifested forms. If, at the close of this writing, the student can grasp somewhat the meaning of those symbolic words,—Radiation, Magnetism, Experiment, Transmutation and Realisation,—and can understand that they embody the purpose and goal of each of the five kingdoms in nature with which we are basically concerned, then the emerging reality of consciousness will be seen, and the prevailing synthesis will be grasped.

a. LIFE—RADIANCE—MAGNETISM

We are told in the *Yoga Sutras of Patanjali* that "By mastery of the binding life comes radiance," and in these words can be found the clue to the relation existing between the mineral and the human kingdoms. In other words, by the conscious control of the static mineral nature, as it expresses itself in man, comes his eventual radiatory activity. Thus "the spark becomes the flame." (Patanjali: III.40, *The Light of the Soul.*) It will be found that in the sutras much effective correlation can be made, particularly when considering any of the various quintuples found in manifestation with such frequency. This book is a basic treatise for initiatory training. Take, as an illustration of this, the words found in Book III.44, and note the illumination thrown upon the evolutionary cycle and on the symbolic development of the five kingdoms in nature:

> "One-pointed meditation upon the five forms which every element takes produces mastery over every element. These five forms are the gross nature, the elemental form, the quality, the pervasiveness and the basic purpose."

You have, therefore, an analogy for consideration:

1. The gross nature .... the mineral kingdom.
2. The elemental form .... the vegetable kingdom.
3. The quality .... the animal kingdom.
4. The pervasiveness .... the human kingdom.
5. The basic purpose .... the kingdom of souls.

Note also the correlation of ideas which can be found as we study the words:

> "By one-pointed meditation upon the relationship existing between the body and the akasha, ascension out of matter (the three worlds) and power to travel in space is gained." (*The Light of the Soul*, page 338.) Patanjali: III.42.

Here it is apparent how valuable is the teaching of this sutra, when the consciousness aspect is held carefully in mind, and how the relationships, on a larger scale than the simply human, become clear:

1. The body .... mineral kingdom ....the dense prison of life.
2. The akasha ... vegetable kingdom .. the fluid conscious life.
3. Ascension out of matter .... animal kingdom .... the evolutionary goal of the relation between body and akasha.
4. Power to travel in space ..... human kingdom .... the goal of the human consciousness through the realisation of the above three.

It is the inner relations with which I deal in this treatise,

The Kingdoms in Nature 237

and with the inner ray influences, which bring about the desired outer results. It is the goal of the evolving consciousness which I seek to make clear. Science can handle with skill and insight the evolution of form. I shall endeavour to lay the ground for that coming science (of which modern psychology is the experimental beginning) which will deal as easily with the evolution of consciousness as modern science deals with the form expressions of life. Only when that newer science has been brought to the point of development at which material science now stands will it be possible to consider the evolution of life, through consciousness in form. I have here made a basic and synthetic statement which needs grasping. Those whose consciousness is expanding out of the human to the egoic will follow my reasoning with a measure of facility.

A very apposite question might here be asked: What determines the ray which should govern or predominantly influence any or all of the various kingdoms in nature? It should be remembered that every kingdom, viewing it as a whole, is an entity, and (from its form side) the sum total of all forms constitutes that entity's body of manifestation. In the last analysis also, the aggregate of self-initiated influences, or the magnetic radiation of that particular kingdom, is an expression of that entity's basic quality or qualities,—the aura of that entity's personality. Two rays govern each kingdom in nature, except in the case of the vegetable kingdom, where three rays indicate the nature of that kingdom's life. Students will possibly find it helpful to consider this problem from the angle of analogy, and to realise that they (as well as every other human being) are governed or actuated by two rays, i.e., the personality ray and the egoic ray. After the third initiation, the disciple has three rays active in him, for the ray of the Monad begins then to make its presence felt. An analogous condition is found in all the kingdoms in nature. Two rays are dominant in each kingdom, but in the vegetable kingdom three rays control, for that kingdom is more evolved (along its own peculiar lines) than any other. What might be regarded as the monadic ray of the Life of that kingdom is functioning. This whole matter must not be viewed from the standpoint of human consciousness, and the human standards of unfoldment and of awareness must not be regarded as holding prominent place in this evolution of divine life. This living entity has a different objective to the Life which informs the fourth kingdom in nature. Nevertheless three basic logoic influences, three major breaths, or three ray vibrations account for this kingdom's life-quality and appearance. This whole matter is too intricate for real comprehension, and the reader would do well simply to accept the statements I make, with reservations, and realise that when he himself is a member of the great company of initiates of the wisdom, that which is at present inexplicable to him may be made clear, and when fitted into its rightful place in the scheme of things will not seem so extraordinary or peculiar.

b. The Five Secrets of the Kingdoms in Nature

There is a secret anent each of the five kingdoms in nature. These secrets concern the relation of the human evolution to the whole, and they are revealed to the initiate at the five initiations. At each initiation one of the five secrets is explained to the initiate, and they are called by the following five names, which are an attempt on my part to interpret symbolically the ancient name or sign:

1. The mineral kingdom . . . . . . The secret of the brilliance of the light.
2. The vegetable kingdom . . . . The secret of the sacred perfume.
3. The animal kingdom . . . . The secret of the following scent.
4. The human kingdom . . . . The secret of the double path or of the double breath.

5. The kingdom of souls . . .The secret of the golden rose of light.

The symbolic forms in which these five secrets are hidden, and so conveyed to the intelligence of the initiate, are as follows:

1. The mineral secret . . . . A diamond, blue white in colour.
2. The vegetable secret . . . . A cube of sandalwood in the heart of the lotus.
3. The animal secret . . . . A bunch of cypress, over a funeral urn.
4. The human secret . . . . A twisted golden cord, with seven knots.
5. The egoic secret . . . . A closed lotus bud with seven blue rays.

Be all this as it may, certain of the seven logoic influences are at this time dominant in the five kingdoms; in four cases, two rays control; in the case of the vegetable kingdom, three rays control. It must not be forgotten that these rays are related to each other, and in the great interfacing and interlocking of the planetary and the solar forces every kingdom comes under the influence of every ray, yet with certain rays always controlling and certain others dominating cyclically. The rays determine the quality of the manifesting life and indicate the type of the appearance.

In resuming our consideration of the three divisions of the vegetable kingdom it might be stated that . . .

Ray VI . . . .determines the type, family, appearance, strength, size and nature of the trees upon our planet.

Ray II . . . . .is the beneficent influence, expressing itself through the cereals and flowers.

Ray IV . . . .is the life quality, expressing itself through the grasses and the smaller forms of vegetable life,— those which provide the "green carpet whereon the angels dance".

An important symbolic happening has been consummated at the close of this Piscean Age, which is the period of the sixth ray influence. This has been the world-wide devastation of the forests of the world. Everywhere they have been sacrificed to the needs of man. Thus have been brought under the influence of fire, those vegetable forms of life which were ready for the initiation. The major agency in the development of this kingdom has been water, and this new development, this bringing together of fire and water in this kingdom, has constituted the subjective fact which brought the steam age into being. The vast forest fires, which form such a menace at this time in different parts of the world, are also related to this "initiation by fire" of a kingdom hitherto controlled and directed in its growth by the element of water.

Similarly, the coming in of the seventh ray inaugurated a tremendous event in the mineral kingdom. This I referred to in an earlier book. Through the effect of sound and fire, the mineral kingdom has also been initiated, and in the great world war, in the steel factories and the other factories where metal is transmuted into articles for the use of man, the world of minerals, and the entity which informs that world, are passing through a major initiation. This was made possible by the personality ray of the entity, manifesting through this kingdom, subjecting itself to the initiatory fire. This is of course expressed symbolically,—the only way in which any aspect of this planetary truth can be grasped by man. It is an interesting, though quite unimportant fact, that at all the initiations of the kingdoms in nature, the planetary Logos of a particular ray always functions as the Initiator. This ray cyclically alters. In the major initiations at this time, for instance, in connection with humanity, not only is the first Initiator, the Christ, officiating, not only is the Ancient of Days, the embodiment of our planetary Logos, participating (either actively or behind the scenes), but behind *Them* both stands now the Lord of the fifth Ray of Knowledge and Understanding.

One point of interest might here be noted. It is known esoterically that the vegetable kingdom is the transmitter and the transformer of the vital pranic fluid to the other forms of life on our planet. That is its divine and unique function. This pranic fluid, in its form of the astral light, is the reflector of the divine akasha. The second plane therefore reflects itself in the astral plane. Those who seek to read the akashic records, or who endeavour to work upon the astral plane with impunity, and there to study the reflection of events in the astral light correctly, have perforce and without exception to be strict vegetarians. It is this ancient Atlantean lore which lies behind the vegetarian's insistence upon the necessity for a vegetarian diet, and which gives force and truth to this injunction. It is the failure to conform to this wise rule which has brought about the misinterpretations of the astral and akashic records by many of the psychics of the present time, and has given rise to the wild and incorrect reading of past lives. Only those who have been for ten years strict vegetarians can work thus in what might be called the "record aspect of the astral light". When they add to their purified astral and physical bodies the light of reason and illumination of the focussed mind (which is very rarely found), then they become accurate interpreters of astral phenomena. Their link with the vegetable kingdom is then very close and unbreakable, and that link or binding chain will lead them through the door to the scene of their investigations. But unless the goal of a vegetarian diet is this field of service, the arguments for its following and for that form of diet are usually futile and of no real moment. From the standpoint of the eternal verities, what a man eats or wears are seen in a connotation very different to that of the one-pointed fanatic. Let me again reiterate that this whole problem of the taking of life (whether in the vegetable or the animal kingdom) is a far bigger one than we know, and should be approached from an angle different (not only in degree but in kind) to that of the taking of life in the human family. The three aspects of divinity meet in man, and with the destiny of a divine son of God no one must interfere. Where the two aspects of divinity are concerned, as in the subhuman kingdoms, the attitude can be otherwise, and the emerging truth is different to that which the little minds believe.

The influence of the three rays, blended together in the vegetable kingdom, being also the three rays of even numbers, 2. 4. 6, has produced a fourfold perfection in this kingdom which is unparalleled in any other. The rays are responsible for this result, and their effect can be seen in the following analysis:

Ray II . . . . The result of this influence, pouring cyclically through the kingdom, has been to produce its magnetism, its attractiveness.

Ray IV . . . . This ray of struggle and of conflict has as its objective the production of harmony between form and life, and has brought about the synthesis and the harmony of colour in nature. As we say the words, "colour in nature", automatically we think of the vegetable kingdom and its achievement of harmony in vegetation.

Ray VI . . . . Growth towards the light is the effect of this ray influence, plus the normal tendency of all lifeforms to evolve. It has brought the latent seeds of the vegetable kingdom, inherent within the soil, to the surface. It constitutes the energy of externalisation.

The united effect of these three rays, working in unison, has been to bring forth the fourth result, the perfume of the flowers, as found in the higher units of the vegetable kingdom. This perfume can be either deadly or vitalising, and can either delight or repel. It attracts and constitutes part of the aroma of this kingdom which is sensed in the planetary aura, though unrecognised as a whole by humanity. You isolate a perfume. Yet the perfume of an entire kingdom is a well recognised phenomenon to the initiate.

Students would find it of interest to trace similar analogies in the other kingdoms in nature, remembering however that this kingdom is esoterically ahead of the others, for there are three rays participating in its perfecting. It might be stated that three rays will ultimately affect each of the other three kingdoms.

During the next subrace, ray two will begin to influence the mineral kingdom.

In the next root race, ray five will commence to pour its power into the animal kingdom, gradually stimulating the instinctual mind of the animal until it vibrates to the ray of the intellect, of knowledge. This will bring about an organising of the animal brain, and the transfer of the power of the solar plexus centre to the head centre, and consequently a shift in the animal polarisation and an added activity of the brain in the head.

Towards the close of this round, the monadic ray of the advanced units of humanity will be so powerful that there will be a marked pouring in of ray one, with its stimulation of the individual will. You will therefore have in this unfoldment of the will aspect of mankind the following stages, which are of psychological importance.

1. Instinct.	2. Emotional aspiration.
3. Intellect.	4. Mental one-pointedness.
5. Egoic purpose.	6. Spiritual will.
7. Divine intent.	

These stages are latent in all of us, and are related to the seven principles of man. They will express themselves in advanced humanity as "aspects of the psyche", and therefore psychologically, during the later stages of human development. They should begin to be of greater interest to investigators and to educators who should seek to develop them in the child and the adolescent. They work out today as marked stages in the development of all disciples and initiates. They indicate place upon the Path. Hence their practical usefulness.

In the kingdom of souls, ray four will complete the work of the next two rounds, but this period is so far distant that with it we need not concern ourselves.

In the vegetable kingdom, the work of the second ray of Love-Wisdom is seen, symbolically, in one of its major consummations. Attractiveness, in the sense of beauty, of colour, of form, of distribution, and of perfume, is to be seen on every hand, and had you but the eyes to vision the reality, the synthesis of life would appear to you in all its glory. But just as the last of the five senses to make its presence felt in man, the sense of smell, is as yet but little understood, and its implications are not realised, whilst its relation to the analytical and discriminative mind is not appreciated scientifically, so the "attractiveness" (esoterically speaking) of the vegetable kingdom remains uncomprehended. It is the radiant garment of the planet, and is revealed by the sun; it is the achieved expression of the informing life of this kingdom in nature, and is the effect of the manifestation of the three divine and functioning aspects of this "peculiar" son of divinity, as he works out his destiny in form and through matter.

The entire problem of magnetism is closely connected with the problem of sex. In the occult study of the dissemination of the seed life and the germs of the vegetable kingdom, and in the understanding of the part played therein by those miraculously developed organisms,—the ants and bees—and later in the investigation of the work of the etheric builders, the elves and fairies, by those with awakened vision will come a new light upon sex and upon the function it serves in the interrelation of lives and the creation of forms. With this aspect of this deeply esoteric truth I cannot here deal, for it is the effect of activity in the solar lives of the solar system, and with these we cannot concern ourselves. It is not possible to handle the subject in such a way as to make it of constructive value to the average reader. What is not of immediate esoteric value at this time of world urgency may well be relegated to a later time.

c. THE PLANETS AND THE KINGDOMS

In the vegetable kingdom the influence of Venus is predominant, amazing as this may seem to some occult students. Venus and Jupiter together powerfully influence this world of forms.

It might be of interest to note that all the planets have a close relation to all the kingdoms, but that this relation should not be confounded with the planetary rays or with the fact that some of the planets are considered as "sacred planets" and some are not. I am here using the words "planetary influence" in the same sense as the astrologer uses them, for he is not dealing, either, with the basic planetary rays. It might be stated therefore that the planetary relations in this cycle are as follows:

1. The mineral kingdom . . . . Pluto and Vulcan.
2. The vegetable kingdom . . . . Venus and Jupiter.
3. The animal kingdom . . . . The Moon and Mars.
4. The human kingdom . . . . Mercury and Saturn.
5. The kingdom of souls . . . . Neptune and Uranus.
6. Synthesising these five . . . . The Sun.

There are other planetary influences to be felt, and hidden forces likewise play upon our planetary life, but these are the major influences bringing about the desired results in the kingdoms of nature under the Plan. It must be remembered that these are the cyclic influences dominant at this time, and that they change from cycle to cycle. For instance, a disciple who is upon the path is strongly influenced by Mercury and by Saturn, but when he begins his training for the first initiation he has to contend with the influences of Pluto and Vulcan; the training for the second initiation brings him under Neptunian influences with Venus and Jupiter contending for control. The link with the vegetable kingdom is then strong, and hence the frequent recognition of "astral perfumes" which the disciple can note. Before the first initiation, the static mineral world within him has been broken up.

At the third initiation, the Moon and Mars struggle to assume ascendancy, and there is his battle-ground. Hence at the great Transfiguration, the body is "transfigured" as the indication of triumph. At the fourth initiation, Mercury and Saturn act as the great translators, and bring the disciple to the door of realisation. When the final initiation is taken, it is the activity of Uranus and the in-pouring force of Jupiter that bring about the reorganisation which results in the final emancipation. The vastness and complexity of the subject thus become apparent.

In the emergence of colour in the vegetable kingdom another vast influence is seen, and the problem of the ray influences becomes still more complicated. In the basic colour, green, we have the indication of the potency of Saturn. Esoterically speaking, the vegetable kingdom is upon an advanced stage of the path of discipleship, and hence Saturn and Mars are active. The influence of the latter planet is to be seen in the prevalence of the colours red, rose, yellow and orange in the flowers at this time.

Again, readers would find it interesting to note mentally the relation of growth to the idealism of the sixth ray. They could learn therefrom the part that the Ray of Devotion plays in bringing about the urge to evolve. It is growth towards an ideal, or towards a divine prototype or archetype. Here is where the secret of this kingdom appears. The secret is hidden in the word "transformation," for the rays 2.4.6 are the great transformers. The clue to the secret is to be found in the processes of assimilation and in the building forces that transmute the assimilated minerals, the absorbed moisture, the food in the air, and the proffered offering of the insect kingdoms into the manifested bodies, the radiant colours, the magnetic auras, and the distilled perfumes of this kingdom. Much along this line has been the subject of investigation by the modern scientist, but until he recognises the fact of ray influences, and the part they play in the producing of these factors, he will fail to discover the true secret of the transformations which he notes.

It will appear, therefore, to the careful reader, that in the relation of the rays to the kingdoms in nature, and in the similarity of the rays found functioning in widely differing kingdoms, will be found their point of contact or door of entry, whereby they can contact each other.

For instance, the human and the vegetable kingdoms find their point of influential entry (using the words in the esoteric sense) through ray four, which influences the forms in both kingdoms. The relation between the vegetable kingdom and the kingdom of souls is found along the second ray. Ray two is beginning to make its presence felt in the mineral kingdom, and hence man's work with, and facility in using materially, the forms in this kingdom. Perhaps I should say, misusing them. Ray five will before long, as we have noted, make its power felt in the animal kingdom, and an ever closer relation will then be set up between men and animals.

Again, the rays in incarnation at any time will establish

relations between the kingdoms, increasing the interplay of forces and the interchange of energies, and thus producing new effects, new forms of life, and new wonders in the world of phenomena. Man is also apt to think that his ray influences (the ray predominant in his own kingdom) must be of paramount importance and the most potent. This is not so at this time.

A careful study and a true analysis of the effect and work of the rays in connection with the animal kingdom is not possible. Yet it must be remembered that the roots of human psychology lie hidden in this expression of God. Humanity is an expression of two aspects of the soul,—the animal soul and the divine soul,—and these two, blended and fused in man, constitute the human soul. It is this fact that is the cause of man's special problems, and it is these two factors which involve him in the long struggle which eventuates in the liberation of the divine soul, through the sublimation of the animal soul. In these words lie much food for thought. "The twain shall be one". This work is begun in the animal kingdom, and constitutes its "secret", and hence the use of the word "transfusion" in this connection. Individualisation was the first result of this secret process. Its final consummating effect can be seen in the five stages of the initiatory process, leading to eventual transfiguration and liberation. The entire work is, however, one great unfolding revelation of the soul of God, and it is only when we divorce humanity from that process of revelation that we find the secrets, the problems, the difficulties and the mysteries insoluble. A consciousness, an awareness and a sensitivity to an ever-widening and more inclusive contact is gradually being developed, and this is the consciousness of God, the awareness of the solar Logos, and the sensitivity of the cosmic Son of God.

The form through which that Life expresses Itself, the sensitive response apparatus through which that Consciousness works, are of secondary importance, and are in the nature of an automatic mechanism. It is the mechanism, nevertheless, with which we have hitherto identified ourselves, and we have forgotten that that mechanism is but an expression of an aspect of consciousness, and that it indicates, at any particular time, the point of evolution of the informing entity. Let me reiterate: The two factors which are of major importance, during manifestation, are the evolving consciousness and the manifesting life. When this is borne in mind, it will be noted how each stage upon the way can be seen whole as a kingdom in nature. Each of these kingdoms carries the consciousness aspect forward to a greater stage of perfection, and demonstrates a greater sensitivity and responsiveness to outer and inner environing conditions, than does the preceding kingdom. Each manifests a fuller revelation of the inner and hidden glory. When, however, a unit of life is immersed in form, and when the consciousness is identified (in time and space) with any particular form, it is not possible for it to realise its divinity or to express it consciously. Its psychology is that of the partial and the particular, and not that of the universal and the whole. The greater and closer the identification with the form aspect, the greater is the lower unity and synthesis, but at the same time, the greater the darkness and, speaking symbolically, the denser is the prison. Such is the consciousness in the lower or subhuman kingdoms in nature. The more the unit of life is identified with "the one who is conscious", the greater again is the higher, yet different, unity and synthesis. Such also is the consciousness of the three higher kingdoms, the superhuman. The tragedy, the problem and the glory of man is that he can identify himself with both aspects—the form and the life; and his psychological state is such that during the period wherein he forms part of the human kingdom, his kingdom, his consciousness fluctuates between these pairs of opposites. He can identify himself with the subhuman forms, and this he invariably does in the early stages. He can identify himself with the life aspect, and this he does in the final stages. In the midway stage of the average man, he is torn violently between both, and is himself the battle-ground.

With this consciousness, incident upon an awareness of the pairs of opposites, is connected the entire problem of pain and of suffering, as we today understand it. The animal suffers, but suffers entirely physically and sentiently. Man suffers, but suffers physically, sentiently, and also mentally, and the mental suffering is due to the development in him of certain aspects of the lower mind—anticipation, memory, imagination, the power to visualise, remorse, and the inherent urge to reach out after divinity, which brings with it a sense of loss and of failure. The sufferings of God Himself (to which the scriptures of the world so often mysteriously refer) are divorced from sentiency, and are mental and intuitive. But on this mystery we need not enlarge. The sufferings of humanity are primarily personal; of God, they are pre-eminently impersonal and related to the whole. I have touched on this as I wanted you to get a picture of the synthesis of the unfoldment from the inchoate to the sentient, from the sentient to the mentally realised, and from the mentally realised to the "divinely appreciated," as it is occultly termed. I give you pictures, but they are pictures of a whole. Endeavour to think in wholes, and try not to fit every point of detail into the whole, but remember that what may appear to be a contradiction may be but a fragment of temporary detail for which you—as yet—see no place or explanation.

In the animal kingdom the first dim indication of sorrow and pain is seen, whilst in the higher and the domesticated animals these two educating processes are still more clearly indicated. Man's work with the animals is potent in results, and will lead eventually to a re-opening of the door into the human kingdom. Some of the work already done by man has outstripped divine expectation and may warrant a hastening of the Plan.

Let us now tabulate our points anent this kingdom and the rays, as we did with the other two kingdoms.

3. *The Animal Kingdom*

Influences . . . . The third Ray of Active Intelligence or of Adaptability is potent in this kingdom and will express itself increasingly as time goes on, until it has produced in the animal world that reaction to life and to environment which can best be described as "animal one-pointedness." Then, at this point and cyclically, the sixth Ray of Devotion or Idealism can make its pressure felt as the urge towards a goal, and thus produce a relation to man which makes of him the desired goal. This is to be seen through the medium of the tamed, the trained and the domestic animals.

Results . . . . In the one case we find the third ray producing the emergence of instinct, which in its turn creates and uses that marvellous response apparatus we call the nervous system, the brain, and the five senses which lie behind and which are responsible for them as a whole. It should be noted that, wide as we may regard the difference between man and the animals, it is really a much closer relation than that existing between the animal and the vegetable. In the case of the sixth ray, we have the appearance of the power to be domesticated and trained, which is, in the last analysis, the power to love, to serve and to emerge from the herd

A Treatise on the Seven Rays

into the group. Ponder on the words of this last paradoxical statement.

Process .... This is called concretisation. In this kingdom we have for the first time a true organisation of the etheric body into what are called by the esotericist "the true nerves and the sensory centres." Plants also have nerves, but they have in them nothing of the same intricacy of relation and of plexus as we find in the human being and in the animal. Both kingdoms share the same general grouping of nerves, of force centres and channels, with a spinal column and a brain. This organisation of a sensitive response apparatus constitutes, in reality, the densification of the subtle etheric body.

Secret .... This is called transfusion, which is a very inadequate word to express the early blending, in the animal, of the psychological factors which lead to the process of individualisation. It is a process of lifegiving, of intelligent integration and of psychological unfoldment, to meet emergency.

Purpose .... This is called experimentation. Here we come to a great mystery, and one that is peculiar to our planet. In many esoteric books it has been stated and hinted that there has been a mistake, or a serious error, on the part of God Himself, of our planetary Logos, and that this mistake has involved our planet and all that it contains in the visible misery, chaos and suffering. Shall we say that there has been no mistake, but simply a great experiment, of the success or failure of which it is not yet possible to judge? The objective of the experiment might be stated as follows: It is the intent of the planetary Logos to bring about a psychological condition which can best be described as one of "divine lucidity". The work of the psyche, and the goal of the true psychology, is to see life clearly, as it is, and with all that is involved. This does not mean conditions and environment, but Life. This process was begun in the animal kingdom, and will be consummated in the human. These are described in the *Old Commentary* as "the two eyes of Deity, both blind at first, but which later see, though the right eye sees more clearly than the left". The first dim indication of this tendency towards lucidity is seen in the faculty of the plant to turn towards the sun. It is practically non-existent in the mineral kingdom.

Divisions . . . . First, the higher animals and the domestic animals, such as the dog, the horse and the elephant.

Secondly, the so-called wild animals, such as the lion, the tiger, and the other carnivorous and dangerous wild animals.

Thirdly, the mass of lesser animals that seem to meet no particular need nor to fill any special purpose, such as the harmless yet multitudinous lives found in our forests, our jungles and the fields of our planet. Instances of these in the West are the rabbits and other rodents. This is a wide and general specification of no scientific import at all; but it covers adequately the karmic divisions and the general conformation into which these groupings of lives fall in this kingdom.

Objective agency . . . Fire and Water,—fierce desire and incipient mind. These are symbolised in the animal power to eat and drink.

Subjective agency . . Smell or Scent,—the instinctual discovery of that which is needed, from the activity of ranging forth for food and the use of the

| | power to scent that food, to the identification of the smell of a beloved master and friend. |
| Quality .... | Tamas or Inertia,—but in this case it is the tamasic nature of mind and not that of matter, as usually understood. The chitta or mind-stuff can be equally tamasic. |

The two problems which are of immediate concern to mankind in relation to the animal kingdom are:

The problem of human relations and responsibility.
The problem of animal individualisation.

A. Human Relations to Animals

Only a few hints can as yet be given, and those must be along the line of information anent the rays at work in both kingdoms. The two problems, particularly the second one, are of vast intricacy, and would require many volumes to be properly elucidated. Right exegesis is not yet possible, nor could man yet understand.

The first point to be emphasized in connection with human responsibility in relation to the animals is that the animal world embodies two divine aspects, two divine principles, and two major rays are concerned with their expression or manifestation. These two aspects are found also in man, and it is along these two lines, which man shares in unison with the animals, that man's responsibility and work lie, and through the use of these two aspects of divine energy will he realise his task and carry it to completion. The same divine activity and the same divine innate intelligence are found in the form aspect of both kingdoms. They are inherent in matter itself. But this third Ray of Divine Intelligence functions more potently and influences more powerfully in the animal kingdom than in man. This is an item of information not hitherto given out.

The Kingdoms in Nature 255

The second ray is of course present in its form-building aspect, as herd instinct and as the basis of the sex relation among animal bodies. It is found performing a similar function among human beings, and along these two lines of energy will the points of contact be found and the opportunity to assume responsibility. Yet it should be noted that, in the last analysis, animals have more to give men than men have to give animals, where these particular powers and functions are concerned. In the human family another divine aspect is found functioning. which is that of the will, of directed purpose, of planned objective, and of intelligent design or plan. These qualities are inherent in man, and constitute an aspect of the divine mind not found actively present in the animal, as a rule. However, as the animal kingdom comes increasingly under human influence and the steady trend towards domesticity makes itself felt, we shall see emerging a measure of purposive objective; and one means towards this end is to be found in the turning of the animal's love and attention towards his master. In this illustration some of the responsibility of man to the animal world is expressed. The domestic animals have to be trained to participate in the action of applied will. This, man seems as yet to interpret as the will of the animal to love his master, but it is something deeper and more fundamental than the satisfying of man's love to be loved. The true and intelligent training of the wild animals, and their adaptation to the conditions of ordered living, are part of the divine process of integrating the Plan and of producing an ordered and harmonious expression of the divine intent. It is through the power of thought that man will eventually bridge the gap existing between the animal kingdom and man, and it must be done by man's directed, controlled thought, controlling and directing the animal consciousness. It is not done through the evocation of love, fear or pain. It is intended to be a purely mental process and a unique mental stimulation.

The relation of the animals to man has been purely physical in the long past ages. Animals preyed upon men in the days when animal-man was but little removed from them. It is oft forgotten that there was a stage in human development when animal-man and the existent forms of animal life lived in a much closer relation than today. Then, only the fact of individualisation separated them. It was, however, an individualisation so little realised that the difference between the mindless animal (so-called) and infant humanity was scarcely appreciable. In those distant aeons, much transpired which has been lost in the dark silence of the past. The animal world was then far more potent than the human, men were helpless before the onslaughts of the animals, and the devastation wrought by animals upon early animal-men in mid-Lemurian days was terrible and appalling. Little nomadic groups of human beings would be completely wiped out, age after age, by the powerful animal life of the period, and though instinct taught the animal-men to take certain precautions, it was an instinct but little removed from that found in their enemies. It was only as the millenia of years passed away, and human intelligence and cunning began to assert themselves, that humanity became more powerful than the animals and in its turn devastated the animal kingdom. Up until two hundred years ago the toll of life exacted by the animal world from the human, in the forests of the western continents, in Africa, in the primeval lands of Australia and in the islands of the tropic seas, was incalculable. This is a fact often forgotten in the sentimentality of a moment, but it lies at the root of man's cruelty to animals. It is but the inevitable karma of the animal kingdom working out. The question must be viewed from a larger scale than has hitherto been the case, and its true historic values must be better understood before man can intelligently decide what constitutes his problem of responsibility and how it should be met and solved.

In Atlantean days the purely physical relation was tempered by an astral or emotional relation, and the time came when some of the animals were swept within the orbit of human life and were tamed and cared for, and when the first of the domestic animals appeared. A new era began, wherein certain of the animals evoked affection from certain humans, and a new influence was brought to play upon this third kingdom in nature. This started during a cycle when the second ray and the sixth ray were both functioning simultaneously, and wherein their major and their lesser cycles coincided. This is a rare occurrence, and when it happens the guardians of the race seize the opportunity to produce major results or to inaugurate new moves whereby the divine Plan may be more rapidly developed. To offset the fear found in humanity as a whole (as far as the animal world was concerned), the opportunity was offered by the guardians of the race to bring men and animals into a closer relation, and because a cycle was present in which love and devotion were pouring upon, into and through all forms, a good deal of the fear present was offset. Since that time the number of the domestic animals has steadily increased. The relation between the two kingdoms is now dual—physical and emotional.

To this there has been added, during the past two hundred years, a third relation, that of the mind. The mental power of humanity will, in the last analysis, be the controlling factor, and through its means the three subhuman kingdoms will be brought under the control of man. This has been happening with great rapidity in the mineral kingdom and in the vegetable kingdom. It is not yet accomplished where the animal kingdom is concerned, but the process is rapidly going forward. Not much progress will be made during the incoming seventh ray cycle, though as law and order and rhythm are imposed upon the planet, and as chaos gives place to organisation, we shall see those areas on the planet wherein the animals still rule increasingly lessened, and certain species will die out unless they are preserved in sanctuaries.

B. INDIVIDUALISATION

It is of course apparent that the effect of the interrelation existing between animals and men is to produce in the former that step forward which is called *individualisation*. This event is a consummation of the process of transfusion, and indicates the appearance of the three divine aspects in a unit of life in form. A son of God, a Lord of dedicated and directed Will, is born, and the third divine principle of purposive energy is fused with the other two and brings about an entire reorganisation within the animal form. As esotericists have long pointed out, individualisation is a great planetary experiment, and when it was instituted it superseded the earlier method, employed upon the Moon, wherein the urge to reach out and on (called aspiration where man is concerned) was the method employed. This really means that, when the evolving life within the form had reached a certain stage of growth in sentiency and awareness, and the inner urge was adequately strong, the life forced itself into contact with another stream of divine expression, with another major ray manifestation. This union of various activities caused a new being to emerge into manifestation. This is the basic truth lying behind the ideas put out at this time and classified under the general term "emergent evolution." It governs still in many departments of nature, and used to govern the appearance of human beings upon the planet. The urge and the development are from within the organism itself, and are the result of growth, of a reaching out and of an expansion.

But the method usually employed at this time is in the nature of a great second ray experiment. This involves an activity from without, from above, from a higher or from the divine side, if such a use of relatively meaningless words can avail to depict the process. The urge or push in this case does not originate from the lower two expressions or earlier fusions of divine energies. It is the higher aspect of divinity which takes the initiative and which, through a stimulation applied from without, causes a response from the life in form. Hence the process is really in the nature of an initiation.

The animals which individualise are, in every case today, the domestic animals, such as the horse, the dog, the elephant and the cat. These four groups of animals are at this time in the "process of transfusion", as it is occultly called, and one by one the life units are prepared and brought to the door of that peculiar initiatory process which we call—for lack of a better term—individualisation. They wait in that condition until the word goes forth that that door may be passed which will admit them to

> ". . . the triple way that leads to the dual road, by treading which they stand at last before the golden door. This final door ushers them upon that Path which is the one, alone and single, and disappears into the Light".
>
> *Old Commentary.*

The factors which determine individualisation are several in number, and some of them might be enumerated as follows:

1. The response of the instinctive nature of the animal to the mental atmosphere of the human being, or beings, with which it is surrounded.
2. The outgoing love and interest of the people to which

the animal is attached by the bonds of affection or of service.
3. The ray impulses which are active at any time. These are, amongst others:
   a. The ray of the animal itself. Elephants are upon the first ray; dogs are expressions of the second ray; the cat is a third ray life manifestation, and the horse is sixth ray. Animals upon other rays are not yet ready for individualisation.*
   b. The ray of the particular person or persons with whom the animal is associated.
   c. The ray or rays of a particular periodic cycle.

I could give you the techniques with which the guardians of the races and kingdoms work when seeking to bring about individualisation, but of what purpose would it be and what use would such information serve? Each ray affects the units found upon it at such a crisis as individualisation in a manner differing from any other ray; each ray finds its point of prime contact through one or other of the centres in the etheric bodies of animals and men. It must be remembered in this connection that, in the animal, four centres are functioning, and three are present but latent in their effect and use. The process followed is that each ray works or pours its energy through one or other of the centres in the etheric body of that Entity Who informs an entire kingdom in nature, and then through that particular centre galvanises the individualising unit into the needed activity. Later, when the ray effects, psychologically speaking, are better understood, and the centres, with their seven ray vibrations, have been more deeply studied, it will be found that through a particular centre and along a particular ray vibration, forms of life and centres of consciousness can be contacted and known. This

---

* See page 164 for a different enumeration of the rays. The apparent contradiction may be due to the use of the word "ray" without indicating whether a major ray, one of the seven subrays of a major ray or a complementary ray is implied.   The Publishers.

applies to all forms in all kingdoms, subhuman or superhuman. One of the first ways in which man is learning this truth is through the discovery of that vibration—emanating from a particular Master—which produces a reaction in himself, and which calls forth a response. Thus he is enabled to find out upon which ray his soul is found and to which ray group he should be attracted. This is of importance to the aspirant, and should be considered more carefully than has hitherto been the case, for by it the aspirant determines the nature and the quality of his soul type, and of the centre through which he (occultly speaking) goes out upon the Path. He discovers likewise the group of forms and of lives with which he is linked, to which he must render service, and by which he can be served.

The relation of the rays to the centres in the average aspirant might be classified as follows:

1. Head centre . . . . Ray of Will or Power. First Ray.
2. The Ajna centre . . . . . . Ray of Concrete Knowledge. Fifth Ray.
3. The Throat centre . . . . Ray of Active Intelligence. Third Ray.
4. The Heart centre . . . . . Ray of Love-Wisdom. Second Ray.
5. The Solar plexus . . . . . Ray of Devotion. Sixth Ray.
6. The Sacral centre . . . . . Ray of Ceremonial Magic. Seventh Ray.
7. Base of Spine . . . . .Ray of Harmony. Fourth Ray.

These rays and their corresponding centres warrant most careful study. They are comprehensive and revealing. Note, for instance, that at this time the seventh ray governs and expresses itself through the sacral centre, that which controls the sex life and the building of forms of expression. Therefore it swings now into activity and pours through this particular centre in order to organise and produce the appearance of those new forms through which all life in the new cycle (astrologically understood and periodically and cyclically understood) may express itself. Thus it was necessary for the sex life to be controlled by this type of energy in order to bring about the needed changes, and hence also one of the great results of the influence of the incoming seventh ray has been the increase in the mental interest in sex. A study also of the ray influences in this present historic period, and their relation to the rays, will reveal the accuracy and suggestiveness of the above ray tabulation.

The relation of man to the animals is, as we have seen, physical, emotional and increasingly mental. Each race of men, in its turn, and working under the ray influences, produces definite effects upon the three subhuman kingdoms. Through humanity, when the great experiment of individualisation was initiated, the energies or ray influences from the superhuman kingdoms were focussed and the great function of humanity began, which is the transmitting of the ray forces cyclically. Though the six-pointed star is, at this time, the symbol of the creative work (viewing the work as a whole), the downward pointing triangle, balanced on an upward pointing triangle, will some day present a truer picture of the creative and preserving function of the fourth kingdom.

C. The Five Points of Contact

There are five points of contact whereby the material world can be occultly "raised" up into life and power, just as there are five centres always to be found in our planet, through which life and energy pour into the natural world. I refer here to certain centres which are active where the physical and material life of the planet are concerned. There are also, as I told you in my writing anent the developments during the next three years, five centres through which a new and energising spiritual force is flowing, and these are the planetary correspondences to the five senses in man, both subjective and objective. But we find the rays pouring through humanity as a whole, and through the five races of men (our present race, the Aryan, being the third—two are yet to come). This particular aspect of ray energy is that which stimulates the consciousness aspect, and it will raise and awaken the consciousness hidden in all material forms, both in man and in the three subhuman kingdoms. These five points, with their five "elevating" influences, are as follows, omitting the two earlier and intangible races which are not strictly human at all, and beginning with the first of the five races which are human throughout:

1. The Lemurian Race . . . fifth ray . . . The coming of the Sons of Fire.
2. The Atlantean Race . . . . sixth ray . . . The devotion of the Lords of Love.
3. The Aryan Race . . . . . . third ray . . . The activity of the Men of Mind.
4. The Coming Race . . . . . fourth ray . . The vision of the Units of Light.
5. The Final Race . . . . first ray . . . . The will of the Lords of Sacrifice.

The two earlier races were governed by the second and seventh rays, respectively, and embody the activity of the form builder and the constructive energy of the magical organiser. The reader must bear in mind, as he studies these major ray cycles, that they cover inconceivably long periods of time, and produce two effects which must be considered.

First, the ray energies, five in number, play upon the human kingdom itself, and in the course of the ages raise man from the dead to life; they lift him out of the dark prison of matter into the light of day. These are the five life-giving forces that raise the human consciousness to heaven, and the form to under-standing. I know no word to express the concept except the word "understanding," and its true sense is seen when divided into its two component parts.

Secondly, these ray energies, working this time through

the human kingdom, raise the subhuman kingdoms in nature also (after much effort) to life and conscious understanding. Through the five points of spiritual contact, in each of the three kingdoms, is life brought to nature itself. For this "the whole creation groaneth and travaileth together in pain until now". Herein is found the secret of the resurrection, viewing it in the planetary sense,— a resurrection enacted also individually by each achieving son of God. This is the great Masonic secret, and the central mystery of the sublime or third degree in Masonry. It is sometimes occultly referred to as "the relation of death to the five life-giving energies seen working upon the third day of revelation" or, speaking still more symbolically:

> "In the chamber of death, the blue light of dawning day reveals the group of workers who seek to raise the dead. Naught avail their efforts until they blend the five great forces of the Lord of Magic. When thus they work as one, in unity complete the work is done they fuse the life-giving force; the dead are raised, and the work of building can proceed. The temple can be glorified and the Word be uttered forth within a chamber of life-giving force and not of death. Through death to life, from struggle in the dark to building in the light! Such is the Plan. Thus do we enter into life that is a death; pass onward through the door whose pillars twain stand there forever as a sign of strength and truth divine; thus do we enter quick within the tomb and die. Thus are we raised again upon a Word divine, upon a fivefold sign, and—springing forth—we live."

Then in relation to humanity, the *Old Commentary* says:

> "The Lords of the fifth great ray of mind have sent us on our way. The Lords of the sixth great ray forced us to suffer in the cause, yet love it too, and through our deep devotion learn. The Lords of the third great ray bring us, through mind, unto the funeral pyre, to the stage wherein we die, yet rise again. In the third room, and on the third dark day, the Master disappears. He dies; is lost to sight. But the five great

Lords unite their forces. In fellowship sublime, they work to raise the dead. Only thus can that Word be spoken which brings the dead to life. Such is the work of man for God, of God for man."

D. Cyclic Manifestation

So the work proceeds. The rays stream forth in:
1. A solar cycle, such as the present one, in which the second Ray of Love-Wisdom is the major ray, and all the others are but subsidiary to it.
2. A planetary cycle, such as those we have just considered in connection with the races,—the five above enumerated and their five controlling rays.
3. Cycles connected with the twelve signs of the zodiac.
    These are primarily two in number:
    a. Those which are connected with a complete zodiacal round, about 25,000 years.
    b. Those which are connected with each of the twelve signs, and which come in and out of manifestation approximately every 2,100 years.
4. Those cycles when certain rays are in power for a period of racial evolution, such as the five major racial periods to which we have referred.
5. The lesser cycling in and out of manifestation, as referred to earlier in this treatise.
6. Cycles of ray activity which are determined by their numerical figures.

The first ray, for instance, governs all cycles such as those of one million years, one hundred thousand years, one thousand years, one hundred years and one year. The seventh ray controls such similar cycles as seven thousand years and seven million years. The interchange and interplay of these ray cycles is so intricate and so great that it would serve only to confuse should I further elaborate. Remember, however, that all of the seven rays are forever functioning, and functioning simultaneously, but that cyclically and under the directed plan of the Minds (who are embodied by the rays), certain of these influences and forces are more dominant at one time than at another, and certain lines of activity and certain results of this activity are demonstrated under one ray influence more than under another. These influences pour through all forms in all kingdoms, producing specific effects, definite and different forms of life, peculiar types of realisation, and particular expressions of consciousness in form which are, for that period, the product of the united and concerted plan of the building forces, working in complete harmony, but temporarily under one or another of their number. They enter into constructive activity; they pass through that particular cycle; they then pass out, or die to that activity, and are then "raised into heaven," until such time as their cycle again comes round. This process they constantly enact and re-enact, repeating the drama of birth, death and resurrection.

In this ray activity will be found the true significance of the Law of Rebirth, and it lies behind the process of incarnation and of reincarnation. Upon this I may not here dwell, beyond pointing out that men's ideas and teaching anent reincarnation are as yet childish and inaccurate. Much readjustment must be made, and much re-arrangement of ideas is necessitated, before a true understanding of this basic cyclic law will be possible.

Cyclic appearance, therefore, governs the rays as well as the kingdoms in nature and the forms contained therein. It determines the activity of God Himself. Races incarnate, disappear and reincarnate, and so do all lives in form. Reincarnation or cyclic activity lies behind all phenomenal activity and appearance. It is an aspect of the pulsating life of Deity. It is the breathing out and the breathing in of the process of divine existence and manifestation. It is that which lies behind the science of chemical affinity, of the relation of the polar opposites, and of the marriage relation, whether that of men and women or of the soul and its expression, the personality. It is the cause of the sex relation in the world, which works under the great Law of Attraction and Repulsion. Perhaps as we are considering the work of one kingdom with another and the relation between positive and negative groups of lives (such as that of the fourth kingdom in nature to the third), it might be apposite next to deal briefly with this subject of sex, which is to be so deeply and widely considered, and more wisely understood, through the influence of the incoming seventh ray.

I have little more to add to this teaching anent the animal kingdom and the rays, for—as said before—it profits not. Man's work is to raise the dead to life, to bring brotherhood into expression on the physical plane, and to transmit divine energy to a waiting world of forms. As the rays play their part with humanity and bring man forth into manifestation as he is in essence and reality, his work with the animal kingdom and with the other kingdoms will proceed steadily and inevitably. Scarcely knowing how or why, humanity will play its part in the work of building. The creative work will proceed and the Plan materialise. Man's work for the animal kingdom is to stimulate instinct until individualisation is possible. His work for the vegetable kingdom is to foster the perfume-producing faculty, and to adapt plant life to the myriad uses of man and of animals. Man's work with the mineral kingdom is to work alchemically and magically. With that process of transmutation and of subsequent revelation I cannot here deal.

E. The Problem of Sex

I have stated that the incoming seventh ray plays through the planetary sacral centre, and then through the sacral centre of every human being. Because of this, we can look for the anticipated developments in that human function which we designate the sex function. We shall see consequent changes in the attitude of man towards this most difficult problem. In speaking on the subject of sex, and in outlining what it is possible to say at this time, I seek to be as simple as I can, and to express my thoughts in such a way that something constructive may eventuate, and a note may be struck which will sound forth clearly in the present welter of discordant sounds, of conflicting views, and of varying ideas.

It is obvious that the matter is a difficult one to approach. So why is it so difficult? In the last analysis, we shall find that the difficulty is based on the prejudices in men's minds, and upon their inner assurance that their particular point of view is necessarily the right one because they themselves live and act in accordance with it, and it suffices for them; it is based on the fact that sex is one of the fundamental primeval urges, one of the substantial instincts, and is consequently the dominating factor in the animal side of man's nature; it is based upon the excessive intimacy of the subject,—an intimacy which was transmuted into an indecent secret during the periods wherein the race succumbed to an excessive puritanism and prostituted a natural function into a prurient mystery. This intimacy relating to the subject of sex caused it to be regarded as an unmentionable episode, and as a topic to be shunned by decent people, instead of being regarded as an instinctual and natural process,—as instinctual and as necessary as the functions of eating and drinking. It is a function, however, which has not been reduced to rhythm in the

The Kingdoms in Nature 269

daily life and regarded as one to be followed and satisfied only when need arises and right demands. Herein lies a great distinction and a clue is offered to the problem.

Again, the difficulty of the problem can be found in the widely diverse attitudes of men's minds to the subject. These attitudes range all the way from an ill-regulated promiscuity to a monogamy which has worked out into a cruel imposition and restraint upon women, and an unbridled license on the part of men. Attendant upon these difficulties, and growing out of these wrong attitudes, the legalities and the illegalities, the license and the restraints, have produced points of infection (if I may so call them) in our civilisation. Because of them, we find a lax morality which is based on bewilderment, "red light" districts which are but an unhappy compromise with vicious tendencies and unsatisfied desires, divorce courts which devastate the life of the family and in time undermine the national life (of which each family unit should be a wholesome part), and the steady growth of disease as the result of the prevalent promiscuity and the many illicit relations. There is also a psychological factor to be found, of real importance. This fact is the militancy expressed by the many groups of people who are seeking to impose their own ideas and their peculiar solution of the problem upon their fellowmen.

Behind all these results of an age-long wrong attitude to the sex function lie two major evils, or rather two major effects of man's actions, mental and physical. These are of dire significance. There is, first of all, the development within man's consciousness of those complexes, those psychoses and psychological disruptions and inhibitions, which have so seriously undermined the health and the serenity of hundreds and thousands of men. There is, secondly, the threatening of the very life of humanity itself, as it is embodied in the family unit and family life. On the one hand, you have promiscuity and over-indulgence in sex relations, which are resulting (and have always resulted) in over-population and an over-production of human beings. On the other hand, you have an enforced sterility which—though in many ways the lesser of the two evils—is eventually dangerous. This sterility is rapidly on the increase. It leads finally to physical conditions which are undesirable. Nevertheless, at this time, it is the lesser of the two evils. Two points might incidentally be noted here. Out of the first of these evils, and as a result of over-production, we have brought about an economic situation of such a drastic and serious nature that the very peace and stability of the world are threatened; out of the second, we should have a gradual disappearance of humanity itself, if enforced sterility should become a universal practice. This would lead to the consequent dominance of the animal world and an immense increase of animal life, and we should have a period of retrogression and not of progress.

In dealing with this subject of sex I shall have to generalise, and the exceptions to the rules laid down and to the suggested classifications will, of course, be many. I am dealing with the subject as a whole, and my topic therefore is the menace of the present attitude, the need for a fuller understanding, and the importance of a re-arrangement of men's ideas on this vital matter. The attitude of the unthinking savage to the sex life, and the attitude of the mentally polarised and spiritually oriented initiate to the same subject, may seem so widely dissimilar that on the surface there may appear no point of resemblance; yet basically both of these attitudes are nearer to each other and to the reality than is that of the average man today. The one is controlled by the rhythm of his animal nature, and knows no more of the evil side and of the vile promiscuity of the civilised man

The Kingdoms in Nature 271

than does the animal in its wild state; the other lives his life in a controlled fashion, governing through the power of the mind, and animated by desire for the good of humanity. In between these two approaching extremes, we have the many points of view, the many dissimilar ideas, the many customs, the many types of relation (legitimate and illegitimate), the many animal and psychological reactions, the many forms of marriage, and the many perversions of a natural process which distinguish modern man in all parts of the world. These again vary in the different civilisations and under the influence of the differing climatic conditions.

It is therefore obvious—is it not?—that it is no part of my service to the readers of this book to enter into a detailed analysis of the marriage customs of the ages, past and present. It is not my work to enlarge in detail upon the mistakes, the evil consequences, the many types of perversion, and the sadistic cruelties which have grown out of man's misuse of the natural processes and of his mate, nor to elucidate his foolish misunderstanding of the Law of Attraction and Repulsion. It would serve no useful purpose if I put forth, in this brief discussion of an immense subject, any of the theories which men have formulated in their search for a solution. Their name is legion. All have in them a measure of the truth. Most of them express the depths of man's ignorance, and they can be studied at any time by any student who has the time to read, the intelligence to see clearly and without prejudice, and the money to purchase the needed literature.

I cannot and I will not touch upon the medical and physiological aspect of vice, whether it be the vice of promiscuity or the vice of an unhappy marriage. I can best serve you at this time by pointing out the laws which should govern the life of man, particularly where sex is concerned, and by indicating—as far as I can and dare—why and how the present peculiar and unique conditions have been brought about. I may also be able to make certain suggestions which, when duly considered, may help to clear from the mind those false and illusory views which prevent man from seeing truly, and I may thus help him to find the golden thread of light which will lead him to his solution in due time.

One thing I will say, sad though it may seem to you to be. There is no immediate solution of the problem of sex with which we are at this time confronted. For ages men have misused and wrongly employed a God-given function; they have prostituted their birthright, and through their laxity and license, and through their lack of control, they have inaugurated an era of disease, both mental and physical, of wrong attitudes and illusory relations which it will take several centuries to eradicate; they have also brought too rapidly into incarnation myriads of human beings who were not yet ready for the experience of this incarnation, and who needed longer interludes between births wherein to assimilate experience. Those souls who are unevolved come into incarnation with rapidity; but older souls need longer periods wherein to garner the fruits of experience. They are however open to the magnetic attractive power of those who are alive on the physical plane, and it is these souls who can be brought prematurely into incarnation. The process is under law, but the unevolved progress under group law as do the animals, whilst the more evolved are susceptible to the pull of human units, and the evolved come into incarnation under the Law of Service, and through the deliberate choice of their conscious souls.

I shall divide what I have to say into four parts, for the sake of clarity and rapid reference:

The Kingdoms in Nature 273

1. Definitions of sex, of virtue and of vice.
2. Sex in the New Age.
3. Some suggestions for the present moment.
4. Sex and the life of discipleship.

I deal not with history nor with the details of racial evolution. These are necessarily all connected with the problem of sex, but are too vast in their implications for my present purposes. As I said before, I deal not with the physiological aspects of sex, nor with the diseases incident upon the misuse of the function, nor shall I deal with the subject of sterility, except as it enters into our consideration of modern man. I cannot touch upon the quarrels of the various schools of thought, for I am not writing from any specific angle, such as that of religion or of morality or of partisanship. The whole question is wider and bigger than any religious view or the moral affirmations of the little minds. What is morality in one country or in one specific relation can be quite the reverse in another. What is deemed legal in one part of the world is found illegal in another. What constitutes a difficult problem under one climatic condition presents totally different possibilities under another. Polygamy, promiscuity and monogamy have been and are cyclically dominant in different parts of the world, down through the ages, and are to be found functioning simultaneously on the earth today. Each has been, or is, in turn right, legal and suitable, or wrong, illegal and unsuitable. Each of these forms of interpreting the sex relation has been the subject of attack or defence, of virtuous horror or of specious argument; each has been the common custom and the rightful method, according to the location, the tradition, training and attitude of the men who practiced it. In one part of the world, one woman may have many husbands; in another, one husband is legally entitled to four wives, if so he choose, and in the harem and the kraal such conditions are always to be found. In the West, a man has legally one wife, but through his promiscuity and his so-called "romantic" adventures, he really has as many as an African chieftain; and today, women are little better.

I have enumerated the above conditions with no thought of criticism in my mind, but simply as a statement of fact, and in order to awaken in the average reader a realisation of a world-wide condition which is probably quite different to their ordinary surmise. I write not for the specialists, but for the average intelligent student who needs a world-wide picture of existing conditions.

It is divinely true that the trend of men's thoughts and desires is towards an established monogamy, but as yet this has never been universally achieved. If one faces this issue with courage and with truth, one will be forced to the conclusion that down the ages men have never been monogamists. Women have been more so in the past than men, but are perhaps less so now, as modern knowledge is inculcating modern methods of protection from the risk and pain of childbirth. Up till now, the act of bearing children has been regarded as deterrent and as a penalty for legal or illegal sex relations. Think of the horror unfolded in those words! Women, practicing the ancient trade of promiscuity, have of course always existed, but I am referring here to women in the home.

Will you believe me if I tell you that the world situation today where sex is concerned, is so critical and so serious that there is not a thinker to be found who can yet see the solution, or who can find—no matter how clear his brain or erudite his mind—the way out of the present impasse? The traditions of customs and of practices, with their inevitable consequences and long established tenure, serve to bewilder

The Kingdoms in Nature 275

the clearest minds. The physical results alone of sexual intercourse, carried on within or without the legalised marriage relation, have produced not only the world of every-day human life, but much of the disease, the insanity, the evil tendencies, and the perverted impulses which today fill our hospitals, our homes for neurotics, our sanatoriums, our prisons and our lunatic asylums.

Our young people, especially the idealistic types and the clear-thinking boys and girls, find themselves faced with a situation which defies their best efforts. They do not know what to think or what to believe. They look into, or form part of, homes which are sanctified by legal marriage, and find (on a large scale) nothing but unhappiness, legalised prostitution, ill-health, the seeking of illicit relations outside the home, neglected and unwanted children, the friction produced by wrong mating, divorce, and no answer to their many intelligent questions. They look then elsewhere, into the lives of those who have avoided the responsibility of marriage, and find naught but discontent, frequently a secret and hidden sex life, ill-health as a result of the frustration of the natural instincts, psychological conditions of the worst kind, sometimes illegitimate children, sexual perversions, and a growing tendency towards what is called homosexuality. They are overwhelmed by complete bewilderment and the failure to find an answer to their questions. They ask the worldly-minded for a solution and for help, and get no clear reply, no sound philosophy and no fundamental instruction. They may be offered sound common sense, and the injunction to avoid excesses and those conditions which would impair their health or lay on them the burden of straitened economic conditions. The moralities of the past may be pointed out to them, and they may be warned of the results which inevitably follow when the laws of nature are broken and the physical body is prostituted to ill-regulated desire. They may have the virtues of "straight living" eulogised to them, and even the fact that they are sons of God may be emphasized to them. All this is good and right and useful. But no true solution is offered, and no light is thrown upon their problem, and their confusion remains unrelieved. They may perhaps turn to the religiously minded people and seek out the orthodox churchman. They may be told to be good; the example of the saints may be cited to them; they may find themselves deluged in a flood of puritanical injunctions, in righteous platitudes, and with unsatisfying explanations, based often on personal prejudice and predilection. But seldom is a clear note sounded, and seldom is it possible to do more than enunciate the great Mosaic law, "Thou shalt not..." To the bulk of the young and seeking enquirers of the present generation the fact that God says thus and so, or the Bible ordains this, that or the other, does not satisfy their longing to know the reason why. The hope of an ultimate heaven, where self-discipline, self-control and sexual abstinence will receive a just reward, seems too far away to offset the temptations of the outer environing world and the insistent urges arising within the man himself.

That many do withstand the "temptations of the flesh" is indeed wonderfully true. That there are men and women everywhere who pass through life clean and uncontaminated is equally and wonderfully a fact. That there are advanced souls whose life is divorced from the animal nature and whose minds control their daily acts is the glory of humanity. But many of them, living in another world of thought and interest, are not tempted as are the more animally inclined of the sons of men. There are, again, of course, those who refrain from wrong doing because they fear the results, either today in the physical body or hereafter in the other world of penalty. But which of all these people, even the most good and saintly, can speak with real wisdom and understanding of this universal problem? Which of them can see the way out for humanity at present? Which of them understands the reason for all the distress, sin and wickedness which have grown up around the sex relation? Which of them really comprehends the true significance of the sex life, its place in the great scheme of things, and the reason for the relation between the sexes? Which of them can say with true vision what the next evolutionary step will be, whither we are going, and what will be the next development?

1. *Definitions of Sex, of Virtue and of Vice*

Cosmically speaking, sex is a short word used to express the relation existing (during manifestation) between spirit and matter, and between life and form. It is, in the last analysis, an expression of the Law of Attraction,—that basic law which underlies the entire manifestation of life in form, and which is the cause of all phenomenal appearance. Humanly or physically speaking, sex is the word used to denote the relation between men and women which results in the reproduction of the species. Speaking in terms of modern usage as it is found among the unthinking and the average, sex is a word which denotes the alluring satisfaction of the animal impulses at any cost and with no rhythmic regulation. Sex is essentially an expression of duality, and of the separation of a unity into two aspects or halves. These we can call spirit and matter, male and female, positive and negative; and they are in the nature of a stage upon the evolutionary ladder towards a final unity or homo-sexuality which has no relation to that perversion which is, today and inaccurately, called "homosexuality". This latter manifestation is rampant at this time in a mental and modern conception of the phenomenon, but it is rare indeed to find a person who truly combines within himself the two sexes, and is,— physiologically and mentally—entirely "self-satisfying, self-sustaining and self-propagating". Down the ages, here and there, we find the true homo-sexual emerging as a guarantee of a distant racial and evolutionary achievement, when the world cycle will have been run and the two separated halves will again be merged in their essential unity. In the above phraseology I do not refer to any doctrine of twin souls, or to any perversion of reality, as ordinarily understood today. I refer to the divine Hermaphrodite, to the true androgynous man, and to the perfected human being. But the word has been distorted from its true significance and applies in nine cases out of ten (nay, in ninety-nine cases out of one hundred) to a type of mental perversion, to a distorted attitude of mind which results often in physical practices and reactions which are—in their manifestation—so old that their very antiquity gives the lie to the idea that this attitude marks a step forward on the path of progress. It marks indeed a point of retrogression, the swinging back into an ancient rhythm, and the resumption of ancient practices.

These perversions are ever found when a civilisation is crumbling and the old order is changing into a new. Why should this be? It is due to the fact that the newer impulses pouring into the old, and the impact of the new forces upon humanity, awaken in man a desire for that which is, for him, a new and untried field of expression, and for that which is unusual and oft abnormal. Weak minds then succumb to the impulse, or strong experimenting souls fall victim to their own lower natures, and investigate in unlawful directions. You have, then, under these new energies, a definite progress forward into new and untried spiritual realms, but at the same time, you find an experimenting in the realm of

The Kingdoms in Nature 279

physical desire which is not for humanity the line of progress.

As the world of forms responds cyclically to the inflow of the higher energies, their effect is to stimulate all parts and aspects of the form life, and this stimulation will produce results that are bad as well as good. Evil will temporarily emerge as well as lasting righteousness. If the effect of the impact of these energies is to produce material reactions, and if man then lays the emphasis of his interest upon that which is material, then the form nature becomes dominant, and not the divine. If energy is prostituted to material ends, such as the expression of physical plane sexual relations for purely commercial objectives, then evil is the result. But it must be remembered that the same divine energy, when working in the realm of brotherly love, for instance, would produce naught but good. Let me illustrate my point in two ways, both of which account for the present orgy of sexual expression and for the widespread interest in the subject.

We live today in a period of the world's history wherein three events of major importance are taking place, mostly unrealised and unobserved by the majority of people.

The seventh Ray of Law and Order is coming into manifestation; we are transitting into a new sign of the zodiac, and the "coming of Christ" is imminent. These three great happenings are the cause of much of the present upheaval and chaos; at the same time they are responsible for the universal turning to spiritual realities which all true workers at this time recognise, and for the growth of understanding, of welfare movements and of the tendency to cooperation, of religious unity and of internationalism. Types of energy which have hitherto been latent are now becoming potent. The consequent world reaction is, in the initial stages, material in its manifestation; in its final stages, divine qualities will manifest and change history and civilisation. The interest being shown today in the so-called cosmic rays indicates a scientific recognition of the new incoming seventh ray energies. These rays, pouring through the sacral centre of the planetary etheric body, have necessarily an effect upon the sacral centres of humanity, and hence the sex life of mankind is temporarily over-stimulated, and hence also the present over-emphasis upon sex. But hence also (and this must be remembered) the keen impetus now being mentally expressed which will eventually result in man's thinking through to a solution of this problem of sex.

The coming in of the Aquarian age also stimulates in man a spirit of universality and a tendency towards fusion. This can be seen working out in the present trend towards synthesis in business, in religion and in politics. It produces an urge towards union, and among other unions, towards religious understanding and tolerance. But these influences, playing upon the sensitive bodies of the undeveloped and the over-psychic, lead to a morbid tendency towards unions, legitimate and illegitimate; they produce an extreme aptitude to sexual intercourse in many directions, and to relations and fusions which are not along the intended or the evolutionary line, and which outrage oft the very laws of nature itself. Energy is an impersonal thing, and is dual in its effect,— the effect varying according to the type of substance upon which it plays.

The incoming seventh ray expresses the power to organise, the ability to integrate and to bring into synthetic relation the great pairs of opposites, and thus produce the new forms of spiritual manifestation. But it will also produce the new forms of what, from the standpoint of spirit, may be regarded as material evil. It is the great impulse which will bring into the light of day all that is to be found clothed with matter, and will thus eventually lead to the revelation of spirit and of the hidden glory, when that which has been revealed of the material form has been purified and sanctified. This it was to which Christ referred when He prophesied that, at the end of the age, the hidden things would be made plain, and secrets be shouted from the housetops.

By means of this process of revelation, within the human family as well as elsewhere in nature, we shall have the development of the power of thought. This will come about through the development of the faculty of discrimination, which will offer choices to man, and thus develop a truer sense of values. False and true standards will emerge in man's consciousness and those choices will be made which will lay the foundation of the new order, which will inaugurate the new race, with its new laws and novel approaches, and so usher in the new religion of love and brotherhood, and that period wherein the group and group-good will be the dominant note. Then separateness and hatreds will fade out and men will be merged in a true unity.

The third factor under consideration, the coming of the Christ as it is called, must also be noted. Everywhere we find the spirit of expectancy, and the demand for a manifestation and a symbolic happening which we call by various names but which is usually referred to as the advent of Christ. This, as you know, may be an actual physical coming, as before in Palestine, or it may connote a definite overshadowing of His disciples and lovers by the Great Lord of Life. This overshadowing will call forth a response from all those who are in any way spiritually awakened. Or again, the coming may take the form of a tremendous inflow of the Christ principle, the Christ life and love, working out through the human family. Perhaps all three possibilities may be found simultaneously on our planet very shortly. It is not for us to say. It is for us to be ready, and for us to work at preparing the world for that significant series of events. The immediate future will show. The point I seek to make, however, is that this inflow of the Christ spirit of love (whether it comes through a Person in bodily form or through His felt and realised Presence) will again be twofold in its effect.

This is a hard saying for the unthinking and the illogical. Both the good and the evil man will be stimulated; both material desire and spiritual aspiration will be awakened and fostered. Facts prove the truth of the saying that a heavily fertilised garden and a carefully tended and watered plot of ground will produce its crop of weeds as well as flowers. Yet in this fact you have two reactions to the same sun, the same water, the same fertilising agency and the same care. The difference exists in the seeds found in the ground upon which these factors play. The inflow of love therefore will stimulate earthly love and earthly desire and animal lust; it will foster the urge to possess in the material sense, with all the evil consequent upon this attitude, and the resulting growth of sexual reactions, and the many expressions of an ill-regulated mechanism, responding to an impersonal force. But it will also produce the growth of brotherly love and foster the development and the expression of group consciousness, of universal understanding; it will produce a new and powerful tendency to fusion, to at-one-ment and to synthesis. All this will be brought about through the medium of humanity and the Christ spirit. Steadily the love of Christ will be shed abroad in the earth, and its influence will grow stronger during the coming centuries, until at the end of the Aquarian age, and through the work of the seventh ray (bringing the pairs of opposites into closer cooperation), we can look for the "raising of Lazarus from the dead," and the emergence of humanity out of the tomb of matter. The hidden divinity will be revealed. Steadily all forms will be brought under the influence of the Christ spirit, and the consummation of love will be brought about.

Owing to these three causes we have at this time a worldwide interest in sex, leading as a natural consequence to two things:

First, to an outburst throughout the entire world, and primarily in our large centres of population, of an increase in sexual relations, but distinguished at this time by no corresponding increase in population. This is due to the modern understanding of birth control methods and secondly to the increased mental focussing or polarisation of the race, which leads to sterility or to a reduction in the size of the families raised.

Second, to a reorganisation of the racial ideas on marriage and on sexual relations. This is due to the breakdown of our present economic situation, to the widespread interest in medical hygiene (an interest hitherto confined to the specialists), to the general recognition of the varied marriage customs of the nations in the East and in the West, which has led to a general questioning, and also to the failure of the legal machine to safeguard the family unit and to interpret human relations in a satisfactory manner.

Out of this universal interest and discussion we shall work towards a solution and an objective which exist as yet on purely abstract mental levels and in the world of ideas. Even the foremost thinkers of the race sense only vaguely and nebulously what these hidden ideals may be.

The question at issue is not primarily a religious one, except in so far as social relations are basically divine relations. It is fundamental in its connotation, and when it is solved we shall see the establishment of equality between the sexes, the removal of those barriers which at present exist between men and women, and the safe-guarding of the family unit. This will involve therefore the protection of the child, so that he may be given those essentials to right physical growth and that true education which will lead to emotional unfoldment along sound lines, and a mental development which will enable him to serve his race, his time and his group to the best possible advantage. This has always been an ideal, but it has never yet been satisfactorily accomplished. The solving of the sexual problem will release the minds of men from an inhibition and an undue concern, and so produce a mental freedom which will admit of the inflow of new ideas and concepts. We shall discover that vice and virtue have no real reference to ability and inability to conform to man-made laws, but to man's attitude to himself and to his social relation with God and his fellowmen. Virtue is the manifestation in man of the spirit of cooperation with his brothers, necessitating unselfishness, understanding and complete self-forgetfulness. Vice is the negation of this attitude. These two words signify in reality simply perfection and imperfection, conformity to a divine standard of brotherhood or a failure to achieve that standard. Standards are shifting things and change with man's growth towards divinity. They vary also according to man's destiny as it is affected by his time and age, his nature and surroundings. They alter also according to the point of evolutionary development. The standard for attainment is not today what it was one thousand years ago, nor a thousand years hence will it be what it is today.

Yet all periods of the world's history have not been as critical as today, for—apart from the great cyclic opportunity to which I have earlier referred—we have in humanity itself a unique attainment. For the first time in racial history, we have the expression of a true human being, of man as he essentially is. We have the personality, integrated and functioning as a unit, and we have the mind and the emotional nature fused and blended, on the one hand with the physical body, and on the other with the soul. Also, the shift of emphasis is today away from the physical life to the mental life, and in an increasing number of cases to the spiritual life. There is therefore little real cause for depression, if what I have here noted is true. There is today, on a wide scale, a true "lifting up of the heart unto the Lord," and a steady turning of the eyes towards the world of spiritual values. Hence the present upheaval.

Apart from the coming in of the new age, apart therefore from the inflow of the Christ spirit, with its transforming power and regenerating force, and apart from the cyclic return of the seventh ray energies, we have mankind in a condition where the response to the deeper spiritual energies and to the new opportunities is, for the first time, adequate and synthetic. Hence the increasing problem. Hence the great day of opportunity. Hence the wonder of the dawn which can be seen brightening in the east.

I should like here to approach the problem of sex from another angle and point out that it is a basic symbol. A symbol, as we well know, is an outward and visible sign of an inward and spiritual reality. What is this inward reality? First of all, the reality of relationship. It is a relationship existing between the basic pairs of opposites,—Father-Mother, spirit-matter; between positive and negative; between life and form, and between the great dualities which—when brought together in the cosmic sense—produce the manifested son of God, the cosmic Christ, the conscious sentient universe. Of this relation the Gospel story is a dramatic symbol, and the historical Christ is the guarantee of its truth and reality. Christ guarantees for us the reality of the inner significance and the true spiritual basis of all that is and ever shall be. Out of the relation of light and dark that which is invisible emerges into visibility, and we can see and know. Christ, as the light of the world, revealed that reality. Out of the darkness of time God spoke, and the Fatherhood of Deity was revealed.

The drama of creation and the story of revelation are depicted for us, if we could but see truly and interpret our facts with spiritual exactitude, in the relation of the two sexes and in the fact of their intercourse with each other. When this relation is no longer purely physical but is a union of the two separated halves on all three planes,— physical, emotional and mental—then we shall see the solution of the sex problem and the restitution of the marriage relation to its intended position in the Mind of God. Today it is the marriage of two physical bodies. Sometimes it is the marriage also of the emotional natures of the two people concerned. Rarely indeed is it a marriage of minds as well. Sometimes it is the union of the physical body of one party, with the physical body of the other party left cold and uninterested and uninvolved, but with the emotional body attracted and participating. Sometimes the mental body is involved with the physical body, and the emotional nature left out. Seldom, very seldom, do we find the coordinated, cooperating fusion of all the three parts of the personality concerned in both parties to the union. When this is indeed found, then you have a true union, a real marriage, and a blending of the two in one.

It is here that some of the schools of esoteric teaching have gone sadly astray. The false idea has crept into their presentation of truth that marriage of this kind is essential for spiritual liberation and that without it the soul remains in prison. They teach that through the marriage act, at-one-ment

The Kingdoms in Nature

with the soul is brought about, and that there is no spiritual deliverance without this marriage. At-one-ment with the soul is an individual interior experience, resulting in an expansion of consciousness, so that the individual and specific becomes at-one with the general and universal. Behind the erroneous interpretation, however, lies truth.

Where this true marriage and these ideal sexual relations on all three planes are found, the right conditions exist in which souls can be provided with the needed forms in which to incarnate. Sons of God can find forms in which to manifest on earth. According to the scope of the marriage contact (if so unusual a form of words can be used in this connection), so will be the type of human being attracted into incarnation. Where the parents are purely physical and emotional, so will be the nature of the child. Thus is the general average determined. Today we have a world of men which is rapidly reaching a high stage of development. We have therefore a dissatisfaction with the present views on marriage, preparatory to the enunciation of certain hidden principles which will eventually govern the relations between the sexes, and provide, as a consequence, the opportunity to men and women to furnish, through the creative act, the needed bodies for disciples and initiates.

Under the symbol of sex, you have also the reality of love itself expressing itself. Love in reality connotes a relation, but the word "love" (like the word "sex") is used with little thought and with no attention to its true meaning. Basically, love and sex are one and the same thing, for both express the meaning of the Law of Attraction. Love is sex, and sex is love, for in those two words the relation, the interplay and the union between God and His universe, between man and God, between a man and his own soul, and between men and women are equally depicted. The motive and the relation are emphasized. But the impelling result of that relation is creation and the manifestation of form through which divinity can express itself and come to be. Spirit and matter met together, and the manifested universe came into being. Love is ever productive, and the Law of Attraction is fruitful in results. Man and God came together under the same great Law, and the Christ was born,—the guarantee of the divinity of humanity and the demonstration of the fact. Individual man and his soul are also attempting to come together, and when that event is consummated the Christ is born in the cave of the heart, and Christ is seen in the daily life with increasing power. Man therefore dies daily in order that Christ may be seen in all His glory. Of all these wonders, sex is the symbol.

Again, in man himself the great drama of sex is enacted, and twice over in his body, within his personality, the process of union and fusion takes place. Let me briefly refer here to these two symbolic happenings, for the use of esoteric students, so that the great story of sex may be comprehended in its spiritual sense.

Man, as you know, is the expression of energies. These energies galvanise the physical man into activity through the medium of certain force centres in the etheric body. These, for our immediate purposes, can be divided into three centres below the diaphragm and four above.

These are:

I. Below the diaphragm:
   1. The base of the spine.
   2. The sacral centre.
   3. The solar plexus.

II. Above the diaphragm:
   1. The heart centre.
   2. The throat centre.
   3. The centre between the eyebrows.
   4. The head centre.

We know that two fusions have to take place and, in these two we have two enactments of the symbolic sex process, and two symbolic events that externalise a spiritual happening and picture forth to man his spiritual goal and God's great objective in the evolutionary process.

First, the energies below the diaphragm have to be lifted up and blended with those above the diaphragm. With the process and rules for so doing we cannot here deal, except in one case,—the raising of the sacral energy to the throat centre, or the transmutation of the process of physical reproduction and of physical creation into that of the creativeness of the artist in some field of creative expression. Through the union of the energies of these two centres we shall come to that stage in our development wherein we shall produce the children of our skill and minds. Where, in other words, there is a true union of the higher and the lower energies, you will have the emergence of beauty in form, the enshrining of some aspect of truth in appropriate expression, and thus the enriching of the world. Where there is this synthesis, the true creative artist begins to function. The throat, the organ of the Word, expresses the life and manifests the glory and the reality behind. Such is the symbolism lying behind the teaching of the fusion of the lower energies with the higher, and of this, physical plane sex is a symbol. Mankind today is rapidly becoming more creative, for the transfusion of the energies is going on under the new impulses. As we develop the sense of purity in man, as the growth of the sense of responsibility is fostered, and as his love of beauty, of colour and of ideas proceeds, we shall have a rapid increase in the raising of the lower into union with the higher, and thereby the beautifying of the Temple of the Lord will be tremendously accelerated.

In the coming Aquarian age this will go rapidly forward.

The majority of people today live below the diaphragm, and their energies are turned outward into the material world and prostituted to material ends. In the coming centuries this will be corrected; their energies will be transmuted and purified, and men will begin to live above the diaphragm. They will then express the potencies of the loving heart, of the creative throat, and of the divinely ordered will of the head. Of this relation between the lower and the higher, physical plane sex is the symbol.

But in the head of man himself is also to be found a marvellous symbolic happening. In that living organism is enacted that drama whereby the purely human being merges himself in divinity. The great final drama of the mystical union between God and man, and between the soul and the personality is there enacted. According to the Eastern philosophy, there are in the head of man two great energy centres. One of them, the centre between the eyebrows, blends and fuses the five types of energy which are transmitted to it and blended with it,—the energy of the three centres below the diaphragm and of the throat and heart centres. The other, the head centre, is awakened through meditation, service and aspiration, and it is through this centre that the soul makes its contact with the personality. This head centre is the symbol of the spirit or positive masculine aspect, just as the centre between the eyebrows is the symbol of matter, of the negative feminine aspect. Connected with these force vortices are two physical plane organs, the pituitary body and the pineal gland. The first is negative and the second is positive. These two organs are the higher correspondences of the male and female organs of physical reproduction. As the soul becomes increasingly potent in the mental and emotional life of the aspirant, it pours in with greater power into the head centre. As the man works with his personality, purifying it and bending it to the service of the spiritual will, he automatically raises the energies of the centres in the body up to the centre between the eyebrows. Eventually the influence of each of the two centres increases and becomes wider and wider, until they make a contact with each other's vibratory or magnetic field, and instantly the light flashes out. Father-spirit and mother-matter unite and are at-one and the Christ is born. "Except a man be born again, he cannot see the kingdom of God," said the Christ. This is the second birth, and from that moment vision comes with increasing power.

This is again the great drama of sex, re-enacted in man. Thus in his personal life he three times knows the meaning of union, of sex:

1. In the physical plane sex, or his relation to his opposite, the woman, resulting in the reproduction of the species.
2. In the union of the lower energies with the higher, resulting in the creative work.
3. In the union within the head of the energies of the personality with those of the soul, resulting in the birth of the Christ.

Great is the glory of man and wonderful are the divine functions which he embodies. Through the passage of time, the race has been brought to the point where man is beginning to raise the lower energies into the higher centres, and it is this transition which is causing much of the trouble in the world today. Many men everywhere are becoming politically, religiously, scientifically, or artistically creative, and the impact of their mental energy and of their plans and ideas is making itself felt competitively. Until the idea of brotherhood dominates the race, we shall see these powers prostituted to personal ends and ambitions, and to consequent disaster, just as we have seen the power of sex prostituted to personal satisfaction and selfishness and consequent disaster. Some few, however, are raising their energies higher still and translating them into terms of the heavenly world. The Christ is being born today in many a human being, and increasingly will the sons of God appear in their true nature to take over the guidance of humanity in the New Age.

2. *Sex in the New Age*

Prophecy is ever a dangerous thing, but a forecast, a drawing out of present general tendencies, is often possible.

During the next two hundred years the old influences under which we have been living will gradually die out, and the new potencies will make their presence felt. Three things we are told will characterise the coming Aquarian age, and they will be made possible through the influence of the three planets governing the three decanates of this sign. First, we shall have the activity of Saturn, producing a dividing of the ways and a proffering of opportunity to those who can avail themselves of it. We shall have, therefore, a period of discipline and a cycle wherein choices will be made, and through these discriminating decisions humanity will enter into its birthright. This influence is now being strongly felt.

Then, later, we shall have, through the influence of Mercury in the second decanate, the pouring in of light, of mental and spiritual illumination, and a truer interpretation of the teaching of the Lodge of Messengers. The work of the first decanate will enable many to make those choices and efforts which will enable them to raise the lower energies into the higher centres, and to transfer the focus of their attention from below to above the diaphragm. The work of the second decanate will enable those who are thus ready to fuse the personality and the soul, and thus, as I earlier pointed out, the light will shine forth and Christ will be born within them.

During the third decanate we shall see the rule of Brotherhood inaugurated, and Venus controlling by intelligent love; the group and not the individual will be the important unit, and unselfishness and cooperation will steadily take the place of separativeness and competition.

In no department of life will these coming great changes show more potently than in the attitude of man towards sex, and in the readjustment of the marriage relationship. This new attitude will gradually come about as the slowly developing science of psychology comes into its own. As man comes to understand his own threefold nature, and as the nature of consciousness and the depth of his own subconscious life are more truly grasped, there will take place, gradually and automatically, a change in the attitude of men towards women and of women towards their destiny. This needed change will not be the result of legal measures, or of decisions by the people's representatives to meet the disasters of the hour; these changes will come slowly, as the result of the intelligent interest of the next three generations. The young people now coming into incarnation, and those who will come during the next century, will prove themselves well equipped to handle this problem of sex, because they can see more clearly than the older generation, and will think in wider and larger terms than is common today. They will be more group-conscious and less individualistic and selfish; they will be more interested in new ideas than in the ancient theologies, and will be freer from prejudice and less intolerant than are the bulk of the well-meaning people of today. Psychology is only just come into its own, and only now is its function beginning to be understood; in one hundred years' time, however, it will be the dominating science; and the newer educational systems, based on scientific psychology, will have completely superseded our modern methods. The emphasis in the future will be laid upon the determining of a man's life purpose. This will be brought about through an understanding of his ray, through an analysis of his equipment (and of this, vocational psychology is the faint first beginning), through a study of his horoscope, and through giving him a sound grounding in mind control, as well as training his memory to the impartation of information. The processes by which he can integrate his personality and raise and purify his living qualities will receive careful attention, and all to the end of making him group-conscious and useful to his group. This is the factor of importance. Synthesis, physical purity, decentralisation and group good will be the keynotes of the teaching imparted. Emotional control and right-thinking will be inculcated, and where these are present a knowledge of spiritual realities will be automatically acquired and the life subordinated to the group purpose. Man's relations to others will then be intelligently directed, and his relation to the other sex will be guided not only by love and desire, but by an ordered intellectual appreciation of the true significance of marriage. The above applies to the intelligent, well-intentioned majority whose standards will have developed as the decades pass, so that they will embody the dreams and ideals of the most advanced visionaries of today. The unthinking, the idle and the stupid will still be found, but evolution proceeds apace and order is on its way.

What laws will be enacted for the control of the people on this difficult subject of sex I cannot say; what the marriage laws will be it is no part of my purpose to foretell; how the legislatures of the nations will deal with the problem remains to be seen. I am not interested in speculation.

The Kingdoms in Nature

But I can and I shall put down for you here the basic premises which will underlie the best thought of the future on the subject of sex and marriage. These premises are three in number; when they are understood and grasped, and when they are integrated into the thought of the period, forming the basis of all recognised standards and consistent living, then the details as to how and where and when will take care of themselves.

1. The relation of the sexes and their approach to the marriage relation will be regarded as a part of the group life and as serving the group good; this will not be the result of laws regulating marriage, but a result of education in group relations, service and the law of love, as understood practically and not just sentimentally. Men and women will know themselves as cells in a vital organism, and their activities and outlook will be coloured by this realisation. It will be regarded as a fact in nature and as a product of past evolutionary cycles, and not be looked upon as a theory and a hope, as is the case today. What is best for the group, and what is needed to promote the efficiency of a unit in the group, will be the points considered. Men will increasingly live in the world of thought and understanding, and not so much in the world of ill-regulated desire and of animal instinct; the love of men for women and of women for men will be more truly present than is now the case, for it will not be so purely emotional, and it will be based also on intelligence.

As the creative urge is turned upwards from the sacral centre to the throat, man will live less potently in his physical sexual urges, and more consistently in his creative expression. His physical plane life will proceed along normal lines, but it is necessary for men to realise that the manner in which man today satisfies his sexual nature is abnormal and unregulated, and that we are on our way to a wise normality. The craving for selfish pleasure and for the satisfaction of an animal urge, which is instinctually right when regulated and devastatingly wrong when prostituted purely to enjoyment, will give place to a mutual decision by both of the parties concerned. The decision will meet a natural need in a right and suitable and regulated manner. Today one party or other is usually sacrificed, either to an undue abstinence or to an unseemly profligacy.

2. The second rule is based upon the point of evolution, and for its right fulfillment necessitates the true integration of the personality. This rule might be expressed as follows: True marriage and right sexual relation should involve the marriage of all three aspects of man's nature; there should be a meeting on all three levels of consciousness at once—the physical, the emotional and the mental. A man and a woman, to be truly and happily married, must be complements to each other in all the three departments of their nature, and there should be a simultaneous union of all three. How seldom is this the case, and how rare it is to find! There is no need for me to elaborate in this direction, for this truth is obvious and has oft been voiced. Later, but not for a long while yet, we shall see marriages which will be based upon the point of development of the integrated personality and only those will meet each other in the sacred marriage ritual who have reached the same point in the work of transmuting the lower into the higher centres; a marriage will be regarded as undesirable and the parties ill-mated where one is living the life of the purified personality above the diaphragm, and the other the life of the intelligent animal below the diaphragm. Finally some few will choose their mates from amongst those in whom the Christ has been born again, and who are giving expression

to the Christ life. But the time is not yet, except for the rare and the few.

3. The third governing principle will be the desire to provide good and fair and healthy bodies for incoming egos. This is not possible today, under our ill-regulated system of co-habitation. The majority of the children who are born now have come accidentally into being or are not wanted. Some few, of course, are desired, but even in these cases, that desire is usually based on reasons of heredity, property to be passed on, an old name to be perpetuated, an unfulfilled ambition to be satisfied; yet the day of ordained and desired births is drawing nearer, and when it comes it will make possible the more rapid incarnation of disciples and initiates. Right preparation will take place prior to any fulfillment of the sex urge, and souls will be attracted to their parents by the urgency of those parents' desire, the purity of their motives and the power of their preparatory work.

When these three motives are carefully studied, and when men and women mould their physical plane relationship to each other upon their group responsibilities, upon their union with each other on all three planes simultaneously, and upon the offering of opportunity for incoming souls, then we shall indeed see a restoration of the spiritual aspect of marriage. We shall see the coming in of that era when goodwill will be the outstanding characteristic, and wherein selfish purpose and animal instinct will fade into the background.

3. *Some Suggestions for the Present Cycle*

I have been occupied with indicating a situation which at present exists, and in pointing out an ideal one which lies ahead, but which is not as yet possible. This is valuable, but it leaves a gap in our thought which requires filling. The question now arises which is capable of formulation in the following terms: Given the accuracy of my presentation of the present appalling conditions, given the possibility of an ultimate approximation to the presented ideal in a distant future, is it possible at this time to take steps which will eventually lead to the necessary adjustments in the department of sex? It most certainly is, and my answer takes the following form.

When certain basic postulates, four in number, have been presented and kept before the mind of the public, they will finally lead to such an education of public opinion that the needed activities will follow. But the first step is the education of the public, and their grasp of the four essential laws. Any correction of present conditions will come as a growth from within humanity itself, and not as the imposition of a ruling from without. The training of the public consciousness must therefore go steadily forward, and thus we shall lay the foundation for the later changes.

I should like here to remind you that the coming three generations (in which I include the present one of boys and girls) will bring into incarnation a group of people who will be well equipped to lead humanity out of the present impasse. This fact warrants remembrance, and is often forgotten. There are always those at every epoch in human history who are able to solve the problems which arise, and who are sent in for that very purpose. This sex problem, in the last analysis, is a temporary one, little as you may think it today, and it grows out of a basic mistake,—out of the prostitution of man's God-given faculties to selfish physical ends, instead of their consecration to divine purposes. Man has been swept and carried off his feet by his instinctual animal nature, and only a clear and clean mental understanding of the real nature of his problem will be strong enough to carry him forward into the New Age and into the world of right motive and right action. Man has to learn and deeply grasp the fact that the main purpose of sex is not the satisfaction of the appetites, but the providing of physical bodies through which life may express itself. He has to understand the nature of the symbolism underlying the sexual relation, and by its means grasp the scope of the spiritual realities. The Law of Sex is the law of those relations whereby life and form are brought together in order that divine purpose may be seen. This is a fundamental law of creation, and it is true, whether one is dealing with the informing Life of a solar system, with the birth of an animal, or with the appearance of a plant from a seed. "Sex" is the word we use to cover the relation which exists between that energy we call "life" and the aggregate of force units through which that energy expresses itself and builds a form. It covers the activity which takes place when the pairs of opposites are brought together, and by means of which they become at-one and produce a third reality. That third reality or result bears witness to their relation, and another life in form is seen. You have always, therefore, relation, at-one-ment and birth. These three words deal with the true significance of sex.

But man has prostituted the truth, and the real significance has been lost. Sex now means the satisfaction of the male desire for sensuous pleasure, and the assuaging of a physical appetite through the prostitution of the feminine aspect to that desire and appetite. This relation leads to no result as intended, but to a momentary second of satisfaction, and all of it is confined to the animal nature and the physical plane. I am largely generalising and would remind you that there are exceptions to all generalisations. I should also like to add that no one must here think that I hold the masculine aspect as responsible for our present problem when I say that man uses woman for his pleasure. How can I mean this, when

I know that every human being is cyclically either a man or a woman; that the men of today have been women and the women have been men in previous lives? There is no sex, as we understand it, where souls are concerned; it is only in the form life that sex exists. Only in the process of differentiation for the purposes of experimentation does the incarnating spiritual man occupy first a male body and then a feminine, thus rounding out the negative and positive aspects of the form life. All the race is equally guilty, and all must be equally active in the process of creating the correct conditions, and in bringing order out of the present chaos.

Therefore, the first postulate which must be laid down, and to which the general public must be educated, is that all souls incarnate and re-incarnate under the Law of Rebirth. Hence each life is not only a recapitulation of life experience, but an assuming of ancient obligations, a recovery of old relations, an opportunity for the paying of old indebtedness, a chance to make restitution and progress, an awakening of deep-seated qualities, the recognition of old friends and enemies, the solution of revolting injustices, and the explanation of that which conditions the man and makes him what he is. Such is the law which is crying now for universal recognition, and which, when understood by thinking people, will do much to solve the problems of sex and marriage.

Why will this be so? Because when this law is admitted as a governing intellectual principle, all men will tread more carefully the path of life, and will proceed with greater caution to fulfill their family and group obligations. They will know full well that "whatsoever a man soweth, that will he also reap," and that he will reap it here and now, and not in some mystical and mythical heaven or hell; he will have to make his adjustments in the life of every day upon earth, which provides an adequate heaven and a more than adequate hell. The spreading of this doctrine of rebirth, its scientific recognition and proving, is fast going forward, and during the next ten years it will be the subject of much attention.

The second basic postulate was enunciated for us by Christ when he told us to "love our neighbor as ourselves." To this we have paid, as yet, but little attention. We have loved ourselves and have sought to love those we like. But to love universally and because our neighbor is a soul as we are, with a nature essentially perfect and an infinite destiny, this has always been regarded as a beautiful dream to be consummated in a future so distant, and in a heaven so far away, that we may well forget it. Two thousand years have gone since the greatest expression of God's love walked on earth and bade us love each other. Yet still we fight and hate and use our powers for selfish ends, our bodies and our appetites for material pleasures, and our efforts at living are, in the mass, primarily directed towards personal selfishness. Have you ever considered what the world would today be if man had listened to the Christ and had sought to obey His command? We should have eliminated much disease (for the diseases originating in the misuse of the sex function underlie a large percentage of our physical ills, and devastate our modern civilisation), we should have made war impossible, we should have reduced crime to a minimum, and our modern life would be an exemplification of a manifesting divinity. But this has not been the case, and hence our modern world conditions.

But the new law must, and will, be enunciated. This law can be summed up in the words: Let a man so live that his life is harmless. Then no evil to the group can grow out of his thoughts, his actions or his words. This is not negative harmlessness, but of a difficult and positive activity. If the above practical paraphrase of the words of Christ were universally promulgated and practically applied, we should have order growing out of chaos, group love superseding personal selfishness, religious unity taking the place of fanatical intolerance, and regulated appetites instead of licence.

The two laws I have proclaimed, and the two postulates I have above enunciated, sound like platitudes. But platitudes are the universal and recognised truths, and a truth is a scientific pronouncement. The moulding of the life by these two recognitions (the Law of Rebirth and the Law of Love) would save humanity and rebuild our civilisation. They are probably too simple to evoke an interested recognition. But the power lying behind them is the power of divinity itself, and their recognition is simply a question of time, for evolution will force the recognition at some distant date. The forming of an earlier recognition lies in the hands of the disciples and thinkers of the present age.

The third basic law underlying the solution of our modern problems, including that of sex, grows normally out of the other two laws. It is the Law of Group Life. Our group relations must be seen and acknowledged. Not only must a man fulfill in love his family and national obligations, but he must think in the wider terms of humanity itself, and so bring the Law of Brotherhood into expression. Brotherhood is a group quality. The young people who are now coming in will come into life equipped with a much deeper sense of the group, and with their group awareness much more fully developed than is now the case. They will solve their problems, including the problem of sex, by asking themselves when situations arise of a difficult nature: Will this action of mine tend to the group good? Will the group be hurt or suffer if I do thus and so? Will this benefit the group and produce group progress, group integration, and group unity? Action which fails to measure up to the group requirements will then automatically be discarded. In the deciding of problems, the individual and the unit will slowly learn to subordinate the personal good and the personal pleasure to group conditions and group requirements. You can see, therefore, how the problem of sex will also yield to solution. An understanding of the Law of Rebirth, a good-will towards all men, working out as harmlessness, and a desire for group good-will will gradually become determining factors in the racial consciousness, and our civilisation will adjust itself in time to these new conditions.

The final postulate which I seek to emphasize is that the keeping of these three laws will lead necessarily to an urgent desire to keep the law of the land in which a particular soul has incarnated. That these man-made laws are inadequate I well know, and it is needless to point this out. They may be, and are, temporary and insufficient to the need. They may fail in their scope and prove inadequate, but they do, in a measure, safeguard the little feeble ones, and will be regarded therefore as binding upon those who are seeking to help the race. These laws are subject to change as the effect of the three great laws makes itself felt, but until they are wisely altered (and this takes time) they act as a brake on license and on selfishness. They may also work hardship. This none can deny. But the hardships they bring are not so evil in their nature nor so lasting in their effects as would be the result of their removal and the consequent inauguration of a cycle of law-less-ness. Therefore, the server of the race cooperates with the laws of the land in his daily life, working at the same time for the removal of the injustices they may produce and for the bettering of the legal impositions upon mankind in his country.

In the recognition of these four laws,—of Rebirth, of Love, of the Group, and of the Land,—we shall see the salvation of the race.

4. Sex and Discipleship

I want to write a word on the subject of sex in the life of the disciple. There is much confusion in the minds of aspirants on this matter, and the injunction as to celibacy is assuming the position of a religious doctrine. We are often told by the well-meaning but illogical that if a man is a disciple he cannot marry, and that there is no real spiritual attainment unless a man is celibate. This theory has its roots in two things:

First, there has ever been a mistaken attitude in the East towards women. Secondly, in the West, from the time of Christ, there has been a tendency towards the monastic and conventual conception of spiritual life. These two attitudes embody two mistaken ideas, and lie at the root of much misunderstanding and at the heart of much evil. Man is no better than the woman, nor woman than the man. Yet many thousands regard women as embodying that which is evil and that which is the basis of temptation. But God has from the beginning ordained that men and women should meet each other's needs and act as complements to each other. God has not ordained that men should live herded together, away from women, or women away from men; and both of these great systems have led to much sexual abuse and to much suffering.

The belief that to be a disciple necessitates a celibate life and complete abstinence from all natural functions is neither correct nor desirable. This can be proved by the recognition of two things:

The first is that if divinity is indeed a reality and an expression of omnipotence and omnipresence as well as omniscience, and if man is essentially divine, then there can be no condition possible wherein divinity cannot be supreme. There can be no sphere of human activity where man cannot act divinely and wherein all functions cannot be illumined by the light of pure reason and divine intelligence. I deal not here with the specious and devious argument that that which normally and by all right-minded people is regarded as wrong must be right because of man's inherent divinity. That can be but a loose excuse for wrong-doing. I speak of sexual relations of the right kind, within the permit of the spiritual law as well as the law of the land.

Secondly, a life that is not normally rounded out till all the functions of its nature—animal, human and divine—(and man is all of these three in one body) are exercised, is frustrated, inhibited, and abnormal. That all cannot marry in these days is true, but that fact does not negate the greater fact that man has been created by God to marry. That all are not in a position where they can today live normal and full lives is equally a consequence of our present abnormal economic conditions; but this in no way negates the fact that the condition is abnormal. But that an enforced celibacy is an indication of a deep spirituality, and a necessary part of all esoteric and spiritual training, is equally false, abnormal and undesirable. There is no better training school for a disciple and an initiate than family life, with its enforced relations, its scope for adjustments and adaptability, its demanded sacrifices and service, and its opportunities for the full expression of every part of man's nature. There is no greater service to be rendered to the race than the proffering of bodies to incoming souls, and the giving of attention and educational facilities to those souls within the home limits. But the whole condition and problem of the family life and of child-bearing have been distorted and misunderstood; and it will be long before marriage and children assume their rightful place as sacraments, and longer still before the pain and suffering consequent upon our mistakes and on the misuse of the sexual relation have disappeared, and the beauty and consecration of marriage and of the manifestation of souls in form supersede the present wrong grouping of ideas.

The disciple and aspirant upon the Path, and the Initiate upon his "Lighted Way," have no better training ground therefore than the marriage relation, rightly used and rightly understood. The bringing of the animal nature under rhythmic discipline, the elevation of the emotional and the instinctual natures upon the altar of sacrifice, and the self-abnegation required in the life of the family are tremendous purificatory and developing potencies. The celibacy required is that of the higher nature to the demands of the lower, and the refusal of the spiritual man to be dominated by the personality and the demands of the flesh. The attitude of an imposed celibacy upon the equipment of many a disciple has led to much prostitution and to many perversions of God-given functions and faculties; and even where there has not been this distressing condition, and where the life has been sane, consecrated and sound, there have frequently been undue suffering and much mental distress and disciplining, before unruly thoughts and tendencies could be controlled.

It is of course true that sometimes a man may be called to some particular life wherein he is faced with the problem of celibacy, and is forced to abstain from all physical relations and to live a strictly celibate life, in order to demonstrate to himself that he can control the animal and instinctual side of his nature. But this condition is frequently the result of excess and licence in a previous life, which necessitates stringent measures and abnormal conditions in order to offset and rectify past errors and give the lower nature time to readjust itself. But again it is no indication of spiritual development, rather the reverse. Forget not that here I am dealing with the special case of self-applied celibacy, and not with the present world-wide condition wherein, through economic and other reasons, men and women are forced to live without a natural and full life expression.

The sex problem must, in the last analysis, be solved in the home and under normal conditions, and it is the advanced people of the world and the disciples of all degrees who must thus solve it.

III. *The Rays and Man.*

Introductory Remarks.
1. The Ray of the Solar System.
2. The Planetary Ray—Earth.
3. The Ray of the Fourth Kingdom.
4. The Racial Rays.
5. The Rays in Cyclic Manifestation.
6. The Nations and the Rays.

CHAPTER III

The Rays and Man

Introductory Remarks

I HAVE now dealt with one of the basic problems confronting the race at this time. I interpolated my comments on the subject of sex at that particular point because it made a fitting conclusion to our study of the rays in connection with the animal kingdom.

Man is a living entity, a conscious son of God (a soul) occupying an animal body. Here lies the point. He is therefore in the nature of a link, and a far from missing link. He unifies in himself the results of the evolutionary process as it has been carried on during the past ages, and he brings into contact with that evolutionary result a new factor, that of an individual self-sustaining, self-knowing aspect. It is the presence of this factor and of this aspect which differentiates man from the animal. It is this aspect which produces in humanity a consciousness of immortality, a self-awareness and a self-centredness which make man truly to appear in the image of God. It is this innate and hidden power which gives man the capacity to suffer which no animal possesses, but which also confers on him the ability to reap the benefits of this experience in the realm of the intellect. This same capacity, in embryo, works out in the animal kingdom in the realm of the instincts. It is this peculiar property of humanity which confers upon it the power to sense ideals, to register beauty, to react sensuously to music, and to enjoy colour and harmony. It is this divine something which makes of mankind the prodigal son, torn between desire for the worldly life, for possessions and experience, and the attractive power of that centre, or home, from which he has come.

Man stands midway between heaven and earth, with his feet deep in the mud of material life and his head in heaven. In the majority of cases his eyes are closed, and he sees not the beauty of the heavenly vision, or they are open but fixed upon the mud and slime with which his feet are covered. But when his open eyes are lifted for a brief moment, and see the world of reality and of spiritual values, then the torn and distracted life of the aspirant begins.

Humanity is the custodian of the hidden mystery, and the difficulty consists in the fact that that which man conceals from the world is also hidden from himself. He knows not the wonder of that which he preserves and nourishes. Humanity is the treasure-house of God (this is the great Masonic secret), for only in the human kingdom, as esotericists have long pointed out, are the three divine qualities found in their full flower and *together*. In man, God the Father has hidden the secret of life; in man, God the Son has secreted the treasures of wisdom and of love; in man, God the Holy Spirit has implanted the mystery of manifestation. Humanity, and humanity alone, can reveal the nature of the Godhead and of eternal life. To man is given the privilege of revealing the nature of the divine consciousness, and of portraying before the eyes of the assembled sons of God (at the final conclave before the dissolution) what has lain hidden in the Mind of God. Hence the injunction before us today (in the words of the great Christian teacher) to possess in ourselves "the mind of Christ." This mind must dwell in us and reveal itself in the

The Rays and Man

human race in ever greater fullness. To man is given the task of raising matter up into heaven, and of glorifying rightly the form side of life through his conscious manifestation of divine powers.

To portray adequately the wonder and the destiny of the human kingdom lies beyond my powers or the power of any human pen, no matter how great a man's realisation may be, or his response to the beauty of God's world. Divinity must be lived, expressed and manifested, to be understood. God must be loved, known and revealed within the human heart and brain, in order to be intellectually grasped.

The hierarchy of mystics, knowers and lovers of God, are manifesting this revealed truth in the world of the mental plane and of the emotional plane today. But the hour has now come when the manifestation of this reality can, for the first time and in truth, manifest itself on the physical plane in an organised group form, instead of through the instrumentality of the few inspired sons of God who have, in past ages, incarnated as the guarantee of the future possibilities. The Hierarchy of Angels and of Saints, of Masters, Rishis and Initiates, can now begin to organise itself in material form on earth, because today the group idea is rapidly gaining ground, and the nature of humanity is being better understood. The Church of Christ, hitherto invisible and militant, can now be seen slowly materialising and becoming the Church visible and triumphant.

This is the coming glory of the Aquarian Age; this is the next revelation of the evolutionary cycle, and such is the task of the immediate future. The true drama of this triple relationship (of which physical sex, as we have seen, is but the symbol) will be enacted on a large scale in the life of the modern aspirant during the next fifty years. We shall see what is called symbolically "the birth of the Christ," or the second birth, taking place in many lives, producing on earth a large group of the spiritually new-born. They will be those who have brought together, consciously and within themselves, the two aspects of soul and body, and thus have consummated the "mystical marriage". The aggregate of these individual happenings will produce a group activity of an analogous kind, and we shall see the emergence on the physical plane of "the body of the Christ," and the appearance of the manifested Hierarchy. This is what is happening today, and all that we see going on around us in the world is but the pangs and the travail which precede this glorious birthing.

We are now in the process of this consummation. Hence the difficulty and agony evidenced in the life of every true disciple who—embodying in himself symbolically the two aspects of father-mother, spirit-matter, and having nurtured the Christ child through a period of gestation—is now giving birth to the Christ, within the animal stable and in the manger of the world. In the sum total of the general accomplishment will the entire group achieve and the Christ again appear on earth, incarnated this time in the many and not in the one personality. Yet each member of the group is a Christ in manifestation, and all together present the Christ to the world, and constitute a channel for the Christ force and life.

It is indeed and in truth from glory to glory that we go. The past glory of individualisation must fade away in that of initiation. The glory of the slowly emerging self-consciousness must be lost to sight in the wonder of the group consciousness of the race, and this the foremost thinkers and workers today most ardently desire. The glory that can be seen faintly shining in humanity, and the dim light which flickers within the human form, must give place to the radiance which is the glory of the developed son of God. Only a little effort is needed, and the demonstration of a steady staying power, to enable those who are now on the physical plane of experience to evidence the radiant light, and to establish upon the earth a great station of light which will illumine the whole of human thought. Always there have been isolated light bearers, down the ages. Now the group light bearer will shortly be seen. Then shall we see the rest of the human family (who respond not yet to the Christ impulse) having their progress facilitated towards the path of probation. The work will still be slow, and much yet remains to be done; but if all the aspirants of the world and all the disciples at work in the world today will submerge their personal interests in the task immediately ahead, we shall have what I might pictorially call the opening of a great station of light on earth, and the founding of a power house which will greatly hasten the evolution and elevation of humanity, and the unfoldment of the human consciousness.

There has been for long in esoteric circles much idle and oft foolish talk anent the ray upon which a man may be found. People are as ignorantly excited over being told which is their ray as they are over the portrayal of their past incarnations. The "new teaching on the rays" vies with astrology in its interest. Like the Athenians, men are always searching for the novel and the unusual, forgetting that every new truth and every new presentation of an old truth carries with it the onus of increased responsibility.

However, it is interesting to trace parallels, and it is becoming obvious to the careful student that the emergence of the teaching on the rays has happened at a time when the scientist is announcing the fact that there is naught to be seen and known save energy, and that all forms are composed of energy units and are in themselves expressions of force.

A ray is but a name for a particular force or type of energy, with the emphasis upon the quality which that force exhibits and not upon the form aspect which it creates. This is a true definition of a ray.

The Rays and the Races

We have been told in the past teaching of the Ageless Wisdom that a human being is a triple aspect of energy, and that he is essentially a trinity, as is the Deity. We speak of him technically as Monad-ego-personality. We define him as spirit-soul-body. I should like to point out here that in studying the human family as a unit and as a whole, it also will be discovered to be essentially a Monad, with seven egoic groups, within which all souls (in incarnation and out of incarnation) find their place, and with forty-nine corresponding racial forms through which the seven groups of souls cyclically express themselves. All souls work out their destiny in all races, but certain types predominate in certain racial forms. Where, then, is to be found any reason for racial predilections or antipathies? In the realisation of the truth that we all, at some time, experience incarnation in all racial forms will come the knowledge that there is only unity. The subject may be clarified if we tabulate the teaching and the ray relationship to the races as follows:

Ray	*Full Expression*	*Major Influence*
Ray I. Will. 1st ray souls.	In the 7th rootrace. Perfection of Plan.	1st and 7th subraces.
Ray II. Love-Wisdom. 2nd ray souls.	In the 6th rootrace. Perfected Intuition.	2nd and 6th subraces.
Ray III. Intelligence. 3rd ray souls.	In the 5th rootrace. Aryan race. Perfected Intellect.	3rd and 5th subraces.

Ray	Full Expression	Major Influence
Ray IV. Harmony. 4th ray souls.	In the 4th rootrace. Atlantean race. Perfected astralism. Perfected emotion.	4th and 6th subraces.
Ray V. knowledge. 5th ray souls.	In the 3rd rootrace. Lemurian. Perfected physical.	5th and 3rd subraces.
Ray VI. Devotion. 6th ray souls.	In the 2nd rootrace.	6th and 2nd subraces.
Ray VII. Ceremonial Magic. 7th ray souls.	In the 1st rootrace.	7th and 1st subraces.

Remember that this tabulation refers to the major ray cycles, and remember further that in every rootrace you have a continuous mingling and intermingling of the rays with what might be called the "constant" or dominating ray, which appears and re-appears with greater frequency and potency than do the other rays. There is therefore a close correspondence between certain rays and certain races, with their subraces, and these are coloured by these predominant ray influences. It is interesting also to interpret these ray influences (as I have expressed them) in terms of their quality leading to their objective, as follows:

The first Ray of Will leads from latent purpose in the first race to the fulfilled evolutionary Plan in the seventh race.

The second Ray of Love-Wisdom leads from love or divine desire in the second race to full intuitional understanding in the sixth race.

The third Ray of Active-Intelligence leads from the latent mental awareness of Lemurian man in the third race to the intellectual achievement of the Aryan race, the fifth race.

The fourth Ray of Harmony through Conflict leads from the period of that terrific balancing of forces in Atlantis (the fourth race) to the sanctified and free devotion of one-pointedness in the next or sixth race, with two lines of energy consummating in it. It marks the point of achievement of the Monads of Love, Who arrive at the expression of Love-Wisdom. The final race marks the point of achievement for the Monads of Will, just as the present Aryan race marks, and will mark, the achievement of the Monads of Intelligence. This warrants thought. It is a relative achievement, for this is the fourth round, but there is necessarily a "high-water mark," if I might so call it, for each round.

In the above four races you have the great period of the balancing of the forces for our humanity. The effect of the other three rays upon the Lemurian race and the two earlier and formless races need not here be considered by us. The nature of the consciousness of the forms found in those races, and the pressure exerted in them by the Entity Who informs the human family *as a whole*, are too abstruse for the average reader. He is mainly concerned with the races here enumerated, which summarise for him past and future achievement.

Consequently, in dealing with the human family, we must endeavour to think in larger terms than those of the individual man as we know him. We must look upon humanity itself as an integrated entity, as a Being, as a Life in a form. In this unified form Life every human being is a cell, and the seven races constitute the seven major centres, with the polarisation shifting ever into the higher centres, and the lower centres fading away into quiescence, until the time comes when all of the seven will be coordinated and energised, at the end of the age. We might here make the following suggestions (note this word) as to the relation between the races and the centres in the body of humanity:

The Rays and Man

Races	Centre	Expression
7th and final rootrace	The head centre	Will. Plan.
6th rootrace. The next	The centre between the eyebrows	Intuitive integration.
5th rootrace. The present	The throat centre	Creative power. Occult.
4th and past rootrace	The solar plexus centre	Psychic sensitivity. Mystic.
3rd and first human race	The sacral centre	Physical appearance. Generation.
2nd and etheric race	The heart or vital centre	Life forces coordinated.
1st race	The base of spine	The Will to be, to exist.

It is with only the last four evolving races that we shall concern ourselves (the first four dealt with in the above tabulation), for the first three races are too far off for any one under the degree of initiate to grasp their mode of development, their type of consciousness, and their procedure towards their goal. The point I seek to emphasize is the necessity of seeing the picture whole, and not in terms of individual man.

It may here be helpful if we note down our tabulation of certain points anent the human kingdom, as we did in connection with the three subhuman kingdoms.

THE HUMAN KINGDOM

Influences:

Two rays of divine energy are peculiarly active in bringing this kingdom into manifestation. These are:

1. The fourth Ray of Harmony, beauty and unity, attained through conflict.
2. The fifth Ray of Concrete Knowledge, or the power to know.

The fourth ray is the ray *par excellence* which governs humanity. There is a numerical relation to be noted here, for the fourth creative Hierarchy of human monads, the fourth ray, in this fourth round, on the fourth globe, the Earth, are extremely active. It is their close interrelation and interplay which is responsible for the emergence into prominence of humanity. In other rounds, humanity has not been the dominant evolution or the most important. In this round it is. In the next round, the dominant evolution will be that of souls on the astral level, and the deva kingdom. Humanity now walks in the light of day, symbolically speaking, on Earth, and these two rays were responsible for the process of initiating the human evolution in this major cycle. Our objective is the harmonising of the higher and the lower aspects, or principles, both in the individual and in the whole. This involves conflict and struggle, but produces eventually beauty, creative power in art, and synthesis. This result would not have been possible had it not been for the potent work of the fifth Ray of Concrete Knowledge which—in conjunction with the fourth ray—produced that reflection of divinity we call a *man*.

The human entity is a curious synthesis, on the subjective side of his nature, producing a fusion of life, of power, of harmonious intent and of mental activity. The following should be noted, for it is of profound psychological interest and import:

Rays I, IV and V . . .   predominate in the life of humanity and govern with increasing power man's mental life and determine his mental body.

The Rays and Man

Rays II and VI . . . . . govern potently his emotional life and determine the type of his astral body.

Rays III and VII . . . . govern the vital physical life and the physical body.

Here you have, if you note carefully, a summation of the rays which govern and differentiate the life of the personality forms, and therefore bring in other factors which psychologists will have to consider as time goes on. You will see therefore that:

1. The human soul or ego is found on one or other of the seven rays, in one or other of the seven ray groups.
2. The mind nature and mental body are governed by the Rays of Purpose, of Harmony or Synthesis, and of Knowledge.
3. The emotional nature and form are governed by the Rays of Love-Wisdom and of idealistic Devotion.
4. The vital life and physical body are governed by the Rays of Intelligence in matter and of Organising Power.

But in the midst of this complexity of rays and forces, the third and fifth rays hold paramount place, and govern the major cycles of the individual. He is controlled not only by his own ray cycles (determined by his egoic ray) and by the lesser cycles of the personality, but he comes also under the influence of the major and minor cycles in the ray life of humanity as a whole.

Results

Through the active work of the two rays above discussed, we find the fourth ray producing eventually in man the appearance of the *intuition*. The fifth ray is responsible for the development in him of the *intellect*. Here again we find appearing in man his great gift of synthesis and his prerogative of unification, for—as earlier said—he blends in himself the qualities of three kingdoms in nature, including the one before and the one after his own.

1. The kingdom of souls .... Intuition.
2. The human kingdom .... Intellect.
3. The animal kingdom .... Instinct.

Hence his problem, and hence his glory. We might also say that through the union of the positive intuition and the negative instinct the intellect is born, for man repeats in himself the great creative process as enacted in the universe. This is the inner creative side of consciousness, just as we have the outer creative side in the creation of forms.

Process:

In the human family, owing to the presence within the human physical form of a thinking entity, called by us the Soul, the procedure followed in order to produce conscious control is that of adaptation. All forms in the three lower subhuman kingdoms are also subjected to the process of adaptation, but that is a group adaptation to environment, whereas in humanity we have the adaptation of the individual to his environment. The person who works consciously and intelligently at adapting himself to that situation and those conditions in which he finds himself is relatively rare. Conscious adapting of oneself to circumstances is the result of evolutionary development. The stages by which man arrives at this capacity may be enumerated as follows:

1. That unconscious adaptation to his environment of the man who is primarily an unintelligent animal. Low grade savages are in this class, and many purely agricultural peasants who have not been subjected to modern education. The man at this stage is little better than an animal and is governed entirely by instinct.

The Rays and Man 323

2. An unconscious adaptation to environment carried on by the man who is beginning to evidence some faint flickers of mental perception. This is partly instinctual and is based on a growing self-love. There is more of the "I" consciousness in him, and rather less of group instinctual awareness. You find this growing self-realisation in the low grade slum dwellers, for instance, and in the petty criminal who is instinctual enough and bright enough to live by his wits and to show quickness in reactions and deftness manually. It is the stage of animal cunning.
3. A conscious and purely selfish adapting of oneself to the environment. In these cases, the man is definitely aware of his motives; they are consciously thought out and recognised, and the man makes "the best of his circumstances". He forces himself to live as far as possible harmoniously in his surroundings. In this there is really good motive, but principally the man is governed by a desire for comfort—physical, emotional and mental—to such a degree that he will discipline himself into such a condition that he fits wherever he may be and can get on with anyone.
4. From this stage on the differentiations become so numerous that they are difficult to follow, being mixtures of pure selfishness (developed often to the n*th* degree), of a growing recognition of the group, of an awakening realisation of the right of other people to a similar degree of comfort and harmony, and of a steady effort to adapt conditions of character and personality life, so that the purely selfish interests do no real damage to others, until we arrive at . . .
5. The average really good man who is struggling to adapt himself to his surroundings, to his group relations and responsibilities in such a way that some measure of love

can be seen. I refer not here to that instinctual love for family and children and herd which men share in common with the animals and which often breaks down when the loved individuals assert themselves. The tie is not strong enough to hold, and the motive is too selfish to resist the pull. I refer to that motivated love which recognises the rights of others and consciously strives to adapt itself to those recognised rights whilst tenaciously holding on to the rights of the personality.

6. Then we have the work of adaptation as carried on by the aspirants of the world who are theoretically convinced of their group relation, of its paramount importance, and of the need of every personality to develop its powers to the fullest capacity in order to bring real value to the group and to serve adequately the group need. In true esotericism, there is no such motive as "killing the personality", or of disciplining it to such an extent that it becomes a dead poor thing. The true motive is to train the threefold lower nature, the integrated personality, to the highest demonstration of its powers, latent or developing, in order that those powers may be brought to the helping of the group need, and the personality of the aspirant may be integrated into the group. Thereby the group life is enriched, the group potency is increased, and the group consciousness is enhanced.

What is therefore to be seen going on in the life of the true aspirant today (his developing recognition of group responsibility) can also be seen going on in groups, in organisations and nations. Hence the many experiments. A process is going forward whereby these groups, large or small, are being subjected to a house-cleaning, to a discarding of the rubbish of old and worn-out ideas, and to a period of disciplining and

The Rays and Man

training which must precede all real group life. When this process is over, we shall have these groups approaching each other in a new and real spirit of cooperation, of religious fusion, and in an international attitude which will be new indeed. Then they will have something of a surer and greater value to offer to the whole. Within all these groups which are struggling towards this newer realisation and integration, and which express what we might call "the sixth stage of adaptation," are those who are already at the seventh stage.

7. Here we have complete unselfish adaptation to the group need and purpose. Those who have reached this point in their evolution are decentralised as regards their own personality life. The focus of their mental attention is in the soul and in the world of souls. Their attention is not directed towards the personality at all, except in so far as is needed to force it to adhere to group or soul purpose. These servers who are expressions of soul radiance and attractive power are knowers of the Plan, and in every organisation they constitute the new and slowly growing group of World Servers. In their hands lies the salvation of the world.

8. The final group in this scale of adaptation is that of the higher initiates, the perfected Elder Brethren and Great Companions. They are perfectly adapted to Their personalities, to each other and to world conditions; but as a group They are learning how to adapt the forces of nature, the energies of the rays and the potencies of the zodiacal signs to the world need and the world demand in a practical manner and at any particular time. It is here that the work of the disciples of the world, and of the higher types of aspirants, proves helpful as a field

of experiment, and it is in the new group of World Servers that the process of adaptation goes on.

I have endeavoured to outline these stages of the process of adaptation in terms of consciousness, viewing the subject therefore philosophically and psychologically. It should be remembered that this process, as it goes on in consciousness, produces (surely and inevitably) corresponding changes in mechanism and structure, and in sense perception through the apparatus of the body. On these changes I lay no emphasis in this treatise, for they are beautifully dealt with by modern science, which is steadily forging ahead in the right direction. I lay the emphasis upon consciousness as the predisposing factor, and on the developed sense of awareness which produces an inner demand for improved equipment. The improving of equipment as a result of the demand of consciousness is the secret of the evolutionary impulse, down the ages. This inner demand in man awakens the centres, and the awakening of the centres determines the response of the endocrine system, governs the nervous system in its threefold capacity, and also the blood stream. Thus the outer form or mechanism is ever an indication of the point of evolution of the inner subjective and spiritual man.

The Secret:

This is called, in esotericism, "the secret of translation". I might bring the general concept underlying those words down to the intelligence of the average student by telling him that when a man really understands the elevating power of the aspiration, he can begin to work with the secret of translation. Students must lose sight of the foolish and erroneous idea that aspiration is really an emotional attitude. It is not. It is a scientific process, governing evolution itself. When given free scope and duly followed, it is the mode *par excellence* whereby the matter aspect, or the whole personality, is "raised up into heaven". The effect of continued aspiration, when followed by right action, is to bring about three things:

1. A stimulation of the higher atoms of the three bodies.
2. The discarding, as a result of this stimulation, of those atomic substances which (when present) occultly hold the aspirant down to earth.
3. The increasing of the magnetic attractive power of the higher atoms, which draw to themselves atoms of high vibration to take the place of those of low vibration. One point I should like to make here, in order to correct an almost universal wrong mental attitude. Right atoms of high vibration are attracted into a man's body or bodies by the power of the united attraction of the atoms already present, and not primarily by the will of the soul, except in so far as that will acts upon the high grade atoms already present and responsive.

Aspiration is an activity of an occult and scientific nature, and is instinctual in substance itself. This point needs emphasis when instructing groups.

It is an interesting side-light thrown upon the phenomena of aspiration that the power to levitate the body, which is so oft today the subject of psychic interest and research, is dependent upon having produced a peculiar alignment of the personality through aspiration and an act of the will. It presupposes in the three bodies a certain percentage of atoms of the adequate vibrations and lightness.

This secret of translation is the underlying cause of the caste system, and caste is a symbol of translation. In the last analysis, souls pass from caste to caste as they "translate" their bodies. The clue to the translation is to be found in the fact that no act of translation ever involves one body alone, and no "passing on and up" into another dimension, into another state of consciousness and another "caste," ever takes place unless an alignment has been produced between (for instance):

    a. The physical body and the emotional body.
    b. These two and the mental body.
    c. These three and the soul.
    d. These four and the group of World Servers.

In these four alignments we have the esoteric parallels of which the outer caste system is the prostituted symbol. Ponder on this, for the caste system is universal in the world. It is when the third alignment has been truly accomplished and when the light of the fourth constituent to the relationship dominates the inherent light of the other three, that the objective of man's evolution is reached. This brings us to the point next to be considered.

Purpose:

This purpose is the Transfiguration. This is the esoteric goal set before humanity. This was the tremendous event which was enacted before humanity by the greatest of all the sons of God in His Own Body, Whom I and all true disciples regard as the Master of all the Masters, the Christ. What shall I say about this culminating event for which the entire personality of man waits? This third great initiation marks a crisis in the initiatory work, and produces a further synthesis experienced in the life of the spiritual man. Up to the third initiation, man has been occupied with the process of fusing soul and body into one unity. After the third initiation (and owing to an event which takes place) man is oriented

The Rays and Man

towards, and becomes occupied with, a further fusion in consciousness, that of spirit-soul-body. I speak of a fusion in consciousness. The unity is ever there, and man in evolution is really becoming aware of that which already exists.

Divisions:

These are five in number from the standpoint of this treatise on esotericism. They can here be only briefly indicated, as elucidation of them would involve too much.

1. The *racial divisions.* These can be considered in two ways:
    a. From the standpoint of modern esoteric science.
    b. From the standpoint of *The Secret Doctrine*, with its septenary divisions of mankind and its forty-nine subdivisions.
2. The division of humanity into *seven main ray types*, which might be enumerated as follows:
    a. The power type . . . full of will and governing capacity.
    b. The love type . . . . . full of love and fusing power.
    c. The active type . . . .full of action, and manipulating energy.
    d. The artistic type . . . full of the sense of beauty and creative aspiration.
    e. The scientific type . full of the idea of cause and results. The mathematical type.
    f. The devotee type . . full of idealism.
    g. The business type . .full of organising power. given to ritualistic ceremony.
3. The *twelve astrological groups*. These we shall consider in dealing with *The Rays and the Zodiac*, and so shall not touch upon them here.
4. The division of human beings into *three esoteric groups*:
    a. Those unawakened to the "I" consciousness.
    These are called esoterically "the darkened sparks."

b. Those awakened to the condition of individuality.
   These are called "the flickering lights."
c. Those awakened to the knowledge of the soul.
   These are called "the radiant sons of light."
5. The division of humanity into *three types of aspirants:*
   a. Those watched from a distance by the guiding Hierarchy.
   b. Those awakened by and attracted to the Hierarchy.
   c. Those who, from the angle of the personality, belong to the world of forces, but are awakened souls whose consciousness is being integrated into, that of the Hierarchy. These are the new group of World Servers.

To these three last groups the Hierarchy Itself may well be added.

The table as a whole shows the main divisions into which esoteric psychology divides humanity, and if you study it with care you will note how all-inclusive it is. I commend it to modern psychologists for study.

Objective Agency:

In the case of the human being, in whom the senses (slowly developed in the lower kingdoms) are already functioning, the outer agency whereby he grows is the world of experience, the tangible physical plane world. There he dwells in the flesh, and it is for him an adequate field of unfoldment; in the process of developing group consciousness he finds that multiplicity of contacts which is needed to awaken his response to his environment. This environment itself is part of the life and expression of Deity, and through its means he arrives at a knowledge of some aspects of God's manifestation. Using the five senses, and working with earth, air, fire and water, he thereby gathers to himself all that is available for his use, and works in, and with, and through the outer world of daily living.

Subjective Agency:

Here we find the mind being employed as an organ of sense, as a synthetic or common sense, and as an instrument of discovery by means of which a man unfolds the truly human consciousness. Through the use of the mind, he learns to protect himself, to guard his interests, and to preserve his identity. Through the use of the mind, he begins to discriminate and to cultivate slowly a sense of values which enables him eventually to lay the emphasis upon the ideal and the spiritual, and not upon the material and the physical.

Quality:

This quality is the development of sattva or rhythm within the human kingdom. This is really harmonious response to vibration, and leads to the integration of the unit in the whole and to the production of that "understanding" which will enable the man to eliminate all barriers in his consciousness, and to render (simply and naturally) a rhythmic and complete response to all conditions and states of awareness. Let it ever be remembered that the secret of the quality of humanity (if I may use so cumbrous a phrase) is the power to identify the human consciousness with all other forms of consciousness and of awareness, with all forms of unconscious and instinctual response, and with all forms of the superconscious or divine sense of being. This can ultimately be done at will.

We must now begin what really constitutes an outline of the new psychology This will work out to its fulfillment and true usefulness in the Aquarian age. It will then become the basic and fundamental science of that age, just as electrical science (the electricity of matter) is the basic achievement of the Piscean age. What we are really going to consider are the influences which make a man what he is, and which determine the quality of his appearance. This appearance must be studied in terms of the entire integrated personality, and not just from the outer and objective physical condition. The influences which determine him are his own personal and soul rays which play upon him and affect his consciousness, finding entrance into his form equipment through the energy units of which that form is made. Other determining influences are also the solar, cosmic and environing factors which likewise play upon him.

It might here be asked: What are the differences between the influences which are ray influences and those which are of an astrological nature, such as the rising sign, or the governing planets?

The energies which astrologically affect a human being are those which play upon him as a result of the apparent progress of the sun through the heavens, either once every twenty-five thousand years or once every twelve months. Those that constitute the ray forces do not come from the twelve constellations of the zodiac, but emanate primarily from a world of being and of consciousness which lies behind our solar system, and which themselves come from the seven constellations which form the body of manifestation of the One About Whom Naught May Be Said. Our solar system is one of these seven constellations. This is the world of Deity Itself, and of it a man can know nothing until he has passed through the major initiations. When we come later to study the zodiac and its relation to the rays we shall work this out more carefully and so make the idea clearer. It

The Rays and Man

is with the ray influences that we are dealing here, and not with the zodiacal.

One of the first things we need to grasp, as we study man and the rays, is the large number of these ray influences which play upon him, and which form him, and "enliven" him, and make him the complexity he is. It would be wise for us to enumerate them one by one and consider them for a while. There is no real reason for bewilderment in this connection. As time progresses and the rays are more widely studied, man's relation to them will be subjected to careful analysis, and there will then be possible a wide checking up of information and of facts. There will later come a tabulation and an understanding of the ray forces. This will lead to a science of psychology of a more sure and accurate nature, instead of the speculative science it now is. At present modern psychology concerns itself with the more apparent aspects of incarnated man and with a discussion of certain speculative subjective possibilities.

It might therefore be noted that the following rays and influences must be considered in the case of every individual man, for they make him what he is and determine his problem:

1. The ray of the solar system itself.
2. The ray of the planetary Logos of our planet.
3. The ray of the human kingdom itself.
4. Our particular racial ray, the ray that determines the Aryan race.
5. The rays that govern any particular cycle.
6. The national ray, or that ray influence which is peculiarly influencing a particular nation.
7. The ray of the soul, or ego.
8. The ray of the personality.
9. The rays governing:

a. The mental body.
b. The emotional or astral body.
c. The physical body.

There are other rays, but the above are the most powerful and have the greater conditioning power. Let us briefly consider them:

1. *The Ray of the Solar System*

It must be remembered that the dominating ray, the outstanding influence in our solar system, is the great cosmic second Ray of Love-Wisdom, a dual ray,—that is, a ray combining two great cosmic principles and energies. It is the ray which governs the "personality" of our solar Logos, if such an expression may be used, and (because it is dual) it indicates both His personality and soul rays, which in Him are now so balanced and blended that, from the angle of humanity, they constitute the major ray, the one ray. This major ray determines both His quality and His purpose.

Every unit of life and every form in manifestation is governed by this second ray. Basically speaking, the energy of love, expressed with wisdom, is the line of least resistance for the manifested lives in our solar system. This ray qualifies the life of all the planets, and the attractive magnetic love of God pours through His created universe; it emerges in the consciousness and determines the objective of all evolving forms. Each human being, as a whole, therefore, lives in a universe and on a planet which is constantly the objective of God's love and desire, and which constantly (as a result of this love) is itself attracted and attractive. For this we do not make adequate allowance. Teachers, parents and educators would do well to recognise the potency of this ray force, and trust to the Law to make all things good.

2. *The Ray of the Planet—Earth.*

Each of the seven sacred planets (of which our Earth is not one) is an expression of one of the seven ray influences. These seven planets might be enumerated as follows, and the rays working through them are accurately given. The student however must remember three things:

1. That every planet is the incarnation of a Life, of an Entity or Being.
2. That every planet, like a human being, is the expression of two ray forces,—the personality and the egoic.
3. That two rays are therefore in esoteric conflict in each planet.

I but indicate one of the rays, and I do not tell you whether it is the egoic or personality ray of the particular planetary Logos. Too much accuracy and too detailed information is not at this time good for humanity, which is yet too selfish to be entrusted with it.

THE PLANETS AND RAYS

Sacred	*Ray*	*Non-Sacred*	*Ray*
1. Vulcan	1st ray.	1. Mars	6th ray.
2. Mercury	4th ray.	2. Earth	3rd ray.
3. Venus	5th ray.	3. Pluto	1st ray.
4. Jupiter	2nd ray.	4. The Moon	4th ray.
5. Saturn	3rd ray.		veiling a hidden planet.
6. Neptune	6th ray.	5. The Sun	2nd ray.
7. Uranus	7th ray.		veiling a hidden planet.

I deal here with the major ray cycles and not with the minor cycles. Two rays, you will note, are apparently not expressing themselves through the non-sacred planets; the seventh and the fifth. There are only five non-sacred planets. But the reason which makes a planet sacred or not is one of the secrets of a certain major initiation, and I may not further elucidate here. Suffice it to say that the sacred planets are seven in number, making a totality of twelve planetary manifestations. It will be obvious to the observant reader also that certain sacred planets and certain non-sacred planets have a close relation with each other through the rays which influence them. These are:

Ray I .... Vulcan .... Pluto.
Ray II .... Jupiter .... The Sun.
Ray III .... Saturn .... The Earth.
Ray IV .... Mercury .... The Moon.
Ray VI .... Neptune .... Mars.

These relationships will provide a somewhat new field of investigation for astrologers.

You will note therefore how peculiarly this Earth on which we live is suited to the development of the incarnating sons of God. Man comes forth, as do all lives within the radius of influence of a solar system, upon the inspiration of love, expressed in wisdom. Love is not a sentiment. Love is the great principle of attraction, of desire, of magnetic pull, and (within our solar system) that principle demonstrates as the attraction and the interplay between the pairs of opposites. This interplay provides every needed grade or type of unfoldment for consciousness. Conscious response is first made to the most potent and to the densest kind of attraction in matter, that of the mineral kingdom. Dense as it is, and heavy as is that type of vibration, it is nevertheless an expression of embryonic love. Response again comes, with greater facility and more true awareness and sensitivity, in the next kingdom, and the consciousness of the vegetable world emerges. But this too is love. It responds more freely and reacts to a far wider range of contacts in the animal kingdom, and the basic instinctual desires emerge and can be recognised. They, in due time, become the motivation of the

The Rays and Man   337

life, yet still it is only the love of God which is manifested. It is love between conscious life and conscious form; it is love between the pairs of opposites, leading to an eventual synthesis or marriage; it is relationship between the basic dualities; it is not sentiment but a fact in a great natural process. Always there is the emerging glory and radiance of a growing love, until we come to the human kingdom wherein love enters another plane. Then responsiveness and sensitivity and human sentimental reaction develop into a rudimentary mind. The consciousness of loving and being loved, of attracting and of being attracted, enters through the door of the intelligence and expands into the human state of awareness. Pleasure and pain become definite factors in unfoldment, and the long agony of humanity commences. Love then is seen in its naked selfishness, but also its potential glory can be sensed. Love or attractive desire then attracts to itself that which it feels it needs, but later, that is changed into what it thinks it should have, and this, in time, is transmuted into that which it knows is the divine non-material heritage of a son of God. Ponder on these last few words, for in the true understanding of love as feeling, love as thinking, and love as aspiration will come a clarification of man's problem and his liberation from the thralldom of the lower loves into the liberty of love itself, and into the freedom of the one who possesses all things, and yet desires nothing for the separated self.

The magnetic pull of that which is desired is modified on our planet by the personality ray of our particular planetary Logos. This is the Ray of Active Intelligence, and of selective Adaptability. Just as every cell and atom in the human body is modified and conditioned by the egoic ray and the ray of each of the inner bodies, so every cell and atom in the body of the planetary Logos is conditioned and modified by

His outstanding ray influence, in this case, His personality ray. In this conditioning influence is found a clue to the distress and agony and pain in the world today. The planetary Logos of our Earth is primarily conditioned by a cosmic ray, to be sure, but not by His egoic ray. Perhaps in this condition may be found the reason (or one of the reasons) why our Earth is not one of the seven sacred planets. On this I need not enlarge, but it was necessary to call attention to this great determining factor, the third ray, which is the personality ray of our planetary Logos.

This ray brings in the factor of discrimination through mental activity, and this, in its turn, balances the so-called love nature, and it is in truth the cause of our evolutionary growth. The life in forms passes through discriminative and selective activity from one experience to another in an ever widening scale of contacts. It is this Ray of Intelligent Activity which dominates man at this time. Human beings are largely centred in their personalities; they are "egocentric," in the terminology of the psychologist, which recognises the integrating principle of the ego (in many cases) but does not yet recognise the overshadowing ego or soul, except under such a vague term as "the superconscious". We have therefore a humanity engrossed by a tremendous activity and demonstrating everywhere a vital discriminating and intellectual interest in all types of phenomena. This tendency to be active will go on increasing and intensifying until the Aryan race will merge into the coming major root-race, for which we have as yet no name, though we recognise that in that race the intellect will serve the intuition. Human activity is now regarded as having reached an incredible speed and intensity of vibration, yet from the angle of the world Knowers it is only just beginning to express itself, and is relatively feeble as yet. The growth of the tendency to vital speed can be noted if history is studied, and the pace at which man now lives, and the complexity and the many dynamic interests of his life, may be compared with those of the average man two hundred years ago. The last twenty-five years of man's history have shown a tremendous speeding up as compared with conditions fifty years ago.

The reason for this increase of intelligent activity and rapidity of response and contact is to be found in the subjective fact that humanity is with great speed integrating the three aspects of human nature into a unity, called personality. Men are steadily becoming personalities, and unifying into one expression their physical, emotional and mental aspects; hence they are more able to respond to the ray of the integrated personality of the One in Whom they live, and move, and have their being.

Speaking therefore in terms of man's life problem, we might state that it is affected potently by the two major influences which beat upon the human kingdom, the cosmic ray of the solar system, the Ray of Love-Wisdom, and the cosmic ray of the planet, which is the personality ray of the planetary Logos, the Ray of Active Intelligence or Adaptability. Man might be defined as a unit of conscious life, swept into tangible expression through the discriminating love of God. Through his life experiences he is presented with innumerable choices which gradually shift from the realm of the tangible into that of the intangible. As he attracts, or is attracted by, the life of his environment, he becomes increasingly conscious of a series of shifting values, until he reaches that point in his development when the pull or the magnetic attraction of the subjective world and the intangible mental and spiritual realities are more potent than the factors which have hitherto enticed him on. His sense of values is no longer determined by:

1. The satisfaction of his instinctual animal nature.
2. The desires of a more emotional and sentimental kind which his astral body demands.
3. The pull and pleasures of the mind nature, and of intellectual appetites.

He becomes potently attracted by his soul, and this produces a tremendous revolution in his entire life, regarding the word "revolution" in its true sense, as a complete turning around. This revolution is happening now, on such a universal scale in the lives of individuals in the world, that it is one of the main factors producing the present potency of experimental ideas in the world of modern times. The attractive power of the soul grows steadily, and the pull of the personality weakens as steadily. All this has been brought about by the process of experiment, leading to experience; by experience, leading to a wiser use of the powers of the personality; by a growing appreciation of a truer world of values and of reality, and by an effort on man's part to identify himself with the world of spiritual values and not with a world of material values. The world of meaning and of causes becomes gradually the world in which he finds happiness, and his selection of his major interests and the use to which he decides to put his time and powers are finally conditioned by the truer spiritual values. He then is on the path of illumination. I have sought to express the effects of these two major ray influences in terms of mysticism and of philosophy, but in very truth all that I have here said could be expressed scientifically and in terms of scientific formulas, if man were mentally equipped to appreciate them. But this is not yet possible. All these ray vibrations, no matter which they may be, can eventually be reduced to formulas and to symbols.

The Rays and Man 341

Reaction to environment, sensitive response to the ray influences which govern and express themselves through the forms which compose man's environment, a growing power to discriminate between energies and forces, a slowly developing sense of values (which sense is the one which eventually dispels illusion and glamour and reveals reality), and a shift of the discriminating interest away from the worlds of tangible experience, of emotional life and of mental interest,— all this expresses the effect of the interplay between the two rays of the solar system and of the planet. These, intermingling, pour through and affect mankind.

One of the most difficult things with which the Masters are today confronted is to prove to man that the old and recognised values and the tangible world of phenomena (emotional and physical) must be relegated to their right place in the background of man's consciousness, and that the intangible realities, and the world of ideas and causes must be, for him, in the immediate future, the main centre of attention. When man grasps this and lives by this knowledge, then the glamour which now holds the world will disappear. If you ponder on this you will recognise how the great crisis of 1914-1918 did much useful work in smashing the glamourous material security in which men were living, and in destroying much of their instinctual and sensuous selfishness. The group is beginning to be recognised as of major importance, and the welfare of the individual is important just in so far as the unit is an integral part of the group. This will not eventually destroy initiative and individuality. It is only in our initial experiments, and through our inexpertness in the use of the discriminating faculty, that we are, as yet, making such sad mistakes. This process of destroying the world illusion has been going on on a large scale ever since; in every country, through the various experiments which are going forward, the glamour is breaking down and the truer values of group welfare, of group integration, and of group progress are emerging. The sense of insecurity which is such a distressing aspect of the present upheaval is due simply to this destruction of the old sense of values, to that dispelling of glamour which reveals at present an unfamiliar landscape, and to the fear and instability which man feels when he comes up against the world "Dweller on the Threshold." This has to be broken up and destroyed, for it blocks the way to the new world of values. The great thought form which man's greed and materiality have built, down the ages, is being steadily demolished, and mankind is on the verge of a liberation which will take him on to the Path of Discipleship. I refer not here to the final liberation, but to that liberation which comes from a free choice, wisely used and applied to the good of the whole, and conditioned by love. Note that I say, "wisely used." Wisdom, actuated and motivated by love, and intelligently applied to world problems, is much needed today and is not yet to be found, except among the few illumined souls in every nation,—in every nation, I say, without exception. Many more must love with wisdom and appreciate the group aspiration before we shall see the next reality to be known and to emerge out of the darkness which we are now in the process of dispelling.

3. *The Ray of the Fourth Kingdom*

We now touch briefly upon an obscure and difficult subject, and one that will appeal primarily to those types who work with the Law of Correspondences. Esotericists must remember that every kingdom in nature constitutes a totality of lives. Every atom in every form in nature is a life, and these lives form the cells of a Being's body or vehicle of manifestation. There is a Being embodied in every kingdom

The Rays and Man

in nature. Just as the myriads of atomic lives in the human body constitute a man's body of expression and form his appearance, so it is with the greater Life informing the fourth kingdom in nature. This appearance—as are all appearances—is qualified by some particular ray type, and is determined also by the vital principle or spirit aspect. Thus every form is composed of innumerable lives, which have in them a preponderance of some ray quality. This is an occult platitude. These qualified lives produce a phenomenal appearance, and thus constitute a unity, through the influence of the integrating principle, which is never absent.

The ray which governs the sum total of the human kingdom is the fourth Ray of Harmony through Conflict. It might be symbolically stated that the egoic ray of the Life which informs the human family is this fourth ray, and that the personality ray is the fifth ray of knowledge through discrimination,—the Ray, as it is called, of Concrete Knowledge or Science. Harmony through conflict, and the power to achieve knowledge through discriminating choice—these are the two rays or major influences which sweep through humanity as a whole, and drive it forward towards its divine destiny. They are the predisposing factors upon which a man may count and infallibly depend. They are the guarantee of attainment, but also of turmoil and temporary duality. Harmony, expressing itself in beauty and creative power, is gained through battle, through stress and strain. Knowledge, expressing itself eventually through wisdom, is attained only through the agony of successively presented choices. These, submitted to the discriminating intelligence during the process of the life experience, produce at last the sense of true values, the vision of the ideal, and the capacity to distinguish reality behind the intervening glamour.

Students of esotericism will, of course, bear in mind that

the fourth ray has a natural relation to the fourth kingdom in nature, which is in turn the lowest manifestation of the fourth creative Hierarchy. This unification of the three major results of the activity of a great Life might be enumerated thus:

1. The ray power or life which tends ever towards harmony and an eventual beauty, the fourth ray.
2. The creative hierarchy of human monads, who (little as they may realise it) have already attained wisdom and are veritably at this time the divine sons of God.
3. The fourth kingdom in nature which is the result of the evolutionary activity of the above, who are in their turn impelled to this activity by the fourth ray.

This is essentially the true apostolic succession, for it provides a triple line of directed energy. This produces the human manifestation on the fourth globe of our Earth chain, and in this fourth round is responsible for the tremendous crisis with which our present humanity is confronted. The conflict aspect of the process is at its height, nay, has passed its height, from the angle of physical plane expression. This situation and this triple influence, producing the manifestation of the sons of God, is summed up for us in the terse words of the *Old Commentary*–terse, when we remember that they express the long agony of humanity's test, and the opening to man of the door into the fifth kingdom of spiritual being. They include therefore, in their meaning, his goal and objective and the process whereby he attains:

"*The Holy Four* descend from out the heavenly places and venture forth towards the sphere of Earth. From the fourth great plane they thus control the battle.

"The Lord of Harmony, Who sits on high, pours all His life and force throughout the field of conflict. He sees the end from the beginning nor stays His hand though deep and full the pain and agony. Peace must be the goal. Beauty must be achieved. He cannot then arrest the life and stop its flow.

"*The Middle Four*, rested now from the earlier campaign, gird on their armour and hide themselves behind the outer form. They leave the fourth great sphere of harmony and pass on to the plane of mind. There they fortify the temple of the Lord, illumine it with light and glory, and then they turn their eyes towards the Earth.

"*The Lower Four* take form between the lives that are not human and the three groups of lives which dwell beneath the threshold. They seek to link and blend, to bridge and fuse. Mankind now lives. The higher and the middle four meet in the lower four upon the fourth great globe.

"The battle now proceeds. When the three groups of manifested fours can see each other in the light, and later blend their forces, the goal will be achieved.

"In the fourth globe of action and in the major cycle of the fourth expression will this fusion be completed. The lower four, merged in the middle four, will leave the triple world of conflict, and find their dwelling place, whilst in the form, within the fourth sphere whence came forth the higher governing four. Thus will the government be established; the glory seen; the rule of the hierarchy demonstrated.

"In the fourth race (the Atlantean—A.A.B.) the conflict was begun, and consciousness was born. In the fifth race (the Aryan—A.A.B.) the crisis of the battle will be seen, and then the lower four and the middle four will begin to unite their forces. In the sixth race, the dust of battle dies away. The lower four, the middle four and the higher four will chant in unison the glory of their Lord, the beauty of the love of God, the wonder of the brotherhood of man. This is their paean".

Esoterically speaking (and not speaking symbolically, for there is a distinction between these two forms which students would do well to note), when the lines of forces are adjusted and there is free interplay of energies and a straight aligned channel between the various aspects of divinity, then there is achievement and beauty. This is the theme of the above symbolical and ancient formulation of truth, which is in the nature of a symbolical prophecy. The same idea has been expressed in a still more ancient and terse statement which has to be understood and reduced to a mantric formula when the fourth initiation is taken:

> "When the forces of the four, three times repeated, become the four, then the Life of . . . . . . reveals Itself in beauty".

It is interesting to note that the numerical value of the word "four" is the same in detail as that of the word "force", if you eliminate the number five. For humanity, it is the fifth energy which leads to the battlefield, the energy of the discriminating mind, and when that has been in due time used, controlled and transmuted, "only the four remains and force has gone". Note the detail of the numbering:

F O R C E
6 6 9 3 5 . . . . 29 . . . . . . 11. Number of adept, using energy.
F O U R
6 6 3 9 . . . . . . 24 . . . . . . 6. The creator, unifying the subjective and the objective.

It is apparent that *force* in the first group ends in separativeness, for five is the number of the mind and of man. Number nine, the number of initiation, is hidden midway in force, but the climaxing figures indicate activity and separation. In the second group of figures, activity precedes the nine of initiation, and that nine is the culmination. *But five is left out.* Man is no longer really human or separative. He is the perfected four of the lower three and the soul. Putting the truth quite simply, let it be borne in mind that mankind, the fourth kingdom, which is an expression of the fourth creative hierarchy of human monads, is swept by the instinct or impulse towards harmony, and is thus primarily under the influence of the fourth ray. This harmony is achieved through the use

The Rays and Man

of the energy of the fifth ray of knowledge. Then through gained and applied knowledge, the result is beauty and the power to create. Then the ray of the fifth Lord will be withdrawn from the major cycle governing humanity, and wisdom and intuitional buddhic response will characterise humanity. There is a close interplay in this major cycle, as far as mankind is concerned, between the two ray Lords of Harmony and of Knowledge. It is again in this numerical relation of four and five that the number nine emerges, which is the number of initiation. An adept of the fifth initiation is one who has achieved complete harmony through right knowledge. This takes place at the fourth initiation and is demonstrated or proven at the fifth.

A close study of the tabulations of the rays affecting humanity will have made it clear that they are so many and so diverse that the complexity of the subject is very great. There are numerous influences which tend to make man what he is, and of many of them little is as yet known. In the early stages of his development, it is well-nigh impossible for any one (except an initiate) to deal with the various phases or even to recognise the indications of humanity's reactions to these rays. But as mankind evolves, and as the form aspect becomes increasingly a better and finer response apparatus and a more plastic sensitive reflector of the inner man, definition and analysis become easier. Types emerge with greater clarity in their delineations, and the ray qualities begin to dominate. The impress of the controlling rays can be more clearly noted and the point in evolution can be more accurately realised.

We have now to consider the rays which dominate the races of mankind. The average reader would be wise to take the position that for him, at least, the information hitherto given, and that which concerns the racial, national and cyclic rays, provide an interesting hypothesis which can be intelligently accepted until disproven. This knowledge must necessarily remain hypothetical for several life periods, where the average student is concerned. When, however, we come to the consideration of the final three points of this section of our treatise, it may be possible to check the information, to correlate the ray types, and to discover (by a study of the potencies involved) their emerging characteristics and ray forces.

By the proving therefore of the human detail, we lay the ground for the acceptance of the cosmic, solar and planetary knowledge. What is proven true on the small scale opens the door for the understanding of that which exists on a larger scale. "Man, know thyself" is a potent key to the knowledge of Deity and to the workings of divinity.

4. *The Racial Rays*

The reader needs to remember that three rays are occultly quiescent and four rays are in varying degrees of activity. Let us recapitulate for a moment so that this thought may be clearly anchored in our minds:

Rays one, four and six are at this time out of manifestation, though ray six began to decline in influence only three hundred years ago, and its potency, though greatly weakened, can still be felt.

Rays two, three, five and seven are still potent. The following statement may give some idea of the relative "values" of these ray influences.

Ray three has been the longest in incarnation, but in 1875 it occultly "completed its outgoing, and began to curve upon itself, and thus return". It is therefore just beginning to wane. When this event occurs in connection with any type of en-

The Rays and Man 349

ergy, the effect produced is always of a crystallising nature and is apt to produce "set forms which warrant prompt destruction". This causes mental conditions of a set and static nature. The inference is therefore clear that in the later stages of this ray's activity we have the demonstration of those dogmatic, sectarian and theological attitudes, for instance, which mark the decline and consequent uselessness of the various schools of thought which have in their time embodied man's ideas and sufficed for his helping during the period of their growth.

Ray two has a rapidly recurring cycle. This is due to its excessive potency. Being the major ray of our solar system (of which all the other rays are but aspects), it might be said that this ray is really never out of incarnation. There are nevertheless constant cycles of waxing and waning potency, produced by the interplay of the rays which produce what is called in the ancient archives "the intrusion of one or another of the seven Brothers Who block the door from whence the force emerges", and "the disappearance of that radiant Brother Who passes on His way and leaves behind an open door through which another Brother can pass upon His mission preordained." The symbolism is clear. The cycles of the second ray are dynamic and recur in a regular rhythm at this time and during the twenty-five thousand years of a zodiacal cycle in sequences of five hundred years. Therefore in 1825 the potency of this ray began to decline as the peak of its two hundred fifty years emergence was reached. It was the gradual withdrawal of this ray which led to that growth of separativeness in the world which produced the European wars and the great World War. This ray will continue declining for another one hundred forty years. This does not necessarily mean the growth of physical violence and the prevalence of war. Humanity is now so much more responsive to ray influences that the watching Hierarchy (through egoic stimulation and the sensitivity of certain nations to the inner guidance) can offset the more obvious major effects. This will give an interesting side light upon the vast importance of these cyclic happenings.

Ray five is the latest of the rays to come into activity and is only in process of "coming forth to power." It is steadily increasing in potency, and the result of its influence will be to guide humanity into increasing knowledge. Its energy beats upon the minds of men at this time and produces that stimulation which lies behind all the scientific approach to truth in all departments of human thought. Being also the ray which governs the personality aspect of the fourth kingdom in nature, and being one of the rays determining or conditioning our Aryan race, its present potency is excessive. This is a point to be remembered with care, for it accounts for much that we can see happening in the world of thought.

Ray seven is also in manifestation, and has been since the year 1675. This we shall consider in more detail when we take up our fifth point: The Rays in Cyclic Manifestation.

The interplay, therefore, and the beauty of the blended energies are at this time great, for so many rays are either manifesting simultaneously or are just passing out and are therefore not entirely negligible; or are hovering near at hand ready to pass into the stage of revelation and so continue their cyclic work. Only one ray is today really out of manifestation altogether and functioning entirely behind the scenes, and that is the first ray. Where humanity is concerned, the first ray makes its presence felt, and its potency dominates, when the stage of accepted discipleship is reached. It increases in power as progress on the Path is gained. Thus there is beginning to be gathered on the subjective side of life a steadily growing group of those who can function under the influence of this first ray. When enough of the sons of men can thus function, their united responsiveness will constitute a channel through which this first ray can come into manifestation. This is one of the main activities and objectives of the Hierarchy, and in the right understanding of the result of the responsiveness of humanity to the ray influences shall we arrive at the recognition of a law in nature hitherto undiscovered. This particular law is connected with the department of the Governor of the world, the Manu.

It might be of interest here to note that ray six governs the Path of Probation and nourishes the fires of idealism in the aspirant.

Ray two governs the Path of Discipleship and transmutes knowledge into wisdom, feeding likewise the Christ life in each disciple.

Ray one governs the Path of Initiation, producing detachment from form, the destruction of all that hinders, and fostering that dynamic will in the initiate which will enable him to take the needed steps towards the Initiator.

It should here be noted that the rays divide themselves into two groups, i.e.:

1. The Rays of Aspect . . . . . . Rays 1. 2. 3. The major rays.
2. The Rays of Attribute . . . . Rays 4. 5. 6. 7. The minor rays.

The distinction between these two groups has been well summed up in some sentences from the *Old Commentary*:

> "The seven brothers are all the children of the same Father, but the elder three partake of the Father's nature. The younger four resemble the Mother. The three elder sons go forth into the universe of stars, and there they represent the Father. The younger four go forth into the universe of stars and show the nature of the one the Father loved."

The rays of aspect have longer cycles than the rays of attribute, and their measure is occultly slow, cumulative in effect, and—as the ages pass away—their momentum steadily increases. The rays of attribute have briefer cycles, and produce a steady heart-beat and a regular rhythm in the solar system. The three rays of aspect might be regarded as embodying the will and purpose of the incarnating Logos. The rays of attribute can equally be regarded as embodying the quality and character of the incarnating Logos. Symbolically speaking, the three major rays are the expression (during manifestation) of the egoic aspect of the solar Logos, whilst the four rays of attribute embody His personality aspect. Nevertheless it must be remembered that the seven together are the manifestation in form of what God is, and the measure of the divine intention. Students should bear these points in mind as they study the rays and their cyclic influence on mankind. If they will remember that when a major ray is in manifestation, then the divine intent, the universal purpose and Plan will be seen emerging with greater clarity, they will expect and look for great happenings in the racial development. If a minor ray is demonstrating, we shall have the growth of psychic sensitivity, and the emergence of a form life which will express the divine nature more potently than the divine Plan.

This truth can be applied also to the development of the individual, and will govern and determine his evolutionary growth either from the angle of purpose or from the angle of quality. Lives that are given to the unfolding of purpose will be of a different timbre and nature than those which are given to the development of character and quality. This is a psychological point of real moment.

The statement made above is one of the most significant and important yet communicated in this treatise, and well merits careful consideration. The true import is of course most difficult to grasp, but the general meaning can be recognized and appreciated by the searching student. The rays of aspect produce primarily the unfolding of the Plan. The rays of attribute produce the unfolding of the qualities of Deity. This is true of the solar Logos and of a human being, of the planetary Deity and of humanity as a whole.

The application of this truth can be clearly seen in connection with the Aryan race and the two rays which govern and control its destiny. The third Ray of Intelligent Activity or Adaptability governs the entire career of the race, and through this dominance we can see working out the plan of God, which is the definite fusion of spirit and matter, through the evolution of the soul of man. The result of this fusion may be briefly summed up in the following three statements:

1. A widespread interest in, leading finally to a recognition of, the soul as a result of this fusion and blending.
2. The appreciation of the divinity of substance, and the recognition of the fact that matter is the outer garment of God. This will characterise the intellectual achievement of the Aryan race.
3. The plan of God that humanity should control matter on the physical plane reaches a high point of perfection in the Aryan race. Of this, man's control of the electrical forces of the physical plane is an outstanding instance.

These three important developments indicate the activity of the third ray during the period of time wherein the Aryan race emerges from the general racial background, develops itself as the generations pass away, and then fades out again as do all the races. By this process the souls which have profited by the experience during racial manifestation pass on into another and higher race, the sixth root race, in this case. These are the major results. There are many minor ones which tend to perfect the divine purpose for the race. That purpose aims only at a relative perfection and not at the ultimate consummation. The racial perfection which will be reached as a result of the activity of the third and fifth rays will be seen as only partial from the angle of vision of the seventh root race, for instance, but it will be far ahead of that achieved during the Atlantean or fourth root race, which was under the dominant influence of the second and sixth rays. The flower of any race, and those who guarantee its achievement, are to be seen in the Masters, Initiates and Disciples Who, during any race, reach the goal which Their souls have set. The reader must remember that the goal of adeptship is a steadily shifting one, and that the adepts of the Aryan race will be higher in development, and of a more intellectual order, than those who reached that stage during the Atlantean race. Therefore the requirements for treading the path of discipleship in the present race are steadily increasing in difficulty as the centuries slip away. At the same time, the assets brought by the aspirant to the task of achieving discipleship likewise steadily evolve, and the equipment is as steadily arriving at a greater adequacy, thus measuring up to the opportunity offered. Such books, therefore, as *The Outer Court* and *The Path of Discipleship* by Annie Besant state the requirements for the path of probation, and not for the path of discipleship. *A Treatise on White Magic* gives the needed data for those who tread, at this time, the path of discipleship. In these three books are to be found the requirements for the two stages of the path of conscious unfoldment.

Curiously enough, in Lemurian days the first ray was active. This was because of a special dispensation or effort on the part of the planetary Hierarchy. With the aid of the seventh ray the needed work went forward. At the time of the individualisation of humanity, a third ray, the fifth, was called into operation, and thus with the united effort of the first, the

The Rays and Man

seventh and the fifth rays, the great fusion between the higher and the lower aspects of mankind was made. It is interesting to note that the secondary ray influence in the Aryan race at this time is the fifth, thus linking up the Aryan and the Lemurian civilisations. Both were and are intensely material civilisations, but the Lemurian was material because the whole attention of the Hierarchy was turned to the development of physical man, whilst today the attention is not turned to the physical unfoldment of man, but to an effort to enable man to control the physical forces of the planet. One rather striking instance of the similarity of the ray forces should be here noted. In Lemurian times, the yoga of the age which produced the required at-one-ing or unification (preceding the taking of the initiation of the time) was hatha yoga, the yoga of the physical body. This gave to the initiate the needed physical control—a control which has today been so perfected in the race that it is now automatic and has slipped below the threshold of consciousness. In the great cyclic recapitulations which go on ceaselessly we see today in our Aryan race a tremendous emphasis being given to physical perfection, to sport, to athletics, to dancing and to physical culture. It is the cyclic effect of the same ray forces, playing upon humanity again. The initiatory goal is today a mental at-one-ing. Nevertheless, the physical reaction to the ray forces produces a higher form of hatha yoga or physical coordination. These points will be further elucidated.

The secondary influence which is leading the Aryan race forward is that of the fifth Ray of Concrete Knowledge or Science. This ray, as we have seen, was one of the rays which brought about individualisation millions of years ago, and so launched mankind upon the path of return. Again it comes into power, and though it has had many cycles of activity since Lemurian days, none of them have been of such unobstructed dominance as the present. Hence the tremendous potency of individuals at this time; hence the difficulty, but also the opportunity. This is a ray of quality, and its effect is to stimulate the acquisition of knowledge and the growth of the human intellect, which is an instrument of exceeding sensitivity, producing increased awareness of God.

It might be said that in Lemurian times the effect of this ray was to stimulate the instinctual nature. This gave awareness of the form nature of Deity. During Atlantean days, through the influence of the second ray, the instinct began to merge into the intellect, and that aspect of man's nature was developed which is called (in theosophical books) kama-manas. This phrase simply means a blend of desire-feeling-lower-mind,—a curious synthesis which characterises average man today, and leads to his complicated problem. This development gave man another type of awareness. He became conscious of the sentient universe; he became sensitive to the love of God, and registered an innate reaction to the heart of God. Today, under the fifth ray influence, the intellect is rapidly awakening; instinct is falling below the threshold of consciousness; kama-manas is no longer the outstanding characteristic of the disciples of the world. The intellect (concrete and abstract, lower and higher) is steadily unfolding, and as it unfolds, the will, purpose and plan of the Deity begin to take shape in men's minds. The secondary effects of this development are the power to organise, and to work individually with definite purpose. This is demonstrated today by individuals in all departments of human activity. They evince capacity to sense the Plan of God and to cooperate; they see the broad general outlines of the divine purpose, and comprehend as never before the great evolutionary plan. Men are building now towards the future because they have glimpsed the past and touched the vision.

Later, we shall have a transition period again, analogous to that period wherein kama-manas was developed, and we shall then have the entire race expressing a developed synthesis of intellect-intuition, preparatory to that advanced stage which will come at the close of the next root race, the sixth. This takes us to a period ten million years hence, when the intellect will have in its turn slipped below the threshold of consciousness, as did the instinct. It will then work automatically as does man's instinctual nature, and the race will be intuitive. This will really mean that the fifth kingdom in nature will be manifesting on earth, and that the kingdom of God (as the Christian calls it) will have arrived. This will constitute an event of an importance equal to that of the advent of the fourth kingdom, when men made their appearance on earth. This next great race will be governed by the second and fourth rays, thus demonstrating a relation between the fourth root race, the Atlantean, and the sixth root race. In terms of consciousness, this can be expressed as a relation between an astral-emotional development and an intuitional-buddhic development. The final race will be governed by the first, the seventh and the second rays.

I think I have given you as much on this abstruse subject as can be grasped. The tabulation of the rays governing the races might be stated, therefore, as follows:

Lemurian Race	Rays 1. 7. 5.
Atlantean Race	Rays 2. 6.
Aryan Race	Rays 3. 5.
Sixth Race	Rays 2. 4.
Seventh Race	Rays 1. 7. 2.

5. *The Rays in Cyclic Manifestation*

We come now to a consideration of the forces which are prevailing at the present time and hence have a supreme interest in connection with what I now have to say. It might first be stated that the main problem of today is brought about by the fact that two rays of great potency are functioning simultaneously. As yet their effects are so equally balanced that a situation is brought about which is described in the ancient archives in the following terms: "A time of rending, when the mountains, which have sheltered, fall from their high places, and the voices of men are lost in the crash and thunder of the fall". Such periods come only at rare and long intervals, and each time they come a peculiarly significant period of divine activity is ushered in; old things pass entirely away, yet the ancient landmarks are restored. The seventh Ray of Ceremonial Order or Ritual is coming into manifestation. The sixth Ray of Idealism or of Abstract Visioning is slowly passing out. The seventh ray will bring into expression that which was visioned and that which constituted the ideals of the preceding cycle of sixth ray activity. One ray prepares the way for another ray, and the reason for the manifestation of one ray or another is dependent upon the Plan and divine Purpose. It is not often that two rays follow each other in a regular numerical sequence, such as is now happening. When this does happen, there eventuates a rapid following of effect upon cause, and this today can provide the basis for an assured hope.

a The Outgoing Sixth Ray

The sixth ray influence served to attract men's minds towards an ideal, such as that of individual sacrifice or service, and the mystical vision was the high water mark of the period; the numerous guiding mystics of the Occident and the Orient have appeared. The seventh ray influence will in time produce the magician, but in this age the magician will be predominantly in the class of white magic (not as in Atlantean days, when the predominance was on the side of selfish or black magic). The white magician works with the forces of nature and swings them back into control of advanced humanity. This can already be seen working out through the activity of the scientists which the latter end of the last century and this twentieth century have produced. That much of their magical work has been turned into selfish channels by the tendency of this materialistic age, and that many of their wise and true discoveries in the realm of energy are today adapted to ends which serve man's hatred or love of self, is equally true. But this in no way militates against the wonder of their achievements. When the motive is transmuted from pure scientific interest to love of the divine revelation, and when service to the race is the determining force, then we shall see the true white magic. Hence therefore the need to turn the mystic into the occultist, and to train the modern aspirant in right motive, mind control and brotherly love,– all of which must and will express themselves through harmlessness. The most potent force in the world today is harmlessness. I speak not of non-resistance, but of that positive attitude of mind which thinks no evil. He who thinks no evil and harms naught is a citizen of God's world.

The following relations between the sixth and seventh rays should be held clearly in mind, and students should grasp the relation of the immediate past to the immediate future, and see in this relation the working out of God's Plan and the coming salvation of the race:

a. The sixth ray fostered the vision.
   The seventh ray will materialise that which was visioned.

b. The sixth ray produced the mystic as its culminating type of aspirant.
   The seventh ray will develop the magician who works in the field of white magic.

c. The sixth ray, as part of the evolutionary plan, led to separations, to nationalism, and to sectarianism, due to the selective nature of the mind and its tendency to divide and separate.

The seventh ray will lead to fusion and synthesis, for its energy is of the type which blends spirit and matter.

d. The sixth ray activity led to the formation of bands of disciples, working in groups but not in close relation, and subject to internal dissension, based on personality reactions.

The seventh ray will train and send forth groups of initiates, working in close unison with the Plan and with each other.

e. The sixth ray brought the sense of duality to a humanity which regarded itself as a physical unity. Of this attitude the academic materialistic psychologists are the exponents.

The seventh ray will inaugurate the sense of a higher unity; first, that of the integrated personality for the masses, and secondly, that of the fusion of soul and body for the world aspirants.

f. The sixth ray differentiates that aspect of the universal electrical energy which we know as modern electricity, produced to serve man's material needs.

The seventh ray period will familiarise man with that type of electrical phenomena which produce the coordination of all forms.

g. The sixth ray influence produced the emergence in men's minds of the following knowledges:
1. Knowledge of physical plane light and electricity.

2. Among the esotericists and spiritualists of the world, knowledge of the existence of the astral light.
3. An interest in illumination, both physical and mental.
4. Astro-physics and the newer astronomical discoveries.

The seventh ray will change the theories of the advanced thinkers of the race into the facts of the future educational systems. Education and the growth of the understanding of illumination in all fields will eventually be regarded as synonymous ideals.

h. The sixth ray taught the meaning of sacrifice, and of this teaching the crucifixion was the outstanding emblem, to the initiates. Philanthropy was the expression of the same teaching, to advanced humanity. The nebulous ideal of simply "being kind" is the same motivation, applied to the unthinking masses.

   The seventh ray will bring to the consciousness of the coming initiates the concept of group service and sacrifice. This will inaugurate the age of the "divine service". The vision of the giving of the individual in sacrifice and service, within the group and to the group ideal, will be the goal of the masses of advanced thinkers in the New Age, whilst for the rest of humanity, brotherhood will be the keynote of their endeavour. These words have a wider connotation and significance than the thinkers of today can know and understand.

i. The sixth ray promoted the growth of the spirit of individualism. Groups exist, but they are groups of individuals gathered around an individual.

   The seventh ray will foster the group spirit, and the rhythm of the group, the objectives of the group, and the ritual-working of the group will be the basic phenomena.

j. The sixth ray influence conveyed to men the ability to recognise the historical Christ, and to evolve the structure of the Christian faith, coloured by a vision of a great Son of Love, but qualified by an excessive militancy and separativeness, based on a narrow idealism.

  The seventh ray will convey to man the power to recognise the cosmic Christ, and to produce that future scientific religion of *Light* which will enable man to fulfill the command of the historical Christ to permit his light to shine forth.

k. The sixth ray produced the great idealistic religions with their vision and their necessary narrowness,—a narrowness that is needed to safeguard infant souls.

  The seventh ray will release the developed souls from the nursery stage and inaugurate that scientific understanding of the divine purpose which will foster the coming religious synthesis.

l. The effect of the sixth ray influence has been to foster the separative instincts,—dogmatic religion, scientific factual accuracy, schools of thought with their doctrinal barriers and exclusiveness, and the cult of patriotism.

  The seventh ray will prepare the way for the recognition of the wider issues which will materialise as the new world religion which will emphasise unity but bar out uniformity; it will prepare for that scientific technique which will demonstrate the universal light that every form veils and hides, and for that internationalism which will express itself as practical brotherhood and as peace and good will between the peoples.

I could continue emphasizing these relations, but I have enumerated enough to show the beauty of the preparation made by the sixth great Lord of Idealism for the work of the seventh Lord of Ceremonial.

b. THE INCOMING SEVENTH RAY

It might be wise here to elucidate somewhat the idea underlying ceremonial and ritual. There is so much revolt at this time against ceremonial, and so many good and well-meaning people regard themselves as having outgrown and transcended ritual. They pride themselves on having attained that so-called "liberation", forgetting that it is only the sense of individuality that permit this attitude, and that no group work is ever possible without some form of ritual. The refusal therefore to participate in uniformity of action is no sign of a liberated soul.

The Great White Brotherhood has its rituals, but they are rituals which have for their objective the inauguration and the assistance of various aspects of the Plan, and of the varying cyclic activities of that Plan. Where these rituals exist, but where the meaning (inherently present) remains hidden and unrealised, there must as a consequence be demonstrated a spirit of deadness, of uselessness, and of weariness of interest over forms and ceremonies. But where it is demonstrated that ritual and organised ceremonies are but the evidence of a custody of forces and energies, then the idea is constructive in its working out, cooperation with the Plan becomes possible, and the aim of all the divine service begins to demonstrate. All service is governed by ritual.

The coming in of the seventh ray will lead to this desired consummation, and the mystics who are training themselves in the technique of occult motive and in the methods of the trained magician will increasingly find themselves cooperating intelligently with the Plan, and participating in those basic rituals which are distinguished by their power to:

a. Harness the forces of the planet to the service of the race.
b. Send forth those energies which will produce in some one or other of the kingdoms of nature effects of a desirable and beneficent aspect.
c. Call in and re-distribute the energies which are present in all the forms in the various subhuman kingdoms.
d. Heal through a scientific method of bringing together soul and body.
e. Produce illumination through right understanding of the energy of Light.
f. Evolve that coming ritual which will eventually reveal the true significance of *water,* which will revolutionise its uses and open to man the free passage to the astral plane. This plane is that of the emotional-desire nature, and its symbol is water. The coming Aquarian Age will reveal to man (and hence also facilitate the work of the seventh ray) that that plane is his natural home at this state of development. The masses today are entirely, but unconsciously, polarised on that plane. They must become consciously aware of their activity. Man is on the verge of becoming normally awake on the astral plane, and it will be through scientific rituals that this new development will be brought about.

The sixth ray influence produced the appearance of the modern science of psychology, and that science has been its consummating glory. The seventh ray influence will carry forward that infant science to maturity. Belief in the soul has become widespread during the sixth ray period. Knowledge of the soul will be the result of the incoming ray activity, plus the aid contributed by the energies released during the incoming Aquarian Age.

The new and esoteric psychology will be steadily developed. It will be apparent therefore that *A Treatise on*

White Magic has a definitely seventh ray import, and this *Treatise on the Seven Rays* has also been sent forth in an effort to clarify the incoming spiritual influences. One of the first lessons that humanity will learn under the potent influence of the seventh ray is that the soul controls its instrument, the personality, through ritual, or through the imposition of a regular rhythm, for rhythm is what really designates a ritual. When aspirants to discipleship impose a rhythm on their lives they call it a discipline, and they feel happy about it. What groups do who are gathered together for the performance of any ritual or ceremony whatsoever (Church ritual, the Masonic work, the drill of the army or navy, business organisations, the proper functioning of a home, of a hospital, or of an entertainment, etc.) is of an analogous nature, for it imposes on the participants a simultaneous performance, an identical undertaking, or a ritual. No one on this earth can evade ritual or ceremonial, for the rising and the setting of the sun imposes a ritual, the cyclic passing of the years, the potent movements of the great centres of population, the coming and the going of trains, of ocean liners and of mails, and the regular broadcasting of the radio organisations,—all of these impose a rhythm upon humanity, whether this is recognised or not. Of these rhythms the present great experiments in national standardisation and regimentation are also an expression, as they demonstrate through the masses in any nation.

There is no evading the process of ceremonial living. It is unconsciously recognised, blindly followed, and constitutes the great discipline of the rhythmic breathing of life itself. The Deity works with ritual and is subjected to the ceremonials of the universe. The seven rays come into activity and pass out again under the rhythmic and ritualistic impulse of the divine Life. Thus is the temple of the Lord built by the ceremonial of the Builders. Every kingdom in nature is subjected to ritualistic experience and to the ceremonials of cyclic expression. These only the initiate can comprehend. Every ant hill and every beehive is equally impelled by instinctive rituals and by rhythmic impulses. The new science of psychology could well be described as the science of the rituals and rhythms of the body, of the emotional nature and of the mental processes, or of those ceremonials (inherent, innate, or imposed by the self, by circumstances and by environment) which affect the mechanism through which the soul functions.

It is interesting to note how the sixth ray, which produced in human beings the sense of separativeness and of pronounced individualism, has prepared the way for the organising power of the seventh ray. It is almost as if (to speak symbolically) the executives who were to undertake the reorganising of the world in preparation for the New Age were trained and prepared for their task by the influence now going out. Today a process of house-cleaning is going forward in practically every great nation, preparatory to the coming revelation, and the executives and dictators who are sponsoring this realignment and readjustment are the experts whom the genius of each nation has brought forth to deal with the unique problems with which it is beset. They are predominantly seventh ray executives, whose task it is to reorganise the world as a whole upon the newer lines. They are in the nature of material efficiency experts who have been sent in to deal with internal affairs and to institute that activity which will eliminate those factors which prevent the nation concerned from functioning as a whole, as a unit, integrated and coherent. It is from the lack of internal harmony and synthesis that those internal difficulties and disorders emerge which (if of long continuance) prevent a nation having aught to contribute to the world of nations and lead to that nation's being so intensely disordered that the wrong people come into power and the wrong aspects of truth become emphasized. A disordered inharmonious national unit is a menace to the comity of nations, and therefore the separative house-cleanings and rearrangements must go forward before the Federation of Nations can be an accomplished fact.

The new era is however upon its way, and nothing can prevent that which the stars decree and which the Hierarchy of guiding Minds consequently foresee. The new executives who will succeed the present dictators and powers will take over the control towards the year 1955, and they will be seventh ray aspirants and disciples in the majority of cases; their capacity towards integration and towards fusion along right lines will then rapidly bring about the needed international understanding.

The question emerges in your mind as to whether such a prophecy will indeed be fulfilled; and if unfulfilled, will not that fact militate against much that I have said and prove me unreliable? Let me answer this question by pointing out that those of us who foresee that which may and ought to be are nevertheless well aware that though the fulfillment of the prophecy is inevitable, yet the time factor may not work out as indicated. This will be because the distressed human mechanisms of those to whom the work is given will fail to react either correctly or at the right time. These incoming seventh ray aspirants and disciples may make mistakes and may perform their undertakings in such a manner that delay may eventuate. They are permitted to have the general outline of their task committed to them by their own souls, working under the inspiration of those great and liberated souls we call the Masters of the Wisdom, but there is no coercion under the Plan and no forced and dictated service. Much of the success in the coming momentous years is dependent upon the work done by all who may be affiliated (even slightly) with the New Group of World Servers. If public opinion is educated in the new ideals, the momentum of that growing tide will greatly facilitate the work of these seventh ray executives, and in some cases will constitute for them the line of least resistance. Failure, therefore, will rest upon the shoulders of the world aspirants and disciples, and will not indicate inaccurate prophecy or misinterpreted astrological conditions. In any case, the prophesied end is inevitable, but the time of that end rests in the hands of awakened humanity. The margin of difference will also be only between one hundred and three hundred years. The impulse towards synthesis is now too strong to be long delayed.

Under this seventh ray influence the Masonic Fraternity will come into a new and pronounced spiritual activity and begin to approximate its true function and to fulfill its long-seen destiny. One point it might be of interest here to note. During the period of the activity of the sixth ray the Fraternity fell into a crystallised and sectarian attitude, along with the many other grouped circles. It fell also into the snare of materialism, and the outer form has for centuries been of more importance in the eyes of Masons than the inner spiritual meaning. The symbols and the system of allegories have been emphasized, whilst that which they were intended to convey and to reveal to the initiated has been quite forgotten. Also, the trend of the attention of a lodge of Masons, and the main emphasis, has been potently placed on the function and place of the W.M., and not upon the inner significance of the work upon the floor of the Temple. The lodge has not been regarded as an integrated functioning entity. This must and will be changed, and the potency and the effectiveness of the lodge work and ceremonial will be demonstrated. It will be

The Rays and Man 369

seen that in the regularity of the rituals and the sanctified formality of the ordained ceremonials lies the true meaning of the work and the use of the *Word.* The coming era of group work and power and of organised synthetic ritualistic activity will profoundly affect Masonry, as the importance of a central dominating figure passes out with the sixth ray influence and the true spiritual work and function of the lodge itself is understood.

The prime cosmic function of the seventh ray is to perform the magical work of blending spirit and matter in order to produce the manifested form through which the life will reveal the glory of God. Students would be well advised to pause here and re-read the section of this treatise in which I dealt with the seventh ray Lord, with His names, and with His purpose. When this has been done, it will be apparent that one of the results of the intensified new influence will be the recognition, by science, of certain effects and characteristics of the work being accomplished. This can already be seen in the work done by scientists in connection with the mineral world. As we have seen in an earlier part of this book the mineral kingdom is governed by the seventh ray, and to the potency of this incoming ray can be attributed the discovery of the radio-activity of matter. The seventh ray expresses itself in the mineral kingdom through the production of radiation, and we shall find that increasingly these radiations (many of which still remain to be discovered) will be noted, their effects understood and their potencies grasped. One point remains as yet unrealised by science, and that is that these radiations are cyclic in their appearance; under the influence of the seventh ray it has been possible for man to discover and work with radium. Radium has always been present, but not always active in such a manner that we were able to detect it. It is under the influence of the incoming seventh ray that its appearance has been made possible, and it is through this same influence that we shall discover new cosmic rays. They too are always present in our universe, but they use the substance of the incoming ray energy as the path along which they can travel to our planet and thus be revealed. It is many thousands of years since what are now studied as the Cosmic Rays (discovered by Millikan) played definitely upon our planet, and at that time the fifth ray was not active as it now is. Therefore scientific knowledge of their activity was not possible.

Other cosmic rays will play upon our earth as this seventh ray activity becomes increasingly active, and the result of their influence will be to facilitate the emergence of the new racial types, and above all else, to destroy the veil or web which separates the world of the seen and tangible from the world of the unseen and the intangible, the astral world. Just as there is a veil called "the etheric web" dividing off the various force centres in the human body, and protecting the head centres from the astral world, so there is a separating web between the world of physical life and the astral world. This will be destroyed, slowly and certainly, by the play of the cosmic rays upon our planet. The etheric web which is found between the centres in the spine, and which is found at the top of the head (protecting the head centre) is destroyed in man's mechanism by the activity of certain forces found in that mysterious fire which we call the kundalini fire. The cosmic rays of which the modern scientist is aware constitute aspects of the planetary kundalini, and their effect will be the same in the body of the planetary Logos, the Earth, as it is in the human body; the etheric web between the physical and astral planes is in process of destruction, and it is of this event which the sensitives of the world and the spiritualists prophesy as an imminent happening.

The Rays and Man

Much of profound interest is on its way as a result of this seventh ray activity. For one thing, though the animal kingdom reacts but little to this type of influence, yet there are going to be very definite results within the soul of the animal form. The door of individualisation or of entrance into the human kingdom has been closed since Atlantean times, but under the new influence it will be partially opened; it will be set ajar, so that a few animals will respond to soul stimulation and discover that their rightful place is on the human side of the dividing door. Part of the reorganisation which will go on as a result of the seventh ray activity will concern the relation of humanity to the animal kingdom and the establishing of better and of closer relations. This will lead men to take advantage of another effect of the seventh ray, which is its power to refine the matter out of which the forms are built. The animal body of man has received much scientific attention during the past one hundred years, and medicine and surgery have reached great heights of achievement. The framework of man, his body, and its internal systems (with their diverse rituals) are now understood as never before, and this has been the result of the incoming ray force with its power to apply knowledge to the magical work. When this knowledge is applied intensively to the animal world much new and interesting data will be discovered; when the differences between the physical bodies of the animals and those of humanity have been more closely investigated there will appear a new and very fruitful field of study. These differences are largely in the realm of the nervous systems; not enough attention has been paid for instance to the fact that the brain of the animal is really in the region of the solar plexus, whilst the human brain, the controlling agent, is in the head, and works through the medium of the spinal column. When scientists know exactly why the animal does not use the brain in the head as does man, they will arrive at a fuller knowledge of the law governing cycles.

There is much that could be said, but little of it would, as yet, be comprehended. Until the incoming ray force and all that attends its entry has produced the adequate changes in the nervous system, it will not be possible for more to be made clear. Brain cells, hitherto dormant in even the most advanced thinkers, must be brought into functioning activity and with this consummated, then more teaching and further elucidation will be possible,—but not till then. Some time must yet elapse before the present human mechanisms are adapted to the registration of that which is new and as yet unknown.

Three final points I wish to touch upon. As you may have noted from some of our earlier tabulations, there is a definite relation between the first kingdom in nature, the mineral kingdom, and the final kingdom, the solar kingdom, the seventh and last to appear in manifestation upon our planet. There is a mysterious unity of response existing between the lowest kingdom in the scale of nature and the highest, between that which expresses the densest manifestation of the divine life and that which embodies its final and glorious consummation. This response is fostered by the play of the seventh ray, which produces those initial reactions to organised movement and ritual which, at the close of our great world period, will demonstrate the response of our entire solar system to the same basic seventh ray influence. What can now be seen in the organisation of a crystal, a jewel and a diamond, with their beauty of form and line and colour, their radiance and geometrical perfection, will appear likewise through the medium of the universe as a whole. The Grand Geometrician of the universe works through this seventh ray, and thus sets His seal upon all form life, particularly in the mineral world. This the Masonic Fraternity has always known, and this concept it has perpetuated symbolically in the great world cathedrals, which embody the glory of the mineral world and are the sign of the work of the Master Builder of the universe.

When the great work is consummated we shall see the Temple of God, the solar system, organised objectively and subjectively; its courts and holy places will then be accessible to the sons of men, who will work then without limitation, and will have free access to all parts of the building. Through the magic of the *Word* which will then have been recovered, all doors will fly open, and the consciousness of man will respond to every divine manifestation. More of this I may not here say, but the work of the Craft is symbolic of the ritualistic organisation of the universe. Of this the mineral kingdom (with which the work is done, and through which the geometrical plan expresses itself) is at the same time the symbol and the undertaking, the beginning and also the concrete expression of divine purpose.

Secondly, I referred earlier to the work of the seventh ray in connection with the phenomena of electricity, through which the solar system is coordinated and vitalised. There is an aspect of electrical phenomena which produces cohesion, just as there is an aspect which produces light. This has not yet been recognised. It is stated in *The Secret Doctrine* of H.P.B., and in *A Treatise on Cosmic Fire*, that the electricity of the solar system is threefold: there is fire by friction, solar fire, and electric fire—the fire of body, of soul and of spirit. Fire by friction is coming to be somewhat understood by the scientists of the world, and we are harnessing to our needs the fire which heats, which gives light, and which produces motion. This is in the physical sense of the words. One of the imminent discoveries will be the integrating power of electricity as it produces the cohesion within all forms and sustains all form life during the cycle of manifested existence. It produces also the coming together of atoms and of the organisms within forms, so constructing that which is needed to express the life principle. Men today are investigating such matters as electro-therapeutics and studying the theory of the electrical nature of the human being. They are working rapidly towards this coming discovery, and much will be revealed along these lines during the next fifty years. The principle of coordination about which men talk has reference, in the last analysis, to this concept, and the scientific basis of all meditation work is really to be found in this basic truth. The bringing in of force and the offering of a channel are all mystical ways of expressing a natural phenomenon as yet little understood, but which will eventually give the clue to the second aspect of electricity. This will be released in fuller measure during the Aquarian age, through the agency of the seventh ray. One of its earliest effects will be the increase of the understanding of brotherhood and its really scientific basis.

I referred to the fact that man must before long function as freely on the astral plane and through the astral consciousness as he now does on the physical plane. We are today laying the emphasis upon the vital aspect of man; the nature of the life principle is under discussion, and the need for "vital" action everywhere emphasized. We talk of the necessity of increasing human vitality and the vitality of animals and plants; the quality of the vitality-producing factors—food, sun and the coloured rays so widely used now—is creeping slowly into all medical thought, whilst even the advertisers of the tinned goods of our modern civilisation lay the emphasis upon the quota of vitamins.

This, esoterically speaking, is due to the shift of human consciousness on to etheric levels. Paralleling the growth of modern knowledge as to the "soul as intellect", we find a growth of understanding as to "the soul as life", though it remains as yet the great and apparently insoluble mystery.

There are two happenings of close and imminent occurrence. Today the bulk of human beings are polarised on the lower levels of the astral plane, but are conscious in the physical body. This distinction must be studied. Soon, many will be conscious in the vital body and beginning to be conscious on the higher levels of the astral plane, and some few upon the mental plane. But large numbers of people today are ready to be fully conscious in the astral body and polarised either on the mental plane entirely or centred in the soul. This produces the wonder and the difficulty of the present time.

Through the scientific ritual of meditation (for that is what it really is) this refocussing can be brought more rapidly about. Through the scientific culture of the ritual of service it can be still further developed. The ritual of the solar system is the result of the meditation of God and the act of divine service, carried on throughout the entire period of manifestation. The subordination of the lower life to the ritual of service is literally the tuning-in of the individual to the rhythm of the life, heart and mind of God Himself. From that tuning-in, automatically a spiritual development follows.

c. THE FUNCTIONING RAY LAWS

There are certain great laws, connected with the seven rays, that are effective in determining the lines of demarcation, the cleavages which produce separation and the differentiations of the manifested life of God into...

1. The septenary constitution of the solar system.
2. The ten schemes which indicate solar achievement.
3. The inner constitution, or so-called "chains", which distinguish each planetary existence.
4. The planetary constitution of our Earth into the various kingdoms of nature.
5. The basic distinctions between the kingdoms; these produce the types, groupings, families, branches, empires and nations.

These Laws of Cleavage are too difficult for general comprehension. They govern form life, and are the result of the united working, or rather the simultaneous manifestation, of the three laws dealt with in *A Treatise on Cosmic Fire*. These are:

1. The Law of Synthesis, determining the future, certifying the goal, and concerned with the life or spirit aspect.
2. The Law of Attraction, determining the present, and governing the immediate condition of the planetary types. It is concerned with the consciousness or the soul aspect.
3. The Law of Economy. This law determines the past, conditions the planetary consciousness, and concerns itself with the form or matter aspect.

When these three function together, during this particular cycle and in our particular race, they produce a fusion of forces which imposes a certain rhythm, a definite materialisation of energies, and a specific type of civilisation which functions under what we (esoterically) call the Laws of Cleavage. It is the mind which separates and divides; it is mental activity (divine and superhuman, as well as human) which produces the many differentiations. This process of divisioning comes to its climax during this world period in the Aryan race, the fifth race. We are today governed by the Law of Cleavages,—a divine law and one of fruitful objective. This must not be forgotten.

The activity of the three divine aspects, in relation to the human family in the first nebulous race (of which science knows nothing), produced what we call the Law of Immersion. It caused that growing diversification of matter, clothing the life, which ultimately produced the early manifestation of the incarnating sons of God. It is not a physical incarnation in the sense that we understand that term.

In the next race, of which again man knows little, the fusion of the three divine energies produced a second law. It should be remembered that a law is but the effect of the continued intelligent activity of the Life aspect as it works in conjunction with matter. This second law is called (by those of us who deal with law and energy) the Law of Capitulation, because the momentum set up by the desire of the sons of God to incarnate proved too strong for the opposing forces of matter. Nothing then could stop the coming into tangible existence of the incarnating spirits. Matter capitulated to spirit, the divine desire and the divine will set their signature upon the rapidly assembling forms. It must be borne in mind that these laws are called by names which indicate their relation to humanity. When active in the other kingdoms of nature their influence is different, and they are called by other nomenclatures.

In the next race, the Lemurian, the triple activity of the divine essential attributes demonstrated as the Law of Materialisation, or (as it is sometimes called) the Law of Hidden Radiance. This law concerns the Light which is in man, and the covering of that Light, in time and space, in order to produce its intensification and its consequent and subsequent radiation, so that, through humanity, light may eventually reach all forms of divine expression. Through man's achievement, and through the conquest of darkness by light, the light of consciousness in all forms must be brought to a condition of a "shining glory which will irradiate the planet, and shine forth into the world of planets as a testimony to the glory of . . ."

The fourth law controlling human destiny is known by the curious name of the Law of the Tides. It concerns the life of desire and of sensory perception and of feeling. It is closely concerned with the development of awareness, and is an aspect of the Law of Cycles which controls solar evolution. It is a basic human law, protective and developing. It controls the cyclic or "tidal" life of all souls who are carried by the great river of life—on the crest of desire—into incarnation, and is one of the laws with which the aspirant must work, early in his training. Until he can function as a soul, independent of the cyclic turmoil of terrestrial life, and free from the control of the tides of his emotional existence, he cannot take initiation. It was the inability to do this which brought on Earth the great Atlantean floods which brought that ancient civilisation to an end.

We come now to a consideration of the Law of Cleavages, for our race is controlled by the great heresy of separativeness. Through these cleavages (symbolically speaking) the fires of destruction may emerge and end our civilisation, as the Atlantean civilisation was ended, unless the conscious sons of God can build those bridges and develop that understanding which will offset this law, thus bringing into functioning activity the law which governs the coming race. The work that the disciples of the world must seek to do is analogous to that which they as individuals have to do in their own private development: build the antahkarana, which will bridge the gap between the human consciousness and the spiritual, and make the race eventually as intuitional as it is, today, intellectual.

The law of the coming race is most difficult to express in understandable terms. I can find no better name for it—so as to express adequately its functional effect—than the words, the Law of Loving Understanding. This is a quite inadequate and sentimental phrase for a scientific expression of a great coming evolutionary development in the human consciousness. But until that development is an accomplished fact, we have no means whereby to express the true significance of the underlying idea. The above must suffice.

Let us now enumerate these laws in sequence, so as to gain a better idea of their relation and interrelationship:

1. The Law of Immersion .... first race.
2. The Law of Capitulation .... second race.
3. The Law of Materialisation. .... Lemurian race.
   The Law of Hidden Radiance.
4. The Law of the Tides. .... Atlantean race.
5. The Law of Cleavages. .... Aryan race.
6. The Law of Loving Understanding ..... next race.

By a right understanding of these laws we can gain an insight into the present world situation as far as the nations are concerned, and can grasp more intelligently the ray influence which, in conjunction with these laws, has brought about the various typical national units.

6. *The Nations and the Rays*

In connection, therefore, with our discussion of the rays which govern and influence the leading nations of the world, the student should bear in mind the fact that all are today governed primarily by the Law of Cleavages, but that advanced groups in each nation are beginning to respond to the Law of Understanding,—a law which will eventually emphasize the eternal brotherhood of man and the identity of all souls with the Oversoul, in the racial consciousness, as well as the oneness of the Life which pours through, permeates, animates and integrates the entire solar system. This Life functions therefore in and through all the planetary schemes, with their kingdoms of forms, and with all that can be included (throughout our solar universe) under the phrase "form life". That phrase itself contains three great and basic ideas: the ideas of life, of matter and of evolution.

The functioning of the Law of Loving Understanding will be much facilitated and speeded up during the Aquarian age, and it will eventuate later in the development of the international spirit, in the recognition of one world faith in God and in humanity as the major expression of divinity in this world period, and in the transfer of the human consciousness from the world of material things to that of the more purely psychic, leading in time to the spiritual. It should be remembered that (for advanced humanity) time sequence of the recognition of these expansions of consciousness is as follows:

1. The world of psychical living. This requires the recognition, by the brain consciousness of the aspirant, of the need for mental and spiritual control as a first step.
2. The world of mental unfoldment and control.
3. The world of the soul or ego.

When these three recognitions are stabilised in the aspirant, then there comes the recognition by the disciple of . . .

4. The control of the physical plane life by the soul.
5. The interpretative faculty of the illumined mind.

The Rays and Man 381

6. The functioning and utilisation of the psychic powers, and their place and part in the field of intelligent service.
7. An inspired creative life on the physical plane.

But in the development of the racial consciousness, the process does not follow the above stages and sequence. This is owing to the stimulation and consequent sensitising of the form aspect through the increased radiation and potency of the dynamic New Group of World Servers, whose ranks are filled by those who have passed, or are passing, through the stages of aspirant and disciple, thus learning to serve. Psychic unfoldment in the masses parallels the spiritual unfoldment of advanced humanity. This can be seen going on today on a large scale everywhere, and it accounts for the tremendous growth of the spiritualistic movement, and for the enormous increase in the lower psychic powers. Old Atlantean magic and the lower psychism are upon us again in the great turning of the wheel of life, but this time good may eventuate, if the world disciples and spiritually focussed people measure up to their opportunity.

Today there are many hundreds (and in America, many thousands) coming under the influence of this Law of Loving Understanding. Many in every nation are responding to the broader synthetic brotherly note, but the masses as yet understand nothing of this. They must be led in right ways gradually, by the steady development in right understanding by their own nationals. Bear this in mind, all of you who work for world peace and right relations, for harmony and for synthesis.

a. THE MAJOR NATIONS AND THEIR RAYS

All of the great nations are controlled by two rays, just as is the human being. With the smaller nations we shall not concern ourselves. All nations are controlled by a personality ray (if so we can call it), which is dominant and potent and the main controlling factor at this time, and by a soul ray which is sensed only by the disciples and aspirants of any nation. This soul ray must be evoked into an increased functioning activity by the New Group of World Servers, for this is one of their main objectives and tasks. This must never be lost to sight. Much could be written about the historical influence of the rays during the past two thousand years, and of the way in which great events have been influenced or brought about by the periodic ray influence. But for this I have neither the time nor the inclination. Interesting as it is, and indicative of the present national trends and problems, all that I can now do is to point out the rays governing each nation, and leave you to study and note their effect at your leisure, and to comprehend their relation to the present condition of the world. One thing I would point out, and that is that those rays which govern a particular nation, and which are at this time in incarnation, are very potent, either materially or egoically, whilst some of the problems may be due to the fact that certain rays, governing certain nations, are at this time out of incarnation.

Nation	Personality Ray	Egoic Ray	Motto
India	4th ray of art	1st ray of government	"I hide the Light."
China	3rd ray of intellect	1st ray of government	"I indicate the Way."
Germany	1st ray of power	4th ray of art	"I preserve."
France	3rd ray of intellect	5th ray of knowledge	"I release the Light."
Great Britain	1st ray of power or government	2nd ray of love	"I serve."
Italy	4th ray of art	6th ray of idealism	"I carve the Paths."

U.S.A	6th ray of idealism	2nd ray of love	"I light the Way."
Russia	6th ray of idealism	7th ray of magic and order	"I link two Ways."
Austria	5th ray of knowledge	4th ray of art	"I serve the Lighted Way."
Spain	7th ray of order	6th ray of idealism	"I disperse the Clouds."
Brazil	2nd ray of love	4th ray of art	"I hide the seed."

A close analysis of the above will indicate certain lines of racial understanding. There is a natural rapport indicated between the modern and present personality rays of Germany and Great Britain, and yet a relationship can be seen between France and Great Britain through their esoteric national mottoes and also between the two symbols which are esoterically theirs. The symbol for France is the *fleur de lys*, which she adopted centuries ago under divine guidance, which symbol stands for the three divine aspects in manifestation. The emphasis is upon the third aspect, producing intelligent manifestation. The symbol of Great Britain, under the same divine apportioning, is the three feathers, carried as the arms of the Prince of Wales. The scintillating and brilliant French intellect, with its scientific bent, is accounted for by the interplay of the third Ray of Active Intelligence with the fifth Ray of Scientific Understanding. Hence their amazing contribution to the knowledge and thought of the world, and their brilliant and colourful history. Be it remembered also that the glory of the empire which was France is but the guarantee of a glory of divine revelation which lies ahead in the future, but which will never be theirs till they cease living in the wonder of their past and go forth into the future to demonstrate the fact of illumination, which is the goal of all mental effort. When the intellect of the French is turned towards the discovery and the elucidation of the things of the spirit, then they will carry revelation to the world. When their egoic ray dominates the third ray, and when the separative action of the fifth ray is transmuted into the revealing function of this ray, then France will enter into a period of new glory. Her empire will then be of the mind, and her glory of the soul.

It is obvious that the governing faculty is strongly the outstanding characteristic of Great Britain. England is an exponent of the art of control, and her function has been, as you may realise, to produce the first tentative grouping of federated nations, and to demonstrate the possibility of such grouping. The United States of America are doing a somewhat similar thing, and are fusing the nationals of many nations into one federated state with many subsidiary states, instead of subsidiary nations. These two powers function in this way and with this wide objective in order to give to the planet, eventually, a system of groupings within one national border or one empire, and yet with an international boundary which will be symbolic of the coming new age technique in government. The second Ray of Love or Attraction governs, egoically, the British Empire, and there is a relation between this fact and the fact that the sign Gemini governs both the United States and London. The fluid, mercurial, intuitional mind is closely allied with the divine aspect of love and understanding, producing attraction and interpretation.

It is interesting to note that the fourth Ray of Harmony or Art, which will begin before long to come into power again in its major aspect, is to be found prominent in the destinies of India, Germany, Italy, Austria and Brazil, and it is for this that there is so much preparatory turmoil in the three European countries. The sixth ray is potent in Russia, the United States, Italy and Spain. It is the fanatical adherence to an ideal which is responsible also for the potent changes in these four countries; in Germany and Italy, as we have seen, the harmonising power of the fourth ray is also seen. Hence we have in all these countries a process of breaking down, and of destruction of old forms, prior to an adequate responsiveness to the influence of the incoming ray. It should be remembered that as with individuals, so with nations,—the reaction to an increasing influence of the egoic ray is ever accompanied by a breaking down period, but this demonstration of destruction is but temporary and preparatory.

India hides the light, and that light, when released upon the world and revealed to humanity, will bring about harmony in the form aspect, for things will be clearly seen as they are and freed from glamour and illusion; this harmonising light is sorely needed in India itself, and when it has been manifested it will bring about the right functioning of the first Ray of Power or Government. The will of the people will be seen in the light. It is in this connection that Great Britain emerges into renewed activity, for her personality ray and India's egoic ray are the same. Many British people are subjectively linked with India, by past incarnations and association, and the quarrel between Great Britain and India is largely a family affair in the deeper sense of the term, and hence its bitterness—the bitterness of an elder brother who sees the younger usurping his prerogatives. Today many British administrators are finding their way back to their own home land, little as they may realise it, there to work out that which they initiated in other lives and bodies. As you may know, there is a close link between the fourth and the second rays, and this again emerges in the relationship between England and India, and a destiny is there which must be jointly worked out.

The static stabilising tendency of Germany showing, for instance, in her futile effort to preserve a purity of race now impossible, is due to her first ray personality, whilst her fourth ray egoic force is responsible for her effort to standardise and harmonise all the elements within her borders, to the exclusion, however, of the Hebrew race. With the problem of the Jew I will deal later. Germany cannot help herself, for though the first ray is not in manifestation as we understand the term, yet the bulk of the egos now in power in Germany are on the first subray of the seven different rays, and hence they are from one dominant angle the transmitters of first ray force. A hint is here given. It is for this reason therefore that Great Britain can contact the German race and handle the German psychology more understandingly than can Russia, Italy or France. They share similar qualities, and one of the services therefore that England can render at this time is to come to the aid of world peace, and so live up to the motto, "I serve," by acting as a mediator.

A careful analysis of the idealism of Russia and of the United States may reveal no resemblances in the goal of their idealism, for the Russian is driven by his seventh ray soul towards the imposition of an enforced ceremonial of ordered rhythms, leading to an idealised order and community of interests. Because of this, and because of the enforced magical work, some forces are present and active in Russia which need most careful handling by the Brotherhood of Light; they are not exactly on the white side, as it is called, but are concerned with the magic of form, whereas pure white magic concerns only the soul or subjective aspect. The black forces, so called, are nowhere rampant in Russia any more than elsewhere in the world, but the Russian reaction and attitude to

The Rays and Man 387

enforced rule and order has in it more of the magical seventh ray influence than is the case in other countries, such as Germany, which also enforces a standardised order and rule of life.

You will note that of the major nations only Brazil, Great Britain and the United States of America are definitely under the influence of the second ray. An interesting fact emerges as we consider this grouping. Great Britain is the custodian of the wisdom aspect of the second ray force for the Aryan race, so called. The United States fulfills the same office for the sixth or coming subrace, which is the germ race for the future sixth great race, whilst Brazil will function as the leading division of the great sixth race. These three races embody the attractive cohesive aspect of the second ray, and will demonstrate it through wisdom and wise government, based on idealism and love. The United States will therefore represent a fusion of races, with the Anglo-Saxon element dominating. Brazil will later represent the best of that which the Latin races have eventually to give. This presented fusion will be considered from the angle of the ray types and the basic unfolding principles, and not from the angle of culture and civilisation.

Great Britain therefore represents the aspect of mind which expresses itself in intelligent government, based eventually on just loving understanding. This, I say, is the ideal before her, but not the fulfilled achievement. The United States represents the intuitive faculty, expressing itself as illumination and the power to fuse and blend. Brazil (or rather what that country will then be called, for the time of this expression lies thousands of years ahead) will represent a linking interpreting civilisation, based on the unfoldment of the abstract consciousness, which is a blend of the intellect and the intuition, and which reveals the wisdom aspect of love in its beauty. But the period of the development of this great civilisation lies too far ahead to make speculation possible.

It is too dangerous for me, in these days of upset and of difficulty, to express myself more definitely as to the future lines of unfoldment. The destiny and future functioning of the nations lie hid in the present activity. The readers of this treatise are, in the majority of cases, far too nationalistic in their viewpoint, and too deeply engrossed with the prime importance of their own nation and of its supreme significance, for me to be able to do more than generalise and to indicate the major lines of progress. The role of the prophet is too dangerous, for destiny lies in the hands of the peoples, and no one knows exactly what way they will take to reach their goal. The inevitability of that goal is assured, as is the ultimate achieving of it, but the incidents of travel cannot be revealed, but lie hid in the racial karma. The time has not yet come when the majority of the people of any race can see the picture as a whole and be permitted to know the part their particular nation must play in the history of nations. Every nation, without exception (and this is a platitude which it is seldom fruitful to repeat), has its peculiar virtues and vices. These are dependent upon:

1. The point in evolution.
2. The measure of the control of the personality ray.
3. The emerging control of the egoic ray.
4. The polarisation of the nation.

It is useful to bear in mind, when considering the nations that some are negative and feminine and some positive and masculine. India, France, the United States of America, Russia and Brazil are all feminine, and constitute the nurturing mother aspect. They are feminine in their psychology,—intuitive, mystical, sensitive, alluring, beautiful, fond of dis-

The Rays and Man 389

play and colour, and with the faults of the feminine aspect, such as the laying of too much emphasis upon the material aspect of life, upon pageantry, upon possessions, and upon money as a symbol of that which connotes the form side. They mother and nurture civilisation and ideas.

China, Germany, Great Britain and Italy are masculine and positive; they are mental, political, governing, standardising, group-conscious, occult, aggressive, full of grandeur, interested in law and in laying the emphasis upon race and empire. But they are more inclusive and think in wider terms than the feminine aspects of divine manifestation. The reader would find it useful to consult an earlier tabulation which I gave (see Pages 382-383), and consider the higher and lower expressions of the rays, noting how they work out in relation to the rays personal and egoic of the different nations. Take for instance the emergence into manifestation of the egoic ray of the German nation. Its lower expression is that of architectural construction, and can be seen at this time making its presence felt in the new and modern style in building. Its higher expression is not yet to be noted, but Germany some day will give out to the world a sound form of hierarchical government. It is interesting to note that the higher expression of the egoic ray of France (the fifth) is already being evidenced. The scientific interest shown in psychism and psychology is a reaction to that ray of influence, and though it is as yet only indicated, the guarantee of the future is contained therein. The sixth ray influence governing the personality or form aspect of the United States of America is abundantly evidenced in its diversified religions and in the national aptitude for idealistic organisation; the second ray, the egoic ray, is also making its presence felt, and we have the consequent interest shown in the phenomena and truth of the reality of initiation.

The analysis of the ray characteristics given earlier can be applied to the nations and countries of the world also, and it will therefore be seen how the many septenates of nature, having their roots in the primary septenate of rays, can be dealt with under the Law of Correspondences with amazingly interesting results.

Intuitional relations and the major intellectual cleavages are based on the governing ray influences. Spain, Austria and France, being governed by the seventh, fifth and third rays, have a close interrelation, and this worked out most interestingly in the Middle Ages when the destinies of these three nations seemed closely to interlink. The newly forming country of the United States is likewise esoterically and intimately associated, in its form aspect, with Brazil, Russia and Italy, and hence the early influx of Russians and Italians into America, and hence also the pull of the South American countries upon the American consciousness and the growth of the ideal of Pan-America.

These relations are all on the form side and emerge out of the personality rays. Many such relations will appear if the countries and their rays are subjected to a careful scrutiny. The ray of attraction or inclusiveness (Ray II), the ray of electrical phenomena (Ray III), and the fifth ray of intellect are potentially very active at this time, as they are all in incarnation, and the incoming seventh ray is slowly and surely—in spite of appearances—imposing order and hierarchical control upon the planet. It must be remembered that all natural processes are rightly slow in their tempo, or the effects would be too destructive. The effect of these influences is felt in the following sequential order:

1. The sensing of an ideal.
2. The formulation of a theory.

3. The growth of public opinion.
4. The imposition of a growing "pattern" upon the evolving life.
5. The production of a form based upon that pattern.
6. The stabilised functioning of the life within the form.

It must be remembered that each ray embodies an idea which can be sensed as an ideal. The rays in time produce the world patterns which mould the planetary forms, and thus produce the inner potency of the evolutionary processes. This pattern-forming tendency is being recognised today by modern psychology in connection with the individual human being, and his emotional and thought patterns are being delineated and charted. As with the microcosm, so with the macrocosm. Every ray produces three major patterns which are imposed upon the matter aspect, whether it be that of a man, a nation or a planet. These three patterns are:

1. The emotional pattern. This embodies the aspiration of the man, the nation or the planetary life, and is the sum total of the desire tendency.
2. The mental pattern. This emerges later in time and governs the thought processes of the man, the nation and the planet. It eventually becomes the controlling factor of the personality or form life. The emotional and mental patterns are the negative and positive aspect of the personality ray.
3. The soul pattern. This is the predisposing goal, the ring-pass-not or destiny which the immortal principle, the solar angel, succeeds eventually and much later in time in imposing upon the form life. This soul pattern finally supersedes and obliterates the two earlier pattern-producing processes.

I have here again indicated fruitful lines of study through

which the reader may arrive at some intelligent comprehension of what is transpiring in the life of the nations in the world today.

If, for instance, the fifth ray of the solar angels, the ray of mind, which is the egoic ray of the French nation, can make its potency felt through the stress and toil of the present world condition, then to France may be given the ultimate glory of proving to the world the fact of the soul and the demonstration of the technique of egoic control. The soul pattern may be translated by the genius of the French intellect into terms which humanity can understand and the true soul psychology may come into being. Again, the genius of Germany has often in the past manifested along the line of its fourth ray soul, and through that soul pattern has been given to the world much of the outstanding music and philosophies. When this is again manifested, and the soul pattern is more strongly impressed upon the German consciousness, we shall begin to comprehend the significance of the superman. Germany has caught a vision of this ideal. It is as yet misinterpreting it, but Germany can give us the pattern of the superman, and this is its ultimate destiny.

If England's ideal of justice (which is the pattern of its personality ray) can be transformed and transmuted by her egoic ray of love into just and intelligent world service, she may give to the world the pattern of that true government which is the genius or the latent soul quality of the British. If the idealism of the United States of America, which is today its personality expression and evidenced by the loudly enunciated idea of the biggest and the best, can be illumined by the law of love, then the pattern which underlies the structure of the States may be seen in lines of light, and we shall have the pattern for future racial light in contradistinction to the many separative national lines. Thus the underlying patterns for all the nations can be seen and worked out by the intelligent reader. It could be noted also that the emotional pattern of the United States at this time is expressed in terms of sentiment and of personal desire. It is capable of being translated in terms of true benevolence. The mental pattern for the States is to be seen as mass information through the schools, the radio and the newspapers. Later this can be transmuted into intuitive perception. The soul pattern in the States today works out through the acquisitiveness of the nation and its love of possessions which it attracts to itself through the misuse of the law of love. The eventual expression of this will be the changing of the attitude which loves the material into that which loves the real, and the acquisition of the things of the spirit instead of those of the form.

b. THE JEWISH PROBLEM

In connection with the nations and the rays I want now to indicate to you certain fundamental conditions which partially account for the (so-called) Jewish problem,—a problem which has existed for centuries, and which is, at this time, causing the deepest possible concern to many, including members of the planetary Hierarchy. If this problem can be solved, it will be one of the potent factors in the restoration of world understanding and harmony. It cannot be solved without the cooperation of the men of good will throughout the world. There is little that I can say anent this matter that can be checked and proved, for the clue to the problem is to be found back in the very night of time and, literally, when the sun was in the constellation Gemini. At that time the two pillars were set up which, as all Masons know, are two great landmarks in Masonry. Hence the Jewish colouring of all the Masonic work, though it is not Jewish in the sense that that word conveys today. Who, therefore, if the facts are of such ancient import, shall say that I speak with accuracy, or establish the right or wrong nature of my conclusions? I but present the facts as I know them from my access to records more ancient than any known to man.

The personality ray, the material form ray of the Jewish people, is the third ray. Their egoic ray is the first. Their astrological sign is Capricorn, with Virgo rising. Mercury and Virgo play a prominent part in their destiny. These clues should suffice to give to the advanced student and astrologer those salient points which will give him light upon their strange history. Because of this third ray influence, you have the tendency of the Jew to manipulate forces and energies, and to "pull strings" in order to bring about desired ends. As a race, they are natural law makers, and hence their tendency to dominate and govern, because their egoic ray is the first. Hence also the constant appearance of the goat in their history, and their teaching about the virgin mother who should give birth to the Messiah.

In every grouping,—whether in heaven or on earth—there is always evidenced a tendency by some units in the group to revolt, to rebel and to show some form of initiative different to that of the other units in the same grouping. When our solar universe came into being, we are told in the allegorical language of the ancient scriptures, there "was war in Heaven"; "the sun and his seven brothers" did not function with true unanimity; hence (and herein lies a hint) our Earth is *not* one of the seven sacred planets. There is, as we know, the ancient legend of the lost Pleiad, and there are many such stories. Again, in the council chamber of the Most High, there has not always been peace and understanding, but at times, war and disruption; this is made abundantly clear by several of the stories in the Old Testament.

Symbolically speaking, some of the sons of God fell from their high estate, led, at one time, by "Lucifer, Son of the Morning". This "fall of the angels" was a tremendous event in the history of our planet, but was nevertheless only a passing and interesting phenomenon in the history of the solar system, and a trifling incident in the affairs of the seven constellations, of which our solar system is but one. Pause and consider this statement for a moment, and so readjust your sense of values. The standard of happenings varies in importance according to the angle of vision, and what (from the angle of our Earth's unfoldment in consciousness) may be a factor of prime importance and of determining value may (from the angle of the universe) be of trifling moment. The affairs of an individual are, to him, of momentous import; to humanity, as a whole, they are of small concern. It all depends upon which unit holds the centre of the stage in the drama of life, and around which central factor the happenings, trivial or important, pursue their cyclic way.

Within the radius of power and life which is the expression of the fourth kingdom in nature, the human, there was to be found a correspondence to that "assumption of independence" and to that "breaking away" which characterised the major grouping. Back in later Lemurian times, a group of men of high development, from the point of view of that time, and numbered among the then disciples of the world, took issue with the planetary Hierarchy, and broke away from the "law of the initiates". It was a time wherein the emphasis of the teaching was upon the material side of life, and where the focus of attention was upon the physical nature and its control. The *Old Commentary* expresses what happened in the following terms, and as you read the measured cadences of that ancient script, it would be wise to try and realise that the phrases are referring to that *group of disci-*

ples who were the early founders of the present Jewish race:

> "The law went forth from the inner group which guided the destinies of men: Detach yourselves. Withdraw within yourselves the power to hold and gain and get. The sons of God, who train themselves to leave the world of men and enter into light, they ever travel free. They hold not what they have. Release yourselves, and enter through the gates of peace.
>
> "Some of the sons of God, waiting outside those gates, ready to enter when the Word went forth to roll the gates aside, were laden with the treasure of the earth. They brought their gifts as offerings to the Lord of life, who needed not their gifts. They sought to enter through those gates, not with a selfish end in view, but to present the garnered treasures of the world, and thus shew their love.
>
> "Again the Word went forth: Leave all behind and pass beyond the portal, laden with naught of earth. They waited and discussed. The rest of those who were prepared entered into light and passed between the pillars of the gate; they left behind the loads they brought and entered free, and were accepted, carrying naught.
>
> "Because they travelled as a group, and as a group progressed and grasped, the group responded to the divine command and halted. There they waited, standing before the portal of the Path, grasping the garnered treasures of a thousand cycles. Naught did they wish to leave behind. They had laboured for the riches which they held. They loved their God, and Him they sought to dower with the fullest measure of the riches they had gained. They loved not discipline.
>
> "Again the Word went forth: Drop on the ground all that you hold, and enter free.
>
> "But three revolted from that stern command. The rest obeyed. They passed within the gates, leaving the three outside. Many were raised unto the heights of joy. The three remained without the gates, holding their treasure firm."

In this ancient writing, older than any of the written scriptures of the world, is to be found the secret of the Masonic story and of the slaying of the Master by the three most

The Rays and Man 397

closely associated with Him in His death and burial. Masons will all recognise the three to whom I here refer. These three were the founders of the modern Jewish race. They were three advanced disciples who resented the command to enter, free and untrammelled, the place where light is to be found. They sought to hold that which they had gathered and to dedicate it to the service of God. Their unrecognised motive was love of riches and a desire to hold safe their gains. Ancient tradition, as taught by the teachers of the past, tells us that . . .

> "They turned their faces towards the gates of earth. Their friends went on..... They stayed behind..... The Masters met in conclave and decided what should be the fate of those who, having reached the Gates of Light, loved the possessions of the world more than they loved the service of the light. Again the Word went forth to the revolting three, who waited still without the gates:
>
> " 'Hold what you have and gather more, but know no peace. Garner the fruits of mind, and seek your power in wide possessions, but have no sure abiding place.
>
> " 'Within yourselves, because you are disciples of the Lord, you shall have no share in peace, no sure and certain knowledge of success, nor power to hold your gains.
>
> " 'Always shall there be the knowledge dim of Him Who watches over all. Always the urge to gather and amass. Never the time to hold and to enjoy. Pass on therefore until the time shall come, and again you stand before the Gates of Light, this time with empty hands. Then enter, free, accepted by the Servants of the Lord, and know, forever, peace.' "

The ancient legend tells us that the three went forth in sorrow and revolt, laden with their treasures, and thus the history of the wandering Jew began. It is significant to remember that one of the greatest sons of God Who has worked on earth, and Who epitomised in Himself the way and the achievement, Jesus of Nazareth, was a Jew. He reversed all the earlier conditions. He possessed nothing at all. He was the first of our humanity to achieve, and was a direct descendant of the eldest of the original three disciples who revolted from the *drama of detachment*. The Jew embodies in himself the world prodigal son. He is the symbol of the disciple who has not yet learned the lesson of a just sense of values. He has been the victim of the Law of Light and of his inability to comply with that Law. He sinned wilfully and with his eyes wide open to results. Hence he knows the law as no other race knows it, for he is eternally its victim. He has enunciated the law from its negative angle; the Law of Moses today rules most of the world, and yet fails to bring into life justice and true legality.

The other group of disciples, the representatives (in their day and age) of the race, passed through the ancient portals of initiation and took the first great step. They came back with a latent and dim recollection of the episode which separated them from three of their co-disciples. On their return to life on earth, they spoke of this event. This was their error; the long antagonism started, which persists until today. Those particular disciples have themselves passed through their long pilgrimage and have entered into eternal peace, but the results of their early betrayal of the hidden events of initiation still persist.

Curiously enough, this ancient race, founded by the three who loved that which they had to offer more than that which they longed to take, were the originators of the Masonic tradition. Their history (and incidentally the history of humanity) is embodied in that dramatic ritual. The reward for their sincerity,—for they revolted in utter sincerity, believing they knew best—was the permission to enact each year, on the return of the day when they might have entered into light, the story of the search for light. Because they had been so nearly resurrected from the death of earth into the life of light, the great tradition of the mysteries was started by them. They chose death and slew that which "had lived and which could have claimed reward", and which could have spoken the word of power which would have caused the gates of resurrection to open wide.

We are told that these three swore an everlasting vow to stand together and never to desert each other. This vow down the ages they have kept; it has consequently produced that racial separativeness and community of interests which arouses the antagonism of other races.

Down the ages, the Jew has been wandering, producing much of beauty in the world, and giving to humanity many of its greatest men, but he has (at the same time) been hated and persecuted, betrayed and hounded. He embodies, in himself, symbolically, the history of humanity. The ancient tendency of the Jews to grasp and hold, and also to preserve their racial and national integrity, are their outstanding characteristics. They cannot be absorbed, and yet so ancient is the race that nevertheless today no nation in the world but has its roots in that group which—in old Lemuria—had advanced so far that all its foremost people stood upon the path of discipleship. There are no racial strains in the Western world which are not offshoots of this oldest select people, with the exception of the Finns, Lapps and those nations which show definite mongoloid strains. But the admixture of what is now called Jewish blood is not found to the same extent, and the modern Jew is as much a by-product as is the Anglo-Saxon race, only, through an imposed selective tendency and racial segregation, he has preserved intact more of the original characteristics.

It is the realisation of this common origin which has led

the British-Israelites into their travesty of the truth, and caused them to trace our modern Western history to the Jews of the Dispersion. It is a far more ancient relation than that, and dates back into a period that antedates the history of the Jews as it is related for us in the Old Testament. The original three disciples and their family groups were the ancestors of three major racial groupings, which can be generalised as follows:

1. The Semitic race or races of Biblical and modern times; the Arabs, the Afghans, the Moors and the offshoots and affiliations of those peoples, including the modern Egyptians. These are all descended from the eldest of the three disciples.
2. The Latin peoples and their various branches throughout the world, and also the Celtic races wherever found. These are descended from the second of the three disciples.
3. The Teutons, the Scandinavians, and the Anglo-Saxons, who are the descendants of the third of the three disciples.

The above is a broad generalisation. The period covered is so vast, and the ramifications down the ages are so numerous, that it is not possible for me to do more than give a general idea. Gradually the descendants of two of these three disciples have accepted the legends which were promulgated in Atlantean times, and have ranged themselves on the side of those who are antagonistic to the Jew, as he is today; they have lost all sense of their common origin. There is no pure race in the world today, for intermarriage, illicit relations and promiscuity during the past few million years have been so numerous that there exists no pure strain. Climate and environment are fundamentally greater determining factors than any forced segregation, except that which comes through a constant racial intermarriage. Of this latter factor, only the Hebrew today has preserved any measure of racial integrity.

When humanity awakens to the fact of its common origin, and when the three great major strains in our modern civilisation are recognised, then we shall see the old hatred of the Jew die out, and he will fuse and blend with the rest of mankind. Even the oriental races, who are the remnants of the great Atlantean civilisation, have in them traces of intermarriage with the ancestors of the modern Jews and other racial types, but they have not mixed well, and have therefore preserved their characteristics more successfully than have the groups of our Western men.

If you ponder upon the above, and if you study the Masonic tradition with care, much will become clarified in your mind. Ethnologists may disagree, but they cannot disprove what I have said, for the origins of the present racial world situation lie so far back in the history of mankind that they cannot even prove their own contentions. All they are capable of considering is the history of the past one hundred thousand years, and their work lies with effects of that past and not with originating causes.

7. *The Ray of the Ego*

In starting our study of the ray of the Ego or Soul, certain major premises might be briefly stated and incorporated into a series of propositions, fourteen in number. They are as follows:

1. The egos of all human beings are to be found upon one or another of the seven rays.

2. All egos found upon the fourth, the fifth, the sixth and the seventh rays must eventually, after the third initiation, blend with the three major rays, or monadic rays.
3. The monadic ray of every ego is one of the three rays of aspect, and the sons of men are either monads of power, monads of love, or monads of intelligence.
4. For our specific purposes, we shall confine our attention to the seven groups of souls found upon one or other of the seven rays or streams of divine energy.
5. For the major part of our racial and life experience we are governed sequentially, and later simultaneously by:
    a. The physical body, which is dominated by the ray governing the sum total of the atoms of that body.
    b. The emotional desire nature, which is to be found influenced and controlled by the ray which colours the totality of astral atoms.
    c. The mind body or mental nature, and the calibre and quality of the ray determining its atomic value.
    d. Later, on the physical plane, the soul ray begins to work in and with the sum total of the three bodies, which constitute—when aligned and functioning in unison—the personality. The effect of that general integration is actively to produce an incarnation and incarnations wherein the personality ray emerges clearly, and the three bodies or selves constitute the three aspects or rays of the lower personal self.
6. When the personality ray becomes pronounced and dominant, and the three body rays are subordinated to it, then the great fight takes place between the egoic ray or soul and the personality ray. The differentiation becomes clearly marked, and the sense of duality becomes more definitely established. The experiences detailed in the *Bhagavad Gita* become the experiences

of the path of discipleship; Arjuna stands "at the midway point" on the field of Kurukshetra, between the two opposing forces, and, owing to the smoke of the battle, finds himself unable to see clearly.
7. Eventually, the soul ray or influence becomes the dominating factor, and the rays of the lower bodies become the sub-rays of this controlling ray. This last sentence is of basic importance, for it indicates the true relation of the personality to the ego or soul. The disciple who understands this relation and conforms to it is ready to tread the path of initiation.
8. Each of the seven groups of souls is responsive to one of the seven types of force, and all of them are responsive to the ray of the planetary Logos of our planet, which is the third Ray of Active Intelligence. All are therefore upon a sub-ray of this ray, but it must never be forgotten that the planetary Logos is also upon a ray, which is a sub-ray of the second Ray of Love-Wisdom. Therefore we have:

THE RAY OF THE PLANETARY LOGOS

I.

The Solar Ray of Love-Wisdom
"God is Love"

II.

The Seven Rays

1.	2.	3.	4.	5.	6.	7.
Will.	Love.	Intellect.	Harmony.	Science.	Devotion.	Ceremony.

III.

Planetary Egoic Ray
with seven sub-rays

1.	2.	3.	4.	5.	6.	7.
Will.	Love.	Intellect.	Harmony.	Science.	Devotion.	Ceremony.

IV.

The Personality Ray
of
the Planetary Logos

It should be remembered that our planetary Logos functioning through the planet Earth is not considered as producing one of the seven sacred planets.

9. The work of each individual aspirant is therefore to arrive at an understanding of:

   a. His egoic ray.
   b. His personality ray.
   c. The ray governing his mind.
   d. That governing his astral body.
   e. The ray influencing his physical body.

   When he has achieved this fivefold knowledge, he has fulfilled the Delphic injunction: "Know thyself." and can consequently take Initiation.

10. Every human being is also governed by certain group rays:

The Rays and Man 405

   a. Those of the fourth kingdom in nature. This will have different effects, according to the ray of the personality or soul. The fourth kingdom has:
      1). The fourth ray as its egoic ray.
      2). The fifth ray as its personality ray.
   b. The racial rays, at this time, are the third and fifth, for our Aryan race, and this powerfully affects every human being.
   c. The cyclic ray.
   d. The national ray.
      All of these control the personality life of each man. The egoic ray of the individual, plus the egoic ray of the fourth kingdom, gradually negate the rays governing the personality as the man nears the path of probation and discipleship.
11. Man therefore is an aggregate of forces which dominate him serially and together; these colour his nature, produce his quality, and determine his "appearance", using this word in its occult sense of *exteriorisation*. For ages he is wielded by one or other of these forces, and is simply what they make him. As he arrives at a clearer understanding, and can begin to discriminate, he definitely chooses which of them shall dominate, until he eventually becomes controlled by the Soul ray, with all the other rays subordinated to that ray and used by him at will.
12. In studying the egoic ray of man we have to grasp:
    a. The process followed . . . . externalisation.
    b. The secret to be found . . . . manifestation.
    c. The purpose to be known . . . . realisation.
    We have also to understand the dominant ray influences of the kingdom of souls, the fifth kingdom. These are:
    1). Ray five . . . . working through the personality.

2). Ray two . . . . working through the intuition.

13. The *Personality ray* finds its major field of activity and expression in the physical body. It determines its life trend and purpose, its appearance and occupation. It is selective of quality, when influenced by the egoic ray. The *Egoic ray* has direct and specific action upon the astral body. Hence the battlefield of the life is ever on the plane of illusion; as the soul seeks to dispel the ancient glamour, the aspirant is enabled to walk in the light.

    The *Monadic ray* influences the mental body, after integration of the personality has been brought about. It causes the mind nature to achieve that clear vision which finds its consummation at the fourth initiation, and releases the man from the limitations of form. There is an analogy to this triplicity and an interesting symbolic relation in the three Initiators.

    a. The first Initiator . . . . the soul of man. This controls gradually the personality.

    b. The second Initiator . . . . the Christ. Releasing the love nature.

    c. The final Initiator . . . . the Planetary Logos. Illumining the mind.

14. The egoic or soul ray begins to make its presence actively felt, via the astral body, as soon as alignment has been achieved. The process is as follows:

    a. It plays on the astral body externally.

    b. It stimulates it internally to greater size, colour and quality.

    c. It brings it and all parts of the physical life into activity and under control.

All the above propositions could be summed up in the statement that the personality ray induces a *separative* attitude and causes a detachment from the group of souls of which the personality is an externalisation, and a consequent attachment to the form side of manifestation. The egoic ray induces *group consciousness* and detachment from external forms, causing attachment to the life side of manifestation and to the subjective whole. The monadic ray has an effect which can be understood only after man has taken the third initiation.

We might divide what we have to say in the next section of our treatise, which deals with the egoic ray, into the four following parts:

     I. THE GROWTH OF SOUL INFLUENCE
    II. THE SEVEN LAWS OF EGOIC LIFE
   III. THE FIVE GROUPS OF SOULS
  IV. RULES FOR INDUCING SOUL CONTROL

Some Tabulations on the Rays

THE RAYS IN AND OUT OF MANIFESTATION

Ray I . . . . Not in manifestation.
*Ray II . . . In manifestation since 1575 A.D.
*Ray III. . . In manifestation since 1425 A.D.
Ray IV . . . To come slowly into manifestation around 2025 A.D.
*Ray V . . . In manifestation since 1775 A.D.
Ray VI. . . Passing rapidly out of manifestation. Began to pass out in 1625 A.D.
*Ray VII . . In manifestation since 1675 A.D.

RAY METHODS OF TEACHING TRUTH

Ray I . . . Higher expression: The science of statesmanship, and of government.
　　　　　Lower expression: Modern diplomacy and politics.
Ray II . . Higher expression: The process of initiation as taught by the Hierarchy of Masters.
　　　　　Lower expression: Religion.
Ray III . Higher expression: Means of communication or interaction. Radio, telegraph, telephone and means of transportation.
　　　　　Lower expression: The use and spread of money and gold.
Ray IV . Higher expression: The Masonic work, based on the formation of the Hierarchy and related to Ray II.
　　　　　Lower expression: Architectural construction. Modern city planning.
Ray V . . Higher expression: The science of the Soul. Esoteric psychology.
　　　　　Lower expression: Modern educational systems.
Ray VI . Higher expression: Christianity and diversified religions. Note relation to Ray II.
　　　　　Lower expression: Churches and religious organisations.

Ray VII. Higher expression: All forms of white magic.
           Lower expression: Spiritualism in its lower aspects.

DISCIPLESHIP AND THE RAYS

1st Ray. Force . . . . Energy . . . . . Action . . . The Occultist
2nd Ray. Consciousness . Expansion . . Initiation . The true Psychic
3rd Ray. Adaptation . . . Development. Evolution . The Magician
4th Ray. Vibration . . . . Response . . . Expression. The Artist
5th Ray. Mentation . . . Knowledge . Science . . The Scientist
6th Ray. Devotion . . . . Abstraction . Idealism . . The Devotee
7th Ray. Incantation . . . Magic . . . . . . Ritual . . . . The Ritualist

From: *Initiation, Human and Solar.*

THE RAYS AND THE FOUR KINGDOMS

Note: Much information and several interesting hints are scattered here and there in *A Treatise on Cosmic Fire* and in this series of Instructions. I have gathered some of it together and students would find it useful to familiarise themselves with the tabulations and points noted below. A. A. B.

THE NUMERICAL INFLUENCE OF THE RAYS

       The Mineral Kingdom . . . . Rays 7 and 1.
       The Vegetable Kingdom . . . . Rays 2, 4 and 6.
       The Animal Kingdom . . . . Rays 3 and 6.
       The Human Kingdom . . . . Rays 4 and 5.
       The Soul Kingdom . . . . Rays 5 and 2.
       The Planetary Kingdom . . . . Rays 6 and 3.
       The Solar Kingdom . . . . Rays 1 and 7.

THE EXPRESSION OF THE RAY INFLUENCES

The Mineral Kingdom.......	Ray 7........	Radiation.
	Ray 1........	Power.
The Vegetable Kingdom....	Ray 2........	Magnetism.
	Ray 4........	Harmony of colour.
	Ray 6........	Growth towards light.
The Animal Kingdom.........	Ray 3........	Instinct.
	Ray 6.......	Domesticity.
The Human Kingdom.........	Ray 4........	Experience.
	Ray 5........	Intellect.

The Kingdom of Souls........ Ray 5........ Personality.
                             Ray 2........ Intuition.
The Planetary Kingdom....... Ray 6....... The Plan.
                             Ray 3....... Creative Work.
The Solar Kingdom............. Ray 1....... Universal Mind Will.
                             Ray 7....... Synthetic Ritual.

SOME SETS OF CORRESPONDENCES

I. Mineral .... Gonads .... Sacral Centre.
                                   Base of Spine.
   Vegetable ...... Heart .... Heart.
                   Lungs .... Throat.
   Animal .... Stomach .... Solar Plexus.
                  Liver
   Human .... Brain .... The two Head Centres.
                  Vocal Organs

II Mineral .... Base of Spine .... Adrenals.
   Vegetable .... Heart Centre .... Thymus.
   Animal .... Solar Plexus .... Pancreas.
   Human .... Sacral Centre .... Gonads.
   Egoic .... Throat Centre .... Thyroid.
   Planetary .... Ajna Centre .... Pituitary.
   Solar .... Head Centre .... Pineal.

III.   *Process*   *Secret*   *Purpose*
   Mineral .. Condensation . Transmutation . Radiation.
   Vegetable. Conformation . Transformation. Magnetisation.
   Animal .. Concretisation . Transfusion ... Experimentation.
   Human .. Adaptation ... Translation .... Transfiguration.
   Egoic ... Externalisation. Manifestation .. Realisation.

SOME NOTES ON THE FOUR KINGDOMS

1. The Mineral Kingdom is divided into three main divisions:
   a. The base metals.
   b. The standard metals.
   c. The crystals and precious stones.

   A Treatise on Cosmic Fire, p. 495.

2. The Vegetable Kingdom is . . .
   a. The transmitter of the vital pranic fluid.

    b. A bridge between the so-called conscious and the unconscious.
    c. In an esoteric relation to the deva or angel kingdom.
    A Treatise on Cosmic Fire, p. 564.

3. The four minor rays control the four kingdoms:
    a. The 7th ray controls the mineral kingdom.
    b. The 6th ray controls the vegetable kingdom.
    c. The 5th ray controls the animal kingdom.
    d. The 4th ray controls the human kingdom.
    A Treatise on Cosmic Fire, p. 588.

4. The 4th ray and the 4th kingdom form a point of harmony for the three lower kingdoms.
    A Treatise on Cosmic Fire, p. 588.

5. The 5th ray has a peculiar relation to the animal kingdom in that it is the ray governing the merging of that kingdom in the human.
    A Treatise on Cosmic Fire, p. 590.

6. The human kingdom is seeking to make manifest the desire or the love nature of the planetary Logos.
    The three subhuman kingdoms seek to manifest the intelligent nature of the planetary Logos.
    A Treatise on Cosmic Fire, pp. 1043, 1044.

7. The mineral kingdom is responsive to the lowest type of energy, the lowest aspect of fire.
    The vegetable kingdom is responsive to that type of energy which produces the phenomenon of water.
    The animal kingdom is responsive to the type of energy which is a combination of the two above mentioned, fire and water.
    The human kingdom is responsive to the energy of fire at its highest manifestation in the three worlds.
    A Treatise on Cosmic Fire, pp. 1071, 1072-3.

8. The period of radiation is longest in the mineral kingdom and shortest in the human kingdom.
    A Treatise on Cosmic Fire, p. 1075.

9. The mineral kingdom provides that negative yet vital something which is the essence of the human permanent atom.

The vegetable kingdom provides the negative energy for the astral permanent atom in the human kingdom.

The animal kingdom provides the negative force which when energised by positive force becomes the mental unit.

Sattva . Rhythm . Mental body . . Mental Unit . . . . Animal.
Rajas . . Activity . Astral body . . . Astral permanent atom . . . . Vegetable
Tamas . Inertia . . Physical body . Physical permanent atom . Mineral

A Treatise on Cosmic Fire, p. 1134

10. Each kingdom in nature is positive to the one next below.
A Treatise on Cosmic Fire, p. 1135

THE INCOMING SEVENTH RAY AND THE ANIMAL KINGDOM

1. The animal kingdom is to the human body what the dense physical body is to the seven principles.
2. The animal kingdom is the mother aspect, prior to the overshadowing of the Holy Ghost.
3. The animal kingdom is the field of individualisation.
4. Since Atlantean days the animal kingdom has been occupied with the development of karma.
5. Domestic animals constitute the heart centre in the life of the Entity Who ensouls the animal kingdom.
6. The animal kingdom does not react strongly to the 7th ray.
7. The human kingdom does, but the 7th ray will have three effects in relation to the two kingdoms and their interplay:
   a. It will refine the animal bodies.
   b. It will bring about a closer relation between men and animals.
   c. It will cause a great destruction of the present animal forms.

RAY METHODS OF ACTIVITY

These are twenty-one in number, making in their synthesis the twenty-two methods which are the expression of the great Law of Attraction.

I. The Ray of Will or Power.
   1. Destruction of forms through group interplay. 1.

2. Stimulation of the self, the egoic principle. 2.
3. Spiritual impulse or energy. 3.

II. The Ray of Love-Wisdom.
   1. Construction of forms through group intercourse. 4.
   2. Stimulation of desire, the love principle. 5.
   3. Soul impulse or energy. 6.

III. The Ray of Activity or Adaptability.
   1. Vitalising of forms through group work. 7.
   2. Stimulation of forms, the etheric or pranic principle. 8.
   3. Material impulse or energy. 9.

IV. The Ray of Harmony or Union.
   1. Perfecting of forms through group interplay. 10.
   2. Stimulation of the solar Angels, or the manasic principle. 11.
   3. Intuitional or buddhic energy. 12.

V. Ray of Concrete Knowledge.
   1. Correspondence of forms to type, through group influence. 13.
   2. Stimulation of the Logoic dense physical body, the three worlds. 14.
   3. Mental energy or impulse, Universal manas. 15.

VI. Ray of Abstract Idealism or Devotion.
   1. Reflection of reality through group work. 16.
   2. Stimulation of man through desire. 17.
   3. Desire energy, instinct or aspiration. 18.

VII. Ray of Ceremonial Order.
   1. Union of energy and substance through group activity. 19.
   2. Stimulation of etheric forms. 20.
   3. Vital energy. 21.

A Treatise on Cosmic Fire, pp. 1222-3

THE SEVEN KEYS TO THE SEVEN RAY METHODS
FIRST RAY

"Let the Forces come together. Let them mount to the High Place, and from that lofty eminence let the Soul look upon a world destroyed. Then let the word go forth: 'I will persist.'"

SECOND RAY

"Let all the life be drawn to the Centre, and enter thus into the Heart of Love Divine. Then from that point of sentient Life, let the Soul realise the consciousness of God. Let the word go forth, reverberating through the silence: 'Naught is but *Me*!' "

THIRD RAY

"Let the Army of the Lord, responsive to the word, cease their activities. Let knowledge end in wisdom. Let the point vibrating become the point quiescent, and all lines gather into One. Let the Soul realise the One in Many, and let the word go forth in perfect understanding: 'I am the Worker and the Work, The One that *Is*!' "

FOURTH RAY

"Let the outer glory pass away and the beauty of the inner Light reveal the *One*. Let dissonance give place to harmony, and from the centre of the hidden Light let the soul speak, let the word roll forth: 'Beauty and glory veil Me not. I stand revealed. *I Am*!' "

FIFTH RAY

"Let the three forms of energy electric pass upward to the Place of Power. Let the forces of the head and heart and all the nether aspects blend. Then let the Soul look out upon the inner world of light divine. Let the word triumphant go forth: 'I mastered energy for I am energy itself. The Master and the mastered are but One.' "

SIXTH RAY

"Let all desire cease. Let aspiration end. The search is over. Let the Soul realise that it has reached the goal, and from that gateway to eternal Life and cosmic Peace let the word sound: 'I am the seeker and the sought. I rest.' "

SEVENTH RAY

"Let the builders cease their work. The Temple is completed. Let the Soul enter into its heritage and from the Holy Place command all work to end. Then in the silence subsequent let him chant forth the word: 'The creative work is over. I, the Creator, Am. Naught else remains but *Me*.' "

REFERENCES TO *THE SECRET DOCTRINE*

Ray I . . . . Will or Power

Planet . . . . Sun, substituting for the veiled planet Vulcan.
Day . . . . Sunday.
Exoteric Colour . . . . Orange. S.D.III. p. 478.
Esoteric Colour . . . . Red.
Human Principle . . . . Prana or life-vitality.
Divine Principle . . . . The One Life. Spirit. This is regarded as a principle only when our seven planes are seen as the seven sub-planes of the cosmic physical plane.
Element . . . . The Akasha. "It is written."
Instrument of Sensation . The Light of Kundalini.
Bodily location . . . . Vital airs in the skull.
Plane governed . . . . The logoic plane. Divine Purpose or Will.
Metal . . . . Gold.
Sense . . . . A synthetic sense, embracing all.

Esoterically, this power is viewed as the life principle seated in the heart.

Ray II . . . . Love-Wisdom

Planet . . . . Jupiter.
Day . . . . Thursday.
Exoteric Colour . . . . Indigo with a tinge of purple.
Esoteric Colour . . . . Light blue. S.D.III. p. 461. Note.
Human Principle . . . . The auric envelope.
Divine Principle . . . . Love.
Element . . . . Ether. "It is spoken." The Word.
Instrument of Sensation . Ears. Speech. The Word.
Bodily location . . . . The heart.
Plane . . . . The Monadic.
Sense . . . . Hearing.

Esoterically, this power is the consciousness or soul principle, seated in the head.

Ray III . . . .*Active Intelligence or Adaptability*

Planet . . . . Saturn.
Day . . . . Saturday.
Exoteric Colour . . . . .Black.
Esoteric Colour . . . . Green.
Human Principle . . . . Lower mind.
Divine Principle . . . . Universal mind.
Element . . . . .Fire. "Fire by friction."
Sensation . . . . .Nervous system. "It is known."
Bodily location . . . . Centres up spine.
Plane . . . . The atmic, or plane of spiritual will.
Sense . . . . Touch.

   Esoterically, this principle of creative mind is seen as seated in the throat.

Ray IV . . . .*Intuition, Harmony, Beauty, Art*

Planet . . . . Mercury.
Day . . . . Wednesday.
Exoteric Colour . . . . Cream.
Esoteric Colour . . . . .Yellow.
Divine Principle . . . . Buddhi. Intuition. Pure reason.
Human Principle . . . . . . .Understanding. Vision. Spiritual perception.
Element . . . . .Air. "Thus is Unity produced."
Instrument of Sensation . Eyes. Right eye particularly.
Plane . . . . The Buddhic or Intuitional plane.
Sense . . . . .Sight.

   Esoterically, this is the pure reason, seated in the ajna centre, between the eyes. Functioning when the personality reaches a high stage of co-ordination.

Ray V . . . .*Concrete Knowledge of Science*

Planet . . . . Venus. The Lords of mind came from Venus.
Day . . . . Friday.
Exoteric Colour . . . . .Yellow.
Esoteric Colour . . . . .Indigo.
Human Principle . . . . Higher mind.
Divine Principle . . . . Higher knowledge. "God saw that it was good."

Element . . . . Flame.
Instrument of Sensation . Astral body.
Plane . . . . Lower mental plane.
Sense . . . . Consciousness as response to knowledge.
Bodily location . . . . Brain.

Esoterically, this principle of sentiency is seated in the solar plexus.

Ray VI . . . . Abstract Idealism, Devotion

Planet . . . . Mars.
Day . . . . Tuesday.
Exoteric Colour . . . . Red.
Esoteric Colour . . . . Silvery Rose.
Human Principle . . . . Kama-manas. Desire.
Divine Principle . . . . Desire for form.
Element . . . . Water. "I long for habitation."
Instrument of Sensation . Tongue. Organs of speech.
Plane . . . . Astral or emotional Plane. Desire plane.
Sense . . . . Taste.

Esoterically, this principle of desire is seated in the sacral centre, with a higher reflection in the throat.

Ray VII . . . . Ceremonial Order or Magic

Planet . . . . The Moon. She is the mother of form.
Day . . . . Monday.
Exoteric Colour . . . . White.
Esoteric Colour . . . . Violet.
Human Principle . . . . Etheric force or prana.
Divine Principle . . . . Energy.
Element . . . . Earth. "I manifest."
Instrument of Sensation . Nose.
Plane . . . . Physical plane, etheric levels.
Sense . . . . Smell.

Esoterically, this principle of vitality or prana is seated in the centre at the base of the spine.

Note:—Esoterically speaking, the planets which are the expression of the three major rays are:

Ray   I . . . . Uranus.
Ray   II . . . . . . Neptune.
Ray   III . . . . . . Saturn.

A study of this will make it apparent why Saturn is ever the stabiliser. In this present cycle, the two rays of Power and Love are directing their energies to Vulcan and Jupiter, whilst Saturn's attention is turned towards our planet, the Earth.

Thus we have the ten rays of perfection, the vehicles of manifestation of what H.P.B. calls, "the imperfect Gods," the planetary Logoi. See *A Treatise on Cosmic Fire,* where this is elaborated. Use the Index.

THE RAYS AND THE PLANES

Ray I . . . . Will, dynamically applied, emerges in manifestation as power.

Ray II . . . Love, magnetically functioning, produces wisdom.

Ray III . . . Intelligence, potentially found in substance, causes activity.

THE RAYS AND THE SENSES

1. Hearing . . . . . 7th Ray . Magic . . . . The Word of Power.
2. Touch . . . . . . 1st Ray . Destroyer . . . . The Finger of God.
3. Sight . . . . 3rd Ray . Vision . . . . The Eye of God.
4. Taste . . . . 6th Ray . Idealism . . . . . The Desire of Nations.
5. Smell . . . . . . 4th Ray . Art . . . . The Beauty of Revelation.
6. The Intellect . 5th Ray . Mind . . . . The Knowledge of God.
7. The Intuition . 2nd Ray Love-Wisdom. Understanding of God.

THE RAYS OF ASPECT AND OF ATTRIBUTE

The four rays of attribute, which find their synthesis in the third ray of aspect, produce the varying qualities in greater detail than do the rays of aspect. It might generally be stated that the three rays of aspect find their main expression in relation to mankind through the medium of the three periodical vehicles:

Ray I . . Power . . . . Life . . . . Ideas . The Monad.
Ray II . Love-Wisdom . . . . . Consciousness . Ideals . The Soul.
Ray III..Active Intelligence . Appearance . . . Idols . . The Personality.

They find their secondary expression in the three bodies which form the personality of man:

Ray I ... Power ...... Ideas ... Mental Body .. Purpose. Life.
Ray II ... Love .... Ideals ... Astral Body ... Quality.
Ray III .. Intelligence .. Idols ... Physical Body . Form.

The rays of attribute, though expressing themselves equally on all the planes, and through the periodical vehicles and the three aspects of the personality, find their main expression through one or other of the four kingdoms in nature.

Ray IV .. Harmony, Conflict .. 4th kingdom .. Human.
  The Balance.
Ray V ... Concrete Knowledge . 3rd kingdom .. Animal.
Ray VI .. Devotion .... 2nd kingdom .. Vegetable.
Ray VII . Ceremonial Ritual ... 1st kingdom ... Mineral.

These are their main fields of influence in the three worlds and upon this we shall later enlarge.

In relation to mankind, these four rays of attribute find a wide expression in connection with the four aspects of the personality, or with the quaternary. The relationship is as follows:

Ray IV .. Harmony through Conflict ..... the physical body.
Ray V ... Concrete Knowledge .... the etheric body.
Ray VI .. Devotion .... the astral body.
Ray VII .. Organisation .... the mental body.

KINGDOMS

No. Kingdom	Ray	Expression
1. Mineral	7. Ceremonial Organisation	Radio-Activity.
	1. Will or Power	The basic reservoir of Power.
2. Vegetable	2. Love-Wisdom	Magnetism.
	4. Beauty or Harmony .	Uniformity of colour.
	6. Idealistic Devotion ..	Upward tendency.
3. Animal	3. Adaptability	Instinct.
	6. Devotion	Domesticity.
4. Human	4. Harmony through Conflict.	Experience. Growth.
	5. Concrete Knowledge .	Intellect.

5. Egoic or Soul	5. Concrete Knowledge.	Personality.
	2. Love-wisdom	Intuition.
6. Planetary Lives	6. Devotion to ideas	The Plan.
	3. Active Intelligence	Creative Work.
7. Solar Lives	1. Will or Power	Universal Mind.
	7. Ceremonial Magic	Synthetic Ritual.

THE MINERAL KINGDOM

Influence .... The seventh Ray of Organisation and the first Ray of Power are the dominant factors.

Results .... The evolutionary results are radiation and potency, a static potency, underlying the rest of the natural scheme.

Process .... Condensation.

Secret .... Transmutation. *A Treatise on Cosmic Fire* defines this as follows: "Transmutation is the passage across from one state of being to another through the agency of fire."

Purpose .... To demonstrate the radio-activity of life.

Divisions .... Base metals, standard metals, precious stones.

Objective Agency .. Fire. Fire is the initiating factor in this kingdom.

Subjective Agency .. Sound.

Quality .... Extreme density. Inertia. Brilliance.

THE VEGETABLE KINGDOM

Influences .... The second Ray of Love-Wisdom, working out in a vastly increased sensibility.

The fourth Ray of Harmony and Beauty, working out in the general harmonisation of this kingdom throughout the entire planet.

The sixth Ray of Devotion or (as it has been expressed symbolically in the ancient wisdom) the "urge to consecrate the life to the Sun, the giver of that life," or again, the "urge to turn the eye of the heart to the heart of the sun."

Results	These work out in the second kingdom as magnetism, perfume, colour and growth towards the light. These words I commend to you for your earnest study, for it is in this kingdom that one first sees clearly the glory which lies ahead of humanity.

    a. Magnetic radiation. The blending of the mineral and vegetable goals.
    b. The perfume of perfection.
    c. The glory of the human aura. The radiant augoeides.
    d. Aspiration which leads to final inspiration.

Process	Conformation, or the power to "conform" to the pattern set in the heavens, and to produce below that which is found above. This is done in this kingdom with greater pliability than in the mineral kingdom, where the process of condensation goes blindly forward.
Secret	Transformation, those hidden alchemical processes which enable the vegetable growths in this kingdom to draw their sustenance from the sun and soil and "transform" it into form and colour.
Purpose	Magnetism. That inner source of beauty, loveliness, and attractive power which lures to it the higher forms to consume it for food, and the thinking entities to draw from it inspiration, comfort and satisfaction of a mental kind.
Divisions	Trees and shrubs. The flowering plants. The grasses and lesser green things which do not come under the other two categories. A group of vegetable growths which are found under the general heading of "sea growths".
Objective Agency	Water.
Subjective Agency	Touch.

Quality . . . . Rajas or activity.

MEDITATION AND THE KINGDOMS

"One-pointed meditation upon the five forms which every element takes produces mastery over every element. These five forms are the gross nature, the elemental form, the quality, the pervasiveness and the basic purpose."

You have, therefore, an analogy for consideration:

1. The gross nature . . . . the mineral kingdom.
2. The elemental form . . . . . . the vegetable kingdom.
3. The quality . . . . the animal kingdom.
4. The pervasiveness . . . . the human kingdom.
5. The basic purpose . . . . the kingdom of souls.

All of this is from the standpoint of consciousness.

ANOTHER RELATIONSHIP

1. The body . . . mineral kingdom . . . the dense prison of life
2. The akasha . . vegetable kingdom . the fluid conscious life
3. Ascension out of matter . . animal kingdom . . . . the evolutionary goal of the relation between body and akasha
4. Power to travel in space . . . . . human kingdom . . . the goal of the human consciousness through the realisation of the above three.

THE ANIMAL KINGDOM

Influences . . . . The third Ray of Active Intelligence or of Adaptability is potent in this kingdom and will express itself increasingly as time goes on, until it has produced in the animal world that reaction to life and to environment which can best be described as "animal one-pointedness". Then, at this point and cyclically, the sixth Ray of Devotion or Idealism can make its pres-

	sure felt as the urge towards a goal, and thus produce a relation to man which makes of him the desired goal. This is to be seen through the medium of the tamed, the trained and the domestic animals.
Results	In the one case we find the third ray producing the emergence of instinct, which in its turn creates and uses that marvellous response apparatus we call the nervous system, the brain, and the five senses, which lie behind and which are responsible for them as a whole. It should be noted that, wide as we may regard the difference between man and the animals, there is really a much closer relation than that existing between the animal and the vegetable. In the case of the sixth ray, we have the appearance of the power to be domesticated and trained which is, in the last analysis, the power to love, to serve and to emerge from the herd into the group. Ponder on the words of this last paradoxical statement.
Process	This is called concretisation. In this kingdom we have for the first time a true organisation of the etheric body into what are called "the true nerves and the sensory centres" by the esotericists. Plants also have nerves, but they have in them nothing of the same intricacy of relation and of plexus as we find in the human being and in the animal. Both kingdoms share the same general grouping of nerves of force centres and channels, with a spinal column and a brain. This organisation of a sensitive response apparatus constitutes, in reality, the densification of the subtle etheric body.
Secret	This is called transfusion, which is a very inadequate word to express the early

	blending in the animal of the psychological factors which lead to the process of individualisation. It is a process of life-giving, of intelligent integration and of psychological unfoldment to meet emergency.
Purpose	This is called experimentation. Here we come to a great mystery and one that is peculiar to our planet. In many esoteric books it has been stated and hinted that there has been a mistake, or serious error, on the part of God Himself, of our planetary Logos, and that this mistake has involved our planet, and all that it contains, in the visible misery, chaos and suffering. Shall we say that there has been no mistake, but simply a great experiment, of the success or failure of which it is not yet possible to judge? The objective of the experiment might be stated as follows: It is the intent of the planetary Logos to bring about a psychological condition which can best be described as one of "divine lucidity". The work of the psyche, and the goal of the true psychology is to see life clearly, as it is, and with all that is involved. This does not mean conditions and environment, but *Life*. This process was begun in the animal kingdom and will be consummated in the human. These are described in the *Old Commentary* as "the two eyes of Deity, both blind at first, but which later see, though the right eye sees more clearly than the left". The first dim indication of this tendency towards lucidity is seen in the faculty of the plant to turn towards the sun. It is practically non-existent in the mineral kingdom.
Divisions	First, the higher animals and the domestic animals, such as the dog, the horse and the

elephant.

Secondly, the so-called wild animals, such as the lion, the tiger and other carnivorous and dangerous wild beasts.

Thirdly, the mass of lesser animals that seem to meet no particular need nor to fill any special purpose, such as the harmless yet multitudinous lives found in our forests, our jungles and the fields of our planet. Instances of these in the West are the rabbits and other rodents. This is a wide and general specification of no scientific import at all; but it covers adequately the karmic divisions and the general conformation into which these groupings of lives fall in this kingdom.

Objective Agency .. Fire and water,— fierce desire and incipient mind. These are symbolised in the animal power to eat and drink.

Subjective Agency ..Smell or scent,—the instinctual discovery of that which is needed, from the activity of ranging forth for food, and the use of the power to scent that food, to the identification of the smell of a beloved master or friend.

Quality . . . . .Tamas or inertia,— but in this case it is the tamasic nature of mind and not that of matter, as usually understood. The chitta or mind-stuff can be equally tamasic.

THE RELATION OF THE RAYS TO THE CENTRES

1. Head Centre . . . . . . .Ray of Will or Power. First Ray.
2. The Ajna Centre . . Ray of Concrete Knowledge. Fifth Ray
3. The Throat Centre . . Ray of Active Intelligence. Third Ray.
4. The Heart Centre . . Ray of Love-Wisdom. Second Ray.
5. The Solar Plexus . . .Ray of Devotion. Sixth Ray
6. The Sacral Centre . . Ray of Ceremonial Magic. Seventh Ray.
7. Base of Spine . . . . . Ray of Harmony. Fourth Ray

RAY RELATIONSHIP TO THE RACES

Ray	Full Expression	Major Influence
Ray I .. Will .... 1st ray souls	In the 7th rootrace . Perfection of Plan.	1st and 7th sub-races.
Ray II ..Love-wisdom 2nd ray souls	In the 6th rootrace . Perfected intuition.	2nd and 6th sub-races.
Ray III.. Intelligence .. 3rd ray souls	In the 5th rootrace . Aryan race Perfected intellect.	3rd and 5th sub-races.
Ray IV . Harmony .... 4th ray souls	In the 4th rootrace . Perfected astralism. Perfected emotion. Atlantean race.	4th and 6th sub-races.
Ray V ..Knowledge .. 5th ray souls	In the 3rd rootrace . Lemurian. Perfected physical.	5th and 3rd sub-races.
Ray VI . Devotion .... 6th ray souls	In the 2nd root race.	6th and 2nd sub-races.
Ray VII.Ceremonial .. 7th ray souls	In the 1st root race .	7th and 1st sub-races.

THE RAYS THAT MUST BE CONSIDERED IN CONNECTION WITH HUMANITY

1. The ray of the solar system itself.
2. The ray of the planetary Logos of our planet.
3. The ray of the human kingdom itself.
4. Our particular racial ray, the ray that determines the Aryan race.
5. The rays that govern any particular cycle.
6. The national ray, or that ray influence which is peculiarly influencing a particular nation.
7. The ray of the soul, or ego.
8. The ray of the personality.
9. The rays governing:
    a. The mental body.
    b. The emotional or astral body.
    c. The physical body.

THE RAYS AND THE PLANETS

Each of the seven sacred planets (of which our Earth is not one) is an expression of one of the seven ray influences. The student however must remember three things:

1. That every planet is the incarnation of a Life, or an Entity or Being.
2. That every planet, like a human being, is the expression of two ray forces,—the personality and the egoic.
3. That two rays are therefore in esoteric conflict in each planet.

THE RAYS AND THE NATIONS

Nation	Personality Ray	Egoic Ray	Motto
India	4th ray of Art	1st ray of Government	"I hide the Light."
China	3rd ray of Intellect	1st ray of Government	"I indicate the Way."
Germany	1st ray of Power	4th ray of Art	"I preserve."
France	3rd ray of Intellect	5th ray of Knowledge	"I release the Light."
Great Britain	1st ray of Power of Government	2nd ray of Love	"I serve."
Italy	4th ray of Art	6th ray of Idealism	"I carve the Paths"
U. S. A	6th ray of Idealism	2nd ray of Love	"I light the Way."
Russia	6th ray of Idealism	7th ray of Magic and Order	"I link two Ways."
Austria	5th ray of Knowledge	4th ray of Art	"I serve the Lighted Way."
Spain	7th ray of Order	6th ray of Idealism	"I disperse the clouds."
Brazil	2nd Ray of Love	4th ray of Art	"I hide the seed."

ARCANE SCHOOL TRAINING

Training for new age discipleship is provided by the *Arcane School.* The principles of the Ageless Wisdom are presented through esoteric meditation, study and service as a *way of life.*

****

www.lucistrust.org/arcaneschool

INDEX

A

Adept–
  centres, etheric, 155
  number, 155
Adeptship, goal, 354
Akasha and body, meditation upon, 236
Akashic records, reading, 240
Alchemists, ray, 166
Alignment–
  factor in effectiveness of soul ray, 406
  factor in levitation, 327
  production, 232
  requirement for passing higher, 328
Analogy, law, application, 9
Ancient of Days–
  definition, 155
  See also Logos, planetary.
Anima mundi, light, 131-132
Animal kingdom–
  influence of planets, 245-246
  influences, results, purpose, agencies, and quality, 425-428
  liberation, 198-199
  purpose, 198
  quality, 198-199
  rays, 45, 121, 216, 251, 255, 371, 415
  relation to seventh ray, 415
  sustenance, 219
Animals–
  characteristics and purpose, 252-254
  cruelty to man, 256
  door into human kingdom, 251, 371
  evocation of affection, 257
  human attitude toward, 164, 259-260, 262, 267
  individualisation, 164, 258-262, 267
  initiation, 259, 371
  mental stimulation, 255-256, 257
  rays, 162, 164, 260
  study, 371-372
Antahkarana, function, 379
Antichrist, work, 74-75
Appearance–
  and quality, fusion, 39, 40, 41
  aspects, union, 39
  synonyms, 18
Appearances, world of, source of energy, 43
Aquarian Age–
  astrological significances, 292-293
  characteristics, 95, 292-297, 313-314, 380
  consciousness, 95, 279, 280
  discoveries, xxiii, xxiv
  psychology, 331-332
  revelations, 364, 374
Aquarius, light, 103
Architect, Grand–
  creation, 15, 43-44, 133, 134, 159
  See also Creators, Three.
Architectural construction, 50
Arjuna experience, 154, 403
Art ray, 206
Aryan Race–
  destiny, 353-354
  mental calibre, 121
  ray influences, 67, 263, 316, 318, 353
  revelation, 40

Aspect—
  form, response in subhuman kingdoms, 135
  love, of Logos, 127
  quality or life, or ray manifestations, 157
  second ray, quality, 193-194
  will, of mankind, unfoldment, 241
Aspects—
  synonyms, 18
  Trinity, body of manifestation, 20
Aspirants—
  adaptation, 324-325
  fusion of soul and body, 360
  instruction, 59, 113, 115-116
  intuition, 59
  perfume, 197, 200
  recognition of need for control, 380
  studies, 195-196, 404
  testing, 10
  work, 107, 108
Aspiration—
  persistence, results, 327
  true nature, 326-327
Astral—
  body. *See* Body, astral.
  ills, 123
  light. *See* Light, astral.
  world, web, 370
Astrological significances of Aquarian Age, 292-293
Astrology—
  basis, 58
  ray, 166
Atlantean—
  floods, cause, 378
  mystics, rule, 319
  race, ray and elevating influence, 263, 356, 357
  race, ray influences, 317-318
Atlantis, lore, 241
Atom—
  manasic, 169
  mind of, 55
  potencies, release, 185
  solar, 151
Atoms—
  attraction, 374
  of three bodies, effects of aspiration, 327
  ray influence, 168
  soul, 54, 56
At-one-ment—
  of higher and lower mind, 55
  with soul, 286-287
Attraction. *See* Law.
Aura, human, ray effects, 121
Austria—
  links, 384, 390
  rays and motto, 383
Authority for teaching, 111-112
Awareness—
  development, 378
  fusion with form, 41
  in man, 135-136
  meaning, 129
  new states, 177
  of life of God, 35
  of subjective realm, 98
  soul, of thinkers, 95
  unfoldment, 95-96, 193-197

B

Beauties underlying forms, consciousness of, 196-197
Beauty, creative ray work, 133, 134, 159
Becoming, world process, initiation, 151
Being, true, consciousness of, 96
Bhagavad Gita, quotation, 15-16, 154
Bhakti yoga, ray, 164
Birth, second, 291
Births, ordained and desired, 297
Blavatsky, Helena P. *See* H.P.B.

Bliss, attainment, 46, 49
Blood, shedding, significance, 198-199
Blue–
   colour passing out, 121, 122
   of Logos, 127,
   rays, 127, 163, 164
Body–
   astral, effect of soul ray, 406
   astral, rays, 162
   causal, creation, 169
   desire, identification with, 38
   etheric–
      correspondences, 132
      definition, 54
      developments, 124
      magnetism, 219
      ray, 162
      relation to planet, 132
      soul of atoms, 54
   mechanism, subjection to down-flow, 101
   mental–
      aspect of soul, 55
      identification with, 38
      rays, 162
   of light, 131
   physical, care, 124
   physical, rays, 162
   pituitary, relations, 290
   planetary etheric, radiation, 132
Brahmanism, ray, 167
Brain–
   cells, stimulation, 59, 372
   functions, 132, 133
Brazil–
   contributions, 387-388
   links, 387, 390
   rays and motto 383
Breathing, solar system, 151
Breaths, seven, 60, 150
British-Israelites, error, 400
Bronze ray, 163
Brotherhood–
   basis, 55, 191-192, 361, 374
   challenge to, 187-189
   demonstration, 96, 282, 293, 362, 380, 391
   establishment, 95, 267, 281, 282
   law, 302
Brotherhood of Nations, culture, 173
Buddha–
   aspiration, 156
   diamond-eye, 230
   life, 76
Buddhas of Activity, aspiration, 156
Buddhic response of humanity, 347
Buddhism, rays, 166, 167
Builders–
   seven creative, of solar system, 151, 155, 191, 193
   three synthetic, 155

C

Capitulation, law, 377, 379
Cat–
   individualisation, 259-160
   rays, 164, 260
Cathedrals, symbolism, 373
Celibacy in disciples, 304-307
Centre–
   base of spine–
      race and expression, 319
      vivification, 218
   between eyebrows–
      race and expression, 319
      stimulation, 291
      symbolism, 290
      work, 290, 291
   head–
      awakening, 290
      race and expression, 319
      symbolism, 290
   heart, race and expression, 319
   sacral–
      energy, raising, 289, 295

race and expression, 319
solar plexus, race and expression, 319
throat—
  energising and use, 289,295
  race and expression, 319
Centres—
  awakening, results, 326
  force, study, 99-100
  lower, energies, raising, 289-291
  of adept, 155
  racial aspects, 318-319
  ray activity, 128, 260-262, 428
Ceremonial—
  idea underlying, 363
  order, ray of. *See* Ray, seventh.
Chaldean religion, ray, 167
Character, ray influence, 128
Chelas—
  work, 106, 108
  See also Disciples.
Child, protection, 284
China, rays and motto, 382
Chitta—
  definition, 55
  relation to intuition, 199
Christ—
  advent, 95, 279, 281-283, 314
  aid of devas, 123
  aspiration, 156
  birth, 288, 291, 292, 293, 296, 313-314
  consciousness, 14, 95, 281, 282-283, 285, 297
  cosmic—
    consciousness, 14, 285
    incarnated, form, 44
    revelation, 133-134
    sevenfold expressions, 119
  influence and direction, 155-156
  life in disciples, 351
  mind, 95, 312-313
  of Galilee, 18-19, 281, 285-286, 301
  transfiguration, 328
  work, 96, 285-286
  See also Jesus.
Christianity—
  function, 28-29
  ray, 50 165, 167, 362
Church, protective power, 126
Churches, ray, 50
City planning, modern, 50
Civilisation functioning under Laws of Cleavage, 376
Clairvoyants, training, 100-101
Cleavage, laws, 376
Cleavages, law, 377, 378, 379
Colours—
  and rays, 89, 127-128, 163-164
  in healing, 725, 126
  in vegetable kingdom, 121, 242, 246
  infra-red and ultra-violet, visibility, 103
  of flowers, 121,122
  of rays, 127-128, 163-164
  primary, 127
  relation to sounds, 126-127
  subsidiary, 127,128
Communication, means, ray, 50
Communicator, stage, entrance, 117
Communicators—
  characteristics, 181
  requirements, 117-118
  training, 117
  work, 118
Complexes due to sex, 269
Consciousness—
  applied, ray, 45-47
  Christ. *See* Christ consciousness.
  cosmic, 14, 136, 285
  definition, 129
  divine, sum total, 59
  duality, 13-14, 38, 119-120, 360
  evolution, 14, 237, 249, 375, 379
  expansions—
    by Hierarchy, 171
    by scientific developments, 177-178

etheric vision, 98,125
initiations, 155-156
New Group of World Servers, 381
of aspirants, 97
on Path of Discipleship, 155-156
rapport with devas, 125
spiritualism and psychism, 98, 125, 381
third and fifth rays, 178
under Law of Loving Understanding, 380-381
group, 115, 118, 293, 314, 341, 342
human, quality definition, 331
in meditation, relation to kingdoms, 425
international, development, 172-173
light of, glorification in man, 378
nature of, 22
of Aquarian Age, 95, 279, 280
of Creator, 15
of Eternal Now, 104
of God, 36, 53, 57-58
of initiates, 38, 61, 328-329
of life, mechanisms, 136
of life of planet and solar system, 14
of Logos, 57-58
of soul, 13, 61, 130
of true being, 96
relation to form aspect, 135
source, 22, 94
spiritual, 16-17
synthetic nature, 22
transcendence, 43
unity, 57
See also Prevision; Telepathy.
Constellation–
definition, 152
distinction from solar system, 152
Constellations, twelve energies from, 154-155
Contradictions, explanation, 189-190
Correspondences–
kingdoms, centres, organs, processes, 413
law, 228-229, 342
sets, 413
Creation–
cosmic, 15, 17-18, 43-47, 133, 134, 158-159
work of–
centres, 100, 289
rays, 133, 134, 158-159
soul, study, 99, 100
Creative Hierarchies, twelve, 155
Creative Hierarchy fourth–
definitions, 71, 344
incarnation, 72
ray, 344
Creator, expression, 15
Creators, three–
synthetic, 155
See also Architect, Grand.
Curie, Marie and Pierre, ray, 226
Cycles–
law, 189, 378
life, rays governing, 321
Cyclic manifestation, 265-267

D

Darkness, conquest by light, 378
Death–
abolition, 96
production, 63-65
survival after, 98-99
Deity–
activity, ray, 47
apprehension, 17
consciousness, 57-58
desire of, expression, 45
fifth purpose, 75-79
first purpose, 44, 63-65
fourth purpose, 70-75

hidden purpose, revelation, 44
love, ray, 46-47
manifestation, 17-18, 43-47, 133, 134, 158-159
ray, 46
second purpose, 65-67
seven qualities, 19
seventh purpose, 83-87
sixth purpose, 79-83
solar, expression of solar Logos, 25
third purpose, 67-70
three major aspects, 155
will, ray, 44
See also God; Logos.
Desire–
nature and expression, 45
of Deity, expression, 45
of nations, 133-134
satisfaction, 46
transmutation into love, 46
Destroyer, ray–
nature, 44, 63-65
See also Ray first.
Destruction–
cycle, 189
function of first ray, 133
Devas–
aid to humanity, 123-126
calling, 125, 126
goal, 88
green, 125
healing, 123, 124, 125-126
ray influences, 122, 123
relation to vegetable kingdom, 198
violet, 123-125
Devotees, emanation, 45
Devotion–
in animal kingdom, 45
ray. *See* Ray sixth.
Diamond, significances, 224, 227, 239
Dictatorship, ray influence, 26
Diet, vegetarian, 241-242
Disciples—
characteristics, 53, 56-57, 153, 314
first ray energy, 350-351
group formation, 113, 114-118
growth, 112
incarnation, 297
life of, sex, 304-307
marriage, 304-306
recognition of needs for service, 380-381
testing, 10
training, 113-115, 117
work, 105-107, 108, 378-379
See also Chelas.
Discipleship, ray expressions, 412
Discrimination, ray source, 338
Divinity, supremacy, 304-305
Dog–
individualisation, 259-260
rays, 164, 260
Door into–
fifth kingdom, opening, 344, 371
fourth kingdom, opening, 259
Duality, consciousness of, 13-14, 38, 119-120, 360
Dweller on the Threshold, destruction, 342

E

Earth–
crust, production, 229
rays, 217, 335-342
Economic synthesis, 172-173
Economy, law, 376
Education–
future developments, 177-178, 294, 295, 361
in powers of soul, 105
needs, 82
present, recommendations, 298
Educational systems, modern, 50
Ego–
ray, determination, 87

ray. *See also* Ray of soul.
Egos–
   rays in manifestation, 26-27
   See also Souls.
Egyptian religion, ray, 167
Elder Brethren–
   work, 325-326
   See also Hierarchy; Masters;
      Souls, Kingdom of.
Electricity, work with, 360, 373-374
Electrification of Earth, 102
Electro-therapeutics, work, 374
Elements, mastery over, 236
Elephant–
   individualisation, 259-260
   rays, 164, 260
Eleven, significance 346, 347
Emotion, personal, in would-be server, 231
Energies–
   constituting ray forces, 332
   from twelve constellations, 154-155
   informing personalities, 128-129
   lower, raising, 289-291, 292, 296
   of rays, manifestations, 73-74, 128-729
   of rays, sources, 152,153, 154
   septenary aggregation, 37
   three streams, forces in manifestation, 6-7
   utilisation by ritual, 363-364
   world of, 194-195
Energy–
   cosmic, 150, 152, 153, 370
   distribution, influence of rays, 128
   divine, transmission to forms, 267
   in occult work, 9, 10, 11
   nineteen types, wielders, 155
   of light, 129, 130-131
   of soul, blending with spirit, 131
   subjective centre, 150
   universality, 315-316
England, function, 384
Esoteric sciences, domain and purpose, 195
Eternal Now consciousness, 104
Etheric–
   vision, development, 102-103
   web separating planes, 102
   world, response to, 124, 135
Ethers, prophecies regarding, 122, 123, 124-125
Evolution–
   by ray, 402-403
   conclusion, agency, 134
   emergent, 258-259
   goal, 129, 131
   human, awareness, 135-136
   human, departments, service, 171
   in mineral kingdom, 224-225, 229
   in particles of light, 101
   law of, 153
   momentum, origin, 154
   objective, 57
   of consciousness, 14, 237, 249, 375, 379
   of love, 336-338
   of quality in humanity, 151, 193
   relation to soul and light, 130-131
   root in desire, 135
   story, 14
   under law of attractive magnetic love, 43
   urge toward, 151
Executives, seventh ray, work, 365, 366-367, 368
Exhibitionism, causes, 161
Extrovert, nature of, 160-161
Eye–
   development, 126
   of God, 133
   of vision, use, 182-183
   single, use, 183, 184
   third, 230

F

Family life–
  of disciple and initiates, 305
  threat to, 269-270
Fanaticism–
  ray, 122, 209
  regarding food and clothing, 141-142
Father, contribution to Son, 46-47
Fatigue, avoidance, 124
Federation of nations, 187
Fellowship of Religions, 177
Fifth kingdom, manifestation, 357
Finger of God, 133
Fire–
  by friction, meaning, 18
  electric dynamic, first aspect, 18
  initiatory, 200, 223, 224, 226, 227, 240
  three types, 167
Five, significance, 346
Flagellants, ray, 166
Flame colour, ray, yoga, and planet, 163
Floods, Atlantean, cause, 378
Flowers, magnetism and perfume, 44-45
Force–
  cosmic, central vortex, 21-22, 27
  forty-nine types, 7
Forces, nineteen, nature, comprehension, 155
Forests, world-wide devastation, 240
Form–
  building, initial activity, 44
  building, technique, 47
  coherence, principle, 54
  fusion with awareness, 41
  in manifestation, two deeds, 54
  life, three basic ideas, 380
  nature, glamour, 38
  nature, subsidence, 137
  perfection within, rays, 50
  ray, 210

Formless, love of, 46
Forms–
  all, cohesion within, 374
  all, coordination, 360
  beauties underlying, awareness of, 196-197
  builders, 11, 20, 21
  creation and development, ray influences, 45-47
  destruction, 63-65, 133, 135
  in kingdoms in nature, differentiations, 37
  integration, 57
  linkage, 136, 151, 152
  production, 60
  sevenfold effect, 19
  response in subhuman kingdoms, 135
  spiritualising, 53
  work of fourth ray, 49-51
  work of seventh ray, 52-53, 226, 280-281
  world of, creation, 43
Four, significance, 344-347
France–
  contributions, 383-384, 389, 392
  links, 383, 390
  rays and motto, 382
  symbol, 383
Frustration of mediocre equipment, 161
Fusion of spirit and matter, 55

G

Gemini, increase and decrease, 153
Genius–
  cultivation, 100
  nature, 99, 100, 161
  study, 99, 100
Geometry in minerals, 226, 227
Germany–
  characteristics, 386
  contributions, 389, 392
  links, 383, 384, 385, 386

Index

rays and motto, 382
situation in 1934, 174
Glamour–
dissipation, 341, 342
of form nature, 38
relation to egoic ray, 406
Gland, pineal, relations, 290
Glands, correspondences, 221
Gnostics, ray, 166
God–
consciousness, 36, 53, 57-58
dynamic idea, 159
immanent and transcendent, 21, 57, 58-59
life, expression, 142
love, 154
plan and purpose, 43-44
plan, definition, 353
problem, 182-183
revelation, 142-143
seeing and knowing, 182-183
will. *See* Will of God.
See also Deity; Logos.
Good will, practice, 297
Government, science, 50
Great Britain–
contributions, 384, 385-386, 387, 392
links, 383, 384, 385-386, 387
rays and motto, 382
symbol, 383
Great White Brotherhood, rituals, 363
Green–
devas, 125
of vegetable kingdom, 246
ray, 127, 128, 164
Group–
consciousness, 115, 118, 293, 314, 341, 342
force, 11
life, law, 302
light bearer, 315
ray, attraction to, 261
service, preparatory, 324-325
service, results, 95-96, 111, 297
seven types of force, 11
synthesis, 179, 360
teaching, 112-117, 294
work, 10, 11-12, 294, 295, 360, 361, 363
Groups–
destructive, 188
importance, 113
of accepted disciples, regulations, 114-115

H

H. P. B.–
quotations re. spirit and matter, 17
See also Secret Doctrine.
Harmlessness–
nature of, 359
results, 111
Harmony–
production, 49
ray, functions, 49-51
Hatha yoga, rays, 164, 355
Healing by–
colour and sound, 124, 125, 126
devas, 123, 124, 125-126
ritual, 364
Heavenly Men, seven, 60
Hermaphrodite, divine, 278
Hierarchy–
Council, meetings, 170-173
manifestations, 313, 314
See also Creative Hierarchies; Creative Hierarchy; Elder Brethren; Masters.
Holy Ghost, synonyms, 18
Homosexuality, situation, 277-279
Horse–
individualisation, 259
ray, 260
Human–
being–
astrological factors affecting, 332

description, 53, 55, 56, 61
function as soul, 378
organisation and influence,
    20-21
rays influencing, 333-334,
    404-405
sound and colour, 126-127
true, expression, 284-285
See also Man.
kingdom–
    adaptation, 322-326
    effects of five ray energies,
        263-265
    objective agency, 330-331
    planetary influences, 245-246
    purpose, 328-330
    ray activity, results, 321-322
    rays, 121, 216, 247, 319-321,
        429
    sustenance, 220
Humanity–
    consciousness, forced expansion,
        171, 172, 177, 178
    development, 142-143
    emerging quality, 199-200
    evolution. *See* Evolution,
    ray–
        dominating through Logos,
            338-341
        egoic, 343-344
        personality, 343
        types, 322-326, 329-330
    understanding, 129
    work, 267
    See also Man.
Hylozoism, definition, 149

I

I Am That I Am, realisation, 14
Ideas–
    ideals, and idols, 162
    problem, 179-181
Identification with form and life,
    249-250
Illumination–
    physical, work, ray, 360-361
    results, 101
Illusion–
    of astral plane, 116
    of personality attention, 112-114
    relation to egoic ray, 406
    subjection to, 38
    world, destruction, 341
Immersion, law, 377, 379
Immortality–
    basis, 154
    belief in, 92-93, 94
    disbelief, 91
    demonstration, 96, 98-99
    problem, 183-186
Impersonality–
    need for, 117
    of Masters, 112-116
Incarnation–
    plans of soul, 10-11
    three streams, 6-7
India–
    contributions, 385
    links, 384, 385
    rays and motto, 382
Indigo ray, 127, 129, 163
Individualisation of animals, 164,
    258-262, 267, 354-355
Individualism, ray, 361
Infallibility, papal, 165
Infra-red, visibility, 103
Inhibition, sex, 269
Initiate, Paul, quotations, 16-17
Initiates–
    characteristics, 53, 153
    consciousness, 38, 61, 328-329
    family life, 305-306
    fifth degree, achievement, 347
    incarnation, 297
    light, 131
    marriage, 304-306
    response to planet, 155
    response to synthetic force, 156
    third degree, comprehension, 150
    third degree, soul ray, 128

understanding of life, 150
work, 105-106, 108
Initiation–
  animals, 198-199, 259
  Atlantean, 40
  factors, 200
  first, influence, 155
  fourth, release, 406
  highest. 156
  mineral kingdom, 197, 223, 224, 226, 227, 230
  process, 50
  second. influence, 155-156
  sixth, Chohans of, work, 87, 108
  third, consciousness, 328-329
  vegetable kingdom, 240
Initiations–
  higher, revelation, 37
  planetary influences, 246
Initiators, symbolic relation, 406
Inspiration, sources, 107, 108, 109, 192
Instinctual Purpose of animal kingdom, 198
Intellect–
  causation, 311, 321-322, 356
  definition, 40-41
  merging, 121
Intelligence, principle, 38
Internationalism, ray, 362
Introvert, nature of, 160-161
Intuition–
  causation, 321, 379
  correspondences, 132, 133
  definitions, 134, 199, 200
  exercise, 71
  failure, 160
  future accomplishment, 357
  in sixth root race, 338
  light, 112
  merging, 121
  of–
    aspirants, 59
    groups, 11-12
    Observers and Communicators, 181
    psychologists, 160
    scientists, 123
    second ray, 133, 134, 202, 203, 204, 212, 217
  power and achievement, 153-154
  regarding soul, 93-94
  results, 153-154
  study, 99
  substitution for intellect, 136
  training, 112
  union with instinct, 322
Intuitional–
  buddhic response in humanity, 347
  development of introvert, 161
  energy, 416
  telepathy, 125
Intuitive–
  grasp of synthesised knowledge, 212
  perception, 393
  response to soul nurture, 105
  solution of problems, 179
  spirit of love in masses, 176
Intuitives, development, forced, 171, 172
Invocations, use of, 126
Italy–
  links, 390
  rays and motto, 382

J

Jesus–
  of Nazareth, Poverty and ancestor, 397-398
  See also Christ.
Jewels, precious, 229-230
Jewish–
  nation, relationships, 134
  problem, 393-401

race, modern, founders, 395-397
Jews—
  astrological signs, 394
  original three disciples, descendants, 398, 400
  rays, 394
  separativeness, 399
Jupiter—
  body of manifestation, 23
  ray, 164, 335

K

K. H., Master, work, 108
Kama-manas, definition and development, 356
Karma—
  factor of personal ray, 169
  Law, observance, 300
Kingdoms in nature—
  correspondences, 220-221
  development, symbolic, 235-236
  expression and characteristics, 422-428
  five secrets, 238-245
  key words, 222
  notes from *Cosmic Fire*, 413-415
  rays, 120-122, 162, 164, 422-423
  sustenance, 219-220
  See also under specific names.
Knower, knowledge, and field, cosmic, 47
Knowledge—
  concrete, ray. *See* Ray fifth.
  cosmic, definition, 47
  of God, 134
  synthesised, grasp, 212
  true medium, 132
Kundalini, human and planetary, 370

L

Law—
  definitions, 62, 377
  divine, reign on earth, 95
  of the land, conformance with, 303
Law of Attraction, 193, 287, 288, 376, 415
Law of Attraction and Repulsion, 267, 271
Law of attractive magnetic love, 43
Law of Brotherhood, 302
Law of Capitulation, 377, 379
Law of Cleavages, 377, 378, 379
Law of Correspondences, 228-229, 342
Law of Cycles, 189, 378
Law of Economy, 376
Law of Evolution, 153
Law of Group Life, 302
Law of Hidden Radiance, 377, 379
Law of Immersion, 377, 379
Law of Karma, 300
Law of Love, 301-302
Law of Loving Understanding, 379, 380, 381
Law of Materialisation, 377, 379
Law of Periodicity, 65, 190
Law of Rebirth, 266, 300-301, 302
Law of rhythm, cosmic, 153
Law of Sacrifice, 219
Law of Service, 272
Law of Sex, 299
Law of Synthesis, 376
Law of the Tides, 378, 379
Law of Understanding, 380
Laws of Cleavage, 376
Leader of men, spiritual, equipment, 161
Leadership ray, 201-202
Lemurian Race—
  covering of the light, 377-378
  ray influences, 263, 317, 354-355, 356
Levitation, production, 327
Life—
  aspect, *See* Aspect, life.

consciousness. *See* Consciousness; Life-Consciousness-Form.
  definitions, 18, 50
  One. *See* One life.
  ray, expression, 152
  solar, expression, 152
  taking, 242
Life-Consciousness-Form, synonyms for, 18
Life-Quality-Appearance–
  definitions, 18, 141
  discussion, 14-22
  in human being, 21
  perfect blending and expression, 143
  significance, relation to rays, 149-169
  source of consciousness, 22
  study, 136
  synthesis, 22, 158
Life-radiance-magnetism, 235-238
Light–
  astral–
    knowledge of, 361
    penetration, 102
    reflection, 241
  energy, 129, 130-131
  God in, seeing, 182-183
  in all forms, 362
  in evolving man, 130, 131, 377-378
  in head, increase, stages, 131
  intensification, 102-103
  magnetic radiatory, 130
  of Earth, 131-132
  of initiate, 131
  of soul, 130, 132
  planetary, 131-132
  problem, relation, 135
  quality, changes, 101
  station, 315
  study, effects, 101
  three types, 102
Lives, past, reading, 241
Living, technique, 57

Logoi, planetary–
  of solar system, 151
  seven, nature, 151
Logos–
  embodied, awareness, 15
  of universe, consciousness, 57-58
  outpourings, 168-169
  planetary–
    heart and brain, 27
    initiatory power, 156
    life, 155
    outpourings, 168
    ray influence, 337, 338-341, 403-404
  solar–
    achievement, 88
    colour, 127
    expression, 25, 58, 163-169
    heart and brain, 27
    plan, 24
    ray, 19, 46
    response apparatus, 136
    work, 87
  will of, expression, 48
  See also Deity; God.
Lord of Active Intelligence, manifestation, 23, 67-70
Lord of Adaptability and the Intellect, work, 133
Lord of Ceremonial Order or Magic, manifestation, 25-26, 83-87
Lord of Concrete Knowledge and Science, manifestation, 24-25, 75-79
Lord of Concrete Science, work, 134
Lord of Devotion and Idealism, manifestation, 25, 79-83
Lord of Fourth Ray, work, 134
Lord of Harmony, Beauty, and Art, manifestation, 24, 70-75
Lord of Love-Wisdom, manifestation, 23, 65-67

Lord of Power or Will—
   manifestation, 23
   work, 133
Lord of Ray of Devotion, work, 134
Lord of Second Ray, work, 134
Lords, seven Ray—
   body of expression, 62
   description, 60, 141-143
Lords of Ceaseless Devotion, 48
Lords of Knowledge and of Love, 48
Lost Word, recovery, 53
Love—
   and desire, 45, 46
   aspect of Logos, 127
   consummation, 282-283
   creative, 42
   definitions, 287-288, 336
   embodiment, 42, 295
   in kingdoms of nature, 336-337
   in man, 61
   intelligent, cosmic principle, 40-41
   laws, 44, 379, 380, 381
   magnetic, response to will, 44
   of God in manifestation, 154
   of God, quality, demonstration, 19
   of One Reality, expression, 42
   reign, 95
   results, 111
   solar fire of, production of forms, 43
   synthetic, definition, 199-200
   universal, 301
Love-Wisdom ray. *See* Ray, Love-Wisdom; Ray second.

M

M., Master, work, 108
Magic—
   Atlantean, 381
   black, 9-10, 74-75
   prophecies, 82, 83, 363-375
   ray of, work, 52-53, 363, 369
   ray of. *See also* Ray seventh.
   white, 9-10, 50, 358-359
Magnetic rapport, 152
Magnetism—
   in vegetable kingdom, 234, 244
   radiance, life, 235-238
Mahachohan, work, 88
Man—
   a machine, 90-92
   a synthesis, 33-34
   aggregation of ray forces, 402-406
   definitions, 20-21, 311-313
   differentiation from animal, 311
   evolving, light, 130, 131
   future control of lower kingdoms, 257-258
   latent powers, unfoldment, 178
   life, taking, 242
   objective, 60
   radio-activity, 199-200
   three souls, 248
   understanding, 160-161
   unevolved, light, 131
   will aspect, unfoldment, 243
   See also Human; Humanity.
Manifestation, Cause and Source, 18
Manu, department, 351
Manvantara, end of, rays, 87, 263
Marriage—
   conditions, 273-275, 286
   cosmic, 285-286
   ideas, racial, reorganisation, 283
   of disciples and initiates, 304-306
   relationship, adjustment, 286, 287, 293-297, 305-306
Mars—
   body of manifestation, 25
   ray, 164, 335
Masonic work—
   development, 368-369
   high moment, 52-53

mode of teaching, 50
Masonry–
  effect of rays, 53, 368-369
  Jewish element, 396-397, 398, 401
  knowledge and work, 373
  protective power, 126
  symbolism, 373
Masses, understanding, 129
Master K. H., work, 108
Master M., work, 108
Master P., work, 105
Master–
  aura, 108
  response to, 261
Master Builder, 159
Masters–
  characteristics, 53
  impersonality, 112-116
  work, 105-106, 107, 108, 367
  See also Elder Brethren; Hierarchy; Souls, kingdom of.
Materialisation, law, 377, 379
Mathematical exactitude, ray, 49
Matter–
  and spirit, 17, 20, 130, 369, 377
  ascension out of, 236
  control on physical plane, future, 353
  creative work, 46, 47
  diversification in first race, 377
  in man, 61
  mastery, 156
  properties, 126
  refining, 371
  sentient activity, 130
  sevenfold effect, 19
  soulless, 130
  synonyms, 18
  See also Mother-Matter.
Meditation–
consciousness and the kingdoms in nature, 425
  of God, result, 375
  of groups, 12
  results, 95-96, 100, 375
  upon five forms, 236
  upon relation between body and akasha, 236
  work, scientific basis, 374
Mental–
  plane. *See* Plane, mental.
  science, 50
Mercury–
  influence in Aquarian Age, 292
  ray, 163, 335
Metaphysics, ray, 204
Millikan, Robert A., work, 226, 370
Mind–
  abstract, aspect of soul, 55
  abstract, downpouring, 59
  control, results, 101
  definition, 40-41
  expression, 55
  functions, 16-17
  in atoms, 55
  lower concrete, aspect of soul, 55
  of God, 311-313
  stuff, aspect of soul, 55
  stuff, relation to intuition, 199
  universal, geometry, 227
  universal, sum total, 59, 60
  use, 331
Mineral–
  kingdom–
    activity, 197
    aid of humanity, 267
    characteristics, 223
    etheric substance, 228-229
    evolution, 224-225, 229
    influence of Planets, 245-246
    initiation, 223, 224, 226, 227, 230
    quality, 197
    rays, 44, 121, 216, 217-219, 221-222
    results, agencies and quality, 423
  substances, groups, 225, 229
Minerals, correspondences, 230

Mohammedanism, ray, 167
Monad—
  aim, 128
  career, 13-14
  definition, 48, 142
  evolving, 127
  expression, 142, 162
  eye of, 132
  purpose, 39
  relation to rays and colours, 127
  unity, 128
Monads, human—
  body of ray Lord, 27
  ray, 87, 344
Monasticism, evil, 304-307
Monogamy, discussion, 269, 273, 274
Moon, ray, 164, 335
Mother-Matter—
  functions, 17, 46, 47
  See also Matter.
Mount of Transfiguration, vision, 150, 153-154
Music, manifestation, 24
Mystic—
  nature of, 160
  practical, 161
  transformation, 359

N

Nationalism, ray, 360
Nations—
  federation, 173, 177, 187
  rays, 379-401, 430
  virtues and vices, factors, 388
Neptune, ray, 335
Neuroses, causes, 119
New Age—
  characteristics, 179, 292-297, 298-299, 302-303, 361
  clue, 183
  inauguration, 12, 74, 82, 102, 281
New Group of World Servers—
  creation, 171-172
  personnel, 171, 172, 330, 381
  work, 172-179, 186, 325-326, 381, 382
Nine, significance, 346, 347
Numbers in mineral kingdom, 221

O

Observers—
  characteristics, 181
  training, 117
Old Commentary, quotations, 28, 61, 253, 264-265, 344-345, 351, 395-396
Omniscience of soul, 104
"One About Whom Naught May Be Said," 150, 151, 155, 332
One Life—
  expression, 141, 191
  mystical rhapsodies, nature, 16
  revelation and awareness of, 15
  seven breaths, 44
One Reality, love and life, expression, 42
Opposites, pairs, subjection to, 16
Orange ray, 121, 127, 128
Organisation through form, ray, 49-51
Oriental races, descent, 401
Orientalists, work, 176
Outpourings, three, 168-169
Oversoul, identity of all souls with, 380

P

P., Master, work, 105
Pain—
  cause, 338
  problem, 199, 250
Patanjali, quotations, 235-236
Path of Discipleship—
  centre of gravity, 13

entrance by humanity, 342
ray governing, 351
requirements, 354
Path of Initiation–
glimpse and discovery, 37-38
ray governing, 351
state of being and knowledge, 53
Path of Probation–
centre of gravity, 13
ray governing, 351
work, 106
Paul, initiate, quotations, 16-17
Peace, world, 381
Perfume of–
aspirants, 197, 200, 246
vegetable kingdom, 197-198, 242-243, 246
Periodical vehicles, ray expression, 162
Periodicity, law, 65, 190
Personality–
activities, influence of soul, 129
appearance, 39
constructive high-grade, 161
contact, illusion, 112-114, 116
control by soul, 365
coordinated and developed, 51-52
definitions, 37, 48-49, 56
energies informing, 6-7
expression, 13, 128-129, 162
intent, 42
integration, 296, 339, 360
"killing out," 324
limitations of would-be servers, 231
purification, 290-291
ray. *See* Ray of personality.
relationships, 191-192
transmutation, 327
Phenomena, astral, interpretation, 141
Photography, use, 184
Physicians, aid from devas, 125
Piscean Age–
basic achievement, 332
close, 240
Pisces, lesser cycles, 26
Plan, the–
Agents of, 59-60, 106
comprehension, 43
communication, 118
cooperation with, 134, 223, 363-364
custodians, "push," 184
definition, 53
devotion to, 109
distortions and misrepresentations, 82
formulation, 159, 170
furtherance, 88, 135, 167, 186, 228, 325, 356
new, institution, results, 172
knowledge of, 154, 325
manifestation, 11-12, 109, 133, 170, 353
organisation, 170-179
roots, 141
statement and custody, 143
synthetic scope, 154
Plane–
astral–
illusion, 116
revelation, 364
separation from physical, 102, 370
source of devotional literature, 118
work, requirements, 241
mental–
light from, 102
work of Master P., 105
Planes–
formless, rays on, 51
seven, microcosmic and macrocosmic, 19
Planet–
forces and energies, 152
Life, consciousness, 14
ray life, 38
Planetary Lives, rays, 217
Planetary Logos. *See* Logos, planetary.

Planets—
  expressions, 152
  influences upon kingdoms in
    nature, 245-246
  linkage, 191
  rays, 163-164, 335
  seven—
    expressions, 62, 163-164
    force, 21
    sacred, 142
Plants. *See* Vegetable kingdom.
Pluto, ray, 335
Points of fire, energies, 6
Politics—
  ray seventh, 178
  ray sixth, 172, 178
  work of New Group, 172-176
Prana, transmission and transformation, 141
Prevision, study, 104
Probationers—
  work, 106
  See also Path of Probation.
Prophecies regarding—
  atomic energy, 185
  coming of Christ, 95, 279, 281-283, 314
  ethers, 122, 123, 124
  fact of soul, 96-97, 98, 100-107
  goal of humanity, 185-186
  government, 185
  group light-bearer, 315
  inspirational writing, 99, 118
  intuition and understanding, 136-137
  magic work, 82, 83, 363-375
  religion, 185
  scientific discoveries, 185
  solar system, 373
  soul knowledge, 95-97, 99-105
  work of Communicators, 118
Protection by ritual, 126
Psychic powers, lower, increase, 381
Psychological influences, 157
Psychologists—
  need of esoteric knowledge, 161
  problems, 101, 160
  recognition of soul, 99, 364
Psychology—
  esoteric, 50, 160-161, 364-365
  future developments, 293-294, 364
  modern—
    achievements, 4-5, 118-119
    cul-de-sac, 118-119
    materialism, 90-91
    recognition of self, 101
    weakness, 5
  new, description, 366
  new, developments, 100, 165, 177-178, 364
  of Aquarian Age, 331-332, 364
  schools, error, 160
Psychoses due to sex, 269
Purification, personality, 290-291
Purity, need for, 126
Purpose of evolution, sensing, 40
Pyramid, symbolism, 103

Q

Qualities, world of, energy, source, 43
Quality—
  definitions, 193-194, 331
  expression, 54
  fusion with appearance, 39, 40, 41
  identification with appearance, 39
  of appearing life, 35
  of each kingdom in nature, 197-200
  of God's consciousness, 36
  of human appearance, 332
  search for, 196
  second aspect, 18-19
  seven aspects, 37
  See also Life-Quality-Appearance.
Quaternary, ray expression, 162

Index

R

Race–
  second, capitulation of matter, 377
  seventh, rays, 263, 357
  sixth, rays, 357
Races–
  centres expressing, 318-319
  ray relationships, 316-319
  reincarnation, 316-319
  root, rays, 263, 357
Radiance–
  by mastery of binding life, 235
  hidden, law, 377, 379
  magnetism, life, 235-238
Radiation–
  of soul, 130
  study, results, 101
Radio–
  future use, 184
  mode of teaching, 50
Radio-activity–
  discovery, 369
  of humanity, 199-200
  ray, 225-226, 229
Radium–
  discovery, 369-370
  key to mystery, 44
  nature of, 45
Raja yoga, rays, 163
Ray–
  affecting human Monads, 344
  ceremonial, discoveries, 122-126
  definition, 316
  energies. *See* Energies.
  fifth–
    activity methods, 416, 417
    colours, 128, 164
    correspondences, 133, 134
    energy today, 350
    expression, 51, 121, 162, 320, 356
    future development, 243
    in animal kingdom, 162, 198-199, 215
    in etheric body, 162
    in human kingdom, 121, 216, 343
    Lord, 75-79, 134, 241
    manifestation, 24-25, 26
    modes of group teaching, 50
    nations, 382, 383
    plane, 51
    planet, 164
    qualities, 78-79
    race, 317, 318
    virtues and vices, 207-208
    work of New Group, 177-178
  first–
    activity methods, 415-416
    animals, 164, 260
    colour, 127, 163
    combination with seventh, results, 226, 229
    concept, 159
    correspondences, 133
    cycles, 265
    diversification of matter, 377
    effect on humanity, 320
    energy, manifestation, 351
    energy today, 350
    expression, 23, 26, 44, 51, 159, 162, 320, 351
    in discipleship, 350-351
    in mineral kingdom, 44, 216
    in Monad and mental body, 162
    in Solar Lives, 217
    Jews, 394
    Lord, 63-65, 221
    modes of group teaching, 50
    nations, 382
    plane, 51
    planet, 163
    political work, 172-176, 178
    race, 316, 317
    virtues and vices, 201-202
  forces–
    balancing, 160
    expression, 73, 170
    originating energies, 332

fourth–
   activity methods, 416, 417
   animals, 164
   colour, 164
   correspondences, 133, 134
   disciples, work, 105
   expression, 24, 26, 51, 72, 121, 162
   future development, 244
   in humanity, 162, 320, 343-344
   in vegetable kingdom, 121, 216, 233-234, 239, 242, 247
   Lord, 70-75, 134
   Master, work, 105
   modes of group teaching, 50
   nations, 382, 383, 384, 385
   plane, 51
   planet, 164
   race, 317-318
   virtues and vices, 205-207
influences–
   Aryan Race, 263, 316, 318, 353
   cyclic, 266
   on civilisation, 4
   on consciousness, 4
   on forms, 4, 49-53, 61, 226, 280-281
   on kingdoms in nature, 412-413
   on soul, 61
laws, functioning, 375-379
life, relation to solar life, 152, 191
lives, nature and expression, 141-142, 143
Lords, characteristics, 142
Love-Wisdom–
   vehicle for desire of Deity, 45
   See also Ray second.
methods of teaching, 49-50, 411-412
of beauty, functions, 49-51
of Deity, 46
of Earth, 169, 335-342
of fourth Creative Hierarchy, 344
of Ego. *See* Ray of soul.
of Intelligent Activity–
   function, cosmic, 47
   See also Ray third.
of Monad–
   activity, 237, 243, 406
   of vegetable kingdom, 238
of organisation through form–
   work, 49-51
   See also Ray fourth.
of personality–
   activity, effects, 406-407
   aspects, 160
   of humanity, 343
   of nations, 382
   planetary influence, 167
   rotation, 128, 129
of radio-activity, 225, 226, 229
of Solar Logos, 46
of solar system, 334
of soul–
   activity, 406, 407
   blend, 402
   dominance, 129
   knowledge, importance, 160
   location, 128
   of humanity, 343-344
   of nations, 382
   premises, 401-407
   study factors, 405-406
one great cosmic, 163, 166, 168
physical operations, 128-129
second–
   activity methods, 416, 417
   animals, 164, 255, 260
   colours, 127, 163
   correspondences, 133, 134
   cosmic of solar system, effects, 339, 340-341
   cycles, significance, 349-350
   experiment, 259
   expression, 45-47, 50, 51, 159, 162
   future development, 243
   in kingdom of souls, 217, 247
   in soul and astral body, 162

Index 453

  in vegetable kingdom, 44-45,
    216, 233, 239, 242, 244, 247
  Lord, 65-67, 134
  manifestation, 23, 26
  modes of group teaching, 50
  nations, 382, 383
  plane, 51
  planet, 163
  qualities, 66-67
  quality, 193-194
  race, 316, 317
  vehicle for desire of Deity, 45
  virtues and vices, 202-204
  work, 176-177
seventh–
  activity methods, 416, 417
  body relationship, 162
  close association, 86, 88
  colours, 128, 164
  combination with first,
    results, 226, 229
  contrast with sixth, 359-362
  correspondences, 133
  cosmic rays, 370
  cycles, 265
  date, 165
  effect on humanity, 321
  energy today, 350, 358
  executives, 365, 366-367, 368
  expression of sixth ray vision,
    358, 359
  form building, 226, 280-281,
    369, 373
  government, 26, 165, 279
  healing, 364
  in mineral kingdom, 121, 162,
    216-218, 221, 223, 225-
    228, 369, 372-373
  influence on sex, 267, 268
  Lord, 83-87, 221, 228, 369
  magic, 52-53, 363, 369
  masonic work, 53, 368-369
  modes of group teaching, 50
  nations, 383, 387
  plane, 25-26, 51
  planet, 164
  political work, 178
  qualities, 86-87
  race, 317, 318
  radio-activity, 225-226, 369
  relation to animal kingdom,
    371, 415
  religion, 165, 179, 362
  ritual, 226, 372
  science, 226, 280
  virtues and vices, 210-211
sixth–
  activity methods, 416, 417
  colours, 128, 164
  contrast with seventh, 359-
    362
  correspondences, 133-134
  dominance, 165
  expression, 25, 26, 51, 52, 81,
    162, 321
  in animal kingdom, 121, 164,
    216, 251, 260
  in astral body, 162
  in vegetable kingdom, 162, 198,
    216, 233, 239, 242, 246-247
  individualism, 361
  Lord, 79-83
  modes of group teaching, 50
  nations, 382, 383, 385
  passing out, 25, 79, 81, 121,
    122, 165, 359
  plane, 51
  planet, 164
  political work, 172, 178
  race, 317, 318
  religion, 165-166, 167, 359,
    361, 362
  science, 360-361
  sense of duality, 360
  separativeness, 360, 362
  virtues and vices, 208-210
sound, 8
synthetic, definition, 127
third–
  activity methods, 416, 417
  colours, 127, 163
  correspondences, 133

expression, 23, 26, 51, 69-70, 159, 162, 321
in animal kingdom, 45, 216, 251, 254
in personality and physical body, 162
Jews, 394
Lord, 67-70
modes of group teaching, 50
nations, 382
plane, 51
planet, 163
Planetary Lives, 217
Planetary Logos, 337-338
race, 316, 317
virtues and vices, 204-205
waning, characteristics, 348-349
work of New Group, 178
See also Ray of Intelligent Activity.

Rays–
activity methods, 415-416
and senses, 133
characteristics, 163-164
classification, 162, 167
colours, 127-128, 163-164
cosmic–
effects, 370
energy, 153, 370
path, 370
significance, 226
creation by, 133, 134, 158-159
creation of, 44
cyclic manifestation, 265-266
definitions, 19, 44, 59-60, 141-142
dominating, 88, 123
duality, 48
energies, sources, 152, 153, 154-155
evolution of unit man, 402-403
fires, 167, 229, 240
fourth and fifth, interplay, in man, 342-347
future activities, 243-244, 247-248
goals, 88
governing faculties of man, 320-321
governing Paths, 351
grouping, 88-89, 351-353
in cyclic manifestation, 357-375
in individualisation, 164, 260
major, first differentiation, 44
major, functions, 47
manifesting and out of manifestation, 348, 411
minor four, production, 44
modes of group teaching, 49-50
nature of, 3-4, 17, 79, 20
numerological influence, 412
of aspect, expression, 62-70, 158-159, 162
of attribute, expression, 70-87, 162, 164-167
of kingdoms in nature, 120-122, 215-220, 237-238
of nations, 379-401, 430
of planets, 335, 430
of Will and Love, dominance, 46-47
pattern-forming tendency, 391
period of influence, 164-167
references in *Secret Doctrine*, 418-421
relationships, 128, 19 l-192, 211-212, 428
senses, and expression, 421
seven–
characteristics, 163-164
correspondences, 59, 133
enumeration, 22-27
manifestation, 190, 411
struggle for dominance, 402-403
study, practical application, 8-9, 128-129
study, requirement for, 22
study, three objectives, 3-14
synthetic, 88, 89

third and fifth, activity, 354
vehicles, and expression, 421-422
work, 128, 141-142
zodiacal control, 153
tabulations, 411-430
Rebirth–
law, 266, 300-301, 302
See also Incarnation; Reincarnation.
Recognition, principle, 52
Red ray, 127
Reincarnation–
in races, 316-319
of disciples and initiates, 297
periods between, 272
process, 266-267, 300
Religion–
new, formulation, 29, 177
ray second, 50
ray seventh, 165, 179, 362
ray sixth, 165-166, 167, 359, 361, 362
teaching, 50
work of New Group, 176-177
world, parts, 187
Religions, organised, 50
Religious man, characteristics, 52
Research, ray, 207-208
Resurrection, secret of, 264
Revelation–
aid to, 189, 281
of soul, 96, 97, 102
Rhythm–
in human consciousness, 331
law, 153
of whole, 57
use by soul, 365
Ring-pass-not, solar, 151
Ritual–
definition, 365-366
healing by, 364
idea underlying, 363
of service, 375
Rituals, powers, 126, 363-364
Rose rays, 163, 164

Rosicrucians, ray, 166
Russia–
characteristics, 386-387
links, 385, 385, 390
rays and motto, 383
situation in 1934, 174

S

Sacrifice–
law, 219
views of sixth and seventh initiates, 361
Salvation of the race, 303
Saturn–
body of expression, 23
influence in Aquarian Age, 292
ray, 164, 335
Science–
definition, 120
future developments, 183-185, 186, 369
modern, views of soul, 89-94
ray. *See* Ray fifth.
ray-seventh, 226, 280
ray-sixth, 360-361
work of New Group, 177-178
Sciences, esoteric, domain and purpose, 195
Scientist, true, 51
Scientists–
discoveries, 100-101, 105, 120, 125
future revelations. *See* Prophecies,
Secret Doctrine–
basic theory, 149
central spiritual sun, 150
references, 17, 48, 155, 373, 418-421
Sectarianism, ray, 360
Self, integrating principle, 5-6
Self-awareness, principle, 55, 56, 57

Self-consciousness—
  expression, 35
  production, 55
Self-expression, attainment, 160
Self-reliance, need, 116, 117
Self-training of disciples, 117
Selflessness, need for, 111, 117
Senses—
  rays, and expression, 421
  seven, relations, 132-134
Sentiency—
  consciousness, awareness, comprehension, 135
  expression, 54
  meaning, 129
  principle, 53
Sentient activity of matter, 130
Separateness—
  great heresy of, 38, 378
  of sixth ray, 360, 362
  principle, 16
Servers, personality limitations, 231
Service—
  group, results, 95-96
  instruments of disciple, 380-381
  law, 272
  ritual, 363-364, 375
  sixth and seventh rays, 361
Seven—
  breaths of One Life, 44
  differentiations of quality, 37
  emanations, potencies, and rays, manifestation, 44
  great Lives, manifestation, 20, 22-27
  in writings of initiates, 20, 23
Sex—
  centre and ray, 261-262
  control, 270, 276-277
  cosmic, 285, 286
  definition, 277, 287, 299
  drama, human, 291
  function, 244-245
  in future, 292-297
  in life of disciple, 304-307
  in mankind, purpose, 299
  law, 299
  problem, 268-307
  relation, cause, 267
  seventh ray influence, 267
  symbolism, 285, 287-291, 299
  two major evils, 269-170
Six, significance, 346
Sixth root race, ray and elevating influence, 263
Solar Angels, expression, 76, 77-78, 191, 192
Solar Lives—
  expression, 152, 191
  rays, 217, 218
Solar Logos. *See* Logos, solar.
Solar system—
  activity, 44
  body of manifestation, 20
  breathing, 151
  creation, 151
  definition, 152
  distinction from constellation, 152
  Life, consciousness, 14, 21
  nature, 151, 152
  prophecy, 373
  ray, 334
  ritual, 375
Solar systems, seven, energies, 150, 152, 153, 154-155
Son—
  creation, 46, 159
  nature of, 17-18, 42
Soul—
  appearance in matter, 130
  appearances, symbol, 41-42
  attraction by, 340
  beginning of career, 55
  capacities, 53-54
  communications from, 107, 109
  comprehension, xxiv, 375
  consciousness, 13, 61, 95, 130
  control of personality, 365

definitions, 36-37, 38, 40-41, 42, 48, 53, 54-56, 61, 109, 130, 311
discovery, 39, 96-109, 353
dominance, 39
existence, establishment, 95, 96
expression, 41, 54, 162
eye, 132
factor in introversion and extraversion, 160
faculties, 104
fusion with body, 360
home, ray, 88
identification with matter aspect, 13
influence, growth, 407
intent, 42, 59
knowledge, prophecy concerning, 94-97, 99-105, 364
life, seven laws, 407
light, 102, 130, 132
mastery of technique of contact, 54
monadic ray, 402
nature–
 permanence and change, 142
 questions of psychologists, 5-6
 views, 132
of all things, light, 131-132
of atoms, 54, 56
origin, 59
personality of, intent, 42
plan, 59
plans before incarnation, 10-11
powers, training, 105
qualities, 37, 55, 130, 135, 137
quality. *See* Life-Quality-Appearance; Quality.
rhythm, 365
science, 50
synonyms, 18
type, determination, 261
universal, 57, 58
views of modern science, 89-94
world, appropriation, 54

Souls–
 cyclic life, control, 378
 five groups, 407
 kingdom of–
  planetary influences, 245-246
  rays, 215, 217, 247
  sustenance, 220
  See also Elder Brethren; Hierarchy; Masters.
 nourishment, 112
 rapport with, 59
 ray destiny, 129
 rays, 401
 three in human being, 56
 wisdom from, 118
 See also Egos.
Sound–
 in healing, 124, 125-126
 initiatory, 240
 made by a ray, 8
 secret, 89
Sounds–
 musical, developments, 122, 123, 124, 125, 126
 relation to colours, 126-127
Space travel, 236
Spain–
 links, 385, 390
 rays and motto, 383
Sparks, divine, energies, 6
Spirit–
 and matter, 17, 20, 55, 353
 blending with matter, 369
 capitulation to in second race, 377
 energy, blending with soul, 131
 fact, 154
 man's, 57, 58
 synonyms, 18
 universality, 17
Spirit-Consciousness-Form, first differentiation, 17
Spiritual–
 being, power to stand in, 59
 man, definition, 181
Spiritualism, ray, 50, 166-167

Spiritualistic movement—
  growth, 381
  output, 107
Statesmanship, science, 50
Steam age, significance, 240
Struggle, ray, 206
Study, occult method, 73
Sub-ray—
  definition, 165
  length of influence, 166
Subjective realm, awareness of, 98
Substance, divinity, appreciation, future, 353
Sun—
  central spiritual, 150
  esoteric substitute for planet, 23
  journey through greater Zodiac, 153
  ray, 335
Suns, interrelation, 152
Survival, fact, establishment, 98-99
Symbol—
  definition, 285
  union of aspects, 39
Synthesis—
  at coming of Christ, 282
  divine, sense of, 34-35
  economic, 172-173
  group, 179, 360
  in consciousness, 193, 280, 381
  in manifestation, 36
  law, 376
  new, production, 178
  of appearance and quality, 39
  of intellect-intuition, 357
  of knowledge, 212
  of life, 57, 294
  of life-quality-appearance, 19, 22
  of man, 33-34, 71, 320
  of minds, 11-12
  of quality and purpose, 39
  power, 153
  ray, 87, 88, 360
  subjective, 34
  triplicity, 33-34
Synthetic—
  apprehension of truth, 200
  force of adept, 155
  force, response of initiate to, 156
  indigo, 127, 128
  nature of consciousness, 22
  rays, 88, 89

T

Taurus, relation to mineral kingdom, 230
Teaching—
  authority, 111-112
  by devas, 123, 124, 125
  evocation, 110, 111
  group, 112-117, 294
  laws of thought, 82-83
  ray methods, 49-50, 411-412
Telepathy—
  dictations, 107-109
  intuitional, 125
  study, 100, 125
Thought—
  laws of, teaching, 82-83
  reservoir, 107
Thoughtforms—
  building, 82, 85
  group, 10
Tides, law, 378, 379
Training—
  aspirants, 113, 115-116
  disciples, 113-115
Transfiguration—
  initiation, 150
  of humanity, 328
Transmutation in mineral kingdom, 222, 228, 229
Travel in space, 236
Treatise on Cosmic Fire,
  references, 88, 131, 151, 373, 407, 413, 475
Treatise on White Magic,
  references, 85, 354, 364-365

Treatment—
   by devas, 125-126
   fifth-ray method, 208
   first-ray method, 202
   fourth-ray method, 207
   second-ray method, 203
   seventh-ray method, 211
   sixth-ray method, 210
   third-ray method, 205
Trinity—
   in man, 33, 56, 312
   in manifestation, 159
   meaning, 17, 159
Triplicity in synthesis, 33-34
Truth—
   definition, 302
   distinction, 17
Twenty-two, significance, 155

U

Ultra-violet, visibility, 103
Understanding—
   loving, law, 379, 380, 381
   of God, 133, 134
   prophecy, 136-137
Union—
   between God and man, 290
   in man, 291
   of life and quality, 56
   urges toward, 280
Unit, integration into the whole, 331
United States of America—
   contributions, 384, 387, 389, 392-393
   links, 384, 387, 390
   rays and motto, 383
   situation, 174-175
Unity—
   absolute, basis in mind, 55
   higher, sense of, 360
   highest, cognition, 14
   of consciousness, 57
   realisation, 13, 14, 57
   subjective, in human being, 56
Uranus, ray, 163, 335

V

Vegetable kingdom—
   aid of humanity, 267
   characteristics and purpose, 233-234
   colour, 121, 242, 246
   influence of planets, 245-246
   initiation, 240
   liberation, 198
   quality, 197-198, 234
   rays, 44-45, 121, 216, 233
   relation to devas, 198
   results, agencies, and quality, 423-424
   sustenance, 219
   work with prana, 241
Vegetarians, interpretation of astral phenomena, 241
Venus—
   influence in Aquarian Age, 293
   ray, 163, 335
Vibration, harmonious response to, 331
Vice, definition, 284
Violet—
   colour, incoming, 121, 122
   devas, collaboration with men, 123-125
   light, use, 124
   ray, 121-122, 127, 128, 164
Virtue, definition, 284
Vision—
   etheric, developments, 123, 124, 125, 126, 183-184
   fourth dimensional, 190
   of God, 182-183
   true, cultivation, 136-137, 183, 291
Vitality, factors, 374-375
Vulcan, ray, 335

W

War—
   in heaven, 199
   world (1st), ray withdrawal, 349

world, shedding of blood, 198, 199
Water–
  revelations of seventh ray, 364
  use in initiation, 200, 240
Way, revelation, 78, 79
Web, etheric–
  destruction, 102, 370
  discovery, 125
Whole, divine, parts, 42
Will–
  comprehension, 43
  dependence on expression, 43
  divine, channel, 76
  dynamic, 351
  electric fire of, production of forms, 43
  embodiment, 42, 48
  intelligent, product, 42
  of Deity, embodiment of hidden purpose, 44
  of Deity, production of differentiation, 44
  of God, activity, 47
  of God, impact on divine substance, 44
  of Logos, expression, 48
Will-to-be, origin and nature, 43
Wisdom ray. *See* Ray second.
Women, wrong views regarding, 304
Word–
  in incarnation, 158
  magical work, 373
  use in Masonry, 369
Words of Power, use, 133
World–
  government, problem, 179-180
  government, work of New Group, 173
  religion, coming, 177
  today–
    cleavages, 379
    control of physical forces of planet, 355
    crisis, 344
    dissipation of glamour, 342
    educational systems, 50
    group spirit, 341-342
    house-cleaning, 366-367
    increase in mentality and spirituality, 285, 291-292, 374, 375, 390, 381
    integrated human beings, 284-285
    liberation, 342
    new synthesis, 178
    ray activity and inactivity, 348-350, 355-356, 357-358
    selfish disregard of teachings, 301
    stimulation by Aquarian Age, 280
    stimulation by coming of Christ, 279, 281
    stimulation by seventh ray, 279, 290
World Federation of Nations, 173, 177

Y

Yellow ray, 127, 163
Yoga–
  bhakti, ray, 164
  hatha, rays, 164, 355
  raja, rays, 163
Youth, situation regarding sex, 275-276

Z

Zodiac–
  control of rays, 153
  cyclic manifestation, 265
  greater, journey of sun through, 153
Zoroastrian religion, ray, 167